AN INTRODUCTION TO ENVIRONMENTAL PSYCHOLOGY

An Introduction to Environmental Psychology

WILLIAM H. ITTELSON
HAROLD M. PROSHANSKY
LEANNE G. RIVLIN
GARY H. WINKEL

Environmental Psychology Program, City University of New York

DAVID DEMPSEY
Editorial Associate

HOLT, RINEHART AND WINSTON, INC.
New York Chicago San Francisco Atlanta
Dallas Montreal Toronto London Sydney

To our students, whose challenging questions, genuine insights, and considerable support have made this book possible

Cover photographs by Mark Krastof

Library of Congress Cataloging in Publication Data
Main entry under title:
An introduction to environmental psychology.
1. Environmental psychology. I. Ittelson, William H.
BF353.I5 155.9 73-21953
ISBN 0-03-001346-1

Printed in the United States of America
4 5 6 7 8 038 9 8 7 6 5 4 3 2 1

Preface

Although the preparation for this book has taken about two years, it has a much longer history. In reality it goes back to 1958, when a National Institute of Mental Health grant made it possible for some of the authors to become involved in a series of studies dealing with the influence of psychiatric ward design on the behavior of patients. As our research progressed, an interest emerged that seemed to go beyond the specific psychology specialties of the researchers and the question of psychiatric architecture; one that became defined as environmental psychology. In turn, interest in the field began to expand, and advanced training was set up in the form of the environmental psychology specialization in the doctoral program in psychology at The City University of New York. Faced with the challenge of providing multidisciplined resources for both research and teaching, a wide range of materials was accumulated. This led to preparation of a readings book, *Environmental Psychology: Man and His Physical Setting*, a tentative step in the direction of organizing some of the varied sources that seemed to define our field.

Although we discussed the central problems and issues in the field briefly in the interstitial materials of the book of readings, through the years we have become convinced of the necessity for a more detailed statement, one that would set forth a theoretical approximation of environmental psychology as it appears to us.

Thus, three purposes guided the writing of this book. First, we wanted to build a framework for the various sources from which environmental psychology draws. This effort seeks to organize a vast body of information, growing daily, but all critical to the study of man/environment issues. In addition, we wished to make our theoretical approximation available to the increasing number of environmental courses, both undergraduate and graduate. These courses have many different names and appear in many different departments, but they all revolve around a central core of common issues dealing with the man/environment relationship. Lastly, our purpose goes beyond reporting, categorizing, and organizing a broad body of information. We have attempted to express a point of view regarding useful concepts and methodology. This book thus provides a vehicle to communicate these ideas to a wider audience.

Despite the fact that the field of environmental psychology is new, we feel that a book such as this provides the opportunity to define its concerns and organize the multidisciplined material on which it is based. As a pioneering endeavor, some of our formulations must be considered tentative. We have proceeded convinced that the study of environmental psychology cannot wait for a set of variables defined uniquely for itself. Rather, building on other knowledge, the variables will be selected over the years and, hopefully, a theory of environmental influence will develop as well. But this must be in the future. Although specific portions of theory, in psychology as well as other disciplines, may be helpful, in our judgment no current theory can provide a unified theme. Rather, the framework of this book has followed our own work in this field, representing areas we have found useful to our thinking about environmental issues.

A brief word might be added to answer the question of what is environmental about the topics covered in the book. Many of the issues are as much social issues. We accept this fully. In fact, we have tried to avoid making a sharp distinction between the social and physical aspects of a setting simply because we think this is impossible to do, given our conception of the meaning of an environment and, at this early stage, the development of the field.

The co-authors worked together in preparing the outlines for the book. The writing of each chapter was the responsibility of a single person. Throughout the writing we each commented freely on the drafts in progress. The difficult, if not impossible, task of dealing with the variant styles of four different persons fell to David Dempsey, who contributed both editorial assistance and substantive writing. The order of authors' names as it appears is alphabetical.

In the years of working on environmental issues, many people have contributed to our work in a variety of ways. Our colleagues Maxine Wolfe, Irwin Mussen, and Susan Saegert, and all the students in our program have provided consistent stimulation to our thinking. Specific bibliographic contributions have been made by D. Geoffrey Hayward, Joel Kameron, Emilie O'Mara, Marilyn Rothenberg, and Sheree West. Beth Merritt, Administrative Assistant to the Environmental Psychology Program, has provided more than typing and editorial skills, adding a creative concern throughout. She was assisted in this task by Elizabeth Gay, Beatrice Dellapietro, Lillian Mandelbaum, and Lynn Kadison.

Our research has been enhanced by the cooperation of many people and institutions, but first by a series of grants from the National Institute of Mental Health. Most supportive of our attempts to extend the boundaries of our work have been James T. Cumiskey, Coryl L. Jones, Clyde Dorsett, and their associates.

Many people have facilitated our work over the years, among them Dr. E. Richard Feinberg, Mr. John Melser, and Dr. Herbert Shapiro. We are most grateful to them and to many others who cooperated with us at a time when environmental studies were neither fashionable nor acknowledged as a legitimate academic concern. We appreciate the suggestions of William Michelson and Lance K. Canon, who read an earlier version of the book. Special thanks go to Debby Doty, our Psychology Editor, and Brian Heald, Senior Project Editor, for assistance, patience, and encouragement when each of these was needed.

The responsibility for errors of omission and commission falls on us.

W.H.I. H.M.P.
New York City L.G.R. G.H.W.

Contents

One

Environmental Man

Environmental Psychology: How It Began

Designers and architects have long known that the form and appearance of a building influence certain behaviors that take place within it. Historians of architecture have noted that man's dwelling places in every land reflect the sociocultural values of his time and place, expressing needs that go beyond those of physical shelter and comfort—psychological needs of identity, creativeness, and harmony with the world. When men build houses, they create not only a physical environment but a psychological environment of meanings, a symbolic world that reinforces a particular scheme of tastes and values. Beyond these general notions of the interplay between the psychological aspects of man and his physical environment, however, only in recent years has there been a systematic attempt to uncover the empirical nature of this relationship. The term *environmental psychology* itself was not used in any clearly defined sense until recently.

In 1958–1959, three of the authors of the present volume began preliminary research into the influence of ward design on patient behavior in mental hospitals. Out of this grew a series of studies dealing with the physical environment as part of a therapeutic setting. Others (Izumi; Osmond; Sommer) were working along these lines independently, and the subject in general was expanding to include the noninstitutional milieu. By 1969 a directory of more than 600 persons who were professionally interested in this man/environment relationship had been assembled (Research and Design Institute, 1969). As yet, however, environmental psychology had evolved little in the way of theory to back up its empirical observations, and it enjoyed limited academic acceptance.

Nevertheless, questions had been raised and signposts erected. Funded by the National Institute of Mental Health, the authors' own project developed into a broad-based inquiry of the effects of continuous physical settings on various aspects of behavior. Here was a field that was clearly neither sociology nor psychology, neither architecture nor urban planning. The design professions entered into it, as did—at strategic levels—anthropology and geography. The time was ripe for an integration of the several disciplines that were going their own way in exploring this newly awakened interest in the relationship of man's physical world and his response to it. In 1968 the Graduate Center of the City University of New York set up a separate specialty within the psychology program. This book, in part, is an outgrowth of the courses that have been developed in the department and the research carried on by both students and faculty.

Since that time, the subject has acquired many students and not a few scholars and investigators. Universities have established departments in environmental psychology; schools of architecture include courses in this field as part of their regular curriculum; architectural firms employ behavioral scientists to assist the professional designer. In the social and physical sciences the implications of environmental psychology are used to investigate hitherto neglected areas of the man/environment relationship that are now seen as relevant to these fields. Although a sizable body of research literature has grown up, and some theoretical positions taken, this material is widely dispersed and not easily available to the student. Books on the subject, for the most part, deal with specialized areas (for example, Sommer's *Personal Space*; Hall's *The Hidden Dimension*; Pastalan and Carson's *The Spatial Behavior of Older People*). At this writing, no general textbook exists that includes all the major components for a study of environmental psychology. It is the intention of the present volume to furnish just such a comprehensive, albeit introductory, approach to this multidisciplinary subject.

Because environmental psychology is new with many uninvestigated and unsolved problems, our text makes no attempt to emulate the rigorously scientific approach that characterizes more traditional disciplines. In short, there is as yet no official canon in environmental psychology; rather, as a developing field of inquiry it seeks to formulate the theories and constructs that will provide, if not a canon, at least a scientifically rooted charter.

Our approach differs from many textbooks in at least two other respects. Because our emphasis is on the integration of material from widely different sources, no effort is made to write in the technical language of any one discipline. The student will find a minimum of jargon and, hopefully, a maximum of comprehension. Environmental psychology need be neither pedantic nor esoteric. At the same time, the literature pertinent to the field is reviewed in this text only to the extent that it applies to specific topics under consideration; our references are selective, and we have not sought to include all the specialized reports and investigations growing out of environmental psychology simply for the sake of saturation. They are, however, representative of what we believe to be the major lines of inquiry. Our endeavor has been to give some descriptive coherence to the diverse array of findings and theory from the many fields that help us understand the man-milieu phenomenon.

What accounts for the burgeoning interest in environmental psychology? Two reasons suggest themselves. One is the current concern with the problems of cities—the built environment that is becoming, for many of us, increasingly inadequate as a context for living. Population density, inner-city decay, pollution, alienation—these are among the environmental stresses to which urban man is subjected. New Towns, urban studies programs, and a stepped-up emphasis on urban planning testify to the urgency with which we seek a more empirical analysis of the relationship between the behavior of man and his cities.

Our second awareness concerns the natural environment. Here to such a factor as man-made pollution we must add the depletion of natural resources, a vanishing wildlife, and the threat of ecological failure. Again, if man is to live in harmony and inspire, as part of the natural order of things, his deeper self, a better balance must be found between the integrity of this environment and its destructive exploitation. The profound concern which is sweeping the world today on the subject of environment is essentially a recognition that mankind no longer has a free ride at the expense of the earth's resources.

That such, indeed, is no longer the case accounts for the zeal with which we have tried to reverse the trend. And beneath the surface of our concern lies a deeper reality of which we are only now becoming aware. The "unnatural," man-made world that has taken the place of "nature" as a setting for our daily lives is cutting man off from much of his biological past. The centuries-old equilibrium of the human and the natural environment—the physical and psychological accommodation between man and his outer world which allowed him to swim freely in the universe—is dissolving under the impact of a stepped-up technology. What we properly seek today, therefore, is a relationship with the environment that not only preserves what we have, but indeed, may help to recapture what has been lost.

Evolution and Change

When man endeavors to change his surroundings he is doing something that is characteristic of all animal species. Three features of this interchange with the environment however are uniquely human: first, its *extent*; second, its *deliberate and self-conscious implementation*; and third, its *complexity*. The evolutionary niche which man occupies on the phylogenetic scale of life is characterized essentially by this ability to modify the environment to serve a wide range of human needs. In so doing he differs noticeably from other animals, which stress adaptation to the environment in an effort to be comfortable and to survive.

From the long-range view of biological evolution, the extent of this interchange is probably its most significant aspect. Beginning with the earliest stone age, men have gradually reshaped the face of the earth, until today we are leaving our marks in the reaches of space. We speak proudly of conquering nature; yet this very conquest, quite apart from what it has done to nature itself, imposes an unprecedented burden of adjustment on man, both in the magnitude of change and its continually increasing rate of acceleration. It is as though a storm were brewing from which we can find no refuge. Modern technology has assumed a life of its own; the very process of change seems at times to have gotten out of hand, so that our industrial societies no longer reflect the true needs of their inhabitants.

As environmentalists, we are concerned not only with the economic and cultural implications of this phenomenon, but the degree to which man has been psychologically abused and caricatured by the technology which is central to it. Indeed, for many of us, there is a nagging feeling that something is wrong with a world that provides so much in a material sense and yet leaves us vaguely dissatisfied with our lives. Simply to change our environment, therefore, does not necessarily improve our chances of survival. Change must be purposeful in terms of long-range human consequences.

This notion is best expressed by the second feature of the man/environment interaction. Of all creatures, man alone can carry out changes deliberately and self-consciously. He does this, moreover, within the framework of a unique, communicable culture which other species do not possess.

The distinction is important because it gives man a degree of control over his world that no other species enjoys. More than this, it makes possible the planning of the direction and effect of such changes, allowing the individual the freedom to better define himself in the very act of modifying his environment and, above all, to create a world that accords with his philosophical and ethical precepts. To control one's environment is, to a very great extent, to shape one's future.

Important as these aspects are in tracing human response to the physical environment, it is the third feature of our triad—the complexity of man's response—that forms the background and motivating force of this book. To be sure, such an interchange is physically and biologically complex (as the sciences tell us), but it is rather on the psychological and social level of analysis that our interests are focused. Less is known about these areas than the more empirically researched qualities of the physical and biological world. More important from our point of view, however, is that man's psychological environment is largely a product of his own creation; and it is because he is so greatly influenced by his own product that the study of this relationship is a crucial one.

The psychological effect on man of the environment which he himself has created may prove to be the clue to the problem of "ecology," for in the long run of history the product becomes the master. In modifying his environment man has set in motion trends which can only be reversed or rechanneled by a conscious and deliberate effort, and such an effort will succeed only to the extent that the implications of man/environment relationships are fully understood. The general purpose of this book, therefore, is to explore the ways in which these relationships influence and change human behavior.

What Is Environmental Psychology?

It should be clear that environmental psychology is not a theory of determinism. It sees man not as a passive product of his environment, but as a goal-directed being who acts upon his environment and who in turn is influenced by it. In changing his world, man changes himself. A guiding principle in this field is what we have called the *dynamic interchange* between man and his milieu. The traditional conception of a fixed environment to which organisms must adapt or perish is replaced by the ecological view that emphasizes the organism's role in creating its own environment.

Another important feature of environmental psychology concerns the methods it uses to investigate behavior. The traditional psychologist studies man by isolating him from his everyday milieu in order to arrive at descriptions of discrete and quantifiable sub-behaviors. This is usually done in the laboratory or in other experimental and controlled settings.

Recognizing that such methods have a valid place in the investigation of certain behavior attributes, environmental psychology nevertheless prefers to study human beings in their everyday, intact settings. It does not ordinarily isolate and arrange behavior in accordance with the psychologist's curiosities, but looks at behavior as it is, with the environment playing an integral role in the process. Thus, our second focus of interest is the study of man as part of his milieu.

A third feature of the environmental approach is its multidisciplinary character. It endeavors to bring together the relevant aspects of a number of scholarly fields whose interests touch upon, and contribute to, an understanding of human behavior in relation to specific environments. Our source material is drawn not only from psychology, but from sociology and anthropology as well; in addition, the work of architects, urban designers, ecologists, designers, and others who are concerned with the physical environment help us define the substantive boundaries of environmental psychology. In this book we endeavor to give some descriptive coherence to the diverse array of findings and theories from other fields that help us understand this man-milieu phenomenon.

Environmental psychology is also concerned with social problems. It adopts a humanistic orientation in recognition of the fact that in dealing with his environment, man is crucially affecting not only the earth on which he lives, but others who share it with him. At the one extreme we explore the behavioral implications of urban living, with its relation to housing patterns, crowding, stress factors and social identity. At another extreme the natural environment is studied as both a problem area, with respect to environmental degradation, and as a setting for certain recreational and psychological needs. In this connection we posit an environmental ethic based on a behavioral, as well as an ecological, approach to nature.

On a more theoretical level, environmental psychology studies some basic psychological processes. Central to our approach is the role of *perception*, which we view as a crucial element in the man/environment interchange. This is to say that each individual perceives or experiences the world about him in individual and unique ways; perceived as well as objective reality guides his actions and determines whether the satisfactions he seeks will be achieved. As part of this process, the role of *cognition* is important—how we make sense of the inchoate environment around us. In this connection we are interested in the *stimuli* that affect perception; in the *spatial* properties of the environment that influence patterns of behavior; in "real world" *contingencies* to which man must fashion a congruent relationship; and in the *social relationships* that are facilitated by his use of space. The environment as a factor in *growth* and *development*, and its role in *learning*, is considered.

For an understanding of all of these processes a knowledge of the values, attitudes, and the social and cultural norms which man brings to his environment is crucial. Finally, we are concerned with man the builder; with the problems of conceiving and designing an environment that is functional, in the practical sense, yet humanly satisfying. A growing trend in environmental psychology is thus directed toward the immediate living environment of the individual, and as we shall see in later chapters, some efforts have been made toward constructing plausible theoretical models which could guide research in this field.

In addition we are seeking to isolate the finer grained qualities of the environment which bear on our daily lives. Is it true, as Izumi (1969) believes, that the use of plastics to simulate wood, metal, leather, cloth, and even plants sets up an element of doubt in our sensory receptors that is inconsistent with what we instinctively feel the environment ought to be, thus creating an unconscious tension in our relationship with the new technology? Do gleaming, glass-walled schools and office buildings explain the "existential anxiety" so pervasive in industrial nations by cutting us off from the familiar, human milieu of our childhood? Izumi holds that monotony of decor, the endless corridors of large buildings, the rows of desks in an office suggest that we are on a treadmill and hence adversely affect "comfortably perceived psychic time." Do such timeless environments make us anxious because we are unable to see a future? Izumi thinks so.

What, therefore, is the role of the environment in providing us with a sense of the future—or, for that matter, a past? Do we want order in our world? Ambiguity? Novelty? What is the appropriate environment that many biologists believe every organism seeks? Not necessarily a comfortable one, for a countless number of the world's peoples live under conditions of physical discomfort, and they do so quite willingly. This is not always a matter of economic necessity; a recalcitrant earth, a dust bowl, a storm-ravaged seacoast help the inhabitants of such places find a sense of self-worth in their environment and in so doing satisfy one of the deepest psychological needs of man.

We test ourselves against the environment every day, and consequently affirm (or negate) certain values that cannot easily be tested in other ways. This is partly a matter of coming up against the new technology, the world of synthetics, the prevailing urban decay; partly a matter of environmental flux. The physical world is changing. Sheer population pressure is making it necessary to arrange people in relation to each other and to their environment in entirely new ways. Largely without precedent, such changes impose novel demands upon our perception of the world. Yet it seems that out of these perceptions a more suitable environment—a survival environment, if you will—can be fashioned.

The Emergence of Environmental Man

It should be clear from the foregoing that the term *environment* embraces many points of view: how we perceive and experience it in the psychological sense; how we modify and use it to serve our needs; and finally, how we accommodate our behavior to a constantly changing ecosystem. Before we briefly discuss some of the assumptions and themes that are covered in this text, it might be well to look at the environment from another perspective. This can be called environmental awareness; it means, simply, that for purposes of study and investigation, we perceive our role vis-à-vis the environment in terms that are quite different from anything that existed before. Out of this awareness a new set of attitudes and values is emerging. Our assessment of the environment—about space and its uses, about the social process engendered by architectural forms, the ecological message that nature holds for us, the effects of density, the influence of cultural norms on our territorial sense, the importance of urban design, and, not least, our conceptualization of the environment as a source of identity—all this presents us with a new way of thinking about man. Indeed, it presents us with a new man, environmental man, whose relation to his world is uniquely different from that of his predecessors throughout history.

In every age man has had a specific functional relationship to society that determines how he thinks about himself. That is to say, he is a product of the evolutionary demands of his time. How he behaves is ultimately related to what he must do to survive. As we know, in very early times these demands were largely physical; primitive man battled nature in his struggle for existence. Fortunately, from the hindsight of modern techniques, he was neither sufficiently skilled nor of such number as to upset the ecological balance. He was, in retrospect, what has been called *natural man,* dependent upon nature even for his supernatural beliefs.

Such labels can be simplistic but they serve the purpose of letting us focus on those aspects of an evolving society which distinguish one age from another. They identify what people regard as most real about their lives. By the Middle Ages the man-environment equation had acquired a new set of values. Nature was no longer the only mirror in which man could find a reflection of himself. The world was increasingly social and conceptual; ideas played a larger role in defining the self, and the idea that prevailed in Europe was that of God, the product of more than a thousand years of Judeo-Christian tradition. The closed, medieval world with its rigid social hierarchies and its attention to Christian doctrine enforced a belief about man's place in the universe that permeated every aspect of life. That such a place could not easily be challenged is seen by the great crises of belief that attended the discoveries of Galileo and Copernicus.

With the coming of the Renaissance there began a gradual dissolution of Christian man, culminating in the idea of the rational man idealized by the eighteenth century, a revolt prompted largely by the scientific discoveries that were giving men more control over their lives. The nineteenth century saw this development channeled into a factory technology for increasingly large numbers of people—employer and worker constituted, in this sense, economic man, both inextricably bound to an industrial way of life. Such individuals might still believe in God, or even in nature, but it was the machine that called the tune.

Yet beneath the prevailing self-concept of every age there has always existed feeling and thinking humanity, man in his behavioral essence. What characterizes more recent times is a new awareness of this essential self, the concept of identity as psychologically generic. It was Freud who created psychological man, and Freud's legacy dominates our conception of man today as a being who increasingly finds his selfhood in existence, in the finiteness of life detached from the transcendent or spiritual values that shaped so much behavior in the past. In place of these values there has not yet been created a viable substitute except, perhaps, in the idea of man himself, in all his psychological autonomy.

It is from this perspective that our study of environment and behavior properly begins. For if psychological man is a function of his age, it is frequently in the negative sense of being alienated from it; from the social environment and the institutions that have been structured by technology rather than by the deeper and more enduring needs of humanity itself. The danger is not that we will be unable to adjust to our new environment, but that we may adjust too well. René Dubos (1968) pointed out that human adaptability makes it possible for man to accommodate himself to conditions which threaten to destroy the values which are characteristically human. The "social speed up" about which Margaret Mead (1970) writes reveals how adaptable mankind is to the new technology; processes which once took generations are now assimilated into our culture within a few years—although at a price. In his popular book, *Future Shock,* Alvin Toffler describes this phenomenon in terms of our struggle to reach a *modus vivendi* with changes yet to come; yet, although the author rightly sees this as a psychological problem, his solution is basically social.

What must be emphasized here is that social relationships occur in an environment that in itself is a dynamic part of the process of change. Institutions—schools, churches, hospitals—are unique in this respect, not only in their physical form (which may limit or encourage certain types of activities) but in the social message which this form conveys to us. Properly speaking, such milieus may influence behavior over the short term simply by limiting one's choices. But an environment can also enlarge this freedom to choose. In shifting the emphasis from a structured to an unstructured environment, the open classroom encourages children to learn at an individually meaningful pace and more in accordance with their own interests and abilities. To cite a comparable situation: Research into patient behavior in a hospital solarium indicates that simply by rearranging the furniture it is possible to achieve striking changes in the use of the solarium, with therapeutic implications for the patients.

We are dealing with a theory of environment that removes the individual from the physical isolation in which he has usually been studied. This in itself is a significant advance in our understanding of human behavior. More than that, it offers the individual a new role in relation to his environment, which becomes the setting for a new humanism that is no longer exclusively concerned with human relations. It is a humanism redirected toward the otherness of life and away from the psychological preoccupation with self which in the words of Paul Shepherd and Daniel McKinley "leads not to discovery but to an abysmal lack of identity. It would appear that the self is discoverable only in its own loss and that it is not identifiable without an intense sense of environment." [1969: 139]

If this is true, then the kind of environment we create becomes supremely important. Shepard (1969) writes: "The humanness of ecology is that the dilemma of our emerging world ecological crisis . . . is at least in part a matter of values and ideas. It does not divide men as much by their trades as by the complex of personality and experience shaping their feelings toward other people and the world at large." [p. 8] In this sense, not only the environment but an ethos is preserved. For the extent to which we achieve an identity in the environment is not simply in the prudent use we make of it, but in the human values we express through our willingness to shape it to an ethical end. We are discovering our environment because we are in danger of losing it. Environmental man is not only in critical relation to the ecosystem, but to his own sense of self.

Design and Behavior

It is our thesis that only as we understand the relationship of individual and group behavior to the environment at large can we bring about desired environmental change. To state that our physical milieu is more malleable today than it has ever been—that the very forces which propel change are susceptible to positive as well as destructive ends—serves no purpose if man does not know his behavioral role in this continuum. Architecture has always recognized the psychology of physical structures, but it was mainly an applied psychology which cast the occupants of these structures in passive roles. Walls of certain colors are warm or cold. Contemporary houses give a sense of "freedom" (because of the minimal use of partitions and a lot of picture windows). In schools, good lighting promotes better learning. Comfort and convenience are assumed to be psychological attributes, and little effort has been made to distinguish between the differing cultural, economic, and ethnic backgrounds of the users. In brief, architects are prone to confuse the psychic needs of their clients with their convenience needs, although the two do, indeed, frequently coincide. As architects take a more behavioral point of view, the shortcomings of our existing structures become apparent. Form and function no longer dominate; ideally, at any rate, the building becomes a setting in which, according to Amos Rapoport (1967), we "find our own meaning."

This behavioral need is not simply one of convenience or comfort. Too much convenience may explain our alienation from a given environment simply because we find it difficult to involve ourselves in it in any meaningful way. To the extent that a physical setting invites us to participate, Rapoport (1967) believes, both complexity and ambiguity are necessary. When these elements are lacking, we attempt to project our own meaning into it; hence, the subtle sabotage on the part of the office staff of some of the new, and highly "functional," skyscrapers which force their occupants to live with a building on its own terms.

When men designed and built their own houses, no matter how crudely, they intuitively shaped them to behavioral requirements. The architect as designer of homes is a late arrival on the scene, and he comes at a time when the house itself is undergoing a change of function to accommodate the nuclear family, as compared with the extended family of earlier generations. This is simply a continuation of changes that began more than a century ago when industrialism separated man's occupational settings from his living arrangements. Cobbler, storekeeper, furrier, glovemaker—nearly all such tradesmen and handcrafters plied their livelihood at home. The house embraced the family both as consumer of space and producer of goods; it was a total setting in which the inhabitants could and, indeed, did participate in the fullest sense. To the extent that such places were functional they were psychologically satisfying too, despite the fact that life was often hard, and hovels were hovels.

It is true, of course, that the identity of preindustrial man was only partly the result of his place in the environment. He had a place, too, in the scheme of religious and social values of his time; moreover, the very rootedness of these people—their attachment to landscape—encouraged a narrow view of life. Yet, however limited his milieu, man belonged to it in a way that has largely vanished. The roots of this estrangement can be traced to the rapid pace of industrialization in the early nineteenth century. A concern for the more conspicuous byproducts of this industrialization constitutes one of the historical antecedents of environmental psychology. The influx of large numbers of people from the countryside to the city, and their resultant concentration in slum housing; the excessively long hours of work; and the frequent dissemination of the entire family into the mills in order to make a living were factors seemingly linked to a social pathology characterized by poor physical health, criminality, high mortality rates, and alcoholism. Although the efforts of social reformers were directed along a broad sphere of action, the bulk of the concern went to the housing environment of those who worked in the heavily industrialized areas. Much of this action, unfortunately, was trial and error, and in many instances no real attempt was made to speculate on the precise way in which the physical environment itself produced indicators of social pathology. This is still an open question, although a voluminous literature has since come into existence on the relationship of the sociological environment and pathology.

Here the question of population density and its effect on behavior arises. The sociologist Georg Simmel (see Wolff 1950) in his studies of Chicago during the early years of this century spoke of the conservation of psychic energy on the part of urban residents who use this mechanism to cope with large numbers of people and who, in consequence, become acquainted with a far smaller proportion of their neighbors than do residents of the country or a small town. For the farmer, physical isolation necessitates that an effort be made to overcome it. There are fewer neighbors to choose from and one tends to be less selective.

We might ask why, then, apart from the obvious economic reasons, do people live in cities that are so frequently stressful? In the seventy years that have elapsed since Simmel's studies a great deal more has been learned about behavioral response to urban environments. We know that you cannot explain a city—or any other environment—until you understand the kinds of people who live in it: their ethnic and social backgrounds, their cultural habits, income levels, and general scheme of values.

One of the interesting discoveries made by sociologists who have studied urban renewal in the United States is the extent to which slum dwellers resist removal to "better" neighborhoods. In his study of the West End of Boston, Herbert Gans (1962) made the point that although inhabitants of a slum may not consider it a physically desirable place to live—broken plumbing and potholes are seldom coveted, even among the poor—they found it congenial to their style of life and indispensable as a place for which they have an image. To this should be added the social cohesiveness that has been observed in the slums—but not, generally speaking, in the better neighborhoods and suburbs—where strong friendship ties, based on economic, cultural, and ethnic homogeneity, act as a defense against the larger, more impersonal environment of the total city.

Likewise, one of the characteristics of life in the Negro ghetto or Puerto Rican *barrio* is the overcrowded and generally dilapidated housing which drives the inhabitants into a vivifying, congenial, and less punitive street environment. That such activity has value for those concerned is seen in their frequent reluctance to exchange this way of life for the physically improved, but possibly sterile, existence in a housing project. Yet there is the danger of placing too romantic an interpretation on such a phenomenon.

Some Major Assumptions

In this chapter we have introduced the idea of environmental man as integral to an understanding of this process of change—man not as a passive receiver of stimuli, nor as psychologically autonomous, but man in dialectical tension with his milieu, interacting with it, shaping it, and being shaped by it. The boundaries of such a concept are broad, with implications for urban planning, the design of office and living space, the conservation of natural resources, and the building of institutions, such as schools and hospitals, where environmental form is intimately related to the educational or therapeutic process which it serves. These aspects of environmental psychology, along with theoretical approaches dealing with methodology and the use of perceptual and cognitive models, will be treated in succeeding chapters. It will be helpful at this point, however, to anticipate some of our major assumptions about the environment and how it works. We summarize below eight characteristics fundamental to an understanding of this process.

The environment is experienced as a unitary field. Although we perceive the environment as discrete stimuli—sight, sound, taste, smell, touch—the total constellation of stimuli determines how we respond to it. It is the complexity that constitutes the physical setting in which men live and interact over extended periods of time that must be considered in assessing the influence of environment on human behavior.

The person has environmental properties as well as individual psychological ones. He is himself an environmental component, and how he interacts with his setting helps determine the nature of that setting and its effect on his actions. This cyclical feedback process is instrumental in measuring human behavior within a given physical milieu. The individual's relationship to his environment, therefore, is a dynamic one.

There is no physical environment that is not embedded in and inextricably related to a social system. We cannot respond to an environment independently of our role as social beings. Even a solitary person reacts to his setting on the basis of his isolation. The nature of an environment will affect the functioning of groups, whether this environment be a city or a schoolroom. The arrangement of space makes possible certain types of relationships and inhibits others. No small face-to-face group, for example, can function adequately, and therefore achieve its goals, if the physical setting precludes normal social interaction among its members. The sheer density of people in a space becomes an environmental component that influences their behavior.

The degree of influence of the physical environment on behavior varies with the behavior in question. Culture and context are reciprocal, but where values are firmly held the context in which they are expressed becomes relatively less important in determining behavior. Beautiful churches do not turn atheists into believers, nor do beautiful schools necessarily educate the dull. In such cases, the milieu may act as a positive or negative reinforcer for an already determined mode of behavior, but it cannot be expected to change the basic direction of this behavior.

The more complex the experience, the more likely that there will be a variety of factors influencing it, and the less likely that the physical environment will be a major factor in this respect. An inherited cultural tradition may be far more operational in determining a given action than the immediate arena in which such an action is expressed, although it should not be overlooked that we shape our environment to reinforce such traditions.

The environment frequently operates below the level of awareness. It is when our environment is changed that we become most aware of it because it is at this point that we consciously begin to adapt. For the most part, we take our environment for granted, and although we may be aware of the affect—how it feels to function in a given milieu—the effect of this on our actions can be wholly subliminal. Territorial behavior in individuals, for instance, is well established and for all practical purposes automatic (see pp. 142 ff.). To the extent that the shape or size of a space affects group behavior, this behavior is almost never "thought out." It is only later, when we analyze our actions (or they are analyzed by others) that we discover underlying reasons for the behavior.

The "observed" environment is not necessarily the "real" environment. What we see and what exists may be quite disparate, which explains why no two people experience the same milieu in exactly the same way. Depending upon our personality, our ethnic background, religious faith, or simply our passing mood, what we perceive may be a distortion of the objective world. Indeed, all of us at some time look at the environment through the distorting lenses of anger, annoyance, or frustration and this fact may be more important in modifying our actions than the physical properties of that environment. We behave as if the environment is structured in a certain way although, in fact, it may not be. It is the perceived as well as the real world to which we respond.

Such perceptions are frequently influenced by one's previous experience with an environment. When students at Ohio State University were asked to estimate the distance from the campus to various points in Columbus, newcomers were surprisingly accurate, but students familiar with the city greatly overestimated the number of miles to the central business section. Impatience with traffic lights and stop signs and the frayed nerves of downtown driving had made the distance seem farther than it was (Golledge 1973).

The environment is cognized as a set of mental images. Both perceptual distortion and the expectations we bring to the environment affect the role we play in it. People develop selective and unique conceptions of the cities they live in, their schools and hospitals, the route they take to work; these in turn influence how they use, move about in, and, indeed, feel about the space. As a function of cultural background, age, sex, social class, occupation, and other factors, this cognitive environment will vary from person to person and group to group. It is no less functional than the geographical environment, since mental images predispose the manner in which we interact with the actual physical setting.

It is this cognitive structuring of the environment that enables us to organize our world in a recognizable and manageable way. Unless we were able to schematize the environment in terms of mental images, we could hardly hope to live in it with any degree of predictability, although it is quite obvious that we are continually having to correct our distortions against reality. But even with these built-in errors, only because we can code, structure, and store perceived information phenomenologically—that is, in a mental setting—can we order it physically. It is this internalized environment that gives form to the visible world.

The environment has symbolic value. What the environment means to us in terms of literal perception—whether it is coherent, esthetically interesting, jumbled—and what it means in terms of value and function is not always the same. A throne is different from a stool, although both are objects to sit on. Certain landmarks help us find our way about a city, quite apart from their usefulness as buildings or parks. Symbolic communication is implicit in most settings, telling us what to expect of a particular setting, and beyond this how to evaluate ourselves in relation to it. Burnette (1971) had called this role of the environment a "fundamental reference system" by which we interpret the significance of a setting. "We 'read' the meaning of iron bars or open gates . . . and understand a man by being in his home. . . ." [p. 68]

It is this quality of the environment that provides man with that sense of "place identity" which helps to define the role he plays in society. Zeisel (1971) has remarked on the tendency of many women to regard their kitchens not merely as a place to cook in, but, more importantly, as a means of proving that they do their job in society well. Large-scale environments perform this same symbolic function for groups, making possible a sense of social identity, as we have noted in connection with the city slum dweller who finds in his environment a sense of belonging that outweighs the physical disadvantages of decrepit buildings and dirty streets. Indeed, the so-called negative aspects of a given environment may be exactly those which contribute the most to a positive outlook on it. A survey of midwestern dust bowl farmers, many of whom refused to relocate when the opportunity came, revealed that for 88 percent of them the elements of conflict, risk, and uncertainty in their way of life were integral to their self-image. Pride in the ability to "stick it out" overrode the inhospitable environment, which in turn had conditioned them to just such pride (Saarinen 1966).

It is in this sense that the Eskimo is at home in the Arctic and the Bedouin in the desert. The environment provides roots, not only in the immediate present, but in an indeterminate cultural past. This is most strikingly illustrated today in the case of the Jews, who have created in the state of Israel a homeland to enclose their cultural and ethnic history. This patch of desert is not merely a territory colonized by a few, but a country filled with symbolic meaning for many.

"The landscape in general serves as a vast mnemonic system for the retention of group history and ideals," the urbanologist Lynch (1960) has written. It is not surprising, therefore, that groups as well as individuals have always seen their world in vastly different ways, for what they interpose between themselves and reality is a symbolic environment derived from their cultural inheritance. How these attitudes have evolved historically in relation to the natural environment, and how man has responded to this environment over time, will be examined in the following chapter.

References

Burnette, C. The mental image of architecture. In *Architecture for human behavior: Collected papers from a mini-conference.* Philadelphia: Philadelphia Chapter/The American Institute of Architects, 1971. Pp. 65–73.

Dubos, R. *So human an animal.* New York: Scribner, 1968.

Gans, H. *The urban villagers.* New York: Free Press, 1962.

Golledge, R. G., & Zannaras, G. Cognitive approaches to the analysis of human spatial behavior. In W. H. Ittelson (Ed.), *Environment and cognition.* New York: Seminar Press, 1973.

Hall, E. T. *The hidden dimension.* Garden City, N.Y.: Doubleday, 1966.

Izumi, K. Some psycho-social considerations of environmental design. Two lectures given at the University of Waterloo, Waterloo, Ontario, November 13 and December 11, 1969.

Lynch, K. *The image of the city.* Cambridge, Mass.: The M.I.T. Press, 1960.

Mead, M. *Culture and commitment.* Garden City, N.Y.: Natural History Press, 1970.

Pastalan, L. A., & Carson, D. H. (Eds.) *Spatial behavior of older people.* Ann Arbor, Mich.: University of Michigan Press, 1970.
Rapoport, A. Whose meaning in architecture? *Interbuild/Arena,* 1967, *83.* Pp. 44–46.
Saarinen, T. *Perception of the drought hazard on the Great Plains.* Chicago: Department of Geography, University of Chicago, 1966.
Shepherd, P. Introduction: Ecology and man—A new viewpoint. In P. Shepherd and D. McKinley (Eds.), *The subversive science: Essays toward an ecology of man.* Boston: Houghton Mifflin, 1969. Pp. 1–10.
Shepherd, P., & McKinley, D. *The subversive science: Essays toward an ecology of man.* Boston: Houghton Mifflin, 1969.
Sommer, R. *Personal space.* Englewood Cliffs, N.J.: Prentice-Hall, 1969.
Toffler, A. *Future shock.* New York: Random House, 1970.
Wolff, K. H. (Ed.) *The sociology of Georg Simmel.* New York: Free Press, 1950.
Zeisel, J. Fundamental values in planning with the non-paying client. In *Architecture for human behavior: Collected papers from a mini-conference.* Philadelphia: Philadelphia Chapter/ The American Institute of Architects, 1971. Pp. 23–30.

Suggested Readings

Kepes, G. (Ed.) *Arts of the environment.* New York: Braziller, 1972.
Smithsonian Annual II: The fitness of man's environment. Washington, D.C.: Smithsonian Institute Press, 1968.
Wagner, P. *The human use of the earth.* New York: Free Press, 1960.

Two

Historical Attitudes toward the Natural Environment

> Tell me the landscape in which you live, and I will tell you who you are.
>
> —*Ortega y Gasset*

In the first chapter it was noted that apart from their immediate stimulus properties, all environments carry a set of meanings acquired through their specific social, cultural, or economic attributes. These are cognized by the individual in terms of his own perceptions and values. We may admire a field of wheat for its beauty, but we know that its purpose is to produce food. Beyond this manifest function, it may stand as a source of power and prestige to the owner. It represents his ability to buy and sell and exert influence in the community. This is its latent meaning. Finally, if it is farmed by progressive and up-to-date methods, it can be said to symbolize the new agriculture. These environmental meanings—aesthetic, utilitarian, latent, and symbolic—are all responded to in some degree.

They are not, however, static meanings. Wherever man inhabits the earth, the environment is altered dramatically; even natural areas which are not exposed to human activity change ecologically as the result of natural forces—the erosion of a shoreline by tides, for instance, or the destruction of plant life by hurricanes. As human behavior is modified, as new discoveries about the nature of reality come into existence, and new philosophies of life evolve, our attitude toward the world in which these meanings are embedded changes too. This chapter will show how these conceptual attitudes toward the natural world developed over a period of time, and indicate some of the forces behind these changes.

Modern man has a vastly different notion of what is significant about his environment from that held by primitive man, and both ancient and modern attitudes differ considerably from those advanced by the pagan Greeks, and later, the medieval theologians. Moreover, none of these interpretations bear much similarity to the philosophy of the natural world that developed in the Orient. One way of accounting for these differences is to say that man's attitude toward his environment is a reflection of his need to find a secure and meaningful place for himself in it. In the West this has led to a man-centered view of the world, a view that separated him from nature, making him, in Plato's words, "the measure of all things." From such a perspective we can imagine a universe that preceded our arrival on earth, and one that will certainly continue should human life disappear. The day-to-day environment that we live in, however, acquires value only to the extent that we project human meaning into it. This may seem like a rather obvious point; yet Western man has always tended to accept the natural environment as a given, subject to human control but nevertheless independent of human existence. We find a place in nature, but not necessarily as part of nature's scheme. We are more likely to adapt the world to ourselves than the other way around. This Western, scientifically oriented tradition is one of prediction and control, leading to utility. The environment, so to speak, is worthy of its hire.

In comparing this point of view with the Eastern one, we see man not as a creature who is separated from his world, but as a part of nature's organic whole, a being who sensitizes himself to a direct experience of the natural world without the need of scientific models to explain it. This Eastern sense of being at one with nature, of apprehending it as the Divine Ground through which a supernatural being manifests his presence, makes man's relation to the natural order the source of ultimate values. Under these circumstances one's attitude will differ considerably from a Judeo-Christian conception of nature as wholly external to man, and largely indifferent to his well-being.

The Symbolic Landscape

In the language of anthropology such differences are said to be cross-cultural; that is to say, all cultures have their own unique ways of looking at, describing, and signifying their environments. Throughout history artists have taught men different ways of seeing nature, just as writers have shown us various ways of thinking about it. One effect of this has been to make nature imitate art, to create an orderly and meaningful environment out of a natural and chaotic one. In essence, art constitutes a kind of feedback system, a means whereby men send messages to themselves about the nature of reality.

Of course, what these messages will be is partly a matter of taste. In eighteenth- and nineteenth-century England, the ideal landscape was pastoral. Much of the English countryside was landscaped, quite literally, in imitation of the paintings of Salvatore Rosa, Claude Lorrain, and others. These men, in turn, were part of a tradition that modeled its world on the Arcadian landscape of Virgil and Ovid. That such a Golden Age never really existed was not important; what counted was that men believed it had and painted accordingly.

On a more profound level, men alter their landscapes out of religious belief. In medieval Germany forests were destroyed by Christian missionaries —interestingly, not because they were jealous of woodland gods, but because they wanted to prove that contrary to ancient belief, the wilderness was not sanctified. Nothing dire would happen to the person who destroyed it. If the wilderness remained a place of punishment (as it did), it was because man was removed from the works of his fellow men who were made in the image of God.

The persistence of this Teutonic attitude on a secular dimension is found in Grimm's *Fairy Tales*, where the forest remains the menacing abode of witches, wild animals, and ogres. Much later, when conceptions of the natural environment had changed dramatically, our own American wilderness was perceived as a source of adventure and a sanctuary from the ills of urban civilization. This romantic viewpoint was epitomized in James Fenimore Cooper's *Leatherstocking Tales*, but it lingers in our retrospective attitude toward the Wild West. Our guiding principle toward the wilderness is that it must either challenge us to subdue it or provide an escape from the man-made world.

Every country to some extent shapes its view of the environment along such literary axes. Willa Cather gives us a rural midwest that is both more rural and midwestern than probably existed for her contemporaries. It is the essential environment as it affected the lives and shaped the values of her characters that matters to us. In the numerous man-against-nature novels, the environment becomes the protagonist. In others the natural setting gives significance to the actions of the characters. The brooding landscape of Thomas Hardy's Wessex novels symbolizes the agnostic fatalism and impersonal destiny that hangs over the lives of those who are caught in it. Many similar examples come to mind: the English Midlands of D. H. Lawrence and Arnold Bennett; the lake country of Wordsworth; and the Dublin of James Joyce's *Ulysses*, of which Joyce himself said that if the city were to be destroyed, it could be rebuilt street by street from his book. Indeed, with all its changes, it is the Dublin of Joyce that one visits today. Such writers created figurative land- and cityscapes that continue to influence the perception of environments long after they have changed. These are inherited landscapes, so to speak, the mental afterimages that make the immediate world a repository of memories and meanings from an earlier time.

This power of previous generations to impose their ordering of nature on the present is most visible, of course, in the permanent additions to the landscape itself. Charles Madge (1950) has remarked that physical change both expresses a past of existing culture and helps to set a pattern for social behavior in the present and the future. The relative permanence of buildings, roads, and railways has the effect of imposing on later generations the ideas and habits of their forerunners. [Pp. 188–189].

There are many similar influences that shape our attitudes toward the environment—the force of custom, economic and social conflict, the conception of common versus private ownership of the land, and legislative practices. For example, the face of England in the late eighteenth and early nineteenth centuries was drastically changed by the Parliamentary Enclosure Acts which all but eliminated common grazing land in favor of the neat, hedgerow-enclosed fields typical of the country today. In our own country the various Homestead Acts tended to establish the pattern of squared-off, 160-acre farms still common throughout the Middle West.

Nature Worship

One of the oldest and most persistent factors that affects one's perception of the land, in a very broad sense, might be called philosophical. Compare primitive man's animistic view of the natural world with modern man's Newtonian, or even Einsteinian, view. Early peoples held that many objects in nature were inhabited—or animated—by spirits. Gods of the sea, rivers, mountains, and fields were placated through ceremony and sacrifice. In a general way these men worshipped Nature as such. Their gods were found *in* the world, not outside it. Well into the Renaissance, the reluctance of Christians to give up this notion is found in the metaphysical concept of *anima mundi*, the "spirit of nature" through which the will of God becomes expressed in the world of matter. In its nineteenth-century American variant, the Oversoul of the Transcendentalists served a similar role.

Modern scientific explanations allow no room for natural spirits; the lawful universe is measured and understood without recourse to magic or religion.[1] Yet when we come to compare these various points in time, a very curious thing is observed: Man, in his own way, still worships nature. We speak of "communing" with nature and of the healing qualities of the natural world and the "spiritual values" to be found in the wilderness. Prairies and mountains are still perceived as "God's country." Indeed, we set aside environmental sanctuaries closed to human exploitation. One wonders whether the deemphasis on religion in our own time has not resulted in a search for transcendence, but within a natural context. God may be dead but Nature is alive and well.

[1] It is interesting, however, to observe animistic attitudes toward objects in young children. See Piaget (1929), *The Child's Conception of the World.*

No doubt this persistent appeal represents a psychological as well as a spiritual need. Especially today, we find relief in turning away from a man-made world that seems to oppress us with its materialistic scheme of values to an undefiled world—where, in fact, this is still the case—that promises psychic renewal. Beyond this, the ecological crisis has compelled us to think about the natural environment in an apocalyptic way. Conservationists, ecologists, and biologists speak of an imminent breakdown of the ecosystem with much the same urgency that certain fundamentalist religious sects predict the end of the world.

For these reasons it is possible that man is learning to respect nature more than ever. As in ancient times, survival is the issue. But the differences are worth noting. In some ways, primitive man's knowledge was advanced enough to know how to use the environment wisely. Moreover, it was not simply fear of environmental catastrophe or of displeasing gods that animated these people; their religious orientations made room for a joyous and thankful celebration of nature's bounty. Our own efforts to resolve the man/environment crisis is rational, but the assumption is much the same: We cannot remain indifferent to the natural world.

In very recent times we have added a significant element to the idea of nature. We know that the environment can no longer be understood without taking into account the effects of human intervention. This realization in itself has profoundly altered our perception of the natural world. Departing from strict Darwinian ecology, with its emphasis on the hierarchical and predatory aspects of evolutionary adaptation, we stress equilibrium and interdependance. This is the concept of ecosystem. In effect, this environmental system involves the interactions that take place both within and between the organic and inorganic systems of nature, and it relates these systems to each other in a cooperative–competitive whole that is held in dynamic tension. An ecosystem implies homeostasis, or stability, and feedback. Climatic, hydrological, and nutritional aspects of the environment all contribute to the functioning of the system, so that ecological damage occurs when any part of it is irreversibly altered. Such alterations may be and frequently are human in origin.

To see the environment as a system to be maintained, rather than a resource to be looted, offers significant opportunity for a change in attitude toward the natural world, which once again becomes central to all life. This change may simply take the form of fewer beer cans on the highways, a prohibition against strip mining, or the reforestation of cut-over land. Unfortunately, it seems to be the case that environmental looting, insofar as it leads to disaster, is more instrumental in changing our attitudes than positive feelings of respect for the environment. For a change in attitudes to succeed in altering our behavior, it is often necessary for an irrational change to precede them. In any case, the message is clear and remarkably similar to that which influenced the ancients. In primitive times Nature said to man: If you mistreat me, the gods will punish you. In the modern world, Nature says to man: If you mistreat me, Nature will punish you. Our task, then, is to trace the route that took us from animism to the ecosystem.

The Greek World of Ideal Forms

The animistic view of nature held by some, but by no means all, primitive societies, gave way in time to the classical mythologies with which we are more or less familiar today. Although the mythological gods provided a supernatural hierarchy into which the workings of the natural world could be fitted, they did not in themselves explain how this world operated. They had ceased to be thought of as inherent in objects and lived a life outside, although certainly not independent of, the natural environment, directing their attention chiefly to the welfare of the human beings in whose imagination (in the last analysis) they really dwelt. Moreover, as we know, many pre-Christian peoples, from the Babylonians onwards, not wholly enslaved by their myths, were able to deduce cause-and-effect relationships in isolated cases, although careful observation and experiment was in practice extremely limited. The result of this primitive view of nature and its workings was not so much a science of relationships (as we know it today) but a philosophy of things.

The major characteristic of this philosophy, which reached its apogee among the Greeks of Plato's and Aristotle's time, was the belief that objects and forms did not change. The natural world was seen as an orderly hierarchy of elements governed by their own inherent principles, rather than by a contigent relation to other objects, and these principles were subject to rational and logical (rather than empirical) explanation. The Greeks lived in a world of necessity and changelessness in which the modern idea of dynamic movement—of change from within—was missing.

Two important developments stemmed from this conception of a stable, unchanging universe. One of these was the belief that objects could best be explained in terms of their individual essences or intrinsic properties. This idea underlies Plato's concept of the Ideal. It was the "idea-ness" common to a group of objects, rather than the "thing-ness" of the individual object, which gave meaning to the natural world. Things were classified not according to whether they acted on one another in some specific way, but on the basis of a similarity of function. Purpose was what mattered and this purpose could be rationally intuited from formal structures. Greek science, therefore, was the search for essences. It was concerned primarily with logic rather than experiment.

To say this is not to deny the speculative genius of the Greek mind. Euclidian geometry alone, in its logical treatment of spatial relationships, was an achievement without which it is difficult to imagine the Galilean breakthrough of the late Renaissance. But the Greeks possessed almost no analytic tools with which to break down and study their environment—certainly not the high-powered telescopes, centrifuges, spectroscopes, atom smashers, and other paraphernalia of the modern laboratory. They were compelled to deduce the workings of nature from superficial appearances. As a result, it was quite logical that natural objects had meanings in the same way that man-made objects did. Both seemed to have been made for a specific and intelligible purpose.

This is in no sense the same as animism. Although believers in myth, the Greeks were not especially superstitious. And just as many Christian theologians are able to reconcile supernatural doctrine with modern science, so the Greeks found room for a variety of personal gods and a rational view of natural events. To them, it was "what the purpose is" rather than "what's it made of" or "how it works" that mattered. This idea that things were not to be understood through mechanical function, but in terms of ultimate purpose, is what we mean by teleology.

The second development that grew out of this concept of a changeless and purposive world was reflected in the Greek view of time. Actually, it was a view shared by almost all the civilized world before the epoch of the Old Testament Jews. Although time might be experienced on a day-to-day basis as passing, and the days and months themselves marked off by calendars, it was conceptualized in the long run as cyclical, forever repeating itself, and therefore predictable. The idea of a progressive sequence of events—an open-ended universe that was evolving toward a different structure from that apprehended now—went far beyond the limits of the Greek imagination. Classical thinkers certainly had a sense of time, but it was circular in form, based on repetition rather than change. Cyclical time allowed them to find meanings and even the answers to mundane problems in terms of ideals that were embedded in an already structured universe. That these meanings could be contingent on one another, however, was inconceivable since relationships, even though not fixed immutably, would sooner or later exhibit their inherent and intended order.

If this pagan view of the world imposed order on what today we would call an existential chaos, it nevertheless lacked a clear notion of direction and causality. Ancient man lacked the historical sense that is so characteristic of our own era. Nature and time were perceived as givens and man himself, as well as his gods, was very much implicated in their structure, although in a curiously passive way. On one level this attitude is exemplified in the polytheism of the Greco-Roman world—the idea of many gods who were identified with natural phenomena. But also it accounts for that aspect of classical humanism in which man saw himself both at the center of the universe and inseparable from it. It has been said that although the Greeks believed in Fate, they acted as free men. They were free, that is, within a system, and retribution was visited on them when, in overreaching themselves in their pride, or *hubris,* they assumed the roles of gods. This was possible because there had not yet grown up the distinction—so sharply defined in Christian times—between man's universe and God's. Man had not yet been wholly divorced from the objective world.

The Christian Belief in Divine Creation

For Christians, initially there was an adaptation of the Aristotelianism of the Greeks to the requirements of the Church fathers. Toward the end of the medieval period, they abandoned this position and argued that the world was not to be understood by looking into the nature of things; on the contrary, meanings were deduced by examining their relationships. These were expressed in a divine master plan in which the enormous complexity of man's environment was given order and purpose and, at the same time, put at man's disposal. As the Christian era progressed into the Renaissance, this investigation of the natural world became more and more controlled and experimental. Ultimately, it cast doubt on the belief that the universe was, indeed, God's handiwork after all.

It may seem far-fetched to relate Judeo-Christian doctrine to a study of the environment. In fact, it is impossible to understand Western man's attitude toward the natural world today without grasping the nature of .the changes in belief that began two thousand years ago. One belief centered on the dualism of man and nature. Man was not just another object in an organic whole, he was a divinely created being set over the natural world. As a result, he was free to exploit nature without fear of being punished. Finally, Christianity gave men a linear view of time. It fostered the idea of progress and thus provided a world that was capable of change. Let us look briefly at these three developments: the man/environment dualism; the exploitative attitude toward nature; and the idea that time is linear, that it is "going somewhere."

When we say that Christians exploited nature we do not mean to imply that primitive men, for all their animism, magic, and mythology, were any less dependent on the environment for survival. Quite obviously they too used nature for their own ends. Fishing, hunting, quarrying, the cutting of trees and gathering of fruit are practices that hardly need to be justified, nor are they necessarily destructive. Christianity was different in that it provided a religious sanction for these practices which altered man's respect for the forces of nature—a nature which had hitherto been seen as relatively benign and even sacrosanct.

A justification of this new attitude, metaphorically at least, is expressed in the Biblical account of man's fall. Once banished from the Garden of Eden, Adam and Eve were compelled to fend for themselves in a largely inhospitable world. And although they had sinned by trying to usurp God's function —by attempting to discover what only God Himself could know—they never ceased to be reflections of God's image rather than Nature's.

The Greeks called this prideful challenge to divine power *hubris*. For the early Christians, who had no clear conception of psychology, the equivalent idea was a lack of humility. God was the "maker of heaven and earth," and yet there was never any doubt that earth had been made for man's benefit. Although the world was to be apprehended rationally, such apprehension was guided by divine inspiration as radiated by the Church Fathers. Indeed, it was Adam's attempt to experience nature directly and sensuously that resulted in his banishment from the Garden of Eden.

An important consequence of this attitude was that the natural world ceased to have the same meaning it had had before the time of the Judeo-Christian prophets. Lynn White, Jr. (1969) sums up this change when he writes that the study of nature was carried on "for the better understanding of God . . . Nature was seen primarily as a symbolic system through which God speaks to men. . . ." [p. 348] In this sense, it had no great value in and of itself; the idea of beauty in the natural environment gave way to a supernatural beauty expressed in the idea of the good. And it was to this idea, rather than to nature as such, that men related. When one looked at nature, it was to realize that God was reflected there nowhere so clearly as in man himself and his creations.

Painting and the Christian Vision

This reflection of God-in-man—essentially a belief in the divine goodness of man—made the natural world of secondary interest to Christian artists. Nature was not painted for its own sake, but as background illustration in pictures that depicted a religious theme. It was not appearances but the moral intention that mattered. Here we see the interrelatedness of art and the changing conceptions of the natural environment that characterizes all societies from the most primitive to the most developed. The painter is a precursor of the styles by which men learn to perceive the world around them. It is he who shows others how to look at nature, and it is in his work that nature is most vividly recorded. To say "this is the way it looked to the artist," however, is not, in any literal sense, to imply that "this is the way it necessarily was." Art has always projected its own vision onto reality; only the camera shows us the naive world.

In the case of early Christian and medieval painting, this vision was wholly didactic. Art taught the exemplary life and celebrated the glory of God; it was concerned least of all with fidelity to natural objects. Technically, the artist also lacked the skill to paint naturalistically, especially when dealing with perspective, but even had he possessed the skill there would have been no incentive to use it for a lifelike portrayal of nature. Christianity was not ready for a sensuous, realistic rendering of the world.

Why was this true? The denial of feeling among the early Christians, the triumph of Logos, the divine Word, over the sensing person, gave them a masculine approach to nature that made it difficult to relate to it in an empathic way. This is explained by the historical attitude that saw feeling and emotion as characteristic of the "lesser vessel," that is, woman. In a male-dominated religion, logic became associated with the masculine way of relating to the world, with feeling of intuition considered too unreliable a means for revealing truth. The result was a devaluation of certain ways of knowing about the world and a devaluation of those who adhered to this "feminine" mode. Thus, insensitive to a direct experience of nature, dominated by a rational model that came to him through revealed propositions, Biblical man was a separate perceiver of his environment rather than an interacting component. Nature was mistrusted. Objects were considered sinful in direct proportion to the number of senses they excited. Moreover, since life on earth was brief, there was little need to pay close attention to one's natural surroundings; what mattered were the spiritual truths that guided the Christian's search for perfection.

In middle- and late-Medieval painting this moral didacticism led to what Sir Kenneth Clark (1946) has called a "symbolic" style. Nature itself was used simply to provide a certain amount of decorative addition to the scene; natural objects such as flowers or trees became highly stylized representations, leading to a kind of abstract patterning of the objects. Interestingly, it was in these patterns that artists began to be concerned with the original objects themselves, the symbols leading to a closer examination of the objects being symbolized.

An example of this approach to nature through its symbols in medieval times was the garden, which could be construed as a foretaste of paradise. Paradise Gardens became extremely popular among the wealthier classes in Europe, and their representation in painting was commonplace throughout the twelfth to fifteenth centuries. (See Plate 1). This recurring theme attempts to unify the disparate objects of nature into a harmonious enclosure. Although the wilderness itself retained much of its old terror, the garden landscape offered viewers a sensuous enjoyment of nature within the framework of theological approval. Even today gardens are separated from the rest of nature as symbols of a "benign and orderly world," as McHarg (1966) has written. Unlike the complexity of nature, they are "reduced to a single and comprehensible geometry" in which "plants are analogous to domestic pets" [p. 527]; a domestication, it might be added, which was compatible with Biblical notions of man as master.

Ah Wilderness!

Compare the Paradise Garden with Domenico Veneziano's "Saint John in the Desert" (Plate 2). Here is nature outside the garden, and a grotesque and baffling nature it is. As in all panoramic landscapes of the early fifteenth century, the mountains are virtually without vegetation; the grotesque angles of these mountains symbolized barren places, part of a pictorial tradition

PLATE 1 Master of Flémalle and assistants. "Madonna and Child with Saints in the Enclosed Garden." Courtesy, National Gallery of Art, Washington, D.C.

dating back to Hellenistic times. The human figure is clearly out of scale; mystery predominates. All this is intentional. Yet there was another reason why these Gothic mountains were unreal: Medieval man did not explore them. Not only was he uninterested, but to do so implicated him in the sinful practice of being carried away by sights which the domesticated garden did not provide. Petrarch, Clark (1946) notes, "was the first man to climb a mountain for its own sake, and to enjoy the view from the top," although he renounced this enjoyment and "turned my inward eye upon myself." [p. 7] Thus, well into the Renaissance, wild country was seen as both a tempting and a dangerous place.

Among other reasons, this explains why Christianity became quite early an urban movement. We should stress here that we are speaking of the relatively small part of the population which was literate—those who understood the church's theology, largely the upper classes. These people were not only urban, but they shunned contact with the natural environment. For them, to be a country dweller was to be a pagan. It was in the cities that one was sur-

PLATE 2 Domenico Veneziano. "Saint John in the Desert." Courtesy, National Gallery of Art, Washington, D.C.

rounded by the works of the mind and these, in turn, were emblematic of a creativity in God that transcended the physical world and gave a higher value to things of the spirit. As we shall see, this trend was to have profound consequences on the development of science, for it was largely in the cities, with their leisure class, their emphasis on learning, and their facilities for experiment that a truly scientific study of nature was possible.

One other point needs to be emphasized in this Judeo-Christian approach to the natural world. Underlying the phenomenal, or experienced, environment was a verbal reality, an abstract meaning. "In the beginning was the Word." Men and things were an incarnation of this creative Logos, and the truth about nature was to be found in the verbal reconstruction of the world considered as a system of law which preceded and underlay it. The architectonic style of Christianity is nowhere clearer than in the idea of God the maker. The world is an artifact constructed in accordance with a divine plan; therefore, it has a purpose and an explanation. Unlike the religions of the Orient, which see their gods as essentially inward-dwelling, mediating the forms of nature with man's innate ethical sense, the Christian God is an outward Being who guides and judges men from on high.

This mechanical model of a universe open to rational investigation was a necessary precedent for later scientific inquiry. By implication, it also put a high value on artifacts, on created over natural things. For nature itself could not be so easily controlled and explained. In its wild state it became the villain, feared as the beguiler and temptress, an abyss of universal flux always threatening to swallow the individual, a cancerous proliferation against which every human work must be defended with perpetual vigilance. Much of our modern ambivalence toward wild places stems from the fear and sense of mystery which they inspired in earlier times. We are not quite certain today whether to hold the wilderness in awe, conquer it for human use, or somehow to do both, for Christian teaching has left us no clear guide.

Probably the most obvious thing about the wilderness is a symbolic environment is its age-old association with evil. In mythology it was the forests and dank places that harbored dragons. The Sphinx waited just outside the gate of Thebes for her ransom of human flesh, casting her spell on the inhabitants of the city. The legendary semihuman wild man of medieval times, his naked figure covered with thick hair, was a common denizen of the wilderness in the art and drama of the period. To this was added in Central and Northern Europe the idea of a supernatural being. In Germany, when storms raged, it was believed that the Wild Huntsman was abroad with his pack of baying hounds. And it was here that St. George slew the dragon. Even in relatively advanced cultures, such as the Greco-Roman, satyrs, not to mention the woodland god Pan, used the wilderness as a place for mischief.

The significance of this continuing attitude, with its representation in mythology, art, and such literary works as *Beowulf*, is threefold: First, the wilderness, little explored, was truly a source of mystery and danger. Roads were nonexistent and one entered the deeper forest, even to hunt, at considerable risk. It was easy to get lost. The "wilderness" was genuinely "wild," and men had not the means of coping with it that they have today.

This actual danger fostered a second level of perception which can be called symbolic danger. Because the wilderness was unknown and untamed, it was logical to fill it with mythological terrors of the imagination. Men separated themselves from such an inhospitable world and made slight distinction between its real and imaginary dangers.

In itself, such an imputation may be thought of as no more important than a child's fear of the dark. Actually, many modern scholars believe that these reactions to wilderness disguised a third and deeper relationship which was psychological. For in addition to being a refuge for objective danger, the unknown regions served as symbolic outlets for the evil that is found in man's own nature. The so-called subterranean tendencies, the "animal," "wild," and "daimonic" qualities that betray man's "higher self," were all projected outward; the darker side of man identified with the dark and unexplored places of nature. A good deal of forest mythology is now seen as an attempt to get rid of one's inner demon by creating an external counterpart. And for this, the wilderness was a highly suitable environment.

Biblical Orientations to Wilderness

The Bible furnished another source of attitudes about the wilderness, but in this case the orientation could be quite ambiguous. A cursed land, associated with the absence of water, it was here that God sent men for punishment. The Fall of Man, in one sense, was Paradise lost to a disorderly and barbaric nature. Yet Biblical accounts left room in this land, as later doctrines did not, for refuge and redemption. The Jews in forty years of wandering found the Sinai desert a sanctuary from persecution. For Christ the wilderness was a retreat in which He could draw close to God. Indeed, the value of such isolated and uncivilized regions was precisely in the hardships they imposed; purged and humbled, people were made ready for the land of promise. One used the wilderness as a means of rebirth, as indeed, in a more secular way, we use it today.

This ambiguity toward that which was essentially mysterious and wild, this conception of the wilderness as an evil place that was yet latently good, persisted throughout the Middle Ages. Because it could not be controlled by man, it was obviously not one of his beneficences. That pagan tribes in Northern Europe celebrated their rites in these sacred groves was all the more reason to destroy them. The great exception to this view, St. Francis of Assisi, who believed that animals had souls and adopted a posture of humility toward the natural world, was declared a heretic—the Church had too much at stake in the notion of man's dominance over nature. Moreover, it preached an aloofness from the world which guaranteed little appreciation of natural beauty for itself. Even as late as the Renaissance, Christians offered considerable resistance to the enjoyment of paintings in which the landscape was meant to delight. Such joy was too sensuous—as it became for the Puritan three hundred years later.

The religious, although not wholly Puritanical, influence on men's perception of wilderness is nowhere better illustrated than in the settling of the New World and the westward movement of the pioneers. Hopes of finding a second Eden were quickly shattered against the reality of the land. William Bradford found Cape Cod "wild and desolate." Frontiersmen used terms such as "howling," "dismal", and "terrible" to describe the country they had to subdue. Longfellow's "forest primeval," with its "murmuring pines and hemlocks," was a later, and somewhat romantic, viewpoint best enjoyed in retrospect. Diaries from the period speak of the wilderness as an enemy to be conquered or subdued by a pioneer army.

On the surface, such reactions are easy to understand. Nature in its wild state did present a threat to human survival; with the land uncultivated, with no forests cleared or streams dammed, the pioneers had to start from the beginning. Settlements were carved out of the wilderness. Not only did nature present hazards, so did Indians who inhabited the region. Conquering the wilderness became the major concern of Americans well into the seventeenth century.

But the pioneers and settlers had a deeper response to nature than that represented by physical frustration; wild country represented a moral vacuum, a cursed and chaotic wasteland. To succumb to it was to revert to a state of savagery. For in conquering the New World, the colonists were also trying to conquer the evil in man, so that the Puritan fear of the wilderness is partly explained by the freedom it offered in escaping the constraints of civilization. Such temptation must be avoided, and in much of the moralistic writing of the seventeenth and eighteenth centuries we find numerous allusions to the wilderness as an unholy world, an environment of evil that must be resisted in the cause of good. Oddly enough, it was this very land which furnished the Puritans their own sanctuary from persecution.

As self-styled agents of God, these early colonists conceived their mission as one of breaking the power of evil. With their attitude toward "barbaric" nature, it is not surprising that they took pride in westward expansion; it was, after all, evidence of God's blessing. Even for such non-Puritans as Lewis Cass (1782–1866), Governor of the Michigan Territory, and George R. Gilmer (1802–1844), Governor of Georgia, Genesis 1:28 could be cited to justify the position that wilderness was waste, and that the proper behavior toward it was subjugation. In later times it became less necessary to find a religious sanction for doing what obviously had to be done—the cutting of timber and the turning of prairies into farmland. Pride of accomplishment was sufficient. One guidebook for settlers advertised: "You look around and whisper, 'I vanquished this wilderness and made the chaos pregnant with order and civilization, alone I did it.' "

Linear Time

In the preceding sections we have emphasized attitudes toward the natural world that grew out of philosophical and religious beliefs. One other important change in the world view must be added at this point—the Christian view of time. By this we mean that time was experienced as sequential, rather than circular, as the Greeks conceived it. True, there are repetitions in nature—the seasons, the life cycle of plants and animals, the ebb and flow of tides, the apparent movement of the solar system—but these were seen as phases in a long-range transformation of the universe. The cyclical repetitions took men back to where they had been; linear repetitions take them ahead to something new.

It is in this sense that Christianity gave the world a beginning (4004 B.C.) and foresaw an end (the Second Coming). It provided its believers with a past and a future, and in so doing imposed a commitment to the notion of change. This idea of one-way time was most systematically worked out by St. Augustine (354–430) in his *City of God*, but for truly scientific application it had to wait for the invention of the mechanical clock in the seventeenth century. Nevertheless, two attitudes that grew out of this concept became important to Christians metaphysically. As Langdon Gilkey (1965) puts it, man became "in some sense transcendent to the repetitive natural order" in which he participated, "conscious of his own unique capacity for self-direction and meaning. . . ." [p. 203]

In turn, this dynamic view made possible the belief that man could act on his environment, change it, and bend it to his purposes as these were manifested in some Divine purpose. For most of us today time is linear without Divine guidance. Modern technology—the sheer capability we have for changing our world—is its own justification.

Of course, beliefs alone do not change the environment. Had the early Christians not invented new tools, their attitude toward nature would have made little difference. Tools were the outgrowth of an empirical approach to the world. If men studied nature the better to understand God, they also discovered relationships that led to the better understanding of nature. Essentially, this derived from the observation that things in the natural world operated not according to a fixed and immutable principle, but in a contingent "cause and effect" relationship. An event might or might not occur depending upon other events that impinged on it; in any case, logical necessity no longer explained the workings of nature.

The significance of the empirical view is seen most dramatically in the theoretical discoveries of Galileo and Newton, but even in the early Middle Ages an elementary technology had begun to alter men's relation to their environment. Lynn White, Jr. (1969) cites the impact on farming methods that followed the introduction of the vertical knife plow in the late seventh century. Supplanting the scratch plow, which could be pulled by one animal, the vertical plow required eight oxen and a new distribution of labor. The size of farming units was expanded and a more intensive cultivation resulted. Whatever intimate link to nature men had brought from earlier times began to dissolve in a new technological distancing, an emphasis on technique and exploitation. "The new Frankish calendars, which set the style for the middle ages . . . ," White points out, "show men coercing the world around them—plowing, harvesting, chopping trees, butchering pigs." [p. 346]

In exploiting these everyday interests, the secular art of the period was intended to delight rather than instruct the viewer. But this was done through esthetic distance; one stood apart from these works, just as he remained aloof, for religious reasons, from nature itself. Still, it was a step forward. Men began to see the natural world in terms of its intrinsic beauty rather than as a collection of symbols and decorative abstractions. In numerous hunting scenes a more intimate contact with nature was both possible and permissible. It should be added that in these paintings the forest, different as it was from the garden, was not particularly remote from it and offered no sense of mystery. Paolo Ucello's "Hunt in the Wood" (Plate 3) illustrates both the proximate conception of the forest wilderness to human activity and its relative naturalism. Trees look like trees, although they remain very much the background element to the human setting.

This pictorial element is also found in religious paintings of the period in which the landscape, heretofore held tightly to foreground figures, suddenly opens up to include the distant features of sky and fields. By the early fifteenth century, nature was no longer represented as purely didactic. In the works of Hubert Van Eyck, for instance, there is a new congruence between the natural world and the painter's perception of it; objects and distances begin to resemble men's personal experience of them, and the ambience of the scene—the light and space with which it is surrounded—takes on a reality of its own. For the first time it is possible to see the world not as an assemblage of fragmented and formal elements related only to one another, but as a naturalistic whole in which the viewer himself is present.

Significant though this artistic breakthrough was, it did not alter the fundamental man/nature dualism on which Christian theology was posited. Here it might be instructive to compare this attitude toward the natural world with that of non-Western peoples, who have historically located the self on quite different axes of time and space. Eastern man is neither more nor less than other objects in the natural world; God is not separate from this world but is

PLATE 3 Paolo Ucello. "Hunt in the Wood" (detail). Ashmolean Museum, Oxford.

discovered within it, immanent rather than celestial. For some Eastern cultures, especially where Buddhism and Hinduism are practiced, time is cyclical and repetitive. History for these people, as Joseph Needham (1969) has phrased it, is a series of "repeat performances."

The Way of Tao

The religions of India and China have been termed the Perennial Philosophy. To our way of thinking they do, indeed, seem more philosophical than religious. The Oriental mind does not make our distinction between "natural" and "supernatural." Followers of Buddha and Lao Tzu, for example, yield to nature's flow and intuit its meanings directly and spontaneously. The Western emphasis on the ego is minimized. The mind itself and the supremacy of ideas play limited roles when one sensitizes oneself to the direct experience of the world. A rational model of the universe is dispensed with and words—the revealed propositions of Christianity that mediate between man and God—are unnecessary for its comprehension. God the maker gives way to the idea of nonmaking, to the spontaneity of creation. This is called an organicist view of nature. Things are understood by being part of them rather than by standing aside and studying their characteristics. Such an approach is facilitated by the contemplative disciplines practiced by many Asiatics as well as through their subjective sense of time.

Much has been written about the fatalism of Eastern thought. Because man is not at the center of the universe, he supposedly accepts his place in nature uncomplainingly, content to adapt rather than alter, resigned to the inevitable hardships of "letting nature take its course." This somewhat simplified view probably derives more from the economic and social realities of conditions in Asia than from religious faith. Moreover, as Needham (1969) has demonstrated, Chinese civilization, with its strong sense of history and its pragmatic control of nature, is really closer to the West in these respects than to India. Yet egocentrism is largely absent in all Eastern cultures, and men acquire dignity and worth through their empathic relation to nature rather than by superiority over it. This view places man within the world he had defined for himself, subject to the knowledge that his existence is inseparable from others and that, collectively, man can know nature only by submerging his ego in the totality of things. The Dharmadhatu doctrine of Mahayana Buddhism, as Alan Watts (1969) notes, sees "the universe [as] a harmonious system which has no governor, that it is an integrated organism but nobody is in charge of it." [p. 147] Likewise the doctrine of Tao involved an Order of Nature, but "no man can say where it dwells." (Huai Nan Tzu) The governing principles of the universe applied to both man and nature, which were ethically inseparable. Needham (1969) sums up one aspect of Tao when he writes: "The harmonious co-operation of all beings arose, not from the orders of a superior authority external to themselves, but from the fact that they were all parts in a hierarchy of wholes forming a cosmic and organic pattern, and what they obeyed were the internal dictates of their own natures." [p. 367]

Decidedly, this is an unscientific and nonpiecemeal approach. Tao did not, however, as Needham has shown, prevent the Chinese from achieving a workable science and a highly advanced technology. Unlike the Christian doctrine, Tao apparently forestalled a mechanical model of the world just as it mitigated against the modern notion of ego. The ego—the "I"—was submerged in nature. This is seen in the Tao concept of *Li*, or "principle," a term originally applied to markings in jade. The lack of symmetry, the fluidity and intricacy of pattern which appealed to the Chinese artisan, became the ideal mode of apprehension for all things. This patternless pattern, however, did not imply lack of form so much as a pattern without clearly discernible features.

Nor is the *Li* unknowable. The artist learns how to handle wood or jade not by imposing his order (or ego) on the material, but by following its dictates—the grain of the wood and the natural configurations of the stone. He is said to discover the underlying order of his medium not through logical analysis but by *kuan*, or silent contemplation. Spontaneity of response is sought. *Kuan* is to observe silently and openly without expecting any particular result. There is no duality between seer and seen; there is only seeing. This approach carried over, in Tao doctrine, to all nature. One's loss of ego did not mean loss of order but simply the emergence of a new order based on the resonance of relations between man and world.

Science and Nature

In spite of this organistically rooted approach to nature, Eastern man was far from unworldly, nor did he lack scientific accomplishments. Needham (1969) shows how progress in mathematics, engineering, and astronomy occupied a central place in Chinese civilization from 400 B.C. to 1600 A.D.

The encouragement of a farseeing central government, the absence of religious superstition, the practical value of scientific advance for the country as a whole, and the prestige enjoyed by those engaged in research all contributed to the development of a strong scientific tradition long before comparable achievements were recorded in Europe. A decimal metrology (first century B.C.) and the seismograph (180 A.D.) are two early examples. Work in optics, acoustics, and magnetism was under way in ancient China, and iron-casting was mastered some fifteen centuries before its discovery in the West. By the twelfth century A.D., mechanical clockwork, the building of iron chain suspension bridges, silk spinning, and printing were all well advanced.[1]

What then is the essential difference between the two traditions? In China such developments were largely pragmatic. Invention bore little relation to a world view; there was no sustained attempt to develop a scientific methodology. In the writings of Chuang Tzu the ideal, or pure, man is seen as a companion to nature who does not attempt to supplant nature's ways with his own. In the West the Christian idea of an underlying plan for the world served as a value matrix in which science could develop. If Eastern man saw himself as within nature, changing as it changed, Westerners perceived the natural world as changing only if man himself changed it. This conceptualization of nature as external to the self, as part of a divine master plan, invited the systematic investigation of its parts. Thus, the Western experiment in changing the face of nature has at its roots the political cosmology of Christian belief.

Historically, such a view may seem strange when we recall that the Church fathers often opposed scientific explanations as heretical and that Galileo was forced to recant for espousing a theory of motion that could not be easily reconciled with Christian doctrine. Yet the foundations of the new world had been laid. Avenues of discovery opened up as Christian scholars began to utilize the Aristotelian concepts of Greek science in a form that was compatible with Church teaching. Such philosophers as Albertus Magnus (1225–1274) helped provide a new outlook on the natural law that made possible a more pragmatic approach to the physical environment. It was a method, however, that was still largely metaphysical.

The Emphasis on Experiment

It remained for a Franciscan, Roger Bacon (1214?–1294), to detach this search for explanations from the wholly metaphysical realm and argue that experimental methods alone give certainty in science. Men like Bacon sensed that in a changing world the natural laws could best be discovered not by abstract reasoning but through careful experiment. Nothing was to be taken for granted. It should be added, however, that experiment was still carried

[1] We should make a distinction between the Chinese way of looking at nature and that of other Eastern peoples, especially the Buddhists for whom the world was, indeed, largely illusory and at times highly subjective and cyclical. In India particularly, technology no less than scientific theory was all but unknown, or borrowed from other nations. Whereas the Indians immersed themselves in the unknown ground of the nouménal universe—a world that transcended knowing—the Chinese found a secure place in a phenomenal world that could be apprehended directly and without the aid of an external God or a metaphysical system. Westerners, as we have seen, approached the natural world somewhat more arrogantly.

out within the Christian belief in a divine plan. Galileo's downfall came not because he was too scientific, but because he tried to be too much the theologian in reconciling his theory with church teaching. In any case, it was the component parts, not the universal scheme of things, that engaged the interest of these early scientists.

Two important consequences resulted from this method insofar as men's attitude toward the natural environment was concerned. One of these has to do with the idea that things and events bear a causal relationship to each other. This is the contingency view of which we spoke earlier. The order of nature was neither teleological nor could it be intuited from its forms; rather, the scientist must manipulate, measure, and study nature if he would discover its workings. For this, sensory interpretation was necessary, and emphasis on quantitative rather than qualitative relationships became paramount.

The other, and corollary, idea posits a mode of thinking in which things must be taken in one at a time. Such a view depends upon one's individual attention, the breaking of the perceptual field into assimilable bits. Once more, in this respect, Western man separated himself from nature. Not only was he outside it as a believer in Christian theology, he also found himself outside the finite world psychologically or, more strictly, perceptually. That is, he not only believed in the duality of man and nature, but he experienced nature itself as a collection of separate things.

This empiricism of Western thought created a dynamic which, in time, was to go far beyond the limits set by the Church. Nevertheless, belief in a universal law of nature based on a monotheistic God formed the premise on which science developed from the thirteenth century on. Because the divine will transcends human understanding, we can only know empirically, and the discovery of an empirical, contingent world led to the classification and description of objects which emphasized not only their differences, but their separateness from the perceiver. Man, in this sense, is removed from nature by words and symbols. He must form a relationship with nature rather than have one. This remains, in our own day, the primary mode of experience—a "thinking about" and "acting on" rather than a "feeling for" the natural world.

In discussing the assumption of Bacon that experimentation was the only way to certainty in science, it is important to note that this remained for some time a largely theoretical stance. It did not, for example, result in the immediate adoption of an experimental approach to problem solving, however it might influence one's conceptual approach to nature. Such an approach had to await the development of new techniques for exploring nature. It should be obvious, too, that Christianity did not purposely invent the scientific method or bring about the technological achievements that began in the late Renaissance. During the Middle Ages scholastics were far more involved in discourse about the metaphysical nature of things than about their physical meaning. Not until later did a truly scientific attitude develop, and the men who advanced it, like the theologians, were at pains to reconcile the new discoveries with Christian doctrine. Newton himself was an amateur theologian who had no intention of upsetting Christian belief. Although it cannot be said that he formulated the laws of gravity because he was a Christian, it is wholly unlikely that he could have done so without the time sense and the mechanical model of the world that Christianity supplied. Only in the seventeenth century did scientists break up the environment in a truly experimental way, and not until the eighteenth century did men feel free enough to dispense with God as a necessary force in their explanations of natural phenomena.

Painting, too, had begun to represent the world naturalistically and was to arrive at a similar fidelity to observed events. Both of these developments had their roots in the fifteenth century. It is useful to look at them separately, beginning with the artist's increasingly realistic depiction of the world, and then go back to scientists such as Descartes and Newton who conceptualized it in the abstract.

Nature as Fact

It was earlier noted that the artist helps men see nature in a new way. At the same time, he is also influenced by those for whom he paints. During the Renaissance this influence was in the direction of a realistic rather than of a metaphysical approach to nature. Men sought an art that represented this palpably different and "reborn" world. They found a new meaning in the here-and-now as the other-worldly aspects of Christianity were relaxed. In addition, the exploration of new continents and the growing commerce among all countries created a powerful merchant class that found its values in recognizable (profitable) things rather than in moral ideas. Finally, painting underwent changes from within. The discovery of "true perspective," a better understanding of physical perception, the scientific sense of relation and comparison, an ability to make light tangible and to give it movement, even advances in the technique of mixing and applying paint—all these factors made it possible for the artist to depict the natural environment in compelling new modes.

In the idealizing sense that all art aspires to, this movement resulted in a landscape much more faithful to the facts of nature than anything that had gone before. In Holland this is well represented by Ruisdael's "Forest Scene" (Plate 4). The remarkable aspect of this painting with its careful attention to natural detail is its starkly modern look. One reason for this is that light is no longer a flat backdrop but is modulated in degrees of intensity, highlighting objects in the foreground, and in general suffusing the scene with a gentleness that makes the wilderness less threatening. Nature is wild, dark in its crags and crevices, but on the whole it is on its way to being domesticated. The human figures, tiny in contrast with their surroundings and very much in scale, are still subordinated to the larger world, unlike those in Italian

PLATE 4 Jacob van Ruisdael. "Forest Scene." Courtesy, National Gallery of Art, Washington, D.C.

paintings where the human element predominates. Here, danger has disappeared, but the mystery of nature has not.

The significance of the painting is its humanizing of nature without loss of realism. Clark (1946) has written that facts become art through love, which lifts them to a higher plane.

This movement toward naturalism, which began with Hubert and Jan Van Eyck, developed chiefly in the Low Countries. Light, whether in the golden and heavenly tones of the Van Eycks, the delicate perceptiveness of Dürer, or the infinitude of Bellini, became the matrix in which feeling for the natural world was quickened. It is not totally accidental that the landscape painters of Holland worked within a context of scientific interest in botany. Men did not simply enjoy nature, they wanted to know its functioning, its secrets. These were seen as amenable to investigation, and painters, in this respect, illustrated the new empiricism. Yet the naturalistic school, at odds with the more rigorously scientific approach of the Florentines, was never a universal mode of painting and by the end of the fifteenth century it disappeared—more accurately, went underground—for 150 years.

Nature as Fantasy

Perhaps this is one way of saying that artists have never agreed, for more than a few generations at a time, on how they should look at nature. For the same countries that gave us a naturalistic approach in the fifteenth century were those that distorted fact into fantasy in the sixteenth. This is seen most powerfully in the works of Hieronymus Bosch (1450–1516) and his followers Pieter Brueghel (1525–1569), two painters with immense powers of observation who saw in nature not so much its serene and loving aspects, but all that was fretful, disturbing, and unpredictable. Brueghel's figures, artisans for the most part, are overwhelmed by their environment; as indeed such men often were in reality. The critic Max J. Friedlander (1963) has written of Brueghel that "The forces of nature determine the doings of man as they do the physiognomy of place. . . . The land is not only his home, it is also his fate, and man is more the slave of the earth than its master. . . . What Brueghel perceived . . . is the activity of the forces of nature, not the worked-upon world but the working world." [pp. 76, 78]

Fantasy was the dominant mode of the sixteenth century, especially in northern Europe, achieving, in men like Albrecht Altdorfer (c.1480–1538) and Matthias Grünewald (c.1480–c.1530), a view of nature that was at once primitive, in which man against struggles for a foothold, and yet consciously romantic, filled with fantastic, knotted shapes, fiery skies, and unearthly doings. Clark calls this art "forest born" and it is consistent with the Teutonic attitude toward nature as inherently threatening. We have seen how this orientation also characterized the Puritan settlers in America who, as Protestants, shared the German fear of wilderness. American painting, however, as we shall note later, was to add grandeur and romanticism to this essentially Protestant mistrust of nature.

This style, exemplified in one degree or another in the landscapes of Giorgione, Dürer, Leonardo, and El Greco (among many) aimed at a direct assault on the emotions. Their fiery heavens and Gothic mountains tapped the unconscious wellspring of feeling, bypassing the gentler moods of nature. The detail from Grünewald's "Isenheim Altar" (Plate 5) is far removed, for instance, from Ruisdael's naturalism in the Forest Scene painting.

In the latter part of the sixteenth century fantasy led to a picturesque and rhetorical style in which a feeling for the independent life of nature gave way to the classical detachment of the mannerists. Much of the excitement was still there, animated by an interplay among the forces of nature, but the result lacks the ring of truth. Landscape reflects not the artist's emotional involvement with the natural world, but his intellectual ordering of it.

Nature as Abstraction

By this time a number of developments had occurred in science which parallel this intellectual ordering of nature by the artist. While the painter was mov-

PLATE 5 Matthias Grünewald. "Isenheim Altar" (detail). Musée d'Unterlinden, Colmar, France.

ing away from the sensuous in nature, and toward a more rational interpretation of events, the scientist was putting reality through a series of geometric reductions. With Galileo the old scholastic substances gave way to an atomistic notion that explained the causality of events in terms of space and time. The real world functioned mechanically, although man retained his teleological place in it. Moreover, it was best understood mathematically. Did this eliminate God? Not yet. Robert Boyle and others hypothesized that the universe was simply a giant clockwork, wound up by a Creator who had no other function but to see to its efficient operation. With Descartes this dualism became more accentuated. For the medieval scholastic, at least, the world had existed in palpable form. For the new scientists, Descartes in particular, it existed as a web of geometrical relationships. Man was reduced to a very small portion of his own brain. The change that this induced in men's thinking during the seventeenth and eighteenth centuries is summed up by E. A. Burtt (1954):

> The scholastic scientist looked out upon the world of nature and it appeared to him a quite sociable and human world. It was finite in extent.

> It was made to serve his needs. It was clearly and fully intelligible, being immediately present to the rational powers of his mind; it was composed fundamentally of, and was intelligible through, those qualities which were most vivid and intense in his own immediate experience—color, sound, beauty, joy, heat, cold, fragrance, and its plasticity to purpose and idea. Now the world is an infinite and monotonous mathematical machine. Not only is his high place in a cosmic teleology lost, but all these things which were the very substance of the physical world to the scholastic—the things that made it alive and lovely and spiritual—are lumped together and crowded into the small fluctuating and temporary positions of extension which we call human nervous and circulatory systems. The metaphysically constructive features of the dualism tended to be lost quite out of sight. [Pp. 123–124]

If science sought to retain the Christian teleology within the new clockwork universe, painting, for which nature was more real than mere geometrical forms—and would remain so until the advent of cubism, much later—reenacted the Christian message within the esthetic framework of classical Greece and Rome. Descartes and his followers broke up the world into ever smaller bits, all but eliminating man in the process; artists like Titian reassembled the natural environment in the image of a vanished culture, with man once more at the center. Perhaps these two diverse interpretations of reality are not wholly unrelated. For two hundred years scientists had been destroying that which was "alive and lovely and spiritual" in the interests of the unseen and abstract. Now the landscape painter presented an ideal view of things, a nature tranquil and serene, reassuring in the civilized values that were depicted in calm waters, grazing sheep, and country pleasures. Things were under human control. An effortless harmony existed between man and nature—a mythical harmony in both senses of the word. For it was in the works of Virgil and Ovid that artists found their inspiration, and the Virgillian landscape became a visionary view of the earth, with the vision turned backwards instead of toward the future. Nature emerged as a source of joy rather than mystery, evoking a sense of the fullness of life and a confidence in the body. For above all, it was scaled to the human dimension. It was not simply a refuge from the outside world, as in the Paradise Gardens; nature opened into the world, symbolizing all that was good in it. But most importantly, nature was tamed and ordered—bent to man's needs. This approach to the natural environment was to figure prominently in later efforts by the colonists in America to bring wild nature under control.

This vision of a Golden Age spread throughout Italy, France, and England. Its practitioners included Giorgione and his student, Titian; Poussin, Claude (Lorrain), and later the English painter Constable. We include here (Plate 6) an example from Claude, "The Judgment of Paris." The first thing the viewer notices about the scene is its extreme tranquility. Claude, who worked directly from nature, has painted the French countryside through Arcadian spectacles. Artistically, the picture is remarkable for its rich observation of natural detail, its effortlessness, the sense of the compositional balance in nature joined with a spontaneous feeling for its beauty.

In contrasting mood, Nicholas Poussin painted what Clark (1946) calls

PLATE 6 Claude Lorrain. "The Judgment of Paris." Courtesy, National Gallery of Art, Washington, D.C.

the "heroic landscape." The purity and softness of Giorgione, the sensual intensity of Titian, Claude's wistful, parklike scenery are replaced by a rigorous and ordered nature; ordered, in part, by the imposition of architectural form or the intervention of a supporting cast of human figures. The scene is structured, as it were, by the mind rather than from its own necessity. But it was no less an earthly paradise, a style that was to endure among landscapists until the Englishman Samuel Palmer completed the movement in the first half of the nineteenth century.

A follower of the poet and mystic William Blake, Palmer introduced a direct spiritual perception into nature, finding God's pattern, in Clark's words, "in every blade of grass and leaf and cloud. . . ." Rural simplicity, however, no longer required classical references, and Palmer's setting is wholly English. But by this time the Industrial Revolution had begun its transformation of the countryside, and Darwin's theory of evolution was casting doubt on its godliness. Palmer's world was soon to become as remote as Giorgione's Greece.

Naturalism and Romance

In discussing the Arcadian painters we have bypassed the revival of naturalism that took place in Holland with the appearance of such masters as Rubens and van Ruisdael from 1625 on. This school of painters influenced, in one form or another, almost all landscape art in nineteenth century England, and to a lesser extent in France. How this came about is worth a moment's consideration.

To begin with, post-Renaissance Europe was becoming increasingly bourgeois. Ordinary citizens replaced the Church, royalty, and the ecclesiastical guilds as the source of patronage for artists. The landscape, like the portrait paintings of the period, should reflect the world that men were familiar with and it should be as comfortable. For the burgher mentality there was no need for disturbing and fantastic visions. They wanted the real thing. Actually, with such men as Rembrandt they got the real and something more—a tidy, bourgeois world opened up and made dramatic by the painter's imagination. Yet the idealization of the scene was never achieved at the expense of recognition. Even when classical themes were used (as in Rubens), the landscape remained Dutch. In Friedlander's (1963) words, Rubens "watches the land like a country squire, like a huntsman—with optimistic vitality." [p. 102]

There were other factors contributing to this revival. Nature itself had become a subject for intense investigation by botanists, as we have remarked. In England Newton discovered new laws of physics; it became possible to conceptualize nature in terms of factual relationships; the theoretical basis for the objective world that men saw could no longer be denied. Thus they felt intimate with nature on a rational, as well as sensuous, plane. Finally, after the disastrous religious wars of the Counter-Reformation, Holland was at peace. The landscape became a symbol of tranquility.

It was not, however, without movement. The element that dominates these Dutch nature paintings—as must have been true in daily life—is the sky. Here, seemingly, topography dictated the mode of perception, for in Holland one looks into the distance for contrasts. In a sense, the sky is the landscape, for it is against the sky that all else is profiled and all movement generated. Light suffuses these spaces; continually shifting, dramatic, sometimes turbulent, it throws the facts of earth onto a new plane of reality. The Dutch taught men how to look at a very plain world through the transforming medium of shadows and sunlight. But by the end of the seventeenth century, as Clark (1946) points out, this gift "had ceased to be an act of love and had become a trick . . . landscape painting became mere picture-taking according to certain formulas. . . ." [p. 33]

The century that followed was in many ways a time of paradox. On the one hand, it rejected the notion that sublimity in nature could be seen only in the well-ordered environment. The wilderness could also please. Although no less solitary, mysterious, and chaotic than before, these qualities were to be coveted, in part because the very complexity of nature, like the complexity of the solar system, was seen as proof of God's handiwork; in part, we suspect, because the age unconsciously sought release from its clockwork universe. Mountains and forests were the sublime, and somewhat disorderly, evidence that God was everywhere. The deists in particular made this aspect of nature cardinal to their faith. The wilderness became the clearest medium through which the Almighty showed his excellence; spiritual truths were more evident in the wild than in man-made settings, and the very obscurity and menace which had tended to repel men were now enhancing.

It should be added, however, that the wild places of the earth were no less fearsome than before; fear simply ceased to be a liability in the apperception of nature. Edmund Burke (1757; 1958) expressed the notion that terror in the face of an unknown wilderness really stemmed from exultation and delight rather than dread and loathing—a prescient insight into the psychology of emotions that was to be extended in more formal terms by Kant. In esthetics the Englishman William Gilpin (1792) defined the picturesque as deriving from the roughness, irregularity, and intricacy of nature (suggestive of the "stimulus complexity" theory held by some environmental psychologists today).

Thus, for all its rationalism, the eighteenth century harbored a strong romantic counterculture. Cities, and the meticulously ordered garden such as Versailles, symbolized an artificial way of life. The New World, too, intrigued these romantics with its *"scene indeterminée des forêts,"* although it must be noted that few of them experienced it from the perspective of the American pioneer. In 1831, when the visiting Alexis de Tocqueville resolved to see the wilderness for pleasure, the frontiersmen thought him mad.

Perhaps the most significant thing about the art of this period, however, was a general disinterest in landscape as an art form. This was the great age of the portrait. Nature was subordinate to man, for in spite of a deistic view of the wilderness on the part of some, it was an age of finite boundaries with man at the center. One had to jump back a century to the bravura style of a Salvatore Rosa for the kind of landscape that liberated one's feelings from the intellectual niceties of the period. And in lining their walls with Rosa's paintings, jump back is just what a very sizable number of Englishmen did.

It was Wordsworth who rescued his countrymen from such second-rate romanticism by giving them, in the *Lyrical Ballads* (written with S. T. Coleridge, 1798) an authentic attitude toward the pastoral landscape. His cardinal idea, "Let Nature be your teacher" is summed up in the lines

One impulse from the vernal wood
Will tell you more of man
Of moral evil and of good,
Than all the sages can.

Wordsworth set the tone for a new appreciation of the natural environment in early nineteenth-century England. In Aldous Huxley's (1919) phrase, "For good Wordsworthians . . . a week in the country is the equivalent of going to church. . . ." [p. 7] Woods, rocks, clouds, waterfalls, crags became the scripture by which men read the meaning of the universe—a deistic universe built to an intimate scale. The English painter Constable illustrated this trend by locating moral perfection in the ordinary representation of familiar, pastoral scenes. He wanted to make facts yield their own divine message. Although a pictorialist, he was never a mere picture-maker. Constable painted from a philosophic stance, however, that rapidly declined under the impact of the technological changes that ushered in the Industrial Revolution. Heretofore human intervention in the natural environment had left few permanently destructive scars. Hollanders who pushed back the North Sea a thousand years ago and the Egyptians of 4000 B.C. who leveed the banks of the lower Nile brought about new irreversible changes in nature. But the insatiable demand of industry for the earth's resources that began in the nineteenth century not only changed the physical landscape but created an environment in which ecological harmony between man and nature was made increasingly difficult. This resulted from the union of the theoretical view of nature that dominated Western thought with man's new-found ability to exploit it.

Turner, who dominated English landscape painting in the latter half of the nineteenth century, organized this new world of machines in a mood of stormy romanticism, adding a sense of the heroic to nature, often building his compositions around dramatic themes—deluges, crashing seas, burning ships. Again, the landscape was heightened to induce strong feelings. Turner gave nature a sense of power rather than piety and this, perhaps, is the kind of England men thought their country ought to be. Constable's countryside, after all, was a little tame for a nation that ruled half the world.

American Pride in the Natural World

If what we have said about Turner is true then one way of seeing nature is through the spectacles of national pride. It is interesting that Constable was largely neglected by his countrymen but much admired in France, where the natural environment was enjoyed for its domestic and pastoral qualities. But if we look at America during and just preceding this period we find that pride, again, is the dominant mood in landscape painting; a pride, however, based not on political power but on physical ruggedness as a major, and certainly the most visible, part of our national heritage.

Every nation, of course, has its patriotic art. But in nineteenth-century America, patriotism was more likely to find expression in the grandeur of nature than in the glory of military victories. As a country we had no power at all. As a culture we still borrowed most of our sensibility from the Old World. But as a people we had conquered the plains and mountains. Our landscape painting—even the relatively subdued and gentle work of the Hudson River school—stirred men to an appreciation of their land as something both intrinsically beautiful and symbolic of a unique American destiny. The seventeenth-century Puritan distrust of the wilderness was supplanted by an affirmation of its role in shaping a national character that invited men to test their manhood in terms of obstacle and challenge. Moreover, in a country with almost no cultural history of its own, the grandeur of nature was one of the few seminal resources we had. If we did not find God in these wild places, we did discover a sense of power and destiny that conformed with the sheer scale of a land that God had put at our disposal

Important to an understanding of this landscape is the knowledge that most of it was painted out-of-doors rather than in the studio—a practice that was not at all common in Europe. Whether it was the stormy coastlines of Winslow Homer or the Great Plains of George Catlin, the artist was recognizably close to his scene. Men like Catlin, for instance, lived among the Indians and buffalo hunters that furnished the inspiration for their work. Realism became the dominant style and little effort was made to glorify artificially what, after all, was quite glorious to begin with. This scenic tradition continues in the picturesque "calendar art" of the present day, but we must remember that the earlier painters saw the West with a fresh eye. Our present-day vision of natural America is borrowed largely from the past. The land has been visibly altered; our perception of it has not.

Parallel with the artist's depiction of the American landscape as a source of beauty and pride there grew up in the latter half of the nineteenth century a pragmatic effort to preserve the wilderness in its natural state. The movement began with selected groups, many of whose advocates, like the naturalist John Muir, found in nature the spiritual values which the Puritans disdained. Others chose to follow Theodore Roosevelt who identified the wilderness as a source of manliness and national character. Rooted in certain features of Transcendentalism, including the "back to nature" philosophy of Thoreau and his admirers, the movement also embraced rural utopias and communes, such as the Oneida colony, in which closeness to nature was seen as essential to a simple, self-sufficient, and moral way of life.

Although Transcendentalism and the commune movement faded, succeeding groups saw nature as a symbol of something precious in our heritage that was in danger of being destroyed: deforestation, mining, and real-estate development left scars that plainly threatened not only the utility of the environment, but the qualities that evoked our pioneering and self-reliant past. The inception of state and national park systems from the mid nineteenth century onwards, along with the designation of forest preserves, represents the earliest effort to keep a selected part of the natural environment intact. Essentially a "museum" approach, it also embraced the important concept of public domain. The wilderness belongs to the people and must be protected from excessive use. Conservationists such as Gifford Pinchot, onetime Governor of Pennsylvania, promoted this attitude through an ambivalent regard for the preservation of nature while managing it for economic ends. The U. S. Forest Service generally represents this point of view.

A third and more technical development growing out of this concern for the natural environment centered not so much on conservation per se, but on the ecological workings of nature. Its most influential spokesman was Aldo Leopold (1949), whose work at the University of Wisconsin and elsewhere emphasized the interdependence of the natural and the biological worlds. Nature was not simply the wonders of the Grand Canyon or the forests of the northwest; it included prairie farmlands, brooks, rolling hills, hedgerows, and the crannies of the countryside that had been largely neglected by conservationists since Thoreau's time. To this mundane landscape, Leopold added the roles that were played by every living creature. His great contribution was to see the interdependence of nature in its ecological details, and although his influence was limited to a relatively small group of professional conservationists, it is on the basis of his observations and those of his colleagues that the foundations of the modern environmental movement were laid.

Today an awareness of the man/nature interdependence has been broadened to include most of our population. In the process, nature is perceived as intimately dependent on the uses to which it is put by man who is himself part of the ecosystem. This awareness, insofar as it provides him with a new experience of his place in the natural world, is a significant dimension of the hypothetical model we have called environmental man.

French Impressionists and the Interior Landscape

To look at Europe during the latter part of the nineteenth century is to see quite a different trend in man's visual response to the natural environment. We are interested here in the artist's vision. The Impressionists are especially important because they recognized that perceptually the world is made up not of things, but of impressions of things. What they painted was the reality of the image, the intimate, everyday revelations expressed in an ambience of light and color. The physical world *as it existed*, not as it might be conceptualized, was all important. The Impressionists wanted to emulate the camera, to give nature the photographic tone and literalness of felt reality. They were psychologists working with paint. "The accent falls on the passivity of the visual process," Friedlander (1963) writes. "The impression which the Impressionists receive is momentary, fleeting; it must be caught hold of quickly, as if in flight." [Pp. 122–123]

Such "painting of sensation," as Clark (1946) calls it, was perfected by Renoir, who sought "truth" through a visual impression that was as close as possible to the phenomenal world. The awareness of *how* one saw, rather than what, gave impressionist painting its verisimilitude. The how was often fuzzy and blurred rather than sharply focused—as perception is in actuality. Monet painted several canvases at once in order to catch the changing angle of the sun. The optic experience was not to be falsified or imagined by the painter. The Impressionists were the last to envision a world that was recognizable to the average person, yet at the same time not simply a copy of it.

With the Postimpressionists landscape painting abandoned all pretense to naturalism; the function of art as public communication was lost to the individual's idiosyncratic vision. Why did this occur? Clark suggests that men "had lost all confidence in the natural order." The religious basis for appreciation of and belief in nature had disappeared and science provided no esthetic equivalent. By the end of the nineteenth century, the lack of a common faith had destroyed the common landscape.

This is exemplified in the works of Van Gogh, Gauguin, and Cezanne. In their hands nature once again became symbolic, reflecting a commitment to personal rather than social meanings, an assertion of individual consciousness against the new chaos. It should be recalled, too, that the camera has made the world that most of us see superficially intelligible—a role formerly reserved for the painter. And science—not least the microscope and the cyclotron—has given the world we cannot see with the unaided eye more threatening qualities than any wilderness. What Western artists found in light and the Orientals in all nature—the manifestation of God's immanent love—is largely missing; the natural world is no longer charged with this feeling, for painters and the camera cannot create it. Nature has become, in effect, a focus for private feelings.

With the Surrealists this takes the form of a dreamscape that distorts reality in accordance with the symbols of the unconscious. Objective nature is regurgitated through the psyche, so that the paintings of this school give us an inner rather than an outer scheme of universals. This trend toward unintelligibility reached its climax in modern Expressionism. Here, pure abstraction replaces any semblance of the real; nature, as we think of it, cannot be said to exist at all It is reduced to a purity of line and geometric form, a conceptualization of the objective world that is cerebral and self-contained. One may admire the painting; one can hardly know the nature that lies behind it, let alone respond to it emotionally. Symbols have become the sole reality.

The Oriental Landscape

Our discussion of landscape perception concludes with a brief resume of its development in China.

This is important for an understanding of basic differences in the response to environment which characterize Eastern and Western man—differences which were outlined earlier in terms of man's conceptualization of his place in nature, but which are even more vividly illustrated by his depiction of nature in art. For in contrast to the West, which took up nature for its own sake only in the seventeenth century, pure landscape is deeply rooted in Chinese painting, achieving its greatest flowering between the third and tenth centuries A.D. The techniques used by the Oriental painter had little in common with those of Western art. An outgrowth of calligraphy, Chinese painting was done on silk or parchment with colored or monochromatic inks. Oil and canvas were not used. The idea of a framed picture was foreign to the artist, who painted on portable screens, on the walls of temples and palaces, or on long scrolls that could be unrolled for study.

The painter in China was also likely to be a poet and scholar, his work influenced by Taoism and Buddhism; in this sense he made no clear distinction between the secular and the religious. Although few examples from the earlier dynasties survive, extensive cataloging and criticism by historians of ancient China have left us with a complete record of the artists' perception of nature and the techniques used in representing it.

As in the West, the styles of the Chinese masters changed over time The archaic and mannered technique of the Six Dynasties (A.D. 211–589) was replaced by a more fluid approach in the Tang dynasty (seventh to tenth centuries) and the fantasized forms, the sublimity, and turbulence of the Sung dynasty (960–1279). Later artists adopted a more concrete and realistic style. In all periods individual painters employed their own distinctive manner in spite of somewhat rigid conventions. Yet the common values that run through their works are more important to an understanding of the Eastern attitude toward nature than individual differences, for the landscape expressed a perception of the natural world that changed little in 2000 years. At once pictorial and didactic, it was the object of meditation as well as enjoyment. We can do no more here than abstract from this long history some salient characteristics that bear on our discussion of the man/nature theme.

1. Eastern art reflects a philosophic and religious view of the world as unitive. G. Rowley writes: ". . . in China not man, but nature was the measure, and that nature was uniquely conceived as the symbol of the universe." [See Sickman & Soper, 1968: 105] Man is not an alien intruder but an integral element in the great operation of nature. This relationship, however, is organic rather than mechanical. In a sense, the Chinese viewer "saw" a painting with his whole being.

2. Although the Chinese landscape is often tranquil, this does not reflect a static view of nature, which was perceived as dynamic and changing, animated by a divine presence. The Buddhist influence is strong here; God lives in all creation. The land was sacred. In addition, Tao expressed the interdependence between the Order of Nature—its hierarchies—and human conduct. The physical world was very real to the Chinese, but it cloaked a deeper reality which could only be known through meditation, and to meditate on nature is to see its capacity for change

3. To our eyes the classical Chinese landscape seems delicate, unreal, and stylized—as, indeed, it is. During the earlier dynasties painters could express their own feelings about nature only in accordance with officially sanctioned styles. In both Japan and China, for example, court painters had to follow certain rules; there were sixteen ways of drawing mountains; the treatment of water, trees, and other motifs was similarly prescribed. Com-

pared with Western orientations, the perception of nature changes relatively little and never reaches the complete disintegration of reality which characterizes modern abstract art. It must be remembered that the country itself was "timeless" and tradition-bound for most of its history, presenting the same face to the artist from one generation to another.

4. An important element in much of this art is the use of reverse perspective and the "moving focus." Western scientific perspective separates the viewer from the landscape by establishing a vanishing point which keeps him at a distance. In Chinese art the problem of depth was handled by using space to imply more space beyond the boundaries of the painting. The scenes shade off imperceptibly in mist-clouded rock masses, in forms half-revealed. Distance is suggested rather than calculated. The finite structure common to the Western view of nature gives way to a world that is unlimited and ultimately unknowable. The spectator is not outside looking at the painting; he is part of it.

The distinction between the natural and the man-made world is further minimized by an intermingling of the two. Many Chinese paintings carry nature into the house proper, in the form of trees that grow through the roof, enclosed courts, fountains and streams that are proximate to the living space. Man lives intimately with nature, which is his true home. The eleventh-century painter Mi Fei is said to have called the favorite rock in his garden "my elder brother."

Finally, the separation of figure and ground so essential to Western painting is deemphasized; people and objects blend into their surroundings, although in detail they may be depicted with intense fidelity. This is seen in the geological structure of rock formations, for instance, or in the effects of erosion. But it is the rockiness, not the rock, that is being portrayed. In these landscapes, "things" as such are not thought of in isolation.

5. Wilderness in Eastern scenic painting does not reflect the presence of evil. In the Chinese view evil is outside of nature. The "towering piles of rocky peaks, rushing torrents and dark cascades, tangled masses of leafless, dormant trees, and lonely temples reached by tortuous and narrow paths." [Sickman & Soper, 1968: 103] suggested beauty, somberness, or even gloom, but nature was seldom threatening. Symbolically it might represent a withdrawal into solitude, a private refuge, or a source of discovery for the traveler; but there is no greater mystery in a mountain than in a rock; the grandeur of the sea is no more or less than that of the pool. All are manifestations of the Divine Ground.

6. The maxim that "Every truth is contained in the behavior of nature" makes the natural world a model for human life. People are not only part of nature but responsible to its hierarchy, its scheme of relative values. One observes the true behavior of this world only by banishing the distractions of the moment. The *li* principles demand submission to the forms and configurations of an object; contemplation becomes the basis for spontaneity. Students

of Japanese brush painting practice breathing exercises first; the painting itself may take no more than five minutes. Thus, in understanding nature the artist learns to control himself.

To Western eyes the Eastern representation of man *in* nature seems strange, somewhat like listening to Chinese music. The perception of both music and art is, to a great extent, culturally determined, a point we will discuss in Chapter 5. Plates 7 and 8 illustrate some of the factors described above. The landscape by Ma Yuan, "High Mountain," is a good example of Chinese Classical painting. Stylization of the rocks and trees rather than naturalistic detail predominates There is no great sense of depth or perspective, and a feeling of immediacy is achieved by compressing distance. Foreground and background are perceived virtually as one. A quite different response to landscape is seen in a panel from "Clear Weather in the Valley" (Anonymous, 10th Century). The merging of mountains and sky in the background give the scene a limitless quality, while the foreground terrain mantles the intimate detail of pavilion and human figures, who are all but lost in the expanse of nature. In Eastern landscape painting the activity, the style, scenery and people are often seen as one mode; strictly speaking, there is no figure and ground.

Summary and Conclusions

Man's assessment of nature is achieved within the context of three broad, not always congruent, ways of looking at the world. One of these is historical. We inherit attitudes that have been laid down in our culture, so that contemporary perceptions are, in part, conditioned by forces that have shaped and evaluated the environment in past times. To this extent we perceive the present through the eyes of the past.

The second mode of response concerns our immediate needs and preferences. This is a functionalist view of nature as subject to human exploitation, limited only by our technological ability to achieve desired ends. "The landscape is worthy of its hire."

Finally, we envision the environment in terms of its future. This is an esthetic-conservation-survival view that has become the basis for an ecology movement. In the long run it is better functionalism than the present functionalism. Yet no such movement can succeed without taking into account the historical factors that have influenced men's assessments of the natural world. It is this perspective that we have been examining.

Earlier in the chapter we asked the question: How did Western man proceed from animism to ecosystem in his view of nature? Primitive peoples made no clear distinction between animate and inanimate things—and in a curious way, considering our present belief that matter is simply pent-up energy, they were surprisingly, if unknowingly, correct. The primitives were superstitious. We are rationalistic, reducing nature, in Bertrand Rus-

PLATE 7 Ma Yuan (Sung Dynasty). "High Mountain." Courtesy, Museum of Fine Arts, Boston.

PLATE 8 Anonymous (Sung Dynasty). "Clear Weather in the Valley" (detail). Courtesy, Museum of Fine Arts, Boston.

sell's phrase, to whatever satisfies the equations of physics. Perhaps this too is a superstition insofar as it explains reality. In any case, we have banished the gods from nature and substituted theories. Our perceptions of the world have changed accordingly.

Four major developments help explain this centuries-long transformation. One of these was the emergence of the Judeo-Christian doctrine of a created universe, with God as the maker and man his servant on earth. This development gradually separated man from nature and put him increasingly outside the world that he sought to know. Christianity gave the individual a strong sense of dignity and self-worth and (in the guise of a soul) an ego. Essentially an urban religion, it regarded the wilderness with ambivalence—as a sanctuary, to which men retreated the better to commune with God, or as a place of mystery and terror where men were punished. Untamed nature was seen as a source of possible temptation, not to be enjoyed for its own sake. This view persisted until well after the Renaissance.

Parallel with this distrust of the natural world was a denial of the sensual aspects of the human body. Rooted in Manicheanism, this aspect of Christianity was most elegantly defined by St. Augustine and achieved its extreme form in Calvinism at the time of the Reformation. The result was an intensification of the man/nature dualism; not only was nature distrusted, but the individual's physical senses were repressed in the cause of a higher, that is, spiritual, good. In both content and design landscape painting was a vehicle for the illustration of religious themes. Not until the seventeenth century was nature itself regarded as worthy of sensuous enjoyment, and only in the eighteenth and nineteenth centuries did it represent a direct source of spiritual values.

A third factor in the externalization of nature was the Christian view of linear time, the idea that events moved forward rather than cyclically. This made possible the notion that change was due to contingent relationships among things rather than self-derived from their nature. The Greek belief that objects were essentially stable and governed by an inherent purpose gave way to the idea that the behavior of the physical world could be explained by cause-and-effect. Until the eighteenth century, these causal relationships were thought to be governed by Natural Law which, in essence, was supernatural in origin.

The fourth major development, and one that would not likely have occurred without the Christian belief in time and change, was the scientific revolution that began in the late Renaissance. On a theoretical level this created a world that was wholly explainable, with man gradually replacing God as the chief knower and maker. On a practical level scientific discoveries provided the basis for an empirical manipulation of the environment. This has been followed by the technological and cybernetic revolutions of our own day. At the same time, theoretical conceptions have reduced nature to ever finer and more discriminable bits, so that we know our environment in terms of its fragments rather than as a unitive and experienced whole. The general theme of this long process is expressed in the phrase, "Man's conquest of Nature."

Disastrous as much of our exploitation of the environment has been, it is to the realm of theory that we must look for the more profound, if less visible, consequences of modern science. To say that science has replaced God as the greater explicator of the universe is commonplace. Nature is no longer subsumed under a system of theological belief. In sum, science asks us to see the world as self-created. Nature's primacy, however, can be understood only by reducing it to smaller and smaller pieces. Ultimately, nature becomes invisible, so that we know the existence of subatomic particles only through their actions in cyclotrons.

Modern science thus represents an extreme instance of selective perception; it is an analytic and abstractive way of focusing attention. More significantly, scientific methodology signals a break with its technological origins, for it is only in the twentieth century that scientists have come to the notion that the laws of nature are not discovered (and were therefore preexistent), but rather that they are invented by the scientist himself. In this view relations among objects are not deterministic but descriptive. In a sense, science is trying to "put the world together" in the holistic images of a universe which man rather than God has created.

Our attitudes toward the natural world are still served by the useful fictions of science that allow us to achieve certain ends. If what is true is what works, we make sure that what works is true. But at the same time that our environment has become increasingly fragmented and reductive, it is also clear that nature can no longer be controlled in a piecemeal fashion. Many environmentalists see this as the real challenge of ecology. What is sought is a design for nature that has as its objective not the mechanics of control within an impossibly complex system of interrelationships, but an ethical response to the "laws" that science has invented. In effect this means reconciling the technological-scientific perception of the world with an ethical-human perception. For if man has invented the world he lives in—if it is no longer God's world—then man is, indeed, responsible for what he has created.

In discussing the foregoing environmental assessments we have compared the attitudes of Western civilization with those of the Orient, principally China. Our purpose here was to show an approach which, although equally rooted in religious orientation, was wholly different in character. Eastern man is seen as psychologically within the natural world rather than separated from it through abstract conceptualizations. His perceptions of nature are direct and organismic, his behavior modeled ideally on the order of nature and directed toward the attainment of harmony with it.

Such a comparison is not intended to imply that either East or West enjoys a superior culture. This is for others to judge. Our point here is simply to indicate how orientations to nature have evolved in two different parts of the world; to inquire whether it is possible to learn from Eastern attitudes in dealing with our own environmental problems. We must add that the East has learned much from us. Without scientific discoveries concerning nature they could not have conquered disease, increased the productivity of the land, eliminated much hard labor, and raised the standard of living for millions of people.

In Chapter Ten, we will approach the subject of nature again, but on a finer-grained and more behavioral level. To what extent does the cultural milieu affect the individual's day-to-day perception of the natural environment? How do such perceptions, in turn, influence his choice of residence, economic use of resources, acclimation to environmental hazards, esthetic appreciation of nature, and concern for the quality of the environment? How do these assessments relate to personality traits, occupation, and socioeconomic class? What are the significant factors involved in environmental decision-making? Finally, how can knowledge be used to formulate an environmental ethic—to project a man/environment relationship that goes beyond the present "state of the art"?

In concluding this chapter some broad determinants are suggested to make such an ethic possible, factors that are likely to guide attitudes toward the natural environment in the coming decades.

1. The environmental crisis will compel (as it is already doing) a radical rethinking of man's relationship to nature. Depletion of natural resources, increasing human population, pollution, esthetic disfiguring of the landscape—these are of critical concern to all of us. Man will be less inclined to impose a scheme on nature without taking into account the ecological consequences of his actions.

2. For a minority of Western man there will be an emulation of Eastern ways—a refeeling as well as a rethinking of the person and nature. For such people the natural world is most deeply apprehended through meditation and personal sensitivity. In the words of one such advocate, George B. Leonard (1972), "the lifeless world comes back to life" as men deemphasize those abstract and general concepts that exercise "hypnotic power over our perceptions." [p. 45] Although small in numbers, this group is articulate, influential, and growing.

3. For most of us, an anthropocentric attitude will prevail, but we will exercise more humility in our dealings with nature. Glacken (1966) has remarked that the man-centered view need not necessarily be identified with "smug utilitarianism" but can also be "hospitable to broader ideas." [p. 364] The values found in nature will be human values, although our approach to them is likely to be rational rather than organismic. The technology that gave us the power to exploit the environment is recognized as a means of preserving it. This approach will occur within the concept of environmental man or, in the broader sense, the ecosystem. Man becomes the conscious decision-maker in the system, facilitating natural processes in accordance with a plan for a better ecological balance between nature and humans.

4. From the practical point of view, how can this be done? We might begin by suggesting a notational system as an aid to thinking. For it should be realized that the apparent complexity of nature is not innate but a consequence of the instruments used to handle, measure, and classify it. There is nothing very complex, for instance, about walking, breathing, or circulation of the blood; complexity arises when we try to describe these processes. A human being is complicated only to the extent that we "mechanize" him in terms of interrelated biological functions. In fact, this is not how we deal with people, unless we are physicians. It is the whole person, the individual who emerges out of his biological, social, and cultural components, that is responded to in ordinary life.

Such, indeed, is the theme of this book. Chapter Three will trace the development of a number of broad theories about the environment that have contributed to this holistic view of the man/milieu relationship.

References

Burtt, E. A. *The metaphysical foundations of modern science.* New York: Anchor Books, 1954.

Burke, E. *Philosophical inquiry into the origin of our ideas of the Sublime and Beautiful* (1757). Ed. by J. Boulton. London: Routledge and K. Paul, 1958.

Clark, K. *Landscape into art.* Boston: Beacon Press, 1946.

Friedlander, M. J. *Landscape, portrait, still-life.* New York: Schocken Books, 1963.

Gilkey, L. *Maker of heaven and earth.* New York: Anchor Books, 1965.

Gilpin, W. *Three essays: On picturesque beauty; on picturesque travel and on landscape painting.* London: R. 1792.

Glacken, C. Reflections on the man-nature theme as a subject for study. In F. Darling & J. Milton (Eds.), *The future environments of North America.* Garden City, N.Y.: Natural History Press, 1966.

Huxley, A. *Do what you will.* London: Chatto & Windus, 1919.

Leonard, G. B. *The transformation.* New York: Delacorte Press, 1972.

Leopold, A. *A sand county almanac.* New York: Oxford University Press, 1949.

McHarg, I. Ecological determinism. In F. Darling & J. Milton (Eds.), *The future environments of North America.* Garden City, N.Y.: Natural History Press, 1966.

Madge, C. Private and public spaces. *Human Relations,* 1950, *3,* 187–199.

Needham, J. *The grand titration.* London: Allen & Unwin, 1969.

Piaget, J. *The child's conception of the world.* New York: Harcourt Brace, 1929.

Sickman, L. C., & A. Soper. *The art and architecture of China.* Baltimore: Penguin Books, 1968.

Watts, A. The individual as man/world. In P. Shepherd & D. McKinley (Eds.), *The subversive science: Essays toward an ecology of man.* Boston: Houghton Mifflin, 1969.

White, L. Jr. The historical roots of our ecologic crisis. In P. Shepherd & D. McKinley (Eds.), *The subversive science: Essays toward an ecology of man.* Boston: Houghton Mifflin, 1969.

Suggested Readings

Caldwell, L. *Environment: A challenge for modern society.* Garden City, N.Y.: Natural History Press, 1970.
Clark, K. *Landscape into art.* Boston: Beacon Press, 1946.
Glacken, C. *Traces on the Rhodian shore.* Berkeley, Calif.: University of California Press, 1967.
Nash, R. *Wilderness and the American mind.* New Haven: Yale University Press, 1967.
Needham, J. *The grand titration.* London: Allen & Unwin, 1969.

Three

The Search for Environmental Theory

The previous chapter looked closely at man's attitudes toward the environment as a function of historical time and cultural setting. Our focus and purpose here narrows considerably as we move from cultural ethos to scientific thought concerning man's environment, from time-related beliefs and attitudes to systematic attempts at theoretical elaborations. If the reader followed the previous discussion closely, then he should have arrived at two conclusions about science in relation to understanding environment and environmental process: first, that science itself is an attitude and means of looking at, understanding, and relating to the environment; and second, that its origins are rooted deeply in those environmental beliefs and attitudes of Western man that began with the demise of medieval conceptions of the earth as the center of the universe.

At root was the view that man was separate from his physical world; that because he was no longer the center of the universe, he could stand apart from his own world, view it and study it with detachment; in the end, he could manipulate it, change it, and make it serve him. This was and is the credo of modern science. Its inexorable search for knowledge is not just to understand, but to control and determine events; and most particularly, those events that are distinguished from man himself, environmental events. If the salvation of man was to be found in God, then science would save him from the awesome, unpredictable, and often catastrophic character of these events.

Under these circumstances, as one might expect, the nexus for the growth of modern science was the study of the physical and natural settings of men. By the nineteenth century, the efficacy of a scientific empirical approach to knowledge with respect to environmental phenomena had not only been assured but acclaimed. Small wonder, therefore, that by that time burgeoning efforts were being made to treat behavioral man himself as an environmental event and subject him to the same kind of scientific or systematic empirical study being made of other events in the physical world. After all, he too was part of nature and there was no reason why he too could not be viewed with detachment and objectivity. Thus, the more general attempts by philosophers and theologians to resolve such issues as the mind-body dualism, the nature of human thought and perception, and the problem of free will were raised in more precise and empirical terms by physiologists, physicists, and a small but growing group of "psychologists." Depending on approach and the way the new science was conceived, particular problems were formulated and studied in order to answer one or more of the questions of how men learn, think, feel, see, hear, become aroused, and engage in complex behaviors.

These "schools of psychology" will not be considered in a systematic fashion in the present discussion; rather, we will look primarily at some of the more prominent attempts to conceptualize the environment, particularly the physical environment, in relation to human behavior. More detailed and comprehensive accounts of these various approaches that laid the groundwork for modern theory and research in psychology—including some developments in environmental psychology—can be found in Heidbreder (1933), Boring (1942), Wolman (1968), and Woodworth (1948). Of course, none of these schools or approaches to psychology simply emerged. Their origins were rooted not just in developments that led to modern science, but in philosophical, theological, economic, and political conceptions of the nature of man and the universe going back to the time of the Greeks and even before.

From the point of view of environmental psychology, the student who reviews these various schools of psychology will recognize a feature common to all of them. Stated simply, none systematically conceptualized or established a theoretical framework for the description and analysis of the environment per se. Human behavior and experience rather than its setting was the focus of concern. Sometimes directly—although in very general rather than specific terms—but far more often indirectly, these approaches to man's behavior and experience had, at best, implications for his environmental setting. In general this setting was taken for granted and as a result its definition in a theory or an approach was far more implicit than explicit.

The reason for this neglect of the environment is easy to understand. The concern of a science of psychology was man and not his environment. The critical task was to replace metaphysical and other philosophical and theological conceptions of man by empirical descriptions and analyses in a context of reasoned elaborations or theoretical schemas. But there were far more subtle and more sustaining reasons for the failure to describe and conceptualize the environmental context in relation to human behavior and experience.

Not only was psychology concerned almost exclusively with the behavior of the person, but, as was suggested in Chapter Two, the person was not really considered part of his environment so much as an object in the environment. Moreover, this environment was studied as a physical and not a social problem. An understanding of the environment indeed had been established by the newly emerging physical and natural sciences, particularly physics, which easily specified the precise nature and details of many relevant aspects of the physical world.

Of course there was a wide array of complex environmental events—both social and physical—that these sciences did not consider that were conceivably of equal significance in understanding human behavior in natural settings. The natural sciences of that time precluded such an approach. If man was separate from the environment, and if the latter was exclusively a physical problem, then all environmental events of a social nature could be safely ignored.

However, a separate point must be stressed. It was crucial to a beginning psychology that these complex physical and social events be rejected as the legitimate concern of a science of man. And so they were. To be a science—to be guided by the methodological and rational precepts of the already established physical and natural sciences—meant defining human problems and their study in ways that guaranteed that these ways of knowing would be met. The environment had to be dealt with in simple, objective, and verifiable terms, a matter that to a large degree was already being taken care of by the physical and natural sciences. Thus, at the time, the study of how human beings learned meant the presentation of pure learning units (nonsense syllables) each exposed after an exact interval of time, with all other measurable environmental conditions in the room kept constant. The physical environment was treated in atomistic and additive terms. This involved a concern with specific environmental objects, and the environment in general was the collection of all of those objects that could be specified and measured. It has only been in relatively recent times that natural scientists have begun to recognize the environment as a network or system of interrelationships, such that any part or level of structure in it that is studied derives its nature and function from, and in turn has consequences for, the nature and function of all other parts or structures of the environment in which it is embedded. The human body viewed in terms of the origin, nature, and function of any of its parts, for example the heart, illustrates this holistic or systems approach to scientific understanding.

Approaches to Man: Psychoanalytic Theory, Behaviorism, and Gestalt Theory

Our discussion begins with three quite different theoretical orientations to man: psychoanalytic theory, behaviorism, and Gestalt psychology. Each of these theories constitutes an historical watershed for the development of still other viewpoints. Indeed, in some instances one finds modern theoretical points of view that have integrated selected aspects of at least two of these different approaches if not all three. It will be helpful if the reader considers these theories as the three points of a triangle with subsequent integrated theories falling between the points of this triangle, or some place inside it when all three theories have been tied together.

Psychoanalytic Theory

Was the environment important in Freud's view of man? Unquestionably so. Did he develop a conceptual scheme for this environment? The answer to this second question is not simply a "no"; rather, it can be said he did not need one. For Freud (1933) put all of his theoretical eggs, so to speak, in one basket. He conceived of man, and all events that followed from his exalted position at the apex of the phylogenetic scale, as rooted in a set of inherited instinctual drives, the life (Eros) and death (Thanatos) instincts. These drives were universal, fixed in an inexorable sequence of development, and ultimately the basis for all human behavior and experience. At the root of Freud's system was the concept of intrapsychic conflicts, for example the Oedipus complex, whose particular form, the ways that they were constrained, and the kinds of consequences they had all depended on the socialization experiences of the individual. To a considerable degree these conflicts, the defense mechanisms made necessary to control them, and indeed the real meaning of what the individual thought, did, and felt remained at an unconscious level. It was at this level that Freud conceived the more conscious and reality-oriented drives and attitudes, which he called the *ego*, that reconciled the demands of the instinctual drives (the *id*) and the physical, social, and cultural mores of organized society.

Freud was an environmentalist in the sense that he felt the social and interpersonal environment shaped and guided the form and consequences of the person's life and death strivings. An inherent succession of psychosexual stages beginning at birth and extending through early adolescence unfolds under the influence of particular people (for example, parents, siblings, friends, and teachers) who are responsible for overseeing the child's basic experiences and activities (eating, playing, sleeping, learning, defecating, and so on) in prescribed human settings (home, playground, school, and so forth). These people, in these settings, establishing the specific form and content of experiences and activities, determine the level, the particular patterning, and ultimate adult consequences of the process of psychosexual development. It is in this sense that Freud can be described as the consummate reductionist. All human events, activities, forms, and concepts, whether of the person, group, or society at large, were manifestations and expressions of the psychosexual system and its development, and therefore could be explained on this basis.

What implications, if any, can be drawn from Freud's psychoanalytic theory about the nature and meaning of the physical environment? At least three major implications can be specified. First, the physical environment is experienced rather than being observed or responded to as if it existed in some objective sense. If all human behavior and experience express the ego–id relationships and intrapsychic conflicts in some modified and disguised forms, then this implies that in meaning, significance, and function the individual's environment itself must be rooted in the underlying intrapsychic system. This implication in turn brings us to still another. Physical environments, their form, content, and meaning, express the unconscious needs, values, and conflicts of the person. In Freud's system the often-referred-to expressive symbolism of man's built environment does not reflect so much the underlying value system of the culture as it does the underlying psychodynamics of individual behavior and experience. In sum, man's cultural, social, and physical systems express a universal basic personality structure that is rooted in the conflicts among and the satisfactions of instinctual drives.

Much of Freud's system of psychosexual development has implications for the design and use of physical settings. The feeding and toilet training of the child, the sexual relations of the parents, the social interactions of siblings, and many other aspects of this developmental approach depend not only on the people involved but also on settings in which these activities occur. Given the centrality of the Oedipus and Electra complexes in Freud's theory, for example, privacy is crucial in the sexual relations of parents. If the small boy has strong sexual attachments for the mother, then what he can see and hear when his parents are involved in any form of "love and romance," either in their bedroom or out, is significant. Given the emphasis on toilet training in Freud's theory, it is not only important how and by whom the child is trained, but where as well. The design of the bathroom, particularly with respect to its privacy aspects, is important. Similar conclusions can be drawn about the design of kitchens in the light of Freud's theory of the oral stage in children and the significance of feeding.

Freud's approach, however, goes well beyond these specific implications. The rationale of man's built environment—regardless of cultural differences —reflects his unconscious desires, his attempts to sublimate these desires, and his ways of both satisfying and restraining his instinctual drives. In its broadest sense and in quite specific terms Freud's theory stands ready to give "underlying" meaning and purpose to modern technology, for example the car or jet plane, regardless of how quickly it progresses in man's attempt to master his physical environment.

Behaviorism

In its origin and development, behaviorism stands in sharp contrast to Freud's psychoanalytic theory. Its setting was the academic animal laboratory rather than the psychiatric treatment room. Unlike Freudian theory it was as much concerned with establishing the precepts for a science of human behavior as it was with understanding man himself. Indeed, our allusion earlier to a "beginning scientific psychology" that used as its model the methodology of the physical and natural sciences, describes a mantle of scientific respectability that was worn more proudly and self-righteously by behaviorists than by any other group of psychologists. Yet the success of behaviorism as a major force in the development of American psychology involved more than its use of this model. It borrowed heavily from the pragmatism of Charles Pierce and William James, and this in turn was consistent with the technocratic, manipulative faith that Americans had in their environment, especially during the decade of the 1920s.

Although classical behaviorism has been modified considerably during the last five or six decades, its basic tenets remain the same. Science, it asserts, is by definition an approach to knowledge in which empirical analysis must be constrained at all times by objectivity. In the case of human behavior only those events that can be observed and empirically specified have any legitimacy for a science of man. The unit of analysis therefore is the S–R or stimulus-response relationship in which observable behavior is elicited by equally observable and measurable stimuli. Some basic S–R units are biologically determined and innately rooted; all other behavior rests upon these essential response systems and is learned through a process of forming new S–R relationships. Wherever problem situations arise in which available S–R units no longer provide an adequate solution to the problem, new responses are evoked and those that lead to satisfaction for the organism become established as new S–R units. Such satisfactions may either be responses that lead to drive-related objects, food or water, for example, that are intrinsically satisfying to the organism (positive reinforcers or rewards), or they may result from responses that help to avoid objects, situations, or events that are threatening or painful to the organism (negative reinforcers or punishments). In one fell swoop behaviorism eliminated consciousness, cognitive activity, and, more generally stated, the "inner life" of the person as the legitimate concern of the psychologist. Behaviorists did not deny that there were internal processes; it was simply that their study and understanding required them to be translated into observable responses. These forms of observed behavior included simple verbalizations tied to equally defined and observable stimulus situations. The individual then becomes a "black box," but a box that can be described in terms of an aggregate of habitual responses (S–Rs) to recurring or similar situations. Whether these were eating, need for privacy, aggressive behavior, sympathy feelings, desire for power, voyeurism, or voting the Republican ticket, what was involved were habitual responses to S–R-connected stimuli or stimulus situations. Indeed, such words as "need," "feelings," and "desire" were mentalistic and therefore neither necessary or useful.

It should be apparent that the environment—physical, social, or cultural—does play a crucial role for the behaviorist. Indeed, behaviorism comes close to conceptualizing the environment in the manner of the natural and physical scientist, which means therefore that it is real, measurable, and existing in its own right. But in understanding behavior the significance of the environment as such is not substantive. In other words, the particular objects, things, or people involved does not matter. The significance is structural in the sense that regardless of the nature or complexity of the environment it can be described in the simplest terms, namely, as a stimulus or stimuli which evoke behavior. By understanding the process of human behavior and learning in this way, those responsible for the development or change in the behavior of others (for example, teachers, master craftsmen) would by definition know what the appropriate activities, behaviors, or responses to be learned were, and could even establish the conditions necessary for learning them.

The environments that people create are simply a function of which environments, or objects in the environments, lead to positive or negative reinforcements. Not only are environments assortments of stimuli, but these stimuli determine when, how, where, and with whom we will behave. Even in this respect, behaviorism's conception of the environment, or the stimuli of which it was composed, fell far short of what was needed. Almost all of the attention was given to the response side of the S–R "equation." The nearest approximation to dealing with the environment in any explicit way is the conception of "setting events," that is, certain stimuli (virtually any stimulus will do) become signals for the receipt or nonreceipt of a reinforcer. In this sense the stimulus sets the occasion for the response. Thus, the environment is a complex set of discriminable stimuli signalling the reinforcement possibilities which may occur there. In Chapter Five we consider the limitations of an object-oriented or stimulus-oriented approach to perception of the environment.

Behaviorism's leading spokesman today is B. F. Skinner (1953) whose chief contribution has been his studies of operant behavior, in which environmental stimuli evoke responses which lead to reinforcements, positive or negative. For example, if the child consistently gets candy or some other reward for speaking softly at home, then according to Skinnerian theory he will learn to be a quiet member of the household. According to the Skinnerian approach, environments are often said to gain "meaning" or "value" as a consequence of secondary reinforcement. The quiet house just described takes on reward significance in its own right. The operant behaviorists have reared a formidable theory of culture based on reinforcement, viewing democratic and liberal societies as basically positive (rewarding) reinforcers and authoritarian states as "punitive." Skinner himself, who is a utopian in his spare time (Skinner, 1971), is decidedly positive in his approach, although this has led him into realms of social engineering which many advocates of democracy find somewhat uncongenial.

Gestalt Theory

Our triangle of major theoretical approaches is completed with Gestalt psychology. Like behaviorism its origin is also the academic research laboratory, but here similarity between the two schools ends. Indeed, Gestalt psychology and behaviorism stand as the antithesis of each other in purpose, theoretical approach, and subsequent influence on the development of psychology as a science. Its original focus was not behavior but human perception and other cognitive processes, and its setting was the academic research laboratories of German universities, in which the visual perception of movement was the initial problem being considered. Its leaders, Köhler (1929) and Koffka (1935), were essentially protesting all forms of analytic reductionism that attempted to understand complex human psychological processes by establishing their irreducible basic elements. In the case of behaviorism, which developed concurrently with Gestalt psychology, the S–R unit was basic. At an earlier period, but still highly influential when Gestalt psychology emerged, the experimental approach of the psychophysicists attempted to establish functional relationships between measurable stimulus attributes, (intensity of light for instance), and discrete psychological reactions (for example, subjective judgments of the brightness of light) (Boring 1942). Still another experimental approach condemned by the Gestaltists were the German, English, and American association psychologies (structuralism in America). The emphasis here was on human consciousness and experiences with a directed attempt, by means of systematic introspection, to establish the fundamental and irreducible units of human cognitive and affective responses (sensation). All of these analytical reductive approaches seeking the basic units of human behavior and/or experience in relation to measurable and definable stimulus properties assumed that once these relationships were established, the apparent complexities of psychological process and human behavior could easily be described and understood (Heidbreder 1933; Woodworth 1948).

If Gestalt psychology was unalterably opposed to this kind of reductionistic analysis, then what did it stand for? The term *Gestalt* is the obvious clue. The word, which has no exact counterpart in English, suggests "form" or "configuration." The important idea, however, is that what is perceived is the whole, whether an object, a person, an event, or a physical setting. To subject any of these to analysis and study, in terms of its parts, as though these add up to the whole, is to violate the integrity of the phenomenon being studied. Any event, object, behavior, or experience consists of the patterned relationship among the various parts. The now famous Gestalt dictum that "the whole is more than the sum of its parts," is no more mysterious than the belief that because of the patterned interrelationships among parts, properties emerge that cannot be found in the parts themselves.

To use a modern analogy: You do not understand the way a city functions by considering its residences, offices and industries, its transportation system, theaters and other recreation facilities, schools, and hospitals on an individual basis, that is, as distinct and unrelated institutional settings. Only when one sees each of these settings operating in relation to the others does the concept of city make sense. Indeed, it is the city as a total reality which explains the functioning of each of its specific settings. In a later chapter the notion of ambience is introduced to describe one aspect of large-scale environments. In a sense this concept helps to integrate psychologically the various inputs whose continuing interactions make a "city."

The theoretical formulations of Gestalt psychology, despite the focus on perception and other cognitive processes, embrace the study of man in general. Our concern here, however, is its particular significance for the study of man in relation to his physical setting. For environmental psychology at least three of its basic assumptions have very great importance. Whether one accepts them or not, they are crucial, for by either accepting or rejecting them one chooses between vastly different approaches to this new field.

Unlike behaviorism, Gestalt psychology was not rooted in American pragmatism but in German phenomenology. Heidbreder (1933) writes that the Gestaltist "attempts to get back to naive perception, to immediate experience 'undebauched by learning'; and [he] insists that [he] finds these not assemblages of elements, but unified wholes; not masses of senses, but trees, clouds and sky." It is in this sense that Koffka (1935) distinguishes between the geographical environment—the environment as it really exists—and the behavioral environment, or the environment as the person experiences it. It is the latter that Koffka sees as the determinant of an individual's behavior. He assumes that in some instances what is actually there and what we perceive to be there may be quite different. (We shall have more to say about this distinction in Chapter Five.) However, the Gestaltists believed that the properties of geographical environments, under normal circumstances, become part of the behavioral environment experienced by the individual; in addition, although each individual in principle perceives uniquely, the perception of geographical environments leads to commonalities in the behavioral environments of different people. This is because of common neurological mechanisms that are innate in people and common superimposed socializing experiences.

Finally, explicit in the Gestalt approach was the view that behavior was rooted in cognitive process. It was not determined by stimuli but resulted from and had consequences for the meaning or conceptions that emerged from the perception of some setting, object, person, or event. In this sense environments not only had structure but substance as well. Different environments in effect—or the same environment at different times—could change in meaning and thereby evoke corresponding changes in behavior.

Lewin's Field Theory

Perhaps no other theorist has had such varied influence on psychology as Kurt Lewin (1935). Although a Gestalt psychologist, he extended and deepened this approach by turning to such issues, rarely considered by the classical Gestaltists, as child development, personality structure and process, the dynamics of group functions, intergroup conflict, research methodology for the study of man, and the nature of human motivation. In all of these considerations Lewin was acutely aware of the significance of the environment and provided both a broad general approach as well as a very preliminary notation system for conceptualizing this environment. In the main he formulated a broad methodological strategy for the formulation and analysis of problems about human behavior and experience, with the theoretical and empirical details to be filled in by means of continuing systematic research. In this limited review we can only touch upon those significant aspects of Lewin's approach that are relevant to the present concern with attempts to conceptualize the individual's environment.

While the concept of behavioral environment was no less evident in Lewin's approach than in any other Gestaltist's, his interest was not in cognitive process per se but rather in its role in determining behavior. Lewin's field theory represents a formal attempt to provide a set of analytical tools that would take account of all the factors that determined behavior (1951). In essence Lewin believed that the stream of activity we call human behavior resulted from the continuing interaction of factors within the person, for example, needs, values, feelings, and predispositions, with other external factors as they are perceived in a given behavioral setting. Thus, it was neither needs nor stimulus objects that determined how, when, and in what way a person behaves, but the constellation or pattern of inner and outer influences that he experiences. This reasoning was at the nexus of Lewin's concept of the *life space*, which he defined as $B = f(PE)$ in which behavior (B) is seen as a function (f) of the interaction of personality and other individual factors (P), and the perceived environment of the individual (E).

Although Lewin gave no special consideration to the physical world, it is clear that his concept of life space included more than just social and cultural environments. Important at this point are some of the terms he employed to describe the environment generally. Thus, objects, situations, or other people in the person's life space may have positive or negative *valences* depending on their ability to reduce or increase respectively the needs or intentions of the person. *Locomotion*, which could either be social, conceptual, or physical, means a change of position with respect to some goal region. The thirsty man going across the street to get to drink at a water fountain in the park employs physical locomotion toward the goal region "water fountain." By contrast, the young man on a blind date, trying to impress a not-so-interested female companion, is also attempting to locomote toward the socially desirable goal of being liked by her. A *barrier* is a boundary in the life space of the person that offers resistance to locomotion. It may be a physical barrier if the gate to the park is closed, or it may be a social barrier if the young man sees his companion as older and more sophisticated.

We have not done justice to the extensive theoretical framework developed by Lewin in his attempt to conceptualize the content, structure, and dynamics (motivational forces) of the life space. However, as a final comment, Lewin never viewed the life space, or the experienced world of a person, as so supreme in relation to behavior that reality and nonconscious events (for example, a wall the person is unaware of) had no place in his approach. Thus he pointed out that consciousness, or what the person was actually aware of, could not be used as a criterion of what existed psychologically. "There is no question, for instance, that when a person is in a familiar room, the part of the wall which is behind him belongs to his momentary environment." [1936: 18] And, we would add, whether he was aware of it or not. In this sense Lewin believed that what was real and therefore to be included in the life space was anything that had effects. Lewin was keenly aware of the fact that beside factors of which the person was unaware, still other factors outside the life space and therefore not subject to psychological laws also influenced behavior. In Lewin's formulation the influence of this kind of reality was not to be denied. Thus, the *foreign hull of the life space* was defined as "'facts not subject to psychological laws but which influence the state of the life space." [p. 206] If our thirsty man gets to the fountain and suddenly finds the water discolored and polluted because the city failed to purify its reservoir, we can be sure he will not drink it. The action—or better said, the inaction of the Water Department—clearly had consequences for his behavior.

Barker's Ecological Psychology

Roger Barker (1963a, 1963b, 1968), a colleague of Lewin's, was also trained in the Gestalt tradition. Barker, however, formulated the problem of human behavior in very different terms. His "ecological psychology" can be defined as the psychology of environment, or what he calls a "behavior setting." A behavior setting is bounded in space and time and has a structure which interrelates physical, social, and cultural properties so that it elicits common or regularized forms of behavior. Barker's objective was to determine the relationships between what he calls the extraindividual pattern of behavior—that is, the behavior that all people en masse reveal in a behavior setting—and the structural properties of that setting. Any institutionalized setting such as a church, a school, a hotel terrace, a cocktail lounge, or a playground, is of concern to the ecological psychologist. To take the example of the hotel terrace, it would qualify as a behavior setting in the sense that its physical properties (arrangement of chairs, small tables, railings, and so forth) as well as their implicit purpose (relaxation, conversation, drinking, card playing, and so on) impose on those entering it an explicit mode of behavior. The uses of all behavior settings and their objects are to a relatively large extent socially defined.

It is evident from Barker's approach that the environment he is talking about has a reality of its own. This is the objective rather than the psychological environment which is at the core of Lewin's life space. However, if we take a closer look it only seems as if this environment has a reality of its own, for Barker does not come to grips with the social definitions applied to different spaces. Although he speaks of behavior settings in terms of space and place, far more is involved conceptually than a physical setting. He stresses the fact that "behavior episodes" are embedded in a physical framework—"tough, highly visible features of the ecological environment"—but far more important is the fact that the physical setting itself has a social and cultural definition resulting from the intended purposes of the setting, the kind of people who will use it, and what activities and immediate outcomes will occur. A behavior setting is not simply a space with any set of boundaries and a random array of objects. On the contrary, its physical dimensions, the nature of its objects, where and how they are placed, and so on, are all determined by the socially defined character of the situation.

Given his concern with relating behavioral settings with en masse behavior, Barker's approach can be erroneously conceived of as behavioristic or S–R in character. Such an interpretation is not valid because his theoretical focus is not the psychology of individual behavior but actually aggregates of people responding to physical settings, in which he hopes to establish how nonpsychological factors of environment have consequences for typical behaviors in typical behavioral settings. Of course in seeking those relationships he holds in abeyance the inner individual psychological processes that determine by definition all human behavior and experience.

At the core of Barker's definition of behavior setting is a social purpose or meaning involving a set of social rules which unifies or integrates into an orderly system what people do, how they do it, with whom they do it, and when and for what intervals of time. Think of a baseball game, a college prom, a funeral, or a school classroom and the full meaning of Barker's ecological behavior theory becomes evident. What emerges in its own right is that Barker's environment is hardly the geographical environment defined by Koffka. Its reality is not physical but socially defined.

Barker's ecological psychology dictates its own methodology, and it is clearly not that of the laboratory or other kinds of contrived human settings. Behavior is to be observed in everyday, ordinary situations, to be recorded under so-called "free-fall" conditions. "Psychology has been so busy selecting from, imposing upon, and rearranging the behavior of its subjects," he writes, "that it has until very recently neglected to note behavior's clear structure when it is not molested by tests, experiments, questionnaires and interviews." [1963:24]

It might seem that Barker is proposing the obvious: We have defined the purposes of various behavior settings in terms of the behaviors necessary to satisfy these purposes. This may be true, but the fact is that beyond the obvious appropriate behaviors (for example, people eat in dining rooms), we know little else about these settings because we have rarely studied them. There are many questions to ask: What nonappropriate behaviors occur? What happens when behavior settings having the same purposes vary in their physical dimension or in other ways? What consequences does the activity of one behavior setting have on the events in another that is related to it in time and/or space? What occurs when the stable structure of a behavior setting is only partially maintained (for example, sometimes the juke box in the local school snack shop works and sometimes it doesn't)? We must even ask what the properties of the common en masse behaviors revealed in behavior settings are. Worth quoting in this respect is Barker's own statement:

> Both science and society ask with greater urgency than previously: What are environments like? . . . How do environments select and shape the people who inhabit them? What are the structural and dynamic properties of the environments to which people must adapt? These are questions for ecological psychology, and in particular, they pertain to the ecological environment and its consequences for men. [1968:3, 4]

Barker's methods for observing the ecological relationship between individuals and their sociocultural setting are discussed in Chapter Eight. The significance of his findings is illustrated by an exhaustive study of schools, in which he was able to show that because smaller schools provide greater opportunities for participation in voluntary activities, students attending them are regulated to a degree that is not possible in large schools, where students are more likely to end up as spectators rather than participants. And since it is from the nonparticipating students that many drop-outs come, the size of the setting may be the critical factor as to whether one graduates.

Some Microtheoretical Approaches

In considering the major psychological theories of human behavior at least two environmental questions are implicit. What is the environment like, and how do we know the environment? Some theorists have attempted to answer either or both of these questions in specific and direct terms. Important in this respect is the work of Brunswik (1949, 1956), who directed his attention primarily to perceiving or "knowing" the environment. Although

Brunswik was Gestalt-oriented, his conception of the individual's psychological environment was quite different from the simple distinction between geographical and behavioral environments made by Lewin and Koffka. Brunswik was concerned with stimuli not as a source of stimulation but as a source of *information* from and about the environment. The view taken by him was simple enough: The cues and other forms of information provided by an object, a constellation of objects, or even a large-scale environment are many and varied. For this reason the information the individual receives from these objects is never perfectly correlated with its source, that is, some information is more valid than other information. This means, in effect, that in the process of getting information from the environment we must also determine the probability of it being correct, to decide whether it is valid information.

Thus Brunswik speaks of "ecological cue validities" and "environmental probabilities," which mean simply that the perceiver becomes part of the perceptual process; given the complexity and the equivocality of his environment, he judges it or gives it meaning by attributing validity to one set of cues rather than another. Given these "educated guesses" or probabilities, the individual then behaves in a way consistent with these judgments. To the extent that these actions confirm the accuracy of his percepts, he builds up particular probabilities about his environment which serve to guide his perceptual judgments in subsequent transactions with his environment. However, since the environment is constantly changing, the hypothesized probabilities we have used in the past may not always be correct; and the organism, if it is not to go under, must acquire new hypotheses. The process of learning, whether in the perceptual system or in the means-end system, is just such an acquiring of new hypotheses.

Although Gibson (1950, 1966) too was concerned with stimuli as sources of information about the environment, his conception of how we perceive it was vastly different. Thus, he distinguished between literal perception and schematic perception. Literal perception refers to the direct experiences of environmental stimuli that all of us have because they are rooted in the basic sensory structures and processes of man. Schematic perception, on the other hand, he defines as "the world of useful and significant things to which we ordinarily attend." This is the environment not only as felt, but as organized into a meaningful universe. In this kind of perception we respond not simply to sensation but to the moods, attitudes, values, and desires that various stimuli induce in us. Thus, hot and cold temperatures, a blinding light, a salty taste, and a fragrant smell will affect nearly all of us in pretty much the same way. But the environmental milieu in which we experience these sensations may be perceived with a wide range of differences, depending upon factors that have nothing to do with the immediate and literal stimuli.

Four factors discussed by Gibson as influencing schematic perception are: previous experience or perceptual set, personal needs, values and attitudes, and social consensus. The latter refers to the fact that our environments have order or make sense because we have imposed such sense or order on them. Through social consensus we group particular objects, apply names to them, and use these names and act accordingly when confronted with them. It is necessary that we recognize the world we move around in not only as being the same world from one day to the next, but the same world that others inhabit. The issues posed by these theorists are explored in greater detail in Chapter Five.

Still other theorists have turned their attention not so much to how we perceive our environment as to what our environment is like. Space limitations compel us to refer generally to these theorists as a group rather than to consider the views of any one of them in detail. Thus, Sells (1966), Fiske and Maddi (1961), and Berlyne (1960) have been concerned with the quality of stimulation with respect to its influence on such factors as personality development, learning capacity, and social competence. Still others, such as Wohlwill (1968), are looking at environment as a source of affect and attitudes which elicit feelings of pleasure and excitement, aversion and boredom. These are seen as a function of certain stimulus attributes such as complexity, incongruity, novelty, familiarity, and variety, to which the organism responds either through arousal or in the form of exploratory activity. Rapoport and Kantor (1967) stress the positive value of ambiguity and uncertainty in "engaging" the individual in his environment, and Wohlwill (1968) has stressed novelty, incongruity, and surprise as these responses are evoked by features of the physical environment. And finally, Fiske and Maddi (1961) emphasize the importance of variation and meaningfulness of stimuli (both internal and external) in arousing the organism neuropsychologically.

Two other theorists, Murray (1938) and Chein (1954), influenced by Lewin, Freud, and Gestalt theory generally, have attempted in a preliminary fashion to conceptualize the person's environment. Murray conceived of environmental objects and situations as positive and negative "presses," depending on whether they facilitated or impeded goal achievement or need satisfaction respectively. The environment he dealt with was Lewin's psychological environment; thus desirable, as opposed to undesirable, environmental goal objects were also identified in terms of positive and negative valences. Chein (1954) in his paper, "The Environment as a Determinant of Behavior," points to the "relative neglect of the environment by many of the most influential theoretical viewpoints." He believes that it is important to put together a schema to provide a more adequate means of conceptualizing the environment. Interestingly enough, in his own preliminary attempt, he turns to Koffka's geographical environment rather than to Lewin's behavioral environment, offering two reasons for doing so. First, he thinks the psychologist's present knowledge of the person is not adequate to conceptualize the behavioral environment, since this environment does not tell us anything at all about how the objective environment influences behavior. Second, Chein stresses the point that things in the objective environment do influence behavior although they are not in the behavioral environment as Koffka conceived of it; that is, the physical setting contains objects, spaces, and qualities which the person usually remains unaware of. As we indicated earlier, Lewin took account of just this problem in his elaboration of the life space, although he never focused on the objective environment in any systematic fashion.

In his formulation Chein defines stimuli as "whatever is capable of initiating a change in the stream of activity." This can be a light source or a complex social situation. But stimuli, he believes, at any level of complexity, may have other functions than to serve as a "release or trigger mechanism." They can also serve in the role of a *goal,* something that satisfies, or as a *noxiant,* something that is unpleasant or produces pain; they can act as *supports,* in that particular features of the environment facilitate certain behaviors, whereas *constraints* either preclude or make the occurrence of such behaviors less likely. Finally, they can serve as directors, which are defined as properties of the environment which "tend to induce specific directions of behavior." Chein further differentiates each of these general types of stimuli, and in the end also provides some dimensions for describing the global features of an environment. Thus, an environment can vary in its degree of *organization,* its degree of *stability,* and finally in the *degrees of freedom* it makes available to the person.

The View from Other Disciplines

Physical environmental theory has too many implications to be left just to psychologists. Many other professions and behavioral science fields have also theorized about the nature of the physical environment and man's responses to it. Of course, our discussion in this chapter has been heavily weighted with the views of theoretical psychologists, because, at least within the context of a scientific approach, psychologists either explicitly or implicitly have had most to say about the physical environment in relation to human behavior and experience. Sociologists are by definition dedicated to environmental concepts, but almost exclusive attention is given to the social environment of man. Yet, as Michelson (1970) notes, it was the sociologist Robert E. Park (1952) who first broached the study of human ecology, or that field of sociology that investigates the relationships among a community or group of individuals and its natural environments. With all of the best intentions—and Michelson takes pains to point this out—human ecology was far more a method than a theory, and the investigations that emerged tended to relate the social properties of given areas with the behavioral characteristics of the various groups of people involved. The relationships between the physical properties of urban settings and the corresponding social properties of these settings, or between the urban settings and the behavior of the people living in them, were largely ignored.

On the other hand, some sociologists, such as Gutman and Gans, have taken an interest in the relationships between the design of physical settings—particularly in housing—and the behavior of individuals and groups. Gutman (1966) has considered the general problem of the contribution of sociological thinking to architectural design and the needs of architects. Gans (1962) has considered the design and organization of urban communities in relation to the behavior and relationships of groups of people living in the communities. His studies of Boston's West End are discussed in Chapters Eight and Nine. More recently, Michelson (1970) himself has posited what he calls an "intersystems congruence theory." This suggests that physical settings by themselves do not determine behavior, but if congruent with the purposes and goals of the individuals who occupy the setting, then they provide supports for the behaviors necessary to realize these goals and purposes. A low-income project, for example, designed for "beauty and expression," but not for meeting the community and "mutual support desires" of its occupants, will be incongruent with the latter's needs.

Anthropologists too have shown interest in physical settings in terms of acquiring a complete understanding of the sociocultural properties of the particular group of people living in a given setting. In dealing with primitive cultures the physical context had to be described and related to the behaviors and experiences of the members in these cultures. Stated differently, the emphasis was on how these peoples adapted to their physical environment. However, not only did a theory of environment not emerge, but in most instances the emphasis moved from the physical environment itself to an emphasis on the psychological properties of physical settings; that is, what was believed, felt, or valued about the physical setting and how these reactions related to the extant behavior patterns and customs of the groups. The physical environment qua physical environment simply became the backdrop rather than the focus of concern. One anthropologist, however, Edward Hall (1966), has given almost all of his time to the question of national and cultural differences in the organization and use of space, particularly with respect to the psychospatial relationships between individuals during social interaction. His approach is called "proxemics," and it is considered in detail later in Chapter Six.

In recent years the behavioral orientation has evolved in the field of geography. This interest has taken a number of forms. One of the major questions is how the terrain and other geographical factors influence the behavior and experience of aggregates of peoples. Also the reverse: How does man influence his geographical setting? But here too there has been much discussion but little development toward conceptualizing an approach to the physical environment. As we move through the remaining chapters of this book, the reader will have occasion to read about the theory and research of some of these geographers.

It is true that architects, designers, and planners concerned with the influence of the natural and built environment on behavior and experience have not waited upon developments in the behavioral sciences. Indeed they should not have, because it has been and will continue to be a long wait. Furthermore, as we already suggested, environmental psychology is an interdisciplinary field that will require the integration not only of the conceptions of different behavioral science disciplines but also of those of the architect, designer, and planner.

As one might expect, some architects, designers, and planners have formulated their own microtheories of environment, although these are more orientations to the problems of the physical settings than actual theories. The work of such people as the architect and planner Kevin Lynch (1960) and the architect-psychologist Constance Perin (1970), come to mind in this context. In our discussions in the chapters on methodology (Chapter Eight), the urban setting (Chapter Nine), and the built environment (Chapter Eleven), and in other places in this volume, their particular views are considered. But here it is important to take note of the considerable influence of the environmental conceptions discussed throughout this chapter on the thinking of these individuals. Thus, Lynch (1960), in his *Image of the City,* takes a cognitive approach to the environment in his attempt to get at the visual quality of the American city. By visual quality he means primarily the "legibility" of the city: that is, the ease with which the parts of a city can be recognized and be organized into a meaningful or coherent pattern which exists as an image in our mind.

His colleague Carr (1967) has called this imaged urban form the "city of the mind." We carry with us a picture of the city (or countryside) that is absent from our immediate perception or beyond our perceptual boundaries. Although in many respects this picture may be a distortion of the actual environment on which it is based, it may be as useful in our day-to-day orientations as an accurate map. This cognitive orientation to city planning is taking its place alongside the traditional economic concerns of land use, esthetic quality, traffic problems, and the like. Lynch's work is discussed more fully in Chapters Five, Eight, and Nine.

Alexander (1964), concerned more with design process than environment per se, takes the view that environmental form follows function. Stated more directly, he argues that only by tracing the functional requirements of human needs and activities can we provide the kinds of forms (solutions to problems of designing built environments) that will fit the context (the problem—human need, activity, and so on). In this respect his view followed Köhler's conception of the "good figure," that is, an environmental object, setting, or event designed so that it relates in the most meaningful way or "best fit" to a human activity, function, or need. We will consider Alexander's views again in our discussion of the built environment later in this volume.

The array of theoretical viewpoints presented in this chapter falls short of providing definitive directions. However, at least one important guiding principle does emerge. Each of the viewpoints attacks one aspect of a broad problem. This, in brief, is the problem of conceptualizing man's environment in relation to the fact that he behaves in and experiences it. Our theories do make sense in the light of their particular focuses. What will be needed in the end is a theoretical approach that is eclectic in the sense that it can integrate all of these points of view.

The fact is that there is an objective world that is experienced in very similar ways by all men. On the other hand, it is no less true that there is a subjective environment which, whatever the commonalities of experience, reflects not just differences in men's values, interests, and past experience, but also the uniqueness to be found in the fantasies of the private world of each individual, for we do interpret, fantasize about, and give special meanings to our particular physical settings. Somewhere between these two extremes is a "constructed objective world": Whatever the hard-data information about the environment provided by each physiological sense system, the sheer integration of all this information in the brain—as part of motivational and other directive state influences—undoubtedly provides a "constructed" view of the environment. To this we must add the fact that the behavior of the person himself changes the very environment that in part produced the behavior.

In terms of a systematic and useful conceptualization, the environment, physical or otherwise, remains a vast unknown insofar as we have been able to establish a viable theory of human behavior and experience. On the other hand, it is possible to pull together from some of the theoretical positions discussed above at least a set of working assumptions about the environment which can serve as a guide to research and the analysis of problems. As the reader knows by now, any theory of the environment must articulate and be consistent with a theory of human behavior and experience. Thus, our first task in the next chapter is to sketch some basic assumptions about the nature of man.

References

Alexander, C. *Notes on the synthesis of form.* Cambridge, Mass.: Harvard University Press, 1964.

Barker, R. G. On the nature of the environment. *Journal of Social Issues,* 1963a, *19,* 17–23.

Barker, R. G. *The stream of behavior.* New York: Appleton, 1963b.

Barker, R. G. *Ecological psychology: Concepts and methods for studying the environment of behavior.* Stanford, Calif.: Stanford University Press, 1968.

Berlyne, D. E. *Conflict, arousal and curiosity.* New York: McGraw-Hill, 1960.

Boring, E. G. *Sensation and perception in the history of experimental psychology.* New York: Appleton, 1942.

Brunswik, E. *Systematic and representative design of psychology experiments.* Berkeley, Calif.: University of California Press, 1949.

Brunswik, E. *Perception and the representative design of psychology experiments.* Berkeley, Calif.: University of California Press, 1956.

Carr, S. The city of the mind. In W. R. Ewald, Jr. (Ed.), *Environment for man: The next fifty years.* Bloomington, Ind.: Indiana University Press, 1967.

Chein, I. The environment as a determinant of behavior. *Journal of Social Psychology,* 1954, *39,* 115–127.

Fiske, D. & Maddi, S. *Functions of varied experience.* Homewood, Ill.: Dorsey Press, 1961.
Freud, S. *New introductory lectures on psycho-analysis.* New York: Norton, 1933. (First German edition, 1930.)
Gans, H. *The urban villagers.* New York: Free Press, 1962.
Gibson, J. J. *The perception of the visual world.* Boston: Houghton Mifflin, 1950.
Gibson, J. J. *The senses considered as perceptual systems.* Boston: Houghton Mifflin, 1966.
Gutman, R. Site planning and social behavior. *Journal of Social Issues,* 1966, *22,* 103–115.
Hall, E. T. *The hidden dimension.* New York: Doubleday, 1966.
Heidbreder, E. *Seven psychologies.* New York: Appleton, 1933.
Koffka, K. *Principles of gestalt psychology.* New York: Harcourt Brace Jovanovich, 1935.
Köhler, W. *Gestalt psychology.* New York: Liveright, 1929.
Lewin, K. *A dynamic theory of personality.* New York: McGraw-Hill, 1935.
Lewin, K. *Principles of topological psychology.* New York: McGraw-Hill, 1936.
Lewin, K. *Field theory in social science.* New York: Harper & Row, 1951.
Lynch, K. *The image of the city.* Cambridge, Mass.: The M.I.T. Press, 1960.
Michelson, W. *Man and his urban environment: A sociological approach.* Reading, Mass.: Addison-Wesley, 1970.
Murray, H. A. *Explorations in personality.* New York: Oxford, 1938.
Park, R. E. *Human communities.* New York: Free Press, 1952.
Perin, C. *With man in mind: An interdisciplinary prospectus for environmental design.* Cambridge, Mass.: The M.I.T. Press, 1970.
Rapoport, A. & Kantor, R. E. Complexity and ambiguity in environmental design. *Journal of American Institute of Planners,* 1967, *23,* 210–221.
Sells, S. B. Ecology and the science of psychology. *Multivariate Behavioral Research,* 1966, *1,* 133–144.
Skinner, B. F. *Science and human behavior.* New York: Macmillan, 1953.
Skinner, B. F. *Beyond freedom and dignity.* New York: Knopf, 1971.
Wohlwill, J. F. Amount of stimulus exploration and preference as differential functions of stimulus complexity. *Perception and Psychophysics,* 1968, *4,* 307–312.
Wolman, B. S. (Ed.) *Historical roots of contemporary psychology.* New York: Harper & Row, 1968.
Woodworth, R. S. *Contemporary schools of psychology.* New York: Ronald, 1948.

Suggested Readings

Boring, E. G. *Sensation and perception in the history of experimental psychology.* New York: Appleton, 1942.
Heidbreder, E. *Seven psychologies.* New York: Appleton, 1933.
Wolman, B. S. (Ed.) *Historical roots of contemporary psychology.* New York: Harper & Row, 1968.
Woodworth, R. S. *Contemporary schools of psychology.* New York: Ronald, 1948.

Four

Man/Environment Transactions

Some Guiding Assumptions*

In the foregoing chapter we outlined a family tree of environmental theory, as it were, which puts our present knowledge in the perspective of historical development. It was pointed out that the objective approach, which had its roots in experimental psychophysics and Watsonian behaviorism, fragmented the physical world into discrete quantifiable stimuli whose specific functional relationship to experience and behavior it has sought.

Taking shape more or less at the same time was the contrasting orientation of Gestalt psychology. Its conception of the environment was not just different, it was radically so. The environment was conceptualized as a complex stimulus field whose properties emerge from and are determined by the organization and interrelationships of its component parts. The person does not respond to an object in isolation from its environmental field, but to the field-like properties of that object created by the environmental context of which it is a part.

It was only in these terms that the behavior and experience of the individual in response to his environment could be understood.

* Some material in this chapter has been reworked from material published in *Environmental Psychology: Man and His Physical Setting* (Holt, Rinehart and Winston, 1970), pp. 27–37.

In fact, the Gestaltists pointed out that a distinction had to be made between a real world and a conceived one. In Koffka's terminology the "geographical" environment is the external setting that exists apart from whoever perceives it; the "behavioral" environment is that setting recreated by the interpretations and meaning given to it by the particular person observing it. The person is himself a component of both of these environments, and his behavior and experience reflect the balance of influences that result from the interaction of these two worlds, the world as is and the world as he perceives it.

Whether conceived geographically or behaviorally, environments for the person vary in scope, complexity, and indeed significance, when we consider that they extend from such large-scale subenvironments or settings as cities, the outdoors, or even regions, to the far more restricted ones of a neighborhood, school, hospital, park, office building, and other such institutional contexts; and to still more confined settings such as a classroom, bedroom, office, playground, hospital ward, and subway car. In our subsequent discussions it will become clear that these are not merely physical settings but that they are also social, cultural, and organizational systems as well. The continuing socialization process of the newborn infant involves as much a definition of the meaning and purposes of the physical settings that circumscribe his existence as it does establishing the definition and meaning of his relationships to all the people who are responsible for this process.

In the history of modern psychology, and to a large extent also of modern philosophy and sociology, the focus of ideas has always been man rather than his environment. Thus many of the theories of the latter discussed in the previous chapter were more implicit than explicit. The experimentalists and Watsonian behaviorists, for instance, were far more concerned with the nature of man than with the nature of his environment. How else explain their simple but almost elegant view that environments, regardless of scope, complexity, or function, were nothing more than accumulations of discrete stimuli? If we go beyond this simple stimulus-response model of behavior to other attempts to explain man, there seem to have been three kinds of questions raised. First is the concern with *basic motivations*, the so-called underlying nature of human beings. Is it power, greed, sex, altruism, pleasure versus pain, competitiveness, affiliation, or love that is the underlying nexus of their desires, interests, and accomplishments? Many if not all of these conceptions of man have played—and indeed some continue to play—a role in the attempts to understand and explain human behavior. The second issue is whether man's behavior, motives, desires, and other properties are innately determined or largely a product of social and cultural learning. Are aggression and altruism in man instinctive, that is, innately determined? Or are they the product of learning and experience, or both; and if both, to what extent does each enter into the picture? The third kind of question raised is reflected in the theories discussed in the preceding chapter and in others that have evolved in the more recent history of psychology. The emphasis here is not so much on content (What are the basic motivations of all men?) or on the origin (learned or innate) of human tendencies, but on the nature of the processes underlying such tendencies. How do men function psychologically? How do they perceive, feel, strive, locomote, achieve, solve problms, think, and behave? To answer this question generally, models of man have been either implicitly or explicitly evolved as a basis for describing and explaining "what makes him tick." Actually such models represent a broad approach to the study of man, rather than detailed statements of significant concepts and principles explaining how individual men function, live, and behave in specific situations.

In the writing of this book the authors too were guided by a model of man. As the reader will soon see it is far more closely related to the Gestalt approach than to the stimulus-response or "machine model" of the behaviorists. However, our model is nothing more than a set of very general assumptions about what man is like, how he functions, and therefore, how he must be studied. What must be emphasized again is that our model of man merely serves as a broad general approach and is not a theory of man with a network of behavioral principles and concepts. This approach in turn, seen against the backdrop of the problems that are of concern to the environmental psychologist—that is, behavior and experience in relation to the design, organization, and other properties of physical settings—has clear implications for how the environment must be conceptualized or defined.

In the discussion that follows we consider two sets of assumptions which, in effect, constitute our man/environment approach. A number of different schools of psychological thought contribute to these assumptions, specifically the works of Lewin (1936), Koffka (1935), Brunswik (1949), Köhler (1929), Barker (1963), Krech and Crutchfield (1948), Murphy (1947), and Murray (1938). In citing these writers, however, we should make it clear that they are not necessarily in agreement about all aspects of behavior. Many held divergent views on specific questions; most of them tended to emphasize the particular facet of behavior they were interested in studying. So it is that we extract from their approaches the building blocks that contribute most usefully to our own working model of human behavior, a model that is intended to help us understand why man's actions in the environment are dynamic and not merely a simple response to a stimulus. Finally, after modeling such a view of man, we derive some rather specific assumptions about the nature of his behavior as it is consistently exhibited in specific environmental contexts.

Man as a Dynamically Organized System

Shakespeare summed up the poet's view of man and his humanness in his famous lines from Hamlet:

> *What a piece of work is man! how noble in reason! infinite in faculty! in form and moving how express and admirable! in action how like an*

angel! in apprehension how like a god! the beauty of the world! the paragon of animals! . . .

In a sense Hamlet's—or rather Shakespeare's—insights concerning the mystery and complexity of man were incomplete. For the unusual and unique nature of man is rooted not just in the existence of his capacity to think, feel, sense, interpret, act, and locomote, but in the interrelated nature of all these functions and processes. Thus we begin our approach with the specific conception that man is a *dynamically organized system* whose behavior and experience at all times expresses the interactive consequences of these processes and functions.

To simply observe the on-going behavior of any individual in any physical setting is to establish the self-evident assumption of the wholeness and integrated nature of his behavior and experience. What better example of this integration and wholeness is there than the synchronization of movement, perceptions, emotional expressions, and sheer desire of, let us say, the tired urban commuter who, after a long day at the office, is now quickly making his way to the one available empty seat on his regular evening train? He practically runs down the aisle to get to it, all the while searching to be sure that no one else just entering the train might just get it before he does. The joy he experiences as he wearily sits down is something to behold.

Our unit of analysis here is not an isolated stimulus-response sequence, but the intact individual behaving and experiencing in the context of a specific ongoing physical setting. To understand the nature of this complex event, which is the primary objective of the environmental psychologist, it is necessary to extract and study particular psychological functions and processes (for example, the commuter's searching perceptions of the train as he enters) but never when removed or in isolation from their relationships to other psychological functions and processes. For most psychologists who conceive of human behavior in these terms, it is generally agreed that the *goal-directed* character of such behavior seems to unify and integrate human activity and experience. This is a key assumption in the present orientation, for in fact it denies that human behavior is simply elicited by appropriate stimuli, or that it simply unfolds in the manner of reflex responses or involuntary biological reactions such as digestion, breathing, and so on. Our tired commuter's behavior, if it tells us anything, expresses his intention and desire to possess that last available seat. Of course, we can get more direct evidence of his motivated or goal-directed state. If we ask him after he is seated why he moved so quickly in the particular direction he did, he is more than likely to tell us: "I am so tired tonight I probably would have stepped on anyone who got in the way of my getting that seat. The thought of standing all the way home was too much!"

Behavioral scientists use such terms as "motives," "desires," and "drives" to describe this goal-directed nature of human behavior. To avoid confusion we shall employ the term *need* to represent all such inferred inner states that are capable of initiating and directing actions in ways and toward ends that will eventually satisfy the individual. These may have to do with hunger, thirst, sex, elimination, or other tissue-related behavioral instigators. They may involve the more complex and socially rooted needs of recognition, power, affiliation, achievement, independence, territoriality, privacy, self-esteem, and success. Finally, they may be relatively simple and tied to immediate situations, for example, the commuter getting that last seat, or they may be far more complex and transcend particular situations, requiring for their satisfaction the satisfaction of a host of more instrumental needs. The strong desire of a young pre-med student to be a great success at medicine is a long-range goal, but it will require for its achievement the satisfaction of such other needs as doing well in courses, being accepted in the best medical school, and getting an appointment as an intern and resident in the best hospitals.

Motivational Processes Underlying Behavior

The reader may think at this point that it is not stimuli but needs which determine behavior. The point cannot be made too strongly that both views are incorrect. Psychoanalytically oriented theories of behavior have fostered the view both among behavioral scientists and laymen that to know the "inner man"—his needs or desires—is to be able to predict his behavior. Such a view commits the "isolation error" of assuming that each human function operates in some isolated fashion, apart from other psychological processes. Given the individual conceived of as a dynamically organized system, nothing could be further from the truth.

To understand human motivation or the goal-directed nature of human behavior, it is important to identify its essential components. The initiation of behavior will depend not just on the existence of a need but the extent of the arousal of that need. Such arousal may result from factors within the person or from events and stimuli in the environment. To take the example of our commuter again, his need for a seat may have been aroused before he even got on the train because of a feeling of being terribly tired and the awful thought of standing all the way home. Or he may have been unaware of just how tired he was until he entered the train and realized he would have to stand unless he managed to get to the last available seat. But even if he was already aware of being terribly tired when entering the commuter train, and therefore already need-aroused, he undoubtedly would not move to get a seat if he saw that all the seats were taken. Indeed he might have immediately gotten off the train to wait for the next one. Thus, we now know that the occurrence of actual behavior depends not only on *need arousal* but also the availability of the appropriate *goal object*.

Now let us suppose that when he entered the train there was a seat available with no other passenger competing for it. However, let us also suppose that the seat's upholstery padding was torn out and its springs exposed. Anyone who took it would experience an uncomfortable ride. It follows, then, that behavior will also depend on the *value* of the available goal object. Clearly, even our tired commuter would behave in a little less determined fashion to get the only seat, if sitting in it would not only cause him discomfort and possibly tear his clothes, but also cause him the embarrasment of sitting in a nonfunctional seat.

But what if the seat available is functional, yet on entering the train our commuter immediately sees that it is at the other end of the car, and that a passenger entering at that end will very likely reach it before he does? Given these circumstances, it is almost certain that our hero would show little if any overt behavior in that direction. Perceived *probability of success* in achieving a goal is thus still another component of the motivational process that determines whether a need will in fact initate behavior.

What we are saying is that need arousal is a necessary, but far from sufficient, condition for determining behavior. All the other conditions cited above—availability of the goal, the value of the goal, the probability of success in achieving it—can be translated into the more general statement that behavior is also influenced and determined by the broader social context in which our relations with other people, social constraints, opportunity, the degree of skill and talent we possess, and the nature of the physical setting all play a role. It is likely that even if he were close to the available seat our commuter would not have taken it if the only other standing passenger was an obviously pregnant woman or someone who was blind.

By now we can specify still another fundamental assumption in our approach to behavior and experience. Man is a *cognitive* animal. He does far more than see, hear, feel, touch, smell, in the simple sense of "recording" his environment. He interprets it, makes inferences about it, dreams of it, judges it, imagines it, and engages in still other human forms of knowing. It is all of these forms of knowing that permit the individual to accumulate a past, think on the present, and anticipate the future. The "poetry" of this human process is the substitution of an "inner reality" of words, images, ideas, feelings, and still other symbols and representations for an "outer reality" of shapes, sizes, objects, movements, sounds, structures, and other attributes of the environment.

If the reader will again consider our tired commuter desperately hoping and trying to get a seat, then the interrelatedness of human psychological processes becomes quite evident. At every step of the way in the unfolding of the motivational episode we described—the arousal of the need, the availability of a seat, the functional usefulness of the seat, the chances of his getting it, the arousal of a competing need (giving a seat to a blind passenger) —cognitive processes in the form of seeing, judging, deciding, concluding, and so on are involved. Need arousal and cognitive process have mutual influences on and interactive consequences for each other.

The Emergent Nature of Experience

For the environmental psychologist there is a critical corollary to the assumption that man is a cognitive animal. Whether he is viewing an object, judging it, interpreting it, or evaluating it, the resulting percepts (or judgments, interpretations, and so forth) are *emergent*. By this we mean they express the interaction of the properties of the object, place, or event being perceived, and the behavioral characteristics of the perceiver—including such things as where he happens to be standing and how significantly his past experience, attitudes, values, interests, and other enduring tendencies become involved as influences. It can be said then that the properties of the "thing out there" and those of the person impose mutual restraints on each other. Conversely, out of the interaction of person and place may come an entirely new, or emergent, kind of experience that is quite independent of the intrinsic nature of either party to the transaction. Thus, in chemistry we know that one part hydrogen and two parts oxygen, when combined, form a new substance, water. Human perception, of course, is not so clear-cut and predictable; yet, metaphorically speaking, something like this happens in the man/environment transaction when an affective need is strongly enough aroused to overcome or suppress the more rational side of our nature. The desert mirage, although at times due to distortions produced by atmospheric phenomena, can involve illusions and fantasies in the desperately thirsty man that have little basis in reality. A more familiar instance is the tired skid-row vagrant caught in a rainstorm for whom a dry doorway is viewed at first as equal to a soft bed in the finest hotel. Once stretched out on the cold ground, he is likely to experience it as something less than that. Fantasy in such cases can soften, enhance, rearrange, and even defy reality. But in its own good time reality has a way of diluting, weakening, intruding on, or even completely dispelling our worlds of fantasy.

A great deal of research has been undertaken by psychologists on the emergent properties of perception and other cognitive processes. Worthy of mention in its own right is the generally accepted proposition that the greater the ambiguity or lack of structure or clarity of the object, place, or event to be observed, the greater the influence of inner or behavioral determinants on the percepts that emerge. Much of the nature of cognitive process as we have described it here is amply demonstrated with respect to environmental perception. Studies by various investigators on the effects of past experience, reward and punishment, personality factors, and cultural factors are reported by Proshansky, Ittelson, and Rivlin (1970) in Part Two, "Basic Psychological Processes and the Environment," of their volume.

Cognition, conceived of as an emergent or transactional process involving the interaction of the characteristics of the person with those of the event to be perceived, turns our attention back to the environment. Our readers may be concerned that if perception is an inner- as well as outer-determined emergent process, then adaptive and meaningful behavior in relation to the real or objective environment is difficult to say the least.

But everyone knows from his own experience that we do, indeed, manage to adapt and behave meaningfully in response to a changing environment. The influence of the behavioral factors we have been discussing determines not only how we perceive the objects and events that concern us, but also what we perceive. As complex changing systems in their own right, the environments that confront goal-directed man must be and are selectively perceived. To behave appropriately and meaningfully our commuter, then, must first find an empty seat and then walk towards it. He cannot at the same time read the ads, or look for a friend, or examine the safety features of the commuter train—if he hopes to get a seat.

But what about the possible distortions in the meaning, definitions, or interpretations we make of the events and objects in the environment? Many factors ensure that the two environments, geographical and behavioral, will not diverge or fail to match in any serious way. First, most objects and situations that the individual encounters in his mundane experiences are not ambiguous or unstructured; thus accuracy of perception is not a problem. Even if the match of the object or setting as "is" and as it "seems" is not perfect, the difference may not be such as to preclude the behavior required to satisfy a particular need. Distortions in cognition will have consequences to the extent that they reach a level that leads to maladaptive behavior. Finally, and perhaps most crucial, as we have already suggested, reality has a way of intruding on fantasy or inner-determined conceptions. Distortions in perception which lead to maladaptive behavior and are accompanied by pain and frustration quickly result in the individual's attempt to improve the match between the object or event and the emergent percept associated with it. Indeed we learn to perceive or cognize with some degree of accuracy, and in the relative stability of day-to-day settings, routine, accurate perceptions lead to routine and appropriate behaviors in periodically aroused goal-directed individuals. Nothing seems so routine, synchronized, "unconscious," and perfectly adaptive as the individual's perception of, and use of, space in the various physical settings that circumscribe his day-to-day experiences.

Affective Determinants of Behavior

If we consider once again Shakespeare's view of man as expressed by Hamlet, conspicuous by its absence is any reference to the *emotional* or *affective* nature of men. Awed by man's capacity to reason, Shakespeare paid homage to him primarily as a rational being. Yet men are no less men because they experience visceral and conscious feelings usually identified as love, anger, hate, sympathy, compassion, guilt, shame, disgust, and still others. What is significant for the present discussion is the fact that the various emotions have the properties of need states. They can initate and guide behavior. They are not merely epiphenomena that accompany other motivated states, but, as reactions to oneself, to others, or to physical settings and their objects, they direct behavior with respect to particular goals or ends.

Spaces and places, no less than people, can evoke intense emotional responses. Rooms, neighborhoods, and cities can be "friendly," "threatening," "frustrating," or "loathsome"; they can induce hate, love, fear, desire, and other affective states. But the individual does more than just experience these states; he may be moved to act on them. He may want to either reduce these feelings or enhance them and in the process he must make adequate and relevant responses to his environment. An unpleasant room will be avoided; a walk through a ghetto at dusk may lead to an increased pace. Of course there is a reciprocal relationship between feelings and places. Places may evoke particular feelings, and already existing feelings may color the individual's perception of places. The fatigue of our friend the commuter undoubtedly was accompanied by some minimal pain and distress as he entered the car. But imagine the joy when he spied the one available empty seat, a joy which undoubtedly helped to propel him down the aisle to get to it before someone else did.

Learning and Behavior

A final consideration in looking at man's behavior and experience is the question of their origin and development, a question that has been asked since the beginning of recorded history. Like all other living organisms, what man is and what he becomes in any given lifetime is rooted to some degree by his place in the phylogenetic scale. What distinguishes him from other living species are both his unique biobehavioral properties and his unusual capacity to learn; and by learning we mean the ability to modify his behavior in response to a changing environment. All complex organisms learn to some degree, but both the nature and level of man's learning capacity set him quite apart from other animal species. His ability to learn, coupled with other cognitive processes, has helped him to build his own environment and, in effect, to modify and control his natural environment. Each new environment he creates evokes new responses, new human interactions, and new problems, which lead him to build other, more complicated, if not more advanced, environments.

Again we find ourselves confronted by the patterning and interrelatedness of human psychological functions and processes. Learning is a process which takes a variety of forms in man. It can be incidental, purposeful, cognitive or reflexive, simple or complex. In most instances it is rooted in the integration of motivational, cognitive, and affective processes in such ways that human behaviors and experiences in relation to environmental settings change in adaptive and satisfying ways. If what the person sees, does, feels, and strives for is the basis for human learning, then it is no less true that what and how he learns subsequently has consequences for all of these psychological processes.

One question remains. Given the integration and interrelatedness of human psychological processes, how do we characterize this "wholeness" or "unity" of the person? Psychologically speaking, the individual represents a dynamic system which is characterized by both constant change and relative stability. At every waking moment—and to a lesser degree during sleep—the person is moving, thinking, seeing, feeling, engaging in activities, satisfying needs, meeting frustration, ad infinitum. But these responses are neither random nor unorganized. In fact, they are in part determined and guided by a relatively stable set of enduring psychological structures which identify and distinguish particular individuals, groups of individuals, or even members of different cultures and subcultures from each other. These structures not only lend consistency and predictability to human behavior, but they provide the continuity to experience that is implicit in the continuing modification of genetic and other biological tendencies.

What emerges, then, out of the continuing interaction of percepts, need states, and feelings, are higher-order and more-or-less enduring psychological structures in the form of attitudes, values, interests, self-concepts, personality traits, abilities, and aptitudes. This points up a final aspect of our commuter's behavior—the values, attitudes, and other behavioral dispositions that he carries aboard with him. Such tendencies or dispositions are a consequence of his earliest cultural and social experiences imposed upon his unique biological and physical tendencies at birth. Thus, a naturally aggressive person may have been taught that it is "bad manners" to scramble for a seat, or that to do so might impair his self-image as a man of dignity. "Well-dressed, well-educated people from my background don't act like this." The workman, however, who has had to struggle for a living may not feel this way. To say that a person has a certain set of values or attitudes is another perspective on his probable behavior in a particular situation.

As yet psychologists differ as to whether all or even more of the analytic tools we have described are needed for understanding human behavior. This need not concern us here. Important for the present discussion is simply the view that psychological structures of this kind do in fact exist and in part underlie the person's behavior and experience in a given situation. For emphasis, however, it must be noted once again that these structures do not by themselves determine such behavior and experience. Any one of them is only one of the conditions along with many others—such as competition from other inner states, the nature of the physical setting, relationships with others, barriers to behavior, the potential consequences of behavior, and so on—that underlie when, how, where, and why the person acts.

This is our view of psychological man. It is now time to ask: What is his environment like? How do we conceive of it? Again, we will make certain assumptions in order to define and establish the general nature of our environmental approach, assumptions that are theoretically and logically consistent with the psychological conception of man sketched above.

We have already distinguished between the observed environment and the real environment, a view that follows theoretically from our conception of man as a cognitive being as well as a goal-directed one. The interrelatedness of these and other psychological functions and the capacity of reality to intrude on fantasy as well as the obverse, immediately dispel or nullify the over-simplified conception that the person's phenomenal world is a poor and inadequate replica of his geographical environment. Not only is this inner world constantly monitored by reality, but its consequences for behavior in relation to goal attainment and emotional satisfaction help to establish structured ways of thinking, believing, acting, feeling, and doing that in most instances establish the efficacy of this inner world in relating the person to a changing environment. As we noted above, these psychological structures—desires, attitudes, values, self-conceptions, interests, and others—are not only enduring but they lend consistency to the behavior and experience of the person.

Patterns of Behavior and the Physical Setting

What follows from this view, and indeed was confirmed by our early space utilization research (Ittelson, Proshansky & Rivlin 1970), and that of others, is that human behavior in relation to a physical setting is enduring and consistent over time and situation. As a consequence, the characteristic patterns of behavior for that setting can be identified. In effect, physical settings such as libraries, bedrooms, station platforms, schoolrooms, dentist offices, and others, as well as individuals, define and structure characteristic patterns of behavior. Our discussion of Barker's behavior setting theory in the preceding chapter bears on this point, although we should keep in mind that Barker is concerned almost exclusively with the social nature of the setting rather than its physical aspects. We emphasize here that the "demand" character of an environment is more than the sum of its ongoing social activities. Individuals, as members of broad social groups, are socialized not just to behave, but to behave appropriately in relation to relevant physical settings; and not simply to the immediate sensory stimuli of the setting, but to its symbolic qualities as well—the "meanings" suggested by outward appearances.

Thus there is a corollary to our first assumption: Other things being equal, patterns of behavior in response to a given type of physical setting persist regardless of the specific individuals involved. Yet within this pattern diversity of behaviors over time and space is also a crucial environmental characteristic. Settings are themselves complex systems involving the behavior of many people over space at any given time. The demand character of any institutional setting for appropriate behaviors is general rather than highly specific. It allows and requires variation and change in the behavior of the person in his continuing reactions to the setting. What this means is that if physical settings require appropriate and relevant behaviors, it is not because as stimulus complexes they automatically elicit responses from individuals (the behaviorist's credo). If man is a cognitive being as we have assumed, then settings have definitions and meanings for the perceiver with respect to his role in them, how they should look and be used, what other people should be involved, what activities should go on in them, what they stand for symbolically, and so on. This is true not just for the moment but over time and with respect to similar physical settings as well.

What we are assuming then is that the regularity and consistency of behavior in given physical settings over time and space occur because such settings are closely and tightly interwoven with the fabric of social, organizational, and cultural systems that circumscribe the day-to-day life of any group of individuals. In effect, any given physical environment is not only a behavioral environment but also a social, organizational, and cultural environment.

It follows therefore that a physical setting that defines and structures any concrete situation is not a closed system; its boundaries are not fixed either in space or in time. A hospital ward, a school classroom, a family apartment, or any other concrete institutional setting may have well-defined physical limits, but its organization, the activities that go on in it, when they begin and end, the number of people involved, and therefore even its properties as a physical setting, will be influenced by and in turn influence the larger, more encompassing and interlocking physical and social system of which it is a part. To take but one example, a governmental decision in a large urban community to save on electric power, which prevents the use of air conditioners and fans during the hot summer months, may have consequences for family living in an apartment insofar as how, where, and when family members interact, sleep, eat, and socialize on the hottest days of this period.

If a physical setting is an open system characterized simultaneously by change and stability because of its interrelatedness with corresponding and more embracing social, normative, and organizational systems, then its organization is dynamic. A change in any component of the setting has varying degrees of effects on all other components in that setting, thereby changing the characteristic behavior pattern of the setting as a whole. The unexpected arrival, for example, of the neighbors down the block just before a family is getting ready to sit down to dinner, may change the entire family behavior pattern associated with preparing, eating, and cleaning up after their evening meal, if these neighbors are invited to stay for dinner. The children's usual pattern of watching TV in the dining room while they eat, with the older members of the family isolated at the other end of the table, may be precluded. The children may in fact be excused from eating dinner with the guests, thereby allowing them to escape to the basement playroom where they can eat and watch TV without being disturbed.

Conservation of Behavior

As part of our research on the behavior of staff and patients on a psychiatric ward we designated such dynamic effects the *conservation of behavior* (Ittelson, Proshansky, & Rivlin 1970). When a change in a physical setting does not permit a characteristic behavior pattern of that setting to occur, that behavior will usually occur at a new time or place. What also must be stressed in viewing the physical setting dynamically is that we can induce just such changes in the characteristic behavior patterns of setting by changing the physical, social, or organizational systems that define the setting. If there were no second TV set in the basement playroom, and if the one in the dining room could not be moved, then the visit of the neighbors, or a breakdown in the heating of the house, or a lively fight between the parents, or some other change, could conceivably lead to the conservation of the children's television-watching behavior by their seeking out a set in the nearby house of a friend.

Notwithstanding the assumptions we have made about physical settings up to this point, it should be clear that regardless of such designations as "physical environment," "social environment," "family," "the individual" and so on, in reality there is only the *total environment.* While the extraction of any one of these environmental aspects is possible and useful for purposes of analysis and research, it cannot be stressed too strongly that first, they are merely different ways of analyzing the same situation, and second, that each one exists and derives meaning only by its relationships to the others.

Let us return for a moment to the example above of the neighbors who visit a family just in time to be invited to dinner. If we view the scene at any given moment while dinner is in progress, then it is apparent that the dining room as a physical setting is not simply a physical space with inanimate objects in it. What makes it a dining room is its relationship to other rooms in the house, the people who use it, the way they use it, what happens in it and what doesn't happen in it, and how, where, and by whom the various objects in it are used. In effect we have objects, people, activities, interactions, relationships, spatial arrangements, as well as other components that interact with and relate to each other. The inclusive environment then is an active and continuing process whose participating components define and are defined by the nature of the interrelationships among them at a given moment and over time.

Given this active and continuing environmental process, it becomes clear that whatever component is abstracted for purposes of analysis and study is both cause and effect. It not only acts upon other components (and as a result changes them), but in so doing induces changes in itself. Let the reader think back to the neighbors who drop in at dinner time and are asked by the wife and mother of the house to stay for dinner. In her invitation to them she becomes a cause; but she herself changes because of the consequences of her action. Once the dinner invitation is accepted, the following things happen: the table is set differently, the "territorial places" at the table change, the children are sent to the basement, the TV is turned off, things are tidied up in the living room, and most importantly, the wife and mother of the house finds herself in the role of "hostess to dinner guests." Her role of wife and mother becomes secondary and other behaviors associated with her new role of hostess emerge. The cause-and-effect consequences of her initial invitation to the visiting neighbors are evident.

But in considering the environment, as we do here, in behavioral as well as in geographical terms, a number of additional assumptions about environmental process follows. In our dining room scene, it is evident that if we study environmental process from the point of view of either the host, hostess, the dinner guests, or any other person in the dining room, we create a situation dichotomized into "the participant" on the one hand and all other environmental components in the process on the other. However similar the points of view of each participant, it is also true that there are as many surroundings as there are persons from whose point of view the environmental process can be examined. By virtue of where each person sits in the dining room, the established role he or she plays (sex, occupation, and so on), who he or she is in the situation (hostess versus guest), and the many, many other possible factors of individual difference, the uniqueness of surroundings for each of them is a self-evident proposition. Even from the point of view of an outsider looking in, given the process we described above, environment is unique at any given time and place. Its stability over time is remarkable in that like the eddy of a whirlpool, it emerges out of a process of constant change.

In establishing both the stability and change involved in environmental process, we touch upon an often-neglected but no less significant aspect of human settings. They have a natural history of use, and, like human beings, are not simply to be viewed at isolated points in time. Rather, they must be conceptualized as time-related phenomena, some of whose properties emerge from the sequence and interactions of a succession of events in the continuous use of these settings. Patterns of behavior in a given setting are rooted not only in the dynamics of the immediate environmental process, but also in the history of that process. Physical settings change as a function both of their continued use and of their place in a changing social system in which technological innovations, altered human relationships, and changing values are at one and the same time the causes and consequences of the changes in this system.

Awareness and Adaptation

Two final assumptions about environment from the point of view of the participants are quite critical for the environmental psychologist. Let us return to the railway car of our friend the commuter or to the dining room scene of our family with unexpected dinner guests. From the viewpoint of any one of the actors in the situation, the surroundings in each of these settings are typically neutral. In other words they enter into awareness only when they deviate from some normative or adaptation level. Much of our research involving hospital wards and other institutional settings confirms the fact that people take their usual physical setting for granted and thus have few opinions, sharp preferences, convictions, or desires to change it. Obviously behavior in an environment, therefore, will be influenced by our awareness of the need to adapt to it. In the case of the dining room, this will be far less true of the mother who was responsible for furnishing it, for she is familiar with the room to an extent which her guests are not. Obviously. too, if our commuter walked into a new and very modern railroad car that he had never experienced before, his awareness of the setting might have been heightened to the point where he momentarily forgot his fatigue and therefore did not look for that one available seat. But if this happened it would be just for the reason we gave: It represents a deviation from some adaptation or normative level in the familiar environment. As he learns the new arrangements and the nature of this new railway car, it too will fade out well beyond the periphery of his awareness.

Our last assumption deals with the constraints a setting imposes on us, whether we are aware of them or not. Indeed, we may not be aware of the walls of a room, yet they will determine how far we can walk in it. The height of a table will influence the way we sit at it; the number of people in a room, how comfortable we feel; the level of noise, how much we really listen. All these factors may be outside the threshold of awareness, for we are possibly preoccupied with other things, yet they profoundly affect the environment/person interaction. In sum, people who live near airports may get used to the constant noise of planes, but this does not mean that the noise has no consequences for them. It may not only keep their friends from ever coming to dinner, but even with adaptation they may experience just that much more tension to make the quality of life just a little less than what it should be.

Below we will summarize the various man/environment assumptions that we have considered in our previous discussion. Before doing this, however, we should take pause to consider the methodological implications of the approach we have taken. The view of the person as a goal-directed cognitive organism, influencing and being influenced by the total environmental process of which he is a part, is in direct antithesis to any form of *environmental determinism* as an explanation of his behavior in relation to his physical world. Neither the physical properties of his environment nor the cognitive processes that give meaning to them by itself determines his behavior and experience. It is the interplay between all events, objective and perceived, in a total environmental context that explains the particular behavior and experiences of the person.

Methodologically speaking, this means, first, that man/environment relationships will have to be studied in their natural ongoing settings in the context of everyday life; and second, that these investigations must seek to establish such relationships by relating the patterning of environmental process with the behaviors, experiences, and activities of the person. This means, in effect, that the more traditional attempts of experimental or causal-hypothesis approaches, in which particular independent variables are extracted and varied as measurable causes of equally measurable behavioral events, simply have no validity in the present approach. To extract and define particular variables representing man/environment relationships is to assume that such relationships are simple in structure and additive in character. Nothing could be further from the truth.

The complexity of environmental process, as evident in the assumptions above, is the reality that environmental psychologists will have to encounter whether they like it or not. Their research will have to be exploratory and descriptive, seeking to establish and test relational hypotheses involving the properties of a patterned environmental setting and their effects on that part of it called the person. Scientific research and the form it takes must be defined by the nature of the problem and its formulation rather than the obverse. Contrary to what some believe, there is not one but many models of scientific research reflecting differences in the essential properties of phenomena and how they can best be understood. Quantitative principles for ordering phenomena represent success in understanding only some of the events in nature. Other events may have properties that may require other levels and forms of analysis for codifying and understanding them.

To conclude our discussion of behavior and experience as it relates to the physical environment, we have briefly sketched ten assumptions.

1. In relation to any physical setting, human behavior is enduring and consistent over time and situation. This is a way of saying that environments define their use.
2. Patterns of behavior in response to a setting persist regardless of the specific individuals involved. This demand character, however, is general and within the setting a person varies his behavior over time and space.
3. The boundaries of a setting are defined not only by the setting's physical properties but through its interactive relationship with other physical and social systems. The environment is an open system.
4. Because of this, its organization is dynamic. The characteristic behavior pattern of the setting as a whole will be affected by a change in any of its components.
5. When such changes preclude the characteristic behavior patterns of the setting, this behavior will be conserved and enacted at a new time or place. In short, another, more adequate setting will be sought out.
6. The environment is inclusive not only of the physical components that are present, but also of social and individual behaviors that occur within it. In this sense it is a process defined by its participants and the nature of their interaction.

7. For the individual, however, the environment will be perceived at any one moment as unique. His vantage point and role will affect behavior vis-à-vis the setting differently from others who perceive the same environment as unique to them.
8. Environments have a natural history of use, and we inherit this history when we participate in them. Such use need not be congruent with the physical character of a setting; custom may dictate that we keep our voices lowered in church, and raise them at a public meeting.
9. Environments are typically neutral. We are most aware of their characteristics when change is introduced or when we encounter an unfamiliar setting.
10. However open they may be as social systems, environments have physical limits. These can be described as resistive, supportive, or facilitative. Behavior in the total environmental context will always be affected by the physical opportunities that exist for expressing a desired behavior.

Having presented our man/environment framework, we now briefly consider the implications for *behavioral process* that follow from it. By this we mean the specific psychological functions involved in relating an individual to his physical setting. In other words, we are asking how individuals respond to physical settings, particularly when there are significant changes taking place in these settings.

In the discussion above we made it clear that when viewed from the participant's point of view, the physical environment is typically neutral and enters into awareness only when it deviates from some adaptation level. For this reason let us focus on a nonadaptation situation, that is, one that deviates from the expected insofar as the individual is concerned. Instead of dealing with the family dining room or the commuter train, we will consider what happens when an individual moves into an apartment in a new urban neighborhood. Typical of the experience of most of us, the individual in this kind of situation is self-consciously aware of his new surroundings. The unfamiliar is yet to become familiar.

In situations of this kind six interrelated types of responses occur: *affect*, *orientation*, *categorization*, *systemization*, *manipulation*, and *encoding*. However, it cannot be emphasized too strongly that although we briefly discuss each of these six types (or levels) of responses in the order just given, in actual experience not only does their order vary to some degree, but they are so interrelated that one blends into the other. What we do here for purposes of analysis should not be assumed to correspond to the actual experience of the person.

It is undoubtedly true that *affect* may be the initial response of the person finding himself in his new neighborhood for the first time. Of course what the affect will be depends on many factors. At a minimum the emotion is probably a heightened awareness or a higher level of tension occasioned by the need to know, predict, and therefore to feel secure in an unknown setting. Aside from this general reaction other affects can emerge because of the particular characteristics of the new setting. To suddenly discover a convenient and all-purpose shopping center could evoke joy; a block of abandoned houses, disappointment and fear; and the loud noise of planes taking off and leaving from a nearby airport, consternation and anger. Such affective responses, both general and specific, may govern the directions that subsequent relations with an environment will take. First impressions (feelings) about places as well as people may have long-range and enduring consequences.

Orientation is a cognitive process. In a new setting, the individual actively seeks to grasp the new setting. It is more likely that it occurs first or at least simultaneously with affective responses to the new setting. Orientation involves—to use a slang expression—"casing the joint." Where are the food stores, how does one get from the house to the train station, what is good in the neighborhood (the tree-lined blocks), and what is bad (the row of seedy looking cocktail bars). Orientation also occurs in smaller settings such as an unfamiliar business establishment, theater, school room, hospital ward, and so on. Orientation expresses the person's desire to "know where he is" physically in relation to the total milieu.

In new situations the individual does more than orient. He also categorizes. In effect he does more than just identify and map out the new settings. He evaluates various aspects of it and in this sense imposes his own unique meanings on it. There is a pleasant route to the train station and an unpleasant one; the neighbor in front is friendly and pleasant, the one in the back aloof; parking is easy in the early afternoon and impossible in the evening. What happens in the case of *categorization* of a physical setting is that the individual is extending its meaning by functionally relating its various aspects to his own needs, predispositions, and values. To know how to drive to the train station in the morning is not half as useful as knowing which route is quickest and least stressful.

Although it is difficult to say where categorization leaves off and *systemization* begins, the latter is a distinct process in the individual's response to a new physical setting. The person begins to organize what he has identified and categorized into more complex and meaningful structures. In time, our newcomer to the neighborhood may begin to relate all his positive experiences (good shopping, safe streets, a place to have a drink, a library for reading, and so on) so that he establishes in a subjective sense "his neighborhood." Indeed, it may not correspond to a simple proximity-distance conception of the neighborhood. Or he may not only know when it is best to park and when it is least possible, but also understand that this is related to the peak activity periods for a near-by shopping center. Out of such systemization or organization of the objects, events, people, and establishments in the new neighborhood, the individual achieves a sense of order and understanding. He not only knows the neighborhood but he can predict it and make it work to his benefit.

This brings us to *manipulation* of the environment. If systemization has occurred—or more simply, if the person has ordered his environment—this usually means he can manipulate it or control it to some degree. Of course just how well he can manipulate it depends not only on his capability to order it, but on what this new neighborhood has to offer. If there is no simple way to the train station, that is, if the environment itself lacks choices and possibilities, or if, on the other hand, it is so complex and unpredictable that order is necessarily of a low level, then manipulation or control will also be correspondingly low. To the extent that the person does have a full grasp of his new setting, he not only can make it work for him, but if part of the setting breaks down (for example, the bus to the train station is not running) he can more readily impose change or manipulate it so that it again works effectively for him.

Finally, to systemize an environment, whether for orienting or manipulative purposes, we must agree on what the component parts of our environment are to be called. For the vast majority of such components, names already exist: tree, street, door, lamppost, house, automobile. The colors, shapes, and sizes of such objects—their adjectival properties—are likewise predescribed for us, so that if someone says "big tree" or "narrow street" or "green car" we have a rough idea of what he is talking about. This process of giving names and qualities to environmental objects is called *social encoding*, and it is something we start to learn as soon as we are able to talk. It enables social man to deal with his fellows on a common ground of understanding. As we shall note below, this coding need not be in the form of words or images; it can be a mathematical symbol or a musical notation. Essentially, however, it must be comprehensible to others (as in music) or learnable (as in mathematics). It permits us to do our systemizing and manipulating cognitively, that is, simply by thinking about the environment.

The Role of Cognition

The single human psychological process most critical for man/environment interaction, and one that underlies all the response characteristics that we have described, is that of cognition. It is this intellectual function and the perceptual process with which it is linked that enable us to transform the chaotic outer world apprehended by our senses into a coherent inner world that we can manage. Equally important, it permits us to do this *when the environment in question is not present.* We create, as it were, a "geography of the mind," classifying and encoding our surroundings so that we can deal with them with some degree of predictability in the future. For, quite obviously, to have to learn an environment all over again each time we encounter it would be highly impractical. Cognition is what our mind does with the raw material of reality; not only with physical images, but with all the information received by our senses.

Many writers have dealt with this question of cognizing reality. In Chapters Nine and Ten, for instance, one such method, called "mental mapping," describes how images of an environment are formed in our mind. Here we want to discuss a more abstract approach, one that helps us understand the actual world by identifying various substitute environments that act in its behalf. This view is cogently summarized by Gerald Holton (1965), who terms the translation of perceived reality into cognitive terms a "cybernetic act" and adds that it is the means by which we grapple with the inchoate world around us for the purpose of deciding how we want to deal with it. For much of our environment is not experienced directly but through interposed, surrogate environments that act as representations of "first order reality." To cite an example: We cannot visit the Grand Canyon in person, but we *see* a film about it; *hear* a lecture on it; *read* of its spectacular beauty; *study* a topographical model of it in a museum; or *listen* to it as a musical composition such as Grofe's *Grand Canyon Suite.* All these media of presentation are ways of learning about something that we do not experience directly, and since they imply the intervention of a substitute environment (the technique by which the presentation is made) they are subject to distortion.

The distortion may be intentional in terms of a desired purpose. The lecturer, for instance, may want to emphasize only the wildlife aspects of the canyon; the film its beauty; the model its geological formation; the music its ambience. Much of our information about the environment, Holton points out, is coded in the form of writing, graphs, slides, and talk and is "similar to the projection of a musical score instead of the performance of the piece itself." Thus we can know of the Grand Canyon without ever being there, and, in fact, this knowledge may simply be that we desire *not* to know it—that is, we have screened it out of our consciousness for lack of interest, and so on.

On the other hand cognitive apprehension may (in certain cases) give us an intuitive insight into the environment that would not be possible simply by looking at it directly. It is the cumulative perception on many levels that gives environmental variables a new pattern of relationships and sparks the flash of inspiration that has no apparent basis in logical thinking: Newton's discovery of the law of gravity, for example. In all such cases we return to primary reality with a new sensitivity to it, seeing the real world differently for having apprehended it on subsidiary orders of meaning. Moreover, because we can predict our reaction to a given event on the basis of cognitive perception, we do not need actually to experience the event to know what our reaction will be. Most of what we know about the environment, in fact, is what we are taught.

Holton has structured environmental reality into seven categories:

1. Experiential—the "phenomena and events in their full context, embedded in rich complexity, burdened with secondary and tertiary 'side' effects that are not suppressed or forgotten . . ."
2. Didactic—the arranged reality of the lecture room.
3. Depiction—films, TV, photographs, and so forth. These are frequently representations of the didactic.

4. Animation and models—"Here the avowed contact with first-order reality has been almost completely broken, and the device shown functions analogically."
5. Condensed coding—the written and spoken words, graphs, slides, and so on, which act as short cuts to the phenomenon itself.
6. Metasymbolism—the "language of direct abstraction" such as a law of physics or mathematical statement.
7. Intuition—"direct apperception of a complex situation in its entirety."

Holton writes:

> Understanding scientific materials, and perhaps understanding anything, depends on a cybernetic act by which one leaves the first level, the realm of the perceived phenomenon . . . and transfers, as rapidly as possible, the internal dialogue to the lowest levels; the decisions reached there allow one then to go back to the field of phenomena itself. . . . It is in this manner that we discover and learn, that we decide what it is in the chaos of events which ought to be looked at and called first-order reality. . . . [1965: p. 58]

To sum up: Our response to the environment occurs on many levels. We have stressed six of these that are central to the man/environment interaction, and we have pointed out that both "man" and "environment" are dynamic systems with profound consequences for this interactive process. Here we should like to make a point that has been intentionally minimized: None of our responses to the environment would mean very much if we did not *perceive* it in some reliable fashion—reliable for ourselves, if not always for others. Indeed, it is doubtful if we can separate the perceptual process from the responses we have discussed, although we have done so for the purpose of explanation. In the chapter that follows, therefore, we will look at this response-to-environment from the point of view of perception.

References

Barker, R. G. *The stream of behavior.* New York: Appleton, 1963.

Brunswik, E. *Systematic and representative design of psychological experiments.* Berkeley, Calif.: University of California Press, 1949.

Holton, G. Conveying science by visual presentation. In G. Kepes (Ed.), *Education by vision.* New York: Braziller, 1965.

Ittelson, W. H., Proshansky, H. M., & Rivlin, L. G. The environmental psychology of the psychiatric ward. In H. M. Proshansky, W. H. Ittelson & L. G. Rivlin (Eds.), *Environmental psychology: Man and his physical setting.* New York: Holt, Rinehart and Winston, 1970.

Koffka, K. *Principles of gestalt psychology.* New York: Harcourt, 1935.

Köhler, W. *Gestalt psychology.* New York: Liveright, 1929.

Krech, D., & Crutchfield, R. S. *Theory and problems of social psychology.* New York: McGraw-Hill, 1948.

Lewin, K. *Principles of topological psychology.* New York: McGraw-Hill, 1936.

Murphy, G. *Personality.* New York: Harper & Row, 1947.

Murray, H. A. *Explorations in personality.* New York: Oxford, 1938.

Proshansky, H. M., Ittelson, W. H., & Rivlin, L. G. (Eds.), *Environmental psychology: Man and his physical setting.* New York: Holt, Rinehart and Winston, 1970. Part II, pp. 101–167.

Suggested Readings

Cantril, H. *The "why" of man's experience.* New York: Macmillan, 1950.

Lowenthal, D. Geography, experience and imagination: Towards a geographical epistomology. *Annals of the Association of American Geographers,* 1961, *51,* 241–260.

Ittelson, W. H. (Ed.) *Environment and cognition.* New York: Seminar Press, 1973.

Proshansky, H. M., Ittelson, W. H., & Rivlin, L. G. The influence of the physical environment on behavior: Some basic assumptions. In H. M. Proshansky, W. H. Ittelson & L. G. Rivlin (Eds.), *Environmental psychology: Man and his physical setting.* New York: Holt, Rinehart and Winston, 1970.

Five

Environment Perception

In the previous chapter we discussed the major assumptions that have guided our thinking in the analysis of problems of man/environment relations and briefly outlined an approach to perception and other psychological processes. This general approach will be developed in more detail here and its implications for environment perception will be explored more fully. We will, however, make no attempt to summarize or discuss the vast amount of knowledge about perception that has been developed by philosophers and experimental psychologists over the years. For this, the reader is urged to look at some of the general works on perception in the list of references and suggested readings at the end of this chapter (Murch 1973; Gregory 1966; Dember 1960). The reader should be warned, however, that if he looks in these and other standard references for the topic "environment perception," he is almost certain to be disappointed. It is a strange fact in the history of psychology that relatively little effort has been devoted directly to finding out how, or even if, people perceive the full-scale environments within which they live. The problem of human perception has been defined by almost all, if not all, theoretical systems in terms of how objects "out there" are experienced by a person who is not part of the "there." If the reader reviews the suggested references he will find almost no mention of how individuals perceive a room they have just entered, or a city, a landscape, or any other large-scale setting. The focus of this chapter will be on just those kinds of experiences, referred to generally as environment perception.

Of course, objects are part of these environments, but that is quite different from saying, as do some writers on perception, that environments are nothing more than collections of objects and surfaces. Rather than considering the perception of environments as built out of the perception of objects, we will treat the perception of objects as only one part of the perception of environments, a topic which presents a much larger area for study. Environments, as we shall see shortly, provide much more information than that necessary for the perception of objects and their spatial relationships. Interest in large-scale or environment perception is, therefore, not simply a matter of "extending the boundaries of knowledge." Any concern with man's physical environment and how the individual influences and is influenced by it has at its root the question of how he perceives this environment as an "environment." As our assumptions about the environment in the previous chapter suggest, the behavior and experience of each individual is part of a total environmental process. The person as one component in that process continually influences all other components, and he in turn is influenced by that pattern of other components described and experienced by him as "his environment."

However, while traditional approaches to perception do not provide the complete answer to questions of environment perception, they are clearly relevant to that issue. Everything that is known about the more traditional perceptual areas of study provides the foundation on which an adequate approach to environment perception must be built, but space prevents our presenting an adequate account here. Once again, the reader is urged to familiarize himself with a standard work on perception as a supplement to the material presented in this chapter. He will find that a fairly complete and comprehensive picture of perception as a psychological process, that is, as activity of the nervous system of a particular individual, is emerging from current work. He will find what are perhaps unfamiliar terms such as sensory register, short-term memory, long-term memory, control processes, coding strategies, and information processing, along with more familiar terms such as figure-ground relationships, spatial orientation, distance cues, size constancy, and others. In this chapter we will not be concerned with these aspects of perception, but rather with the more general problem of how perception serves the individual in the active process of dealing with his environmental surroundings. Murch (1973) has written that perception "involves the study of the way an observer relates to his environment—the way in which information is gathered and interpreted." It is to this general problem that we will address ourselves here.

We have already defined environment as a system of interacting components including the individual whom we label as "the perceiver." In this approach, the distinction between the person and his environment is one that is made for purposes of analysis and not because it represents preexisting and independent entities. Conceiving of the environment in this way and asking how the individual perceives this environment as a total system of which he is a part, immediately suggests that there are basic differences between environment perception and the more traditional object perception.

Up to this point we have asserted that objects are not environments, nor are environments simply collections of objects. This distinction is crucial in understanding and studying environment perception. Therefore, a detailed analysis of this difference is necessary so that we can see what kinds of additional information environments provide for the perceptual process. Perhaps the most obvious starting point is the fact that by definition objects require subjects—the subject-object relationship is part of the very concept of the object itself. In contrast, one cannot be a subject of an environment, one can only be a participant in it. When we speak of a person's perception of his environment, as we do for purposes of analysis and discussion, we are implying a dichotomy which has no factual basis. There is only the total environment of which man is one kind of component in relation to other kinds of components. The very distinction between person and nonperson breaks down. The environment surrounds, enfolds, and no thing and no person can be isolated and identified as standing outside of and apart from it.

Thus, environment perception never takes place "by itself." It can be studied only as part of the situation in which it occurs, and the components into which that situation can be analyzed are determined by the situation in which they are encountered. We literally change the environment by perceiving it, if for no other reason than that we attribute certain aspects of our own experience to the world around us. Of course, this does not mean that we are free to perceive anything we want, to attribute any characteristics to the environment. The environment is as much a part of the situation as we are, and particular environments, as we shall see in more detail later, provide particular kinds of information and offer particular opportunities for action. We experience neither an environment independent of ourselves as participants nor ourselves independent of the situation in which we are participating, but rather we experience ourselves in and of an environment. It is the total event itself that is perceived.

For most of us, this is not an easy concept to grasp. It seems contrary to what is actually happening, for we order the external world as though it existed independently of us. And indeed, common sense tells us that it is often useful to assume such a representational view of the environment, to talk as though its attributes were distinct from our perception of them. If we are to act effectively in our world, we frequently must think about it as being "out there," apart from ourselves. However, this common sense view can also lead to distortions in our understanding of environmental processes, as, for example, in the notion of environmental determinism, which holds that there are particular external environmental conditions that make us perceive and behave in certain ways. We know, in fact, that we are neither captives of our environment nor do we stand outside of it, but, on the contrary, that we experience and contact it through active participation.

Expressed in another way, the environment we know is the product, not the cause, of perception. Perceiving in this sense is carried on by an individual from his own position in space and time and in terms of his own combination of past experiences and needs. It is just this way that transactionalists define perception: the process by which a particular person, from his particular behavioral center, attributes significances to his immediate environmental situation. In fact, only when we order our world with ourselves as part of the ordering transaction, only when our dealings with it are done with a purpose, and only as we relate the environment to our purposes is it truly perceived.

Environments as Sources of Information

The first step in the conventional analysis of perception is the identification of relevant aspects of the external situation. What characteristics of environments are important for environment perception? To ask this question presupposes, as we have already seen, an artificial splitting of the situation into the environment on the one hand and the perceiver on the other. For the purposes of analysis, such a procedure is both necessary and conventional. However, our answers to the question will not be completely conventional, in that we will look for broad categories of informational content rather than specific physical features of the environment. To what extent, if any, the informational content of the environment can be directly related to its physical characteristics remains an open question in the light of current knowledge.

We will consider seven broad categories of information related to any environmental situation and relevant to environment perception: (1) environments have no fixed or given boundaries in space or time; (2) environments provide information through all the senses; (3) environments include peripheral as well as central information; (4) environments include far more information than can adequately be handled; (5) environments are defined by and experienced through action; (6) environments have symbolic meanings; and (7) environmental experience always takes on the systemic quality of a coherent and predictable whole. It will be useful to look at these aspects of environment perception separately, although in fact they may be inextricably related to each other.

The first of these is stated in negative form to emphasize the contrast with everyday experience. We typically perceive our environment as bounded, yet the environment as such does not provide any information as to its spatial or temporal boundaries. The same proposition can be stated in positive form by noting that the perceived boundaries of any environment are a product of information generated through the interplay of the perceiver and his surroundings, rather than being imposed on the perceiver by external conditions.

If a person explores his immediate surroundings, his exploration is neither aimless nor predetermined. It is the person, the explorer himself, who sets his own boundaries for the various settings he experiences. His purposes and actions constantly interact with the environmental information and opportunities for action he encounters, thereby leading to shifts in the boundaries that define the successive situations which he perceives. In some instances, as for example highly "imageable" environments, the environment may appear to set its own boundaries, while at the other extreme no two people may experience exactly the same limits. As in all other environmental situations there is a continuous interplay between environmental information and individual and cultural definitions.

Of course, environmental boundaries change in time and space for each person regardless of whether he is with others or alone. But in all cases it is the individual himself who is the organizing center of his milieu, and the exploratory aspects of his perceiving can and frequently do extend over large spaces and long periods of time. In the most obvious sense this is what happens when a traveler explores a strange land, but even on the level of everyday experience we are constantly searching and creating boundaries which serve our immediate purposes. Such perception involves the use of memory and assumes both a purpose and the ability to discriminate among qualitative differences in the environment.

Perceptual exploration of a setting makes use of all the sense organs through which the environment transacts with an organism and contributes to its behavior. It thus brings us to the second characteristic of environments, that they provide information through all the senses. It is almost impossible even to conceive of an environment which offers information through only one of the senses. In this respect, environments are *multimodal*; the senses function, so to speak, in concert. It should be noted, however, that multimodal effects—the use of all the senses—and crossmodal effects—the influence of one sense on another—are relatively uncharted areas in psychology, and much work remains to be done before we know their precise application to environment perception. We do know, of course, that at a given moment our perception may seem to be dominated by only one modality. A pronounced odor may preclude our seeing a room as visually attractive; a blind person learns to get around through his sense of touch and a kind of private radar closely related to his sense of hearing. But for most of us during most of our waking hours, the environment emits a mélange of information that is transmitted through all the senses simultaneously.

Inasmuch as this is so and because we are able to make qualitative discriminations among the components of any environment, much of the information available will be peripheral to the central focus of interest. Because information is available does not mean that it is always useful. To a certain extent the individual is able to choose his information through focused interest, yet in another sense he is always concerned with its totality. Important or relatively useless, it is there whether he wants it or not. Although much peripheral information may never enter awareness, its long-range effects may be measurable and important. The area behind us is no less a part of the environment than that in front. We assume it to be there, and we make predictions and act on them based on that assumption, even though we do not directly receive sensory input from it at any moment.

Environments almost always provide more information than can possibly be processed. What is central and what is peripheral will depend upon what we are looking for—our particular goals and purposes. Yet even so, the mélange of information that we spoke of may also be redundant, ambiguous, conflicting, and contradictory. The entire mechanism of information processing in the nervous system, which is the focus of much current research, is brought into play.

Many hypothetical models of the way the perceiver deals with this mass of incoming information are being proposed (Haber 1969; Neisser 1967), and the specific consequences of a variety of informational characteristics have been studied. Probably the best-known condition, although rarely encountered except in highly contrived laboratory settings, is sensory deprivation (Zubek 1969), the reduction of incoming information to an absolute minimum. It has been shown to produce profound psychological effects. On the other hand, the opposite extreme, information overload, forces the perceiver to group together greater and greater amounts of possibly disparate information until the ability to process the information at all may break down completely if the information load far exceeds the capacity to handle it. In between these two extremes, dealing with ambiguous or conflicting information poses special problems which are receiving increasing attention in perceptual studies. While our knowledge of how the perceiver processes peripheral, redundant, ambiguous, or conflicting information is far from complete, the fact remains that the environment, considered as a source of information, is continually providing each one of us with information with precisely these characteristics.

We do know that throughout the process of environment perception the individual is never completely passive. This consideration leads us to the fifth characteristic of environmental information, that it is always defined by and experienced through action. The perceiver always acts as a component of the situation he perceives. He learns the kinds of interventions that he can bring about and their consequences. This means he not only behaves in his environmental context, but also records environmental feedback in relation to his own needs and purposes. This relationship between the person perceiving and the person acting is basic to our understanding of the perception of everyday environments. In this process the environment plays a dual role. First, it provides the source of information on which action is based, information which makes it possible for us to predict the probable consequences of alternative courses of action. Second, the environment provides the arena within which the actions do, in fact, take place. The actual consequences of these actions are largely a product of the environmental opportunities and limitations encountered by the acting individual. The environment thus provides information as to the probable consequences of future action and the actual consequences of past action, both of which enter into the active process of environment perception.

Another way in which environments influence the behaviors which take place in them is through their symbolic meanings. In its most obvious sense an environment has symbolic meaning because the purposes and the activities that go on in it have been socially defined. For each of us in American society a football field and a doctor's office elicit immediate percepts of what should go on in each of these settings, who will be involved, and what ends will be achieved. Indeed, it is difficult even to imagine an environment that does not symbolically convey a set of behavioral expectations and thus define the kinds of action that are likely to occur in it. The symbolic meanings and motivational messages emitted by an environment are integral to our perception of it. Every setting induces feelings, associations, and attitudes in the perceiver that can be described as its *ambiance.* Whereas symbolic meanings generally carry cognitive information, ambiance is related to the way we feel about an environment. A setting can be exotic, pleasant, gloomy, or restful. Such feelings can be general across many individuals or unique to one person. When they are perceived as being characteristic of the environment, they are called its ambiance. Let the reader himself think of the coldness of a doctor's tiled examination room, the solemn silence that envelops a chapel in a mortuary, the intimacy of a dimly lighted restaurant, or the warm security of his own particular room or nook. Any setting by virtue of its people, activities, and physical features induces an atmosphere of its own which is difficult to define but is an integral part of one's perception of the environment.

A related, but distinct, characteristic of environments is their esthetic quality. Here, we are not simply being stimulated by our surroundings, or evaluating them in terms of behaviors; we are assessing and experiencing their intrinsic beauty and value. The entire question of esthetics and value judgments has been sadly neglected by all but a few social scientists, but it is forced upon us by the consideration of environment perception. It is to be hoped that the study will accelerate. The experience of the esthetic quality of an environment reflects most dramatically the complex interrelationship between the perceiver and the situation of which he is a part. It will vary from individual to individual, from time to time and from culture to culture, but the perception of all environments necessarily involves a degree of esthetic awareness. In recent years attempts have been made to design esthetically neutral objects, but an esthetically neutral environment is unthinkable.

The final characteristic of environments which is relevant to environment perception is their systematic quality, representing order and regular relationships. The various components of an environment relate to each other in ways that, more than anything else, characterize and define the particular environment that is being perceived. If nature abhors a vacuum, the human observer abhors the random and the chaotic. The seemingly systematic nature of the external world is actually one of our most fundamental responses to it.

We are especially aware of this in studying the ecology of natural environments, where the systematic and dynamic interrelationships among all the organic and many of the inorganic activities have been the subject of extensive study. The ecological principles of natural settings are coming to be fairly well established. Concurrently, there is a growing tendency to refer to the "ecology of the built environment," although it is very likely that there are fundamental differences between the two and that the ecology of natural areas may not have any direct bearing on our understanding of the ecology of the built environment. In natural areas there is generally a close relationship between changes in the physical environment and the various life forms comprising these systems. At the present time comparisons with the built environment are mostly through analogy.

However, whether or not the built environment has an ecology in the same sense that a natural environment does, there can be no question that it has its own inner system of *coherence.* In cities there is a more or less orderly arrangement of streets, sidewalks, and buildings. The buildings themselves consist of rooms systematically laid out, and rooms containing furniture that is appropriately arranged for the function it serves. The chair is put together with a particular function in mind. And in all such cases our behavior within the environment is systematically related to the environment so that reasonably adequate predictions may be made. Of course, all the relationships in the man-made environment are not the result of deliberate planning; many are the unintended and unexpected consequences of technological change. By self-consciously creating order and predictability in the man-made environment and discovering it in both the man-made and the natural world, we are able to adapt to and live in both. Randomness is repugnant to life.

This completes our look at the environment considered as an external situation and the listing of characteristics relevant to environment perception. The environment provides no direct information as to its boundaries in space or time; it provides information through all the sense modalities; this information is of a very complex nature; environmental information is always acquired through action on the part of the perceiver; the information conveys, among other things, symbolic meanings which have cognitive, affective, and esthetic aspects; and, finally, environments have a systematic quality of orderly interrelatedness.

Environment Perception as Information Processing

This view of environmental information almost demands that one treat perception as an information-processing system. This is in contrast to the more conventional concern with the role of the stimulus in perceptual studies. Traditionally in psychology the concept of stimulus has meant a change in physical energy outside the organism, which when it impinges on the organism, initiates processes, the end product of which is a response wholly determined and predictable from the nature of the stimulus. Said briefly, this view conceived of the stimulus as a source of stimulation. In its place, first slowly but then with increasing theoretical and research interest following World War II, there emerged a very different view of the stimulus, one which defined it not as a source of stimulation but rather as a source of information. Today, few perceptual writers speak of stimulus energy, but rather they talk of stimulus information, a change of terminology with profound implications.

Although the information-processing view is directly in the tradition articulated by Helmholtz (1962, originally published 1866) a century ago, the contemporary psychologist who first advanced an approach to perception consistent with the "stimulus as a source of information" view was Egon Brunswik (1956), whose concept of ecological cue validity was mentioned earlier. Brunswik suggests that the individual samples his environment perceptually and then tests the accuracy of his perception by trying out the environment through his actions. His perceptions can only be as accurate as are his samplings of all possible environments. Since, in Brunswik's view, environments are never totally consistent with each other or, indeed, completely internally consistent, and since sampling can never be perfect, the messages the individual receives from these environments are always probabilistic rather than absolutistic. In Brunswik's terms the perceiver builds up probabilities about the environment, and the ecological cue validities are expressed as probabilistic statements. By testing the accuracy of what he perceives through actions, he is then able to decide which cues will give him reliable information about his surroundings and the objects in it.

Since we cannot be absolutely certain about these environmental guides, in practice we posit a probable relationship between perception and cue and then test it for accuracy. As Brunswik himself has stated: "The best [the individual] can do is to compromise between cues so that his posit approaches the 'best bet' on the basis of all the probabilities or past relative frequencies or relevant interrelationships lumped together." [Hammond 1966: 36]

Brunswik developed a "lens model" of perception in which the distal environment is seen as scattering its stimuli, while the organism recombines them as a lens captures light rays and focuses them in a single plane. In Brunswik's words: "The general pattern of mediational strategy of the organism is predicated upon the limited ecological validity or trustworthiness of cues. . . . This forces a probabalistic strategy upon the organism. To improve its bet, it must accumulate and combine cues." [Hammond 1966: 37].

This probabilistic or "best-bet" approach to perception has influenced a large number of perceptual theorists and was probably most extensively developed by Adelbert Ames, Jr., a contemporary of Brunswick who arrived at an essentially similar concept independently (Ittelson 1952, 1960). Both theorists emphasized the probabilistic nature of environmental information

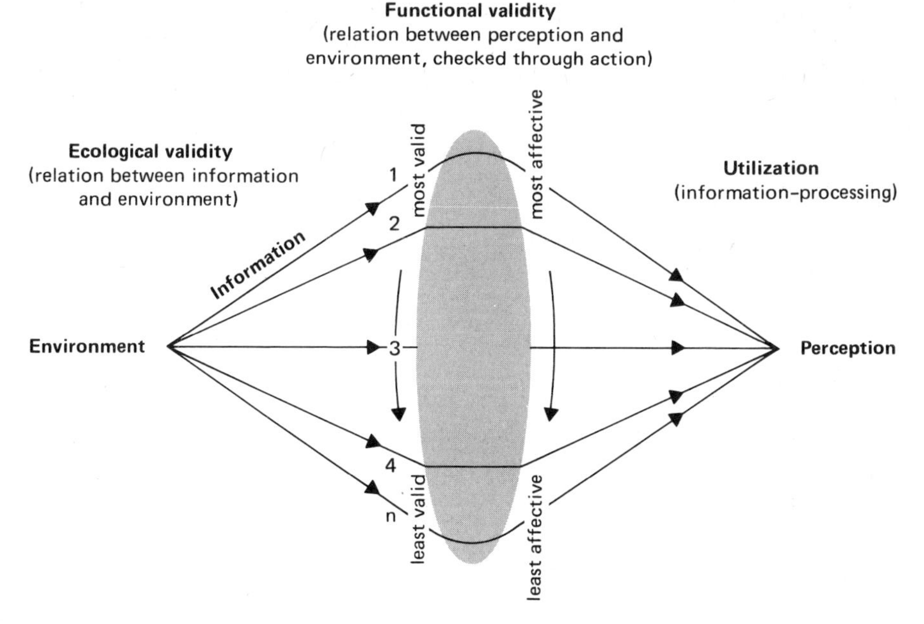

Fig. 5-1 Brunswik's probabilistic theory illustrates one way of relating the information available from the environment to the way the individual perceives that environment.

and the importance of sampling all possible environments in order to maximize perceptual validity or to increase the probability of the "best bet." Ames' most significant elaborations of the approach involved his development of the role of action in building up probabilities and his emphasis on the role of the individual in creating his own probability statement.

If we take as our example the well-known and simple distance cue of *relative size*, we can demonstrate the contributions of both these theorists. As a general rule, large objects (or more accurately, objects subtending large visual angles) are close to us while small objects are distant. But we know that this is not always true. The rule can therefore best be expressed not as a certainty but as a probability. For Brunswik, the ecological validity of this cue of relative size was just that—a probability to be discovered within the external environmental situation. In principle Brunswik in his experiments sampled all environments, counted the times the rule was right and the times it was wrong, and from this computed the ecological validity for that cue. He assumed that the individual through his actions in these environments did essentially the same thing and thus developed for himself the same probable validity figure for this cue. Doing this for all other distance cues as well, the perceiver arrived at a set of probability figures, which he could then apply to any given situation, unconsciously weighing one against the other, resolving conflicts among them, and coming up with the best bet.

This approach can be illustrated by one of Brunswik's experiments in which he accompanied a subject throughout that person's normal daily activities. At randomly determined times he stopped the subject and asked for judgments of the size and distance of objects that happened to be in the scene before the subject at that moment. In this way he obtained a representative sample of the everyday environments of his subject together with judgments of the size and distance of everything from pencils to mountains. In addition, for each scene he took actual measures of size and distance, and a photograph from which he could analyze the visual information available to his subject. Although the quality of the data varied considerably, in principle at least he was able to obtain three sets of measures, the subject's view of his surroundings, the visual information or cues provided by the surroundings, and the physical dimensions of those surroundings. These data showed that the relationship between the physical measures and the various visual cues (the ecological validity of the cues) was varying but relatively low. However, the subject's perception of the objects around him was highly accurate. Brunswik concluded that his subject arrived at a highly valid and functional view of his world by combining a large number of pieces of information, each one of which has a relatively low ecological validity, utilizing some sort of psychological information-processing system.

Brunswik's theory was and is of great importance. It takes into account most but not all of the kinds of environmental information we have discussed earlier, and it is here that Ames rounded out the picture. To the objectively determined probabilities, which he too considered extremely important, Ames added, in his terminology, "sequential significances and value significances." By this he was suggesting the importance of systemic and symbolic information and the role of action, not just in sampling environments but in furthering goals and purposes. Brunswik's "ecological validity," a measure of an objective environmental condition, became for Ames "environmental significance," a measure related to the individual's overall ability to achieve his goals in a particular environmental context. Thus, between them, these two theorists pointed the way to a comprehensive approach to environment perception.

It should be noted, however, that not all theorists of environment perception agree with all of the details of the position just outlined. For example, an important and influential psychologist, J. J. Gibson (1966), while also viewing environment perceptions as an information-processing system, believes that environmental information is absolutistic rather than probabilistic. In his view all the information necessary for environment perception is directly contained in the pattern of physical energy impinging on the sense organs. However, the utilization of this information requires more than merely responding to or interpreting sensory excitation. Rather, the individual must actively explore his environment over space and time and extract the invariant aspects from the constantly changing pattern of incoming information. By doing this, he gains a progressively more and more exact and accurate picture of his environment as it really is. Gibson thus stands in contrast to those who take a probabilistic view, and all the differences in the details of his theory stem directly from his premise of the absolute nature of environmental information.

There are other theorists of environment perception, and there are many other differences in detail among them, but to the reader interested most generally in finding out how our perceptions of our environment came about, their similarities are of more importance than their differences. All agree that environment perception is based on an information-processing system in which the individual actively explores his surroundings and extracts and uses information in constant interaction between himself and his environment. The exact nature and details of this process must await further study, which hopefully will proceed at an accelerating rate.

The particular view presented here obviously draws heavily on the Brunswik-Ames approach, which we believe conforms most closely to the available facts. In this view, the individual is not sensing his environment as though it were wholly external to him with fixed independent qualities of its own. On the contrary, he is sampling it, testing it, giving it a meaning that is unique to him, and seeing it differently from the way others see it. Environment perception does not spring directly from the objective properties of the world out there, but rather, from that world transformed into a psychological environment by a perceiving and cognizing organism. In a very general sense of the term, it is an essentially creative process, actively carried out by the individual who is himself immersed in the perceptual situation. The adequacy of these perceptions is assessed not by comparing them with some hypothetically independent environment, but rather by their utility in aiding the individual in achieving his own personal and social goals.

Environment Perception in Differing Environments

Environment perception, then, is a product of active commerce with the environment. The individual's perception of and action in an environment are inextricably related processes. How we behave in a setting is a function of how we perceive it, but these perceptions in turn are dependent on the information we derive from our own actions in this setting. How one perceives an environment depends on both what a person does in a particular setting and what the setting has to offer him by way of available information.

It follows therefore that different people or groups of people may perceive the "same" environment differently, and that the same person would perceive quite differently had he lived in a different environment. That is, different people will extract different information from the same environment, and different environments offer different kinds of information to the same person. The first proposition has been amply demonstrated in the psychological literature, and social and personality psychology in particular have dealt with individual differences in perception.

In addition to those more dynamically or psychologically determined differences, there are other differences in the environmental information received based not on environmental differences but on the individual selection of certain aspects of the environment and neglect of others. Certain professions, for example, require a high degree of visual imageability, and those who engage in them, such as architects and artists, literally see "better" than —or at least differently from—most people. We speak of the artist as having a trained eye; the lighting engineer is sensitive to subtle differences in lighting; musicians are aware of tonal nuances that escape the nonmusical; the blind man must use his auditory, tactile, and vestibular senses much more than the sighted. Indeed, there is a long and fascinating list of reports of congenitally blind people who have had their eyesight restored by operative procedures. The environment suddenly provides them with a whole new range of information, and the evidence is so overwhelming that it takes a considerable period of time for these people to assimilate this new world into their already existing modes of dealing with environmental information, and eventually to use visual information in ways similar to that of normally sighted people. Without elaborating further we can assert that the role of individual differences in perception based on the individual's unique mode of dealing with his environment is clearly established.

The role of environmental differences in the formation of perceptual differences, apart from some unique attribute as described above, is less easily demonstrated. Studying the effect of living in different environments presents a difficult practical problem which has been dealt with in two very general ways. It is possible, for example, to create artificial environments which differ from one another and from the customary environment of a particular individual. If that individual is then asked to live in that environment for a period of time, it is possible to determine the effects on his perceptual and other cognitive processes. Another approach is to find naturally occurring environments which are significantly different from each other and to study the perceptual characteristics of people who live in these environments. Literally hundreds of studies on this question have been conducted over the years and their general conclusions support the position presented here. The kind of environment a person lives in influences the way he perceives it in relationship to what he himself does in carrying out his activities in that environment.

Experimentally, the easiest way to change the visual environment is to put on a pair of distorting glasses which alter the light rays reaching the eye in one way or another. The visual information has changed while all other aspects of the environment, in particular the action feedback relationship, remain the same. The psychologist then asks the question, "Does the change in the visual information received from the environment eventually lead to changes in the way the person uses that information, that is, to change in his visual perception?" The answer based on a very large number of studies using a wide variety of distorting lenses appears to be affirmative (Rock 1966; Epstein 1967).

Actually, anyone who wears corrective glasses has performed this experiment in miniature. It is an almost universal experience that a new pair of glasses requires "getting used to." The length of time this takes varies from a few minutes to several days or even weeks depending on the nature and magnitude of the correction. But however long or short the period, it involves assimilating the new visual information into the previous perceptual pattern so that a new and stable mode of information processing is established.

Of course, the distortions introduced by distorting lenses are much more extreme than those produced by a new pair of glasses. Historically, the first and still the most dramatic example is the inversion lens which turns the image received by the eye upside down. At first, the person wearing these lenses is quite disoriented; he literally cannot tell which end is up. But the remarkable fact is that after wearing the glasses for an extended period of time, say on the order of a month, he can get along quite well in his everyday activities and perform even such complex skills as riding a bicycle. He may eventually become unaware that his visual world is upside down.

An anecdote from one of the inversion lens studies illustrates this quite nicely (Snyder & Pronko 1952). The subject wearing his inversion lenses and the psychologist doing the study were standing together one evening observing a particularly beautiful sunset. After some time of mutual exclamations of wonder and appreciation, a thought occurred to the psychologist and he turned to his subject and asked if it didn't make a difference to him that the sunset was upside down. The subject turned angrily and said that that question had ruined the sunset for him. Up to that moment he had been totally unaware of anything being amiss and was simply immersed in the beauty of the scene. As soon as the question was asked, the world had almost literally turned upside-down, and he could no longer enjoy the beauty before him. Here—and as would be the case with some other kinds of distorting lenses—the individual after a period of time had become totally unaware of the distortions, but he could make himself aware of them. However, in very few cases have these glasses been worn for longer than a month, and the truly long-term effects remain unknown. But even on this limited basis the general effect is universally replicated. The person wearing distorting lenses over time acquires and utilizes a new set of relationships between environmental information and environmental action.

Another way of experimentally studying the effects of living in differing environments is to construct a strange environment which is different in some ways from a person's usual environment. One can then put a subject in this environment for a period of time and study the effects on his perceptual processes. Technically, of course, the construction of strange environments is both difficult and expensive, and most such studies which have been conducted are quite simple and primitive, in that they have allowed the

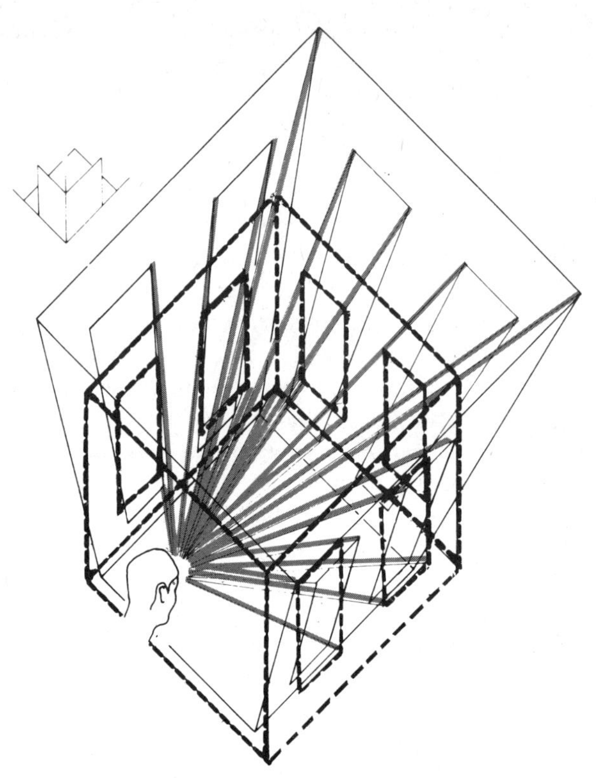

Fig. 5-2*A* The Ames distorted room has been widely used as an artificial environment that produces varied and unusual experiences. (From Ittelson 1952-1968. Reproduced by permission of the Hafner Publishing Co.) *B* One of the visual effects found in the Ames distorted room. (Photograph courtesy of Irving Fitzig, Brooklyn College.)

subject only a very limited range of experiences (Ittelson 1970; Nahemow 1971).

Probably one of the best known of such experiments used the distorted room created by Adelbert Ames, Jr. This room has sides which are trapezoidal in shape and of different sizes. However, when viewed from the proper point, the room appears to be of normal rectangular shape. In an important experiment Kilpatrick (1954) had subjects carry out activities such as throwing balls and touching parts of the room with a stick while viewing the room from this point. He found that after doing this for a period of time the subjects not only saw the distorted room as being distorted but, more importantly, saw a similar but actually rectangular room as distorted and nonrectangular.

This study demonstrates the critical role which action in environment plays in providing feedback to the perceiver. It also suggests that the perceivers began to question the validity of the cues provided by visual inspection alone.

Of course, one can find rather than build environments which differ markedly from each other. Natural environments vary tremendously, from desert to forest, from plain to mountain; and man-made environments as well differ markedly from each other, although perhaps not on quite so dramatic a scale. Existing environments also have the added advantage that for the most part people are already living in them, and one can perform a field investigation in the natural setting without introducing any element of artificiality.

Two well-known studies can illustrate this type of approach. Both have to do with the effects of living in a "carpentered world," that is, a world of straight lines and right angles as opposed to a noncarpentered world. For example, among the Zulus there is no word for, and no real concept of, square and rectangle. Theirs is a world of round doors and windows and villages laid out in circles. They do not "understand" angularity in the same sense as people living in the carpentered world, because they have not been exposed to this world. Allport and Pettigrew (1957) for this reason chose to study the Zulus, using an illusion involving straight lines and right angles, the Ames "trapezoidal window." In this illusion a trapezoid, although actually rotated, appears to be swinging back and forth. In comparison with Westernized people, the Zulus found the illusion (relatively) less compelling.

A similar general idea was held by Segall and his collaborators (1966) who sought out not man-made, carpentered worlds but natural environments which varied in the degree to which they provided examples of straight and vertical objects. In an extensive and carefully controlled study, two visual illusions were shown to a number of groups throughout the world: the Müller-Lyer illusion, which deals with the effect of angles on the apparent length of a horizontal line, and the vertical/horizontal illusion, in which a vertical line appears longer than a horizontal one. It was found that of the two illusions the strength of the vertical/horizontal illusion varied systematically with the extent to which the natural environment provided examples of straight lines,

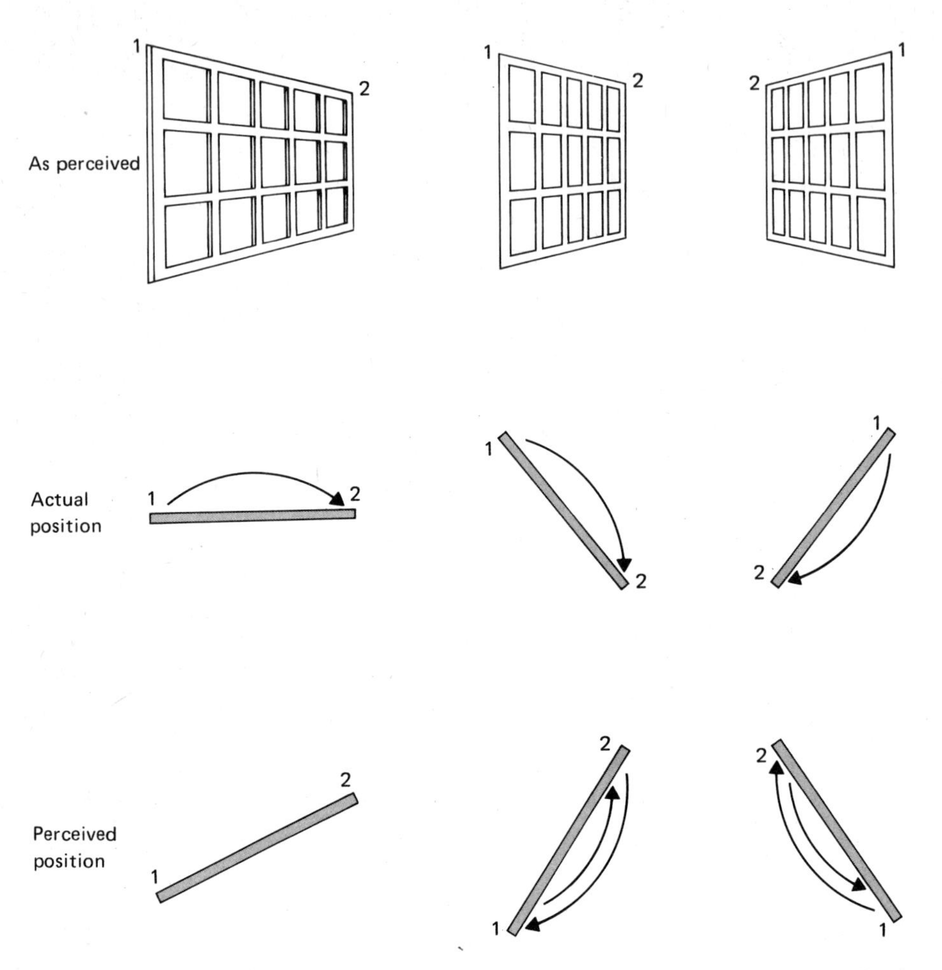

Fig. 5-3 The "trapezoidal window" looks rectangular and appears to swing back and forth though it is actually rotating. The effect is most compelling for people who live in "carpentered" environments. (After Ames 1951)

right angles, and clearly defined verticals and horizontals. These are only two examples using relatively simple measures, but they illustrate the rather important contribution that cross-cultural studies can make to the understanding of environment perception.

We have dealt with these various examples of the effect of differing kinds of environmental information because they illustrate perhaps more dramatically than any other approach the intricacies and complexities of environment perception. However, the available studies are still quite limited. For example, almost all deal primarily with visual perception. But the other modalities cannot be neglected in a full understanding of environment perception. Although people tend to think of the environment in visual terms, the

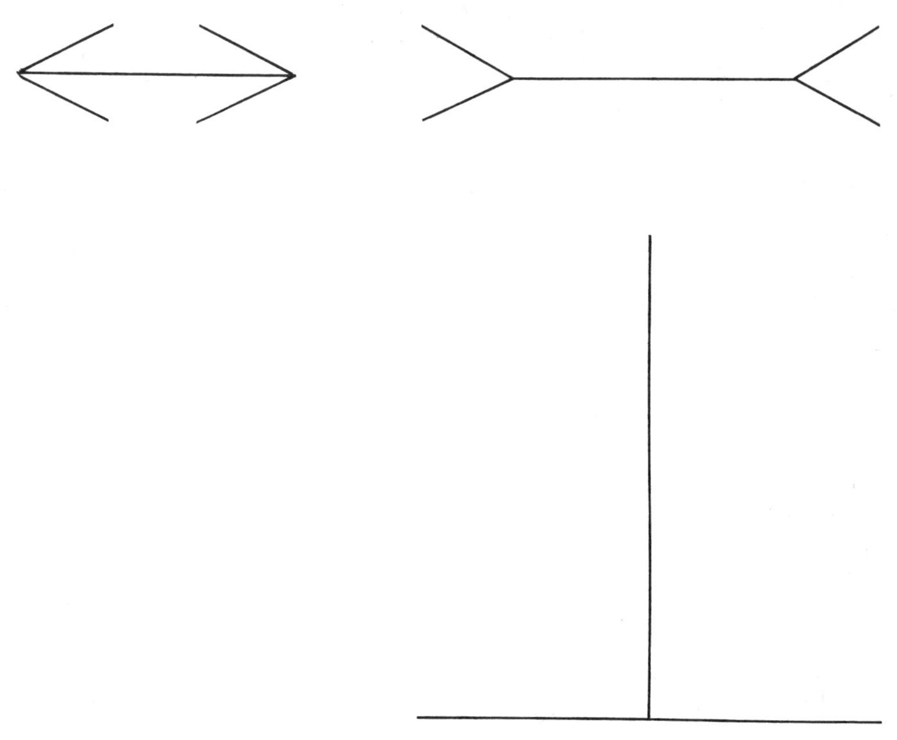

Fig. 5-4. The Müller-Lyer and the vertical-horizontal illusions were used to study cultural and environmental influences on perception.

roles of audition and olfaction, for example, are equally important. City dwellers typically regard environmental sounds and smells to be primarily the source of annoyance and pollution, even though auditory and olfactory information has been shown to provide important information even in the urban setting. One is even more dependent on all the senses in the natural environment. The farmer "smells" the weather; the seaman "tastes" it. Foresters gain much information from the many sounds which only they can interpret. Examples can be multiplied, but they are mostly anecdotal. The systematic study of the environmental information through senses other than vision is still in a primitive stage.

The general conclusion that one comes to from a brief survey of environment perception in different environments is that different environments provide different amounts and kinds of information to the perceiver, afford different contexts for action, and feed back to the individual different relationships between the consequences of his actions and the environmental information. As expected from the general view of environment perception presented here, people who live in different environments develop distinctive ways of recording, processing, and acting on this information.

What Is Perceived

Up to this point we have discussed the relevant characteristics of the environment considered as an external source of information and the ways in which that information enters into the perceptual process. We now turn to the contents of environment perception, what it is that is perceived.

In the case of object perception, such a question presents no great difficulty. For the most part, what is perceived are the common-sense attributes of objects, such as the book you are now reading. You can perceive its size, shape, weight, color, orientation in space, distance and direction from you. You can feel the texture of the pages, hear them rustle as you turn them, perhaps smell the binding. In any case, you can identify it as a particular object, a book.

All these perceptual characteristics apply to large-scale environments as well. But to these we must add other important properties that go beyond the traditional characteristics developed in the study of objects, and a definitive list for environment perception cannot be drawn as yet. The systematic study of environment perception is so new that as yet new variables keep appearing as new studies appear and as new investigators become interested in the field. It is reasonable to assume that the relevant environmental information we have talked about is related to a set of possible features which can be perceived in the environment. For example, it was pointed out that environments do not come with ready-made, externally defined boundaries, yet they are always perceived as bounded. The perceived limits of environments, in space and time, are an important variable for investigation.

Again, we noted that environments provide conflicting information; the process of conflict resolution, and the consequence of this process for experiencing the environment, offers a fruitful area for further study. Similarly, environmental symbols have been briefly touched upon. The whole question of environmental esthetics is virtually unexplored, and has been dealt with primarily in terms of likes and dislikes and preferences of one environmental situation over another. This list of actual and potential variables could be expanded indefinitely. However, rather than presenting an abstract list at this point, we will discuss in detail all those special aspects of environment perception which have been systematically studied as they become relevant to the particular subject matter of the various other chapters throughout this book. For example, the perception of environmental boundaries will be described in detail when cognitive maps are considered in Chapter Nine on the urban environment. Environmental esthetics and preferences will be treated in discussions of both the natural and the built environment. Similarly, other specific content areas will be found at appropriate places throughout the text.

Environment Perception and Other Psychological Processes

The relation of perceiving to other psychological processes is a recurring problem in both the theoretical and experimental study of perception. Particularly in the case of environment perception, distinctions between perception, cognition, and memory at times become meaningless. The fact that environments extend over spaces and times forces memory into play, so that the perception of a large-scale environment is as much a cognitive process as it is anything else (Ittelson 1973). The very use of these words probably should be avoided, except that they carry so much meaning and are so helpful in common usage.

Traditional psychologists would probably throw up their hands in despair at this point, claiming that much of what we have already said does not properly belong to the study of perception at all. Classical psychology very sharply categorized psychological processes into neat pigeonholes, each of which had its fixed limits which set it off from all others. Perception, cognition, and memory were the labels given to three of the most sacrosanct pigeonholes in the history of psychology. In this scheme of thought, if something belonged to cognition, it could not possibly be part of perception, and similarly for the other categories. But contemporary psychology does not recognize any utility in such compartmentalization and is whittling away at the assumed theoretical boundaries between these processes until they are all but invisible.

Consider, for example, your perception of the room you are in, your home, and the city you live in. The instances move progressively further from immediate sensory input, yet they clearly all belong to the same general category of experience; there is no point at which we seem to have moved into a different domain. Each involves the use of information recorded and stored in our memory system. Each is heavily loaded with cognitive meanings as well as with feelings and values. And these and other aspects are not separate elements which can be individually detached and added up somehow to make your perception of your room, home, or city. Perception, cognition, memory, and other psychological processes function together in ways that render meaningless attempts to treat them separately and independently.

The concept of mental or cognitive maps illustrates this complex character of environment perception. It is one way of approaching the perception of your room, home, or city. All of us carry a mental map of our surroundings around with us, and this map is often more important in determining our orientation toward an environment than any particular feature or group of features which may exist in that situation. A cognitive map of an environment, thus, is our internalized image of that environment. It need not necessarily be a correct and accurate representation.

From a practical point of view, mental maps are a mode of ordering an environment that might otherwise be chaotic or meaningless. For this reason they have been particularly applied to the study of cities where the setting tends to be obviously overloaded in terms of available information. We must sort out all the countless aspects of the city—the buildings, streets, parks, sidewalks, and intersections—into some sort of pattern which corresponds with our use of these aspects. As Lynch (1960) has pointed out, special details of a given environment can serve to heighten or reduce its imageability. This imageability is also subject to wide distortion. Two people will map the same neighborhood quite differently. Buildings will be perceived as taller or shorter than they actually are; estimated distances to the same point will vary according to subjective experience in traveling to this point; personal needs, prejudices, expectancies, goals, and past experiences all help determine the map that we carry around of a given environment.

Imageability involves not simply how we perceive a single setting or even a combination of perceptions of a variety of settings, but rather a total picture of the functional utility of the particular environment with which we are concerned. In spite of susceptibility to wide subjective distortion, mental maps are highly practical. They provide the source of our awareness of our surroundings and in the social sense provide a common means of communication and memory through common images. The architect Charles Burnette (1971) has written:

> People are able to act in relationship to their environment and the world because they have some plan in mind, some program to direct their behavior and adapt it to meet the situations which they encounter. . . . A mental image of the environment which we "anticipate" for our actions is a necessary part of this ability to plan our behavior. [p. 65]

Imageability need not be visual. Sounds contribute to our sense of space and our orientation to it; church bells help provide a sonic image of a city, as do boat whistles, traffic roar, splashing fountains, street musicians, and chiming clocks. Likewise, many cities have strong olfactory elements—open markets, fish stalls, food processing, harvest smells—all of which serve as reference points in conceptualizing our environment. Put them all together and you have your own unique cognitive map of that particular environmental setting. It is clear that this map is neither pure perception nor pure cognition nor pure memory in the classical sense of these terms; however, it partakes of all of them, and it is in fact what comes to mind when we ask ourselves to visualize any particular environmental situation.

Functional Relevance of Environment Perception

Like all perceptual processes, environment perception plays a dual role in our lives. First, it is the source of our phenomenal experience of the world; all its sights and sounds and smells, all its simple and subtle meanings, all its ugliness and its beauty, all its sense of value comes to us through the process of perception. Second, perception provides us with a guide to action in the environment, it gives us both the arena within which actions take place and the ability to register and record the consequences of these actions. Environment perception in particular orients us in our surroundings, it provides us with information about the systematic relationships among the components of our world, and it is the means whereby we can relate our own goal strivings to the environment within which we live. Environment perception thus orders our world, with ourselves as part of the ordering process. In this sense the environment can be said to exist for us only in relation to the ways in which it is significant to us.

Environmental significance is, however, not immediately self-evident, and the first step in establishing significances is by exploration and orientation through environment perception. Exploratory and sometimes seemingly random perception is in fact a product both of the need to know, to experience the environment as a pattern of meaningful relationships, and of the need to achieve particular goals and purposes. This search for information is a characteristic feature of our relation to an external world which itself is not a steady-state environment but one that is continually changing, partly because the individual's very presence in the situation affects the kinds of information available from it.

To act in an environment in order to achieve our purposes presupposes that our perceptions are reliable and accurate, that what we think is going to happen by virtue of the way we perceive a situation will actually happen. The validating function of environment perception goes hand in hand with exploration and orientation in the world. It is the process whereby we extract and check out the systematic order of the surroundings. Without the faith that we see things in some kind of predictable and verifiable relationship, it would be impossible to function at all. The bridge that spans the river must get us to the other side; the ball hurtling in our direction will strike us if we do not move; the flower will have a fragrance if we smell it. Of course, we know that in many cases the environment does not work this way. Assessments of size, space, distance, to mention just a few examples, are subject to great distortion. "Appearances are deceiving," and perception is seldom if ever absolutely accurate. In the face of this, we are continually striving to reduce the probability of distortion to acceptable limits. Most of the time our experience with previous situations of a similar nature tells us what will probably take place in this one. We learn to recognize the relevant relationships in the environment that correspond to similar relationships encountered in other environments and in this way build up a pattern of predictable relationships.

This concept of predictability leads us to treat environment perception as the creation of certainty out of uncertainty or probability. And this is possible because the experienced consequences of actions provide a check on the perceptual predictions on which the actions were based. If we don't duck when the ball comes, we discover, rather unpleasantly, that our assumption was correct. Every concrete situation potentially involves an element of choice, and we make the right choices only if we can rely on the predictive accuracy of our perceptions. Predictive accuracy, in turn, has meaning to us only in relation to what we want to accomplish. The validity of our perceptions, whether they work or not, has meaning to us only insofar as they help us achieve our purposes, help us attain those particular satisfactions of living for which each of us is striving.

The overall function of environment perception, then, is not to reveal present reality nor to recall past reality; rather it is to predict the future. Perception is anticipatory. In the words of Ames, "perceptions are prognostic directives for action." Environment perception provides the means whereby we can establish environments within which to carry out our purposes, environments that will accommodate the range of behaviors we have chosen to enact and which are most likely to provide the consequences to our actions which we anticipate. It is the checking out through action of these anticipated consequences of our behavior that provides the key to our understanding of environment perception.

This anticipation is not possible without our experience with the recording of past environments. In an objective sense the recorded and verified relationship furnishes reliable guides to further action. In a subjective sense, the symbolic and value ordering of an environment likewise helps us predict its relation to our own goals and values. The sum total of the assumptions which an individual makes as to the nature and significance of the external world constitutes his only known world. Environment perception reconciles the world we experience anew each day with the world we have already come to know. By referring what we perceive to what we assume on the basis of past perception, we are able to create and maintain a stable environment.

References

Allport, G., & Pettigrew, T. Cultural influence on the perception of movement: The trapezoidal illusion among the Zulus. *Journal of Abnormal and Social Psychology,* 1957, *55,* 104–113.

Ames, A., Jr. Visual perception and the rotating trapezoidal window. *Psychological Monographs,* 1951, *65,* No. 324.

Brunswik, E. *Perception and the representative design of psychological experiments.* Berkeley and Los Angeles: University of California Press, 1956.

Burnette, C. The mental image of architecture. In *Architecture for human behavior: Collected papers from a mini-conference.* Philadelphia: Philadelphia Chapter/The American Institute of Architects, 1971. Pp. 65–73.

Dember, W. N. *The psychology of perception.* New York: Holt, Rinehart and Winston, 1960.

Epstein, W. *Varieties of perceptual learning.* New York: McGraw-Hill, 1967.

Gibson, J. J. *The senses considered as perceptual systems.* Boston: Houghton Mifflin, 1966.

Gregory, R. L. *Eye and brain.* London: Weidenfeld and Nicholson, 1966.
Haber, R. N. *Informational processing approaches to perception.* New York: Holt, Rinehart and Winston, 1969.
Hammond, K. R. (Ed.) *The psychology of Egon Brunswik.* New York: Holt, Rinehart and Winston, 1966.
Helmholtz, H. L. F. von *Helmholtz's treatise on physiological optics.* Translated from the 3rd German edition. J. P. C. Southall (Ed.) New York: Dover, 1962. (Original German edition, 1866.)
Ittelson, W. H. *Visual space perception.* New York: Springer, 1960.
Ittelson, W. H. *The Ames demonstrations in perception.* Princeton, N.J.: Princeton University Press, 1952. [Reprinted by Hafner Publishing Company, 1968.]
Ittelson, W. H. Perception of the large-scale environment. *Transactions of the New York Academy of Sciences,* 1970, *32,* 807–815.
Ittelson, W. H. (Ed.) *Environment and cognition.* New York: Seminar Press, 1973.
Kilpatrick, F. P. Two processes of perceptual learning. *Journal of Experimental Psychology,* 1954, *47,* 362–370. [Reprinted in H. M. Proshansky et al. (Eds.), *Environmental psychology: Man and his physical setting.* New York: Holt, Rinehart and Winston, 1970. Pp. 104–112.]
Lynch, K. *The image of the city.* Cambridge, Mass.: The M.I.T. Press, 1960.
Murch, G. M. *Visual and auditory perception.* Indianapolis, Ind.: Bobbs-Merrill, 1973.
Nahemow, L. Research in a novel environment. *Environment and Behavior,* 1971, *3,* 81–102.
Neisser, U. *Cognitive psychology.* New York: Appleton, 1967.
Rock, I. *The nature of perceptual adaptation.* New York: Basic Books, 1966.
Segall, M. H., Campbell, D. T., & Herskovits, M. J. *The influence of culture on visual perception.* Indianapolis, Ind.: Bobbs-Merrill, 1966.
Snyder, F. W., & Pronko, N. H. *Vision with spatial inversion.* Wichita, Kan.: University of Wichita Press, 1952.
Vernon, M. D. *The psychology of perception.* Baltimore, Md.: Pelican Books, 1962.
Zubek, J. (Ed.) *Sensory deprivation: Fifteen years of research.* New York: Appleton, 1969.

Suggested Readings

Brunswik, E. *Perception and the representative design of psychological experiments.* Berkeley and Los Angeles: University of California Press, 1956.
Haber, R. N. *Information processing approaches to perception.* New York: Holt, Rinehart and Winston, 1969.
Gibson, J. J. *The senses considered as perceptual systems.* Boston: Houghton Mifflin, 1966.
Gregory, R. L. *Eye and brain.* London: Weidenfeld and Nicholson, 1966.
Ittelson, W. H. *Visual space perception.* New York: Springer, 1960.
Segall, M. H., Campbell, D. T., & Herskovitz, M. J. *The influence of culture on visual perception.* Indianapolis, Ind.: Bobbs-Merrill, 1966.

Six

Social Interaction and the Environment

Chapter Four presented some general assumptions dealing with man's individual behavior in relation to the physical environment. Now, we shift the focus to social processes and interactions in specific settings. The environment will be viewed as a component of man's interaction with others in his setting—a component frequently omitted or understressed in considering social interaction processes.

Central to our discussion in Chapter Four was the view of man as a dynamically organized system, capable of learning, able to modify his behavior in response to changes in his environment, but bringing to it a set of enduring psychological structures—the attitudes, values, interests, and personality traits that reflect his sociocultural background. This interaction of social experiences and traits with the setting is our major concern here.

As a member of various social groups and institutions, man is socialized to behave appropriately in relation to specific physical settings, not simply to isolated stimuli, but to symbolic meanings of settings as well. Although we may separate the physical and

* Parts of the discussion on pages 142–160 in this chapter have been reworked from material published in *Environmental Psychology: Man and His Physical Setting* (Holt, Rinehart and Winston 1970), pp. 173–183.

social components of an environment, there really is only a total environment. Our isolation of the social component in this chapter is in no sense an attempt to negate the dynamic quality of man's responses. Rather, it represents a somewhat different frame for the analysis of environmental behavior.

A basic issue is the meaning of social interaction. Very simply it is the behavior and responses that individuals induce in each other. Interaction grows out of the roles we play, the defined relationships we have in various groups. Some of these roles involve face-to-face contacts, as sibling, parent, boss, or teacher. Others involve larger aggregates where we interact with many others. In all cases, some form of communication is involved, whether through speaking, positioning the body, gestures, or various "body" languages. In all cases, too, the interaction has a location and its characteristics are crucial elements in the interaction process.

The "person" components of this process range from the individual alone, to face-to-face groups, to aggregates. A consideration of the social-environmental implications of a person alone might seem like a non sequitur, but in fact individuals are never alone. In the process of living and learning within society, rules and regulations are acquired and internalized, and guide behavior, influencing and modifying it whether or not others are present. In essence, this is what we mean when we say a person has been socialized. However, it does not imply that an individual's behavior when others are present is identical to his activity in isolation, but rather that both are based on his previous experiences with specific groups in specific settings.

Three major issues constitute the second portion of this chapter: crowding, territoriality, and privacy. Although these do not exhaust all relevant areas, they will be discussed as samples of the kinds of issues that are meaningful in analyzing the social implications of man in his environment. They involve groups of varying sizes, made up of persons playing different roles in different settings. In all cases, the constructs are dynamic combinations of persons, interactions, and environments.

SOCIAL INFLUENCES AND ENVIRONMENTAL BEHAVIOR

Social Interaction and Social Processes

To say that much of man's behavior in the physical setting is based on social processes explains why he is able to move about, distance and position himself without consciously thinking through each step he takes. It also means that man moves through settings with expectations of how others will behave as well. Reciprocity underlies socialized behaviors. To do otherwise would be inordinately time-consuming and distracting. A child growing up in the United States quickly learns that motorists "keep to the right." In the

British Isles, however, he understands that they "keep to the left." Such clear-cut examples enable the individual to carry out certain actions without making a new decision each time he acts.

Most norms in our society are far more subtle and complex than traffic rules, and they are not usually given the force of law. In a very broad sense they are the invisible guidelines or sanctions, laid down in a culture over a period of time, that influence people's behavior, thoughts, feelings and attitudes in certain situations. (For a discussion of norms, see Brown 1965: 48–60.) Norms constitute the "house rules" by which society attempts to govern public behaviors, and these behaviors are usually learned through one's contact with a specific group—the family, a street corner gang, a club, or the socioeconomic class to which one belongs. One learns the appropriate sets of behaviors within the context of a smaller unit, on the basis of interaction within that unit, and these behaviors are appropriate to the roles within that unit. Members of a family, for instance, maintain closer physical contact with one another than do strangers. Essentially, this has grown out of the trusting relationships implied in kinship, but equally close symbolic familiarity is expressed in certain groups. Thus, it is quite usual for French males to exchange kisses—a behavior that is decidedly unusual in most Western countries. In a series of exercises, the sociologist Harold Garfinkel (1964) and his students deliberately violated a number of norms, among them the norm of appropriate distance. In reporting these experiences, it became clear that the violators had great difficulty maintaining their unusual roles. It was especially uncomfortable to approach other persons too closely, placing one's face close up to another person. The violators seemed to experience more discomfort than those violated.

Face-to-face cues—postures, gestures, expressions, and interaction distances—are fundamental properties in social discourse and are affected by the context of the situation. Such an environmental context includes the physical reality of one's body, the properties of the surrounding space, of objects and other persons in the setting, and the social rules of one's culture. In some cultures a person feels compelled to sit as close as possible to others who are present; in another culture, the person selects the farthest position from others.

Consider the experience of entering a room. One is likely to have certain responses if the room is vacant, another set if it is partially occupied, and a still different experience if it is crowded. But we do not respond only to the number of people; size, decoration, and coloring are important too. Is the room bare or full of furniture, comfortable or impersonal? The physical attributes can signal that different responses are appropriate. Physical attributes of the person interact with the design. We are able to see and hear just so far. Visual acuity depends on a certain level of illumination. Chairs can be too hard or too soft, too low or too high. Add to this the inside and outside noise levels and a broad range of demands, often contradictory, is placed on us.

All of these factors are mediated by past social experiences and, in turn, mediate the social process. Their importance in face-to-face interaction can be understood if all but the verbal cues are removed, as occurs when one speaks over the telephone. A common physical environment ceases to exist, and we can achieve a high degree of anonymity or, if we wish, an intimacy that may not be possible when one is in the presence of others. In contrast, when verbal speech is not used quite a different set of cues is necessary. Anyone who takes part in a charade knows how effective nonverbal communication can be. Gestures, sign language, postures, and distance take the place of words. One speaks with the whole body. Such movements are highly exaggerated examples of the kinesic movements all of us use in everyday life. Yet, here again, both cultural norms and the role one is enacting at a given time affect the way such movements are carried out. Many public speakers employ sweeping gestures that would be considered quite inappropriate in casual conversation. The speech of certain ethnic groups is accompanied by animated and vigorous movements that would not be seen among less demonstrative groups.

Norms, however much they reflect various cultural patterns and to whatever extent they may be taken for granted, are not carried on for their own sake. Since man's behavior is goal-directed, normative behaviors are in pursuit of cognitive, motivational, and affective goals. But there are times when a goal may be in conflict with a particular norm. Intimate contact with someone of the opposite sex, for example, is usually thwarted if others are present; the desire, or goal, exists but such displays of affection in public are regarded, in our society at least, as inappropriate for all but the young.

Likewise, the existence of spatial norms does not always suggest that, from the individual's point of view, this is the best or healthiest way to behave. Distancing based on class distinctions is frequently awkward for all parties in democratic societies, yet the behaviors tend to persist as residuals from an older, more class conscious age. Discomfort is equally a factor in accommodating oneself to the posture and movement in cultures where these differ radically from one's own. It is usual for the Japanese to sit cross-legged at low tables while eating, but it is decidedly unusual (as well as uncomfortable) for Americans to do so. In some Japanese restaurants the problem is solved (for the non-Japanese) by providing holes in the floor for one's legs.

Another example in our own culture is the implicit rule that furniture arrangements in public areas are to remain set, whether or not they are appropriate for what is taking place. This often leads to hours of physical discomfort and difficulties in communication. Yet, most people are reluctant to move chairs or tables that are not theirs. Even in familiar settings shifting of available props is not usual.

In all such cases it should be clear that the environment itself is "normative" only to the extent that it signifies something to the social agent; it is he who introduces the norms, and indeed, he may alter the environment to make the normative behavior more easily followed. In the physical sense, of course, once this alteration has taken place, it may be difficult not to comply with the particular behavior suggested, as in the case of the Japanese restaurant. The rather formal arrangement of furniture in many sitting rooms or parlors is the cue for a certain type of polite discourse, but only if the participants accept this as normal for the occasion.

We are really saying that man's sociospatial behavior is guided by two forces, both stemming from his cultural context. The first is the cultural rules that govern his positioning in *space*, the distances maintained from others, the orientation of his body, his posture, and his nonverbal communications. The second is the cultural symbols signaling the way a particular *place* might be used, the arrangement that suggests intimacy or formality, talking or eating, conversation or prayer.

What these instances teach us most of all is that a radical alteration of space will seldom change human spatial behavior when the attitudes and norms on which such behavior is based are well established. There are obvious exceptions to this generalization over the short term—submariners and astronauts learn to do without privacy and to live with confinement—but for the most part environments are built to accommodate existing ways of life, no matter how counterproductive or incongruent these may prove to be. Environmental "fit" is seldom achieved simply by changing the environment. If we desire changes in the uses of space, the provision of new spaces is only part of the problem. It is necessary also to understand and perhaps change people's attitudes toward each other and the space itself.

The Individual and Physical Settings

In the preceding examples, discussion centered on three variables: (1) the attributes of the person (particularly those based on cultural norms); (2) the nature of the social interaction; and (3) the setting which acts upon the individual and is acted upon by him. On the most obvious level, such interpersonal relationships involve the conscious give and take of people who participate in a given activity, whether this be an organized group process or simply a casual encounter. It is necessary now to look at some additional factors influencing the individual's response to social situations in which the environment plays a role. These factors in general comprise behaviors that reflect a person's need for some minimum space surrounding him, his response to crowding, his sense of territory, and his desire for privacy. All such factors define physical as well as psychological needs and are rooted both in man's biological makeup and his culturally acquired traits. All have a strong environmental component in the sense that the settings must be manipulated or the person must modify his response in some way to meet the demands of the setting if his goals are to be realized.

One of the first of these constructs to be investigated in terms of human behavior is that of *personal space.* The sociologist Georg Simmel described this concept in the early 1900s (see Wolff 1950), and it has received attention by psychologists over the years. Recently, the notion has drawn widely on the field of ethology for parallels among animal behavior. Hediger (1968) used the phrase "personal distance" to describe the characteristic distances maintained by noncontact species of animals as a means of physical protection. However, unless we expand the notion of protection to include the preservation of intended behaviors, it is difficult to apply this physical self-preservation concept to the complex set of maneuvers used by humans. Some of this preservation may derive from one's sense of self—one's identity as a unique and separate person. On the other hand, such behavior may refer back to physical variables—the distance necessary to develop a clear image of others and of the objects in one's setting. Much of it depends on role behavior—the appropriate spaces necessary to carry out particular roles where appropriate distances and behaviors are associated with these roles.

Hall, an anthropologist, has identified personal space as a "small protective sphere or bubble that an organism maintains between itself and others." [Hall 1966: 119] Hall has analyzed the sensory parameters of these distances, reviewing the role of the visual, auditory, olfactory, tactile, and thermal senses in the perception of distance and as immediate receivers of spatial stimulation (see Chapters IV, V, and VI in *The Hidden Dimension*). The eye emerges as a powerful receiver of stimulation, capable of gathering a vast amount of information from the environment at a distance that far outreaches other senses. In contrast, the other senses are generally understimulated by our setting, and Hall (1966:45) describes Americans as "culturally underdeveloped" in the olfactory senses, surrounded by bland, deodorized spaces.

As Hall (1966) has described them on the basis of studies in the United States, the various culturally defined distances include the *intimate* ones of lovemaking and fondling, *personal distance* (the protective sphere), the *social distance* of most interpersonal and small group discourse, and the more far-flung *public distances*. Each of these has a near and far phase. For example, personal distance among human beings is evident in the ways people arrange themselves in public. Riders on a subway train will leave seats between themselves until the car fills up. When possible, we avoid body contact on the street; if others are unduly threatening, we "give them a wide berth." Embodied in the places we take, positions we hold, postures we maintain is the expectation that others will behave in a reciprocal manner. This is at the heart of the interaction process, learned within specific groups and specific contexts.

That people not only protect their own personal space but respect the space of others is evident from their tendency to maintain conversational distance even when no conversation is taking place. Except for physical assaults, distances are violated only with the stated or tacit permission of the other person, as in the case of lovers, let us say, or men who "rough house" in the locker room, where the intimate distance is more appropriate. On an impersonal basis there is what might look like an invasion of space in crowded elevators and similar situations, but in these instances space is maintained symbolically through deliberate avoidance of eye contact, "hunching up," and similar behaviors.

Reluctance to invade the space of others (which also implies invasion of one's own close space) has been tested empirically. In an experiment by Horowitz, Duff, and Stratton (1964) the distance behaviors of diagnosed schizophrenics and normal males were studied. In the belief that their equilibrium was being tested, the subjects were asked to approach (a) a hatrack on which a coat was hung and (b) a staff member of the same sex as the subject. In all cases the object was approached significantly closer than the person. The schizophrenics' mean distance from the object was significantly larger than the normal group's, although no difference was evident in their distances from people. However, in other studies Horowitz did demonstrate that schizophrenics do, in fact, maintain greater distances from people than do normals. When a variation of the experiment was repeated with a group of normal males, including directions to advance toward a male and a female until they began to feel uncomfortable about closeness, the subjects stopped farther from the man than from the woman. With both male and female, approaches from the rear were closer than those from the front. In these studies Horowitz uses the term "body buffer zone" which he defines as the characteristic area surrounding a person that is seen as an extension of the body image. It is much like Hall's protective bubble. Many researchers have noted that defense against invasion of this sphere is often accompanied by various gestures, eye movements, bodily stances, and so on, which act as self-markers in delineating spacing boundaries. Argyle and Dean (1965), for example, have demonstrated the decrease in eye contact that follows increases in proximity. The reader is invited to invade the personal space of an unsuspecting stranger to learn the variety of ways in which the body responds. Eyes will be averted; weight will shift; there may be fidgeting, a leaning away from the invader, or perhaps a constriction of the body perimeter. Sometimes arms go up in a guarding position. Eventually, if the attack is pressed, the target will retreat. In genuinely threatening or uncomfortable situations, contact will be minimized by shallow breathing. These are all physical and symbolic techniques for maintaining distance.

Although many of these reactions may have some biological roots ("flight or fight"), one should beware of equating spatial behavior with animal models. Hall points out that such "proxemic" behavior is culturally determined. Societies exhibit different space norms, and in addition, such factors as age, sex, role, status, cultural background, race, and environmental conditions such as noise (see Canon and Mathews 1973) operate as variables within a given milieu.

In a review of issues and research dealing with personal space, Leibman (1970) describes a common example of the way roles and their prescribed behaviors maintain personal space. The case of doctor and patient involves a relationship of physical closeness that is acceptable when symbolic distance is maintained by behavior that is impersonal, professional, and appropriate to the roles. If either patient or doctor behaves in any way which would symbolize closeness, through excessive eye contact or inappropriate personal comments or the like, the expected role relationship is undermined and the personal space intruded.

With respect to sex differences in spacing, there is considerable evidence that women tend to place themselves closer to each other than to males (for example, Lott & Sommer 1967; Leibman 1970). Children approach both objects and people more closely than do adults (Argyle & Dean 1965). They also get closer to one another than adults, but adults touch children more often than they do each other. Distances are further modified according to the mood of the individual or the nature of the setting. We "stand away" from a stranger but move closer as we get to know him better. Parties promote a gregariousness in which the space bubble is easily pricked. Telling children ghost stories, as Feshback and Feshback (1963) found, can spontaneously reduce the size of the circle in which they are sitting. At another extreme is the important person or "great man" whose personal space is generally inviolable to an extent seldom experienced by ordinary people. Simmel has written:

> In regard to the "significant" (i.e., "great") man, there is an inner compulsion which tells one to keep at a distance and which does not disappear even in intimate relations with him. The only type for whom such distance does not exist is the individual who has no organ for perceiving distance. . . . [See Lyman & Scott 1967: 242].

Leibman (1970) summarizes a number of factors influencing personal space norms and behaviors, including: (1) characteristics of the physical environment (for example, number of occupants, shape of table, available furniture, arrangement of occupants); (2) characteristics of the individual (for example, personality traits, age, sex, feelings); (3) characteristics of the task or relationship between individuals (for example, cooperation, friendship, conversation); (4) characteristics of the other individual (for example, leadership, attraction, stigma). In each case one can find a series of empirical studies, including Leibman's work on sex and race norms and personal space.

Some of the most extensive studies of personal space have been carried out by Robert Sommer and his associates. Two of these studies (Felipe & Sommer 1966) deserve mention here. Although they were made in widely different settings and among contrasting types of people, they indicate that resistance to the invasion of one's personal space is a rather general response in our culture.

For the first study Sommer deployed himself on the grounds of a 1500-bed state psychiatric institution in California. Male patients who were sitting alone and not otherwise occupied were "invaded" by a male investigator who sat alongside them at a distance of six inches. If the patient moved, the investigator also moved to maintain the close distance. In one condition, the investigator took notes of the patient's reactions and jiggled his keys occasionally, looking at the patient in an effort to assert his dominance. The second condition only involved jiggling the keys. The sixty-four individual sessions with different patients each took a maximum of twenty minutes. At the same time, the behavior of "controls"—other patients in the same vicinity—was observed in order to make comparisons.

The purpose of the study was to find out how long each patient would remain seated before fleeing the invader. The results indicated that 36 percent of the experimental subjects fled within two minutes, while all the controls remained seated. Half of the "victims" left within nine minutes as compared with 8 percent of the controls. By the termination of the twenty-minute session, 64 percent of the invaded subjects had left, but only 33 percent of the controls.

The authors add, however, that in a series of dayroom invasions of five patients on one ward, where the patients were extremely territorial in their behavior, occupying the same chairs day after day, only one of the five subjects reacted by moving away within a few minutes of the intrusion. In two cases "it was like trying to move the Rock of Gibraltar."

The contrasting experiment was made in the study hall of a university library. Subjects were females sitting alone at one of the fourteen large tables. They were invaded by another female who sat at various distances ranging from very close (the chair next to the subject was moved to within three inches of the subject's chair) to a position in which two empty chairs intervened. The investigator also sat directly opposite the subject. Controls at other tables were observed for comparison. Results showed that, in general, the invaded person showed little reaction when other chairs or the table itself intervened. When the investigator sat next to the subject, however, and moved her chair within contact distance, there was a decided flight reaction as well as "more subtle signs of the victim's discomfort." At the end of the thirty-minute session, only 30 percent of the subjects remained at the table, compared to 87 percent of the controls.

Felipe and Sommer note that in both studies violation of personal space or "conversational distance" is followed at first by various accommodations or attempts to "live with" the situation. Flight is usually the final resort. It is apparent from one's experience on buses, subways, and elevators that people tolerate invasions when there is no alternative, but they do this by "turning off" from the invader and by creating symbolic distance. Obviously too, such invasions are normal for these kinds of settings. Even so, people generally seem to find spatial intrusion uncomfortable and a variety of defensive techniques—postural, gestural, the attempt to establish new distance, the use of parts of the body or reading material to buffer the closeness—are called into play. Whereas animals may howl and bare their teeth, humans tend to use more subtle and indirect avoidance devices; it is only when they feel too pressured that they are likely to flee.

Whatever expectations we have regarding the use of space, these can be surrendered to others under certain circumstances. This is especially evident when differences in ages are considered. The personal space "rights" of young children are either nonexistent or at best very limited. One thinks nothing of approaching a young child at a very close distance, even if the child is unknown to us; in general children learn to tolerate if not enjoy the fondling and head patting of admiring strangers. In a sense such invasions are very much tied in with the privacy rights of children, which are also very limited. Conversely, the child is given greater leeway in the exercise of his distances vis-à-vis others. An experimental study of Fry and Willis (1971) illustrates this point. Sixty women and sixty men waiting to enter a movie were invaded by five-, eight-, and ten-year-old children who were instructed to break into the line and stand as close as possible to the subjects without actually touching them. The sex of both subjects and invaders was varied. Reactions clearly indicated that the tolerance for invasion differed according to the age of the invader. For example, subjects were more likely to smile at the two younger groups and speak and turn toward the five-year-olds. More than any other group, the eight-year-olds were likely to elicit no response at all. With the ten-year-olds, however, the subjects tended to move away.

The study points up the nature of personal space norms in the developmental context. Whether it was the size and/or dress of the child, as suggested by the authors, the cues given off by the children elicited different responses from those given by adults.

In addition to age differentials, race and status or "caste" are clearly implicated in distancing behaviors. This is observable where approach distance rather than invasion of personal space is the measure of violation. In a study of caste as it relates to positioning and distancing in northern India, Grant (1971) documented the spatial behavior of "high" (Brahmin) and "low" (Harijan) caste members in several villages. Her experimental conditions revealed rather expected behaviors. For example, in a room set up with a waiting area, a person's seating position on a bench with another person (placed there as a confederate) reflected in large part his own caste and the caste ascribed to the confederate. Level was also used to establish distance, with a low-caste subject (Harijan) often choosing to sit on the floor to maximize his distance from the Brahmin on the bench. Untouchables, although legally eliminated as a caste in India, represent an extreme example of both actual and symbolic space norms that govern behavior. All of these instances are ways of using physical distance to regulate social distance. We might speculate that the physical form of Indian houses and cities may well be a reflection of the people's social values and attitudes with respect to caste, and this, perhaps, is the real significance of studies like these for environmental psychology.

One can speculate about similar experiences along racial and ethnic lines in our own culture. It is widely assumed that most whites, for instance, prefer to maintain greater distances between themselves and blacks than between each other. There is some empirical evidence to support this view, pointing up the influence of race on speaking distances (Willis 1966) and other distancing behaviors (Kleck 1969). However, Leibman's experimental study (1970) in an office setting did not support the predicted differences of white female subjects in their seating behavior with black and white confederates. Leibman suggests that in the safe natural setting of an office, where everyone would be presumed to be fellow employees, it might have been deemed inappropriate and unnecessary to manifest racially influenced behavior.

That racially differentiated behavior may be based on the distances preferred by whites among all people is suggested by Aiello and Jones' (1971) study of a mixed population of first- and second-grade school children observed in New York City school playgrounds. In noting distances between interacting pairs, these investigators found that white children remained farther apart in their free play than did black or Puerto Rican children. This distancing was more pronounced among boys than among girls, although for blacks and Puerto Ricans sex differences were minimal.

A more recent variation of this study (Jones & Aiello 1973) extended the comparisons to first-, third-, and fifth-grade students. Two schools were selected, one predominantly black and the other middle-class white. The teacher paired members of each class with persons of the same sex with whom they would normally talk and play. The experimenters then took two pairs at a time to a room where they were instructed to talk about television commercials. As they spoke, the observer recorded their physical positions, including the orientation of their bodies—the degree to which the pairs' shoulders were turned toward each other. Comparisons revealed no significant distance differences in black and white pairs. (A significant difference in the first grade, with blacks closer to each other than whites, disappeared over time. Thus, the first grade results are consistent with the authors' earlier study.) In terms of body position there were sex and group differences, with black children and males in general less inclined to face each other. This study suggests that there is a gradual acquisition of the spatial norms of the two reference groups through exposure to middle-class values and the more direct socializing experiences within a particular group (black or Puerto Rican). Clearly, social background places different emphasis on distancing behaviors, but children need a certain amount of school and other experiences to acquire the dominant patterns of the larger cultural group.

To sum up our discussion of norms and spatial behavior: Under specific circumstances man has some need for sheer physical separation from others. Differences in separation and distancing behaviors maintained by people in various cultures suggest that this behavior is normative to groups within the culture and that it serves both a social-symbolic and a functional purpose. Space norms are also affected by differences in age, sex, social status, and ethnic background.

The Small Group and Its Setting

Much of our previous discussion has involved the normative aspects of the man/environment interaction. It would be unfortunate if this emphasis were to be construed as an argument for behaviorism, or some other form of environmental determinism. Whatever the context in which they operate, people are not automatons rigidly programmed by their norms, locked helplessly into their "space bubbles," or controlled by the attributes of their personality and the roles they enact. Neither are they manipulated by their environment. That the physical setting plays a part in social interaction, in the manner in which people deal not only with their environment but with each other, is nevertheless a factor in the process that is frequently overlooked.

Take a common example. Almost anyone who has done organized committee work will recognize the extraordinary importance of the group's physical setting. Some of the comfort of the room may relate to the temperature level, the hardness of the seats, the lighting quality. These are certainly important, both in terms of whether the participant leaves with a tired and disgruntled feeling, or whether he is relaxed and pleased. Obviously, the content of the meeting has a bearing on the degree of satisfaction, but it is easy to neglect the environmental contribution. Research suggests that the physical arrangement of the setting can affect the actual group process. On a simple level the willingness to compromise, the ability to see another point of view, in some measure depends on feeling that one has an equal opportunity, that others whose views one is trying to share can be seen.

Perhaps nowhere is this reciprocity more evident than in group functions. One indication can be discerned in the speaking order of the participants, which so often depends merely on where they are sitting. Some of the earliest evidence that seating arrangements do, indeed, influence interactions was provided by Steinzor (1950), who experimented with circular groups of ten members. He found that when a person stopped speaking, someone opposite rather than alongside was next to speak. The explanation, according to Steinzor, was that "opposites" have greater physical and expressive value for one another than "side-by-sides." Whether for this reason or for some other, seating arrangements unquestionably encourage specific interaction patterns. A critical word, of course, is the word "encourage"—for in and of themselves seating arrangements cannot cause or create communication.

A later study by Hearn (1957) approached the problem in terms of the presence or absence of a group leader. Using a six-man U-shaped pattern, Hearn found that in groups with minimal leadership the "Steinzor effect" did seem to operate with comments toward the opposites prevailing. With strong direction by a leader, however, the comments tended to be directed to side neighbors. Hearn suggested that when group members and the leader shared the discussion, other than spatial factors influenced the direction of comments.

Another influence on informal groups is the shape of a table. To many people a round table implies a give-and-take on the part of equals. Although the participants may not be equally qualified, the table layout makes this difficult to determine. Rectangular tables, on the other hand, have a way of putting people in their place; the "head of the table" position is head in more than name, for it symbolizes power. In feudal days commoners sat "below the salt" in deference to the nobles who occupied the "head" end of the table. In many families today this position is still reserved for the father and is looked upon as a mark of authority.

In addition, it has been found that the head position tends to be taken by persons willing to assume power. Among other things, it dominates the group visually. Thus, in studies of mock juries, Strodtbeck and his associates (1958, 1961) related social status, position at the table, leadership, and the results of the deliberation. Using regular jury pools, they created mock juries and played recordings of real trials. After deliberating, the panel returned verdicts. A careful record was made of details of the process and participants. Findings showed that the person chosen to be foreman was generally a male of higher occupational status than the others. The foreman turned out to have a strong influence on shaping the final decisions. Most striking, for an environmental analysis, was that jury members generally elected as foreman the person already seated at one of the head positions. There appeared to be a tendency for higher-status people to select one of the head chairs, and these head positions were more active in the discussion. Their contributions tended to be rated as more valuable by jury members.

Studies of this type are truly meaningful only if the independent variable (chair and table arrangement) is altered for purposes of comparison. In this case, it was not. We want to know, in short, if a nonrectangular table would have produced substantially different results. Something of this sort was taken into account by Harold J. Leavitt (1951) who studied the physical distribution of members within the group and communication patterns in relation to performance and personal satisfaction in the task. Where distribution is contingent on the setting (as it frequently is), the setting becomes instrumental in determining how well the group functions. Leavitt arranged groups of five individuals in the networks shown below.

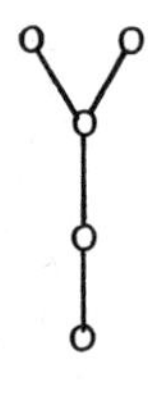

"Y"

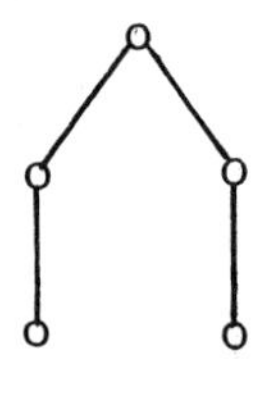

Chain

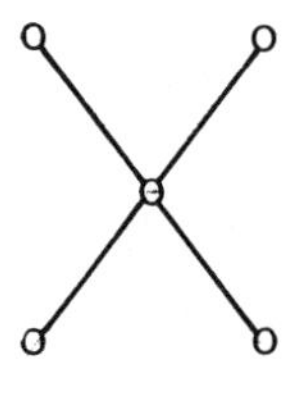

Wheel

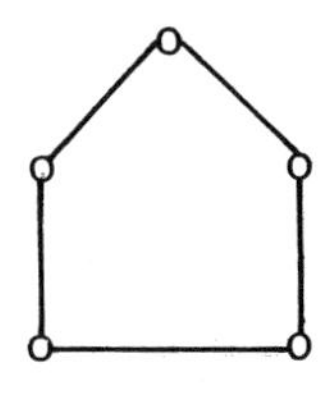

Circle

The task of each group was to solve a common problem. This was possible only by an exchange of information within the group, for no single member possessed enough information to solve the problem by himself. The structure of the network, therefore, was important with respect to the relative facility with which information could be exchanged.

The reader will note that a cardinal feature of two of the networks (the "Y" and the Wheel) is a central, or axis, position through which messages must be channeled in order for all five members of the group to participate. No such centrality exists for the Chain and the Circle networks. Two factors were measured: (1) the comparative time required by the four groups to complete their trials; (2) subjective satisfactions on the part of the members in their work with reference to the type of network to which they belonged.

In general Leavitt's findings revealed a progressive shift in efficiency (in terms of number of messages necessary to solve the problem) from the Wheel through the "Y", Chain, and Circle. The Circle proved the least, the Wheel the most efficient arrangement. However, the latter was also seen as providing the fewest satisfactions to its members. Circle members, although lacking a leader (central link), found their roles highly satisfying.

What conclusions relevant to society can we draw from this experiment? Settings which by their physical structure increase the likelihood of excessive peripheral activity in a group will diminish the satisfactions of its members. Peripheral users become dependent upon the leader, who, almost alone, controls the process. According to Leavitt: "In our culture in which needs for autonomy, recognition and achievement are strong, it is to be expected that positions which limit independence of action (peripheral positions) would be unsatisfying." [p. 48]

An example of concern over table shape in recent history comes to mind. The eight months of deliberations in 1969, preceding the Paris Peace Talks, were largely centered on the issue of the shape of the table to be used in the negotiations. It is unlikely that the final shape that was selected influenced, in any significant way, what finally occurred in sessions, although clearly a round table contrasts with other shapes in ease of communication, eye contact, ease of passing materials about, opportunity for casual conversation, and symbolic meaning. It is important to repeat that in this case and in the experimental studies cited, the physical setting is not the determinant of behavior. The issue of determinism will be considered more fully in the chapter on the built environment, but is raised at this point as a kind of warning in evaluating the contribution of any physical setting that is part of a complicated social interaction process.

The question can be raised as to the extent that the abstracted social arrangements studied by Leavitt are representative of the types of experiences workers have in the real world. The possibility that physical arrangements do, indeed, matter is indicated in recent efforts by the Saab Motor Company of Sweden to substitute group participation for the traditional linear assembly line, on the theory that the worker has been alienated, not only from a sense of creative involvement in his product, but also from necessary social contact with his coworkers. To some degree, the absenteeism that has plagued the automobile industry in the United States is seen as a revolt against the psychological isolation of the assembly line. The network, in effect, represents a preexisting chain of command in which the individual is not expected to participate in decision making.

In quite a different setting it has been found that site placement in housing projects strongly influences the formation of friendships among neighbors. The classic study of Festinger and his associates (1950), conducted in a post-World War II housing development for married students, found the greatest number of friendships among side-by-side neighbors. Of the features of the housing that seemed to influence the presence or absence of social interaction, most basic was the opportunity provided for contact. In particular, the distances between doors appeared to be critical. Festinger considered the ecological basis of friendship in terms of two forms of distance, *physical*—that is, the measured distance "as the crow flies"— and *functional*, the traversed distance required to go from one's own door to a neighbor's via sidewalks, driveways, yards, and so on. Although both influence the number of possible contacts among people, they do not always work together. Physical proximity in the absence of common paths will not lead to contact. Two families may live back to back, in close physical proximity, but without doors that are near to each other or shared back yard space, and there may be little or no interaction. However, Festinger's study involved residents with rather homogeneous interests and backgrounds, encouraging the possibility that contact would lead to friendships. The students, removed from their permanent residences, thrown together in the academic setting, were likely to depend on one another for friendships. Proximity is certainly not the sure path to friendship as any apartment resident can testify. Even in the face of a common lobby, a single elevator or staircase, the anonymity of the city dweller can be preserved over many years.

From the point of view of human social interaction, the functional centrality of an area is only the first step toward face-to-face interactions. It is not the interaction itself. There are at least three factors that influence the possibility that meaningful contacts will occur (Proshansky 1971). One is simply the amount of time people spend in a given area. If the time is short, as in walking through a lobby or walking down a corridor, interaction is not ensured. Another factor is frequency, how often the occupant uses the area. Assuming that there is a high frequency of use, combined with a reasonable amount of time spent doing it, then the third important factor becomes one of facilitation. Is the size of the space adequate for the use intended? Do seating arrangements promote or discourage face-to-face contact?

In this connection it is useful to consider Humphry Osmond's (1957) characterization of *sociopetal* or *sociofugal* spaces. Sociofugal spaces repel interaction, thrusting people apart. Sociopetal spaces, on the other hand, encourage interaction. In one ward of a psychiatric hospital in which the authors conducted research, a potentially attractive solarium was rarely used, in large measure because the seating arrangement was sociofugal, suggesting a waiting-room with a long, hard bench. Sociopetal public spaces on the other hand cannot guarantee that friendships will be made. They can, however, become an area of discovery which leads to the formation of friendships.

Where this is not the case, proximity among several persons may mean very little and can, in fact, limit social interaction. For example, it is commonly assumed that the number of people assigned to rooms in institutions makes for greater contact. Yet a study of bedroom size and use in psychiatric hospitals (Ittelson et al. 1970a, b) found just the opposite to be the case. In rooms holding one to six beds, it was unusual to find more than one patient at a time. Only in the larger rooms (six beds and over) was there a tendency for two or more patients to be present. Moreover, regardless of size, the bedrooms tended to be treated as single rooms, used for isolated kinds of behaviors. It was in the smaller rooms, especially the single-bed units, that one found the widest distribution of activities. Clearly, the occupants of larger rooms felt that their freedom of action was limited by the presence or potential presence of others.

Similar studies have focused on proximity relationships in housing, offices, and schools where social status is a variable. This question is salient, for example, in Deutsch and Collins' (1951) study of the effects of interracial housing, where more favorable attitudes as a result of interracial contact tended to occur within a single social status condition. However, there were prerequisites, as it were, including the requirement that the minority not conform to the prevailing racial stereotype. The majority group in turn had to possess values and be open to experiences that were inconsistent with prejudice. Mere contact is clearly not sufficient for immediate change of view, but contact seems to be important if not essential as a mechanism for attitude change, other conditions being equal. Gans (1961) has pointed this up on a community level, where life style and status have been found to be more powerful agents of neighboring than site plan and propinquity. In noting the complexity of friendship choice, Athanasiou and Yoshioka (1973) found that propinquity may play a part in establishing and maintaining friendships among women who have very little in common other than their stage in the life cycle. For friendships to be maintained over distance, a similarity in social class seems to be essential. Settings, in this sense, are arenas of discovery. It is men and women, not "occupants" and "neighbors," who form friendships.

SOME SOCIAL-ENVIRONMENTAL ISSUES

In this section four concepts will be considered in detail: *territoriality*, *crowding*, *privacy*, and *freedom of choice*. Although these do not exhaust the range of potentially useful constructs, we concentrate on them because of their particular relevance to a number of issues in environmental psychology.

In part they reflect the heritage of animal research that has contributed to our ecological knowledge, especially in the study of crowding and territoriality. And for all of them, but especially for privacy, there is a direct applicability to many aspects of environmental planning. These topics are also areas in which available research adds to philosophic interest. If gaps exist in our knowledge, this in itself makes their study most critical.

Territoriality

One way man achieves a sense of control over his life is through his ability to control significant behaviors in defined areas of space. In recent years the term *territoriality* has been much in vogue. Drawing heavily on the work of biologists, ornithologists, animal psychologists, and ethologists, it assumes implicitly that man too lays claim to his territory—the piece of ground which he will defend against intruders. Because he occupies it, he has the right to determine who may or may not enter his physical domain.

The history of territoriality as a construct goes back to the seventeenth century, when John Ray's study of the nightingale (1678) described its "freehold." More systematic observation of territorial behavior began with the British ornithologist H. E. Howard, whose *Territory in Bird Life*, published in 1920, set forth the intricate ways in which certain species of birds "staked out" a given area and used it to apportion the food supply, mate, rear their young, keep out intruders, and establish a social hierarchy within the flock. The result of Howard's observations was to stimulate research with other types of animals, both in their natural habitat and in confinement.

There is no need here to review the growing literature on territoriality in lower organisms. The interested reader is directed to volumes by Hediger (1964, 1968), Lorenz (1966), Ardrey (1966), and papers by Leyhausen (1965). All add to the systematic and informal evidence that certain species of infrahumans stake out a territory to be defended against members of their own species and by this means establish the appropriate ecological balances for preserving the species. Hediger (1964) provides an especially rich description of animal territories, including the way they operate as external evidence of a fixed time/space system which governs the use of specific sectors of a defined area for various purposes at regular times. Ethologists characterize this aspect of territoriality as reflecting an underlying "respect" for the area acquired. It is reflected in such specialized functions as feeding and excretion, which are usually separated in space (as well as time). It also provides for spacing of a species to prevent overexploitation of resources. The "wisdom" of this is certainly obvious. The question that arises in dealing with the notion of territoriality is where man fits into this picture.

Man certainly gives evidence of territorial behavior. Humans, no less than lower organisms, define particular boundaries of the physical environment and assume the right to determine who can and who cannot move across these boundaries. Whether we speak of a man's home, his office, the turf of a neighborhood gang, or the cubbies of nursery school children, there is evidence that these have a territorial component. On the other hand, the analogy with such behavior in infrahuman species quickly reaches its limit. To begin with, as Roos (1968) points out, territorial behavior in animals is instinctive; in men it is optional. Much of what is called human territory involves the concept of private property. To assume that such behavior serves the same functions in man as in lower organisms, or that it is rooted in innately determined biological mechanisms, simply ignores the properties that distinguish people from other organisms. Whatever the complex social behavior under consideration, and regardless of its essential origins in biology, in every instance it has been so inextricably tied to man's socializing and broader cultural experiences that the biological or animal analogy must necessarily be discarded. It is as a descriptive term rather than an empirically demonstrated behavior that we find the construct most useful.

Earlier we introduced the notion of man both as a living organism and a physical object. To survive as a person and to be free of physical discomfort he requires a minimum amount of space. Under conditions that threaten to eliminate or reduce this minimum something related to his territorial needs will be aroused and expressed. Thus, in the face of severe spatial restrictions the tendency to push others away may be a basically territorial way of reducing discomfort.

The functioning individual, however, requires another kind of minimum space in order to survive. He must be able to move freely within and between physical settings to satisfy not only his hunger, thirst, sex, and similar biological drives, but also his needs for affiliation, achievement, success, and other complex social motives. Under given circumstances, the individual may have to define a space for himself long enough to permit the satisfaction of these drives and motives, including those that are sociospatial in nature. This may explain examples of territorial behavior in two very different settings. In studying psychiatric patients in a hospital ward, Esser and his associates (1965) found many specific instances of territoriality. Particular areas of the ward were claimed by some patients. In the second investigation, reported by Altman and Haythorn (1967), nine pairs of sailors who were initially strangers to each other were studied over a ten-day period while they lived in small rooms with no outside contacts. Comparison was made with controls, also pairs, who lived in regular barracks but worked in an isolated area. As the ten days passed the men showed a gradual increase in territorial behavior and a tendency toward social withdrawal. At the beginning territoriality for the complete isolates took the form of exclusive use of specific beds; later this extended to the side of a table and finally to a more mobile and less personal chair. Among the controls, chair and table territoriality were high at first, then dropped. Bed territoriality began low, then increased to the level of isolates.

Territoriality of this kind was more rigidly maintained in those pairs in which both the sailors were either high or low in dominance characteristics than among pairs who were compatible in this respect, that is, with one high and the other low in dominance. In the study by Esser and his associates (1965), dominance tendencies were also found to influence territoriality, but in this case, territoriality both reflected and maintained a relatively stable dominance hierarchy. The most dominant patients were not always the ones with territories, suggesting that for these people the entire ward served as a kind of territory. The middle groups tended to have territories with great exposure, while the low-dominant persons found secluded spots for their territories.

In both settings, it should be emphasized, individuals were confined to a single area (room or ward) and socially isolated from other settings and groups of people. In this area need satisfactions of all kinds, social as well as biological, were necessarily limited to whatever resources existed within its confines. To be dominant then, or to be high in the dominance hierarchy, was to have potential control of these resources, the actual realization of which depended on guaranteeing that certain spaces and objects would always be available to them. Indeed, territoriality, whether achieved through dominance, mutual consent, aggression, or administrative authority, establishes which individuals have access to what areas of a physical setting and, therefore, to what extent their needs will be satisfied. Such possibilities indicate, again, how fundamentally complex territorial behavior in humans differs from territoriality in animals.

This behavior in man is not limited to situations involving physical isolation and confinement. Territorial behavior is instrumental in the definition and organization of various role relationships. In many instances a social or occupational role establishes who can use and control a given space and who cannot. Doctors and nurses but not patients have access to the nurses' station in a hospital; the boss's office is off-limits to those lower down in the hierarchy when he is away, except for his secretary and executive assistant; the teachers' lounge is a privileged area not open to students, parents, or perhaps not even to the principal.

It has been suggested before that a person's sense of identity is fostered by the places and things that are important to him. The loss of valued objects or places, or the involuntary removal from familiar settings for long periods of time, may contribute in some measure to a blurring if not a loss of self-identity. Considered in this context, territoriality becomes one means of establishing and maintaining one's sense of self. In part this may explain why territorial behavior manifests itself under conditions of isolation. The pairs of sailors in the Altman and Haythorn (1967) study may have laid claim to particular places, beds, and chairs not merely to guarantee the satisfaction of biological and social needs, but perhaps as a means of maintaining or preserving their sense of personal identity. Removed from their usual physical surroundings and confined to a single setting with social interaction severely curtailed, a consistent use of specific spaces might have helped these men define their separate identities. With other means of expression limited, territory becomes more than ever an extension of the self.

The variability of this behavior along personality dimensions is illustrated by Altman and Haythorn's studies (1967) of sailors in isolation. One comparison concentrated on interpersonal compatability and the use of space. The quickly established "high territoriality and high social activity" of these groups is cited as evidence of a successful coping with space in terms of the predictive consequences of "being together" in isolation over a period of time. Groups low in affiliation need tended to isolate themselves as time went on and revealed high territorial behavior; "low-dominant" types, contrary to what might be expected, became increasingly territorial in their use of space. Altman suggests that the stress of isolation in such people creates a need for territorial structuring. In this situation, it is the weak (low-dominant) rather than the strong who seek the emotional security of "place."

Territorial behavior can be seen in a wide variety of contexts. With very young children a specific table or chair, as well as their own cubbies, become very important and are the source of many battles in day care centers and nursery schools. In moments of stress preschoolers generally retreat to their "own" places, seeking comfort as much from these physical sites as from protective adults. For the child these may serve as a reminder of his individuality in the group setting. In the home as well, places, through mutual consent, are acknowledged to be mother's, dad's, or a sibling's. In a study of living spaces in urban ghettos, Scheflen and his associates (1971) videorecorded the daily activities of families in their apartments. Each family seemed to have evolved characteristic patterns of use for the various rooms, including an exclusive use of specific spots for specific family members. At times a priority system seemed to guide who was where. When father was home, he had the right to use the couch and TV, and the children often retreated to the edges of the room. Territories were protected by the posture one assumed in them as well as through verbal means.

Such data visually demonstrate what we remember from our own family experiences. The number of occupants in the house, their age, status, and personal habits guide the use and possession of spaces in a way that minimizes conflict. Life style is an important element and includes the combined factors of ethnic origin, economic level, religious background, and stage in the life cycle. The territorial behavior of a family with young children may be quite different from the neighboring family with teenagers, and both will be distinct from the retired couple down the street. Psychological characteristics of individual members may also determine which rooms "belong" to them at specific times. The aggressive teenager may preempt the television space from his younger sister, who retreats to her own room. An older brother coming home from work may in turn take over this territory as "his." The hierarchical use of space is well established at the family level and is often related to power and status within the family.

A type of temporary territoriality exists when places are personalized for brief periods in pursuit of some defined activity. Roos (1968) has called this "jurisdiction." It was observed by him in a study of shipboard life in which sailors laid claim to specific working areas, such as a boiler room or storage locker, where permission was needed to "invade" the space. Brooms and grease rags became symbols of authority. In such instances jurisdiction combines with territorial behavior to give the impersonal and confined existence on shipboard a sense of order.

Although temporary territories have a different meaning from other spaces in the vicinity, there is a limited investment in them on the part of the individual and a limit to their "survival" value or comfort. Studies by Sommer and Becker (1969) used confederates to "claim" chairs and tables by marking them with personal property. The purpose was to see if they could be defended in this manner. In some cases the marked area was usurped by a second confederate. The type of markers, the density of the setting, and the effects on interaction with a neighbor before leaving a marker, among other things, were varied. Sommer and Becker found four factors related to defense: involvement with a neighbor before leaving the area; having a "usurper" directly ask the neighbor if the seat was empty; the length of time the seat was abandoned; and the use of markers.

Territoriality of Groups

A territorial analysis of neighborhoods, especially in urban areas, may help us understand the underlying social order, or disorder, in an area. Just as territorial behavior reduces conflict and enhances identity within the home, neighborhood territories appear to serve a similar group function. Here again analogies with animal territories are of limited usefulness. Whereas infrahumans are, for the most part, biologically motivated in their use of space, the ultimate motivation in people is directed at some primary goal. In cities, for example, the "turfs" and ethnic enclaves so familiar to many of us, represent ways of dealing with the ambiguity and enormity of urban life, where the habits, dress, postures, and communications of people are unfamiliar.

In a field study of the Addams area of Chicago's South Side, Suttles (1968) analyzed the four ethnic groups that lived there: Italians, blacks, Puerto Ricans, and Mexicans. Suttles focused on the strategies used by these groups within the overall territory to seek out a social order. His emphasis was on the differences among the ethnic groups in the way they "claimed" and used their own neighborhoods. On a broad level, members of each group in a specific sector were assured of contacts with those they knew best. Subgroups, in turn, occupied specific territorial units within the larger space. Although people crossed these invisible partitions between territories, they retreated to their "own" areas for most free-time activities.

Additional demarcations served to segregate, to some degree, various age groups, sexes, and residential groupings. Each territory also had its own character. For the Italians, the youthful street-corner groups continued into the adult years as a social athletic club. Among blacks (unlike other groups) girls were given much the same freedom to roam as boys and to form street-corner groups. Mexican girls and boys both had named groups, but they often operated as allies. The Puerto Ricans, most recent in their arrival to Addams and small in number and area, had groups that were still different, less known by their title than by individual members.

Suttles was especially interested in what went on within rather than between adjacent territories, and he does not imply that the territorial order he observed has created conflictless spatial order. He notes, however, that cohesion among the groups was strongest when there was a problem with an adjoining neighborhood. The reader need hardly be reminded that this is the theme of *West Side Story.* It is also poignantly illustrated by Piri Thomas in *Down These Mean Streets* (1967). In a chapter entitled "Alien Turf," Thomas describes what it means for a Puerto Rican family to move from a Puerto Rican block to an Italian block in the East Harlem section of New York City. Aside from being surrounded by people who act, walk, and talk differently, the block was the territory of another gang and the source of much conflict. Since it was impossible for Thomas to get his old friends to pass through the boundary and fight the Italians, the battle had to be faced alone. Status came from his ability to tolerate a fight that ended in his coming close to being blinded.

With man, territory is seldom absolute; what we do with it is subject to public approval, as anyone who has ever tried to add extra rooms to his house soon discovers. On the other hand, although animals may defend territory, there is no evidence that they look upon it as "theirs," certainly not in the sense that it can be passed on to others of the species. For man, ownership implies not mere possession, but the right to dispose of it as the owner wishes. Man is fluid in his relationship to space in comparison with the territorial mammal, who is restricted to relatively fixed boundares; in a sense, space dominates him.

In the final analysis, man's spatial relations transcend physical boundaries. J. B. Calhoun (1970) sees this conceptual space as a means whereby, through modern telecommunications, people manage physical space without having to take personal possession of it. The empire of Howard Hughes is no less a symbol of power because much of it is never visited by its owner. Finally, the locus in which territorial behavior is expressed shifts continually. At one moment we occupy our own property, at other times we have rights (a theatre seat or a restaurant table) in someone else's. Public space—a park or a portion of beach—is shared by many but may be territorialized on the basis of "first come." The temporal element also affects control of space. The sanctum of a business executive is "invaded" by the cleaning staff at night. The night watchman is "in charge" of the building when the owners quit work. In sum, control of space is not absolute; men occupy so many kinds of places at different times that they are continually adjusting territorial relationships with others.

Crowding

As with territoriality, crowding has been extensively studied among animals. Perhaps best known is Calhoun's (1962, 1966) celebrated series of experiments with Norway rats. Four separate but connected pens were arranged in such a way that two of them were most frequently occupied. By controlling the food supply in these two pens Calhoun created conditions of severe overcrowding, with rather dramatic pathological results. Male rats became increasingly violent; infant mortality rose as the females became less adept at nest building; in addition, some males engaged in sexual deviation and cannibalism. Calhoun termed this convergence in an area, and the accompanying pathological behaviors, the "behavioral sink."

Comparable phenomena have been noted among other types of animals. Even under natural conditions the relationship between crowding and behavior is evident, perhaps the best known example being the periodic, headlong exodus of lemmings into the sea. Once thought to represent a unique suicidal urge, such behavior is now seen to represent an ecological "thinning out" that enables the species to survive. A similar die-off was observed among sika deer in the Chesapeake Bay area (see Christian et al. 1960), with the population reduced from one animal per acre to one for every three acres as breeding rate decreased.

Paradoxically, it is not lack of food that accounts for such a "population crash," but an apparent oversupply of food which leads to increased breeding and subsequent overcrowding. In a sense, this is a reversal of the Malthusian doctrine among humans; food supply out-runs the population and creates an intolerable density among the species. Otherwise "healthy" animals, autopsied following their die-off, were found to have greatly enlarged adrenalin glands symptomatic of a pathological degree of stress. This, it is believed, was caused by overcrowding.

Whatever their zoological significance, animal studies are seldom applicable to human processes. The term "crowding" is usually employed when the number of persons in a given unit of space exceeds an optimum standard for comfort and normal functioning. Among social scientists, especially those involved in epidemiological studies, it usually refers to the number of persons per living unit; in western countries, the threshold is usually considered 1.01 or more persons per room. Crowding is sometimes distinguished from *density* and *congestion*. The former is measured by the number of persons per acre of land, or per census tract. Congestion refers to the number or magnitude of activities in excess of the capacity of an area or facility.

Even without a mathematical formula for determining the optimum number of individuals for a particular space, crowding can be recognized in the extensive anecdotal literature of life in Mexican and Puerto Rican slums (Lewis 1959, 1961, 1965) and the many historical incidents cited by Biderman and his associates (1963). The latter, a descriptive and analytic survey, cites examples from the African slave trade to Japanese-American relocation camps. A striking range of statistics is presented. The family barracks of Japanese-American relocation centers offered 437.5 cubic feet per person; the American Prison Association recommends a minimum of 289.0, yet the typical District of Columbia jail cell of 145.0 cubic feet accommodates two men in a space designed for one. The Black Hole of Calcutta allowed 22.0 and the New York Subway car (maximum legal capacity) provides 20.8.

With such extreme examples as the slave-trade ships, the potential dangers and stress from poor air quality, uncomfortable temperatures, minimal sanitation, and postural constraints on sleep become apparent. Even without a fine distinction of what constitutes an optimal space, these examples clearly indicate "overcrowding." They also reveal man's ability to tolerate and survive such conditions, at least for temporary periods. Even under less extreme conditions human capacities and options in dealing with crowds go beyond that of other species. A person can feel crowded even though few people are present. In particular circumstances he may enjoy masses of people about. His abstract powers also serve him well in crowded conditions as he joins with others to better conditions (an explanation for the ability of some who survived the extreme crowding cited in Biderman). He can plan for a future that extends beyond the specific crowded setting. He also possesses a wide repertoire of behavioral maneuvers such as eye aversion, shallow breathing, going within himself, and fantasy, although these may be more effective in acute temporary crowding rather than chronic situations. To the extent that the optimum number of individuals in a physical setting can be maintained or achieved by increasing or redesigning space, the unpleasant effects of crowding can be reduced. Unfortunately, enlarged spaces are frequently outgrown, just as adaptation to crowding reaches an ultimate threshold.

Crowding is not necessarily close physical contact. For a community center, schoolroom, hospital ward, or similar institutional setting, optimum space must be considered in relation to the facilities and services provided and the number of people using them. The thirty-bed ward in which five extra beds have been installed will generally be perceived as crowded if only because nursing services are spread over a larger number of patients. Even if individuals and places available are matched, the nature of the activity, rather than the number of persons per se, may be the important factor. Ten desks may fit in a large office area, but if the work involves intense concentration this could well be too many for the space.

Our previous discussion suggests that crowding is a psychological as well as an objectively viewed social phenomenon. Its conceptualization as both a concomitant and consequence of modern life goes beyond the question of the number of persons in an available space. How a space is organized, for what purposes, and what kinds of activities are involved are all factors that contribute to the phenomenology of crowding.

Crowding may be experienced as pleasurable as well as painful. There are those who thrill to the excitement of the crowded city. Clearly the crowded theatre, stadium, or party, other things being equal, contribute to defining these situations positively. Of course, crowded areas that have positive effects or are enjoyed because they are crowded are seldom described as crowded. In most cases physical settings cited by the individual as crowded are meant to have negative connotations, experienced by him as unpleasant or even painful and to be avoided.

Under what circumstances, then, does the individual feel crowded? Much will depend on what he has experienced in the past in similar settings and therefore what he is willing to accept in the present. Cultural and subcultural differences in the use and organization of space may also explain acceptable levels of crowd density (Schmitt 1963; Hall 1966; Lucas 1964). The "slick" coats worn by passengers in the Tokyo subways to facilitate their way through the hordes of riders suggest that the range of normative adjustments is indeed extensive. Even so, the tolerance of the Japanese for such conditions eventually gave way, and a mass rebellion of commuters took place in 1973.

When culturally established expectancies in the use of space are not confirmed, this too may induce a sense of crowding. Once having learned to perform a task in a given setting with a given number of individuals, any increase in this number may be experienced as crowding by each person in the situation. It is important to note, however, that the failure to confirm normative expectations with respect to space cannot contribute to a sense of crowding in isolation from other factors. To find that space cannot be used as one expects means more to the individual than just the experience of a lack of fulfilling an expectancy. The addition of another person to a private office may mean many other things for the original occupant: that he can no longer behave in exactly the same fashion; that he must accommodate his working habits to that of another; and that in fact what was once his must be shared.

The phenomenology of crowding must also take into account sheer physical discomfort or pain. The jammed, rush-hour buses in many urban centers or even the crowded shopping centers are cases in point. Although these conditions are indeed normal for these settings, it does not diminish the sense of being crowded. Acceptance is that form of adaptation to negative situations in which the individual's ability to change these situations is neutralized but not his ability to experience the pain and discomfort they induce—although over long periods of time even the intensity of these feelings may be reduced. Conversely, anticipation of crowding may discourage one from going into crowded areas, whether the shopping center during the pre-Christmas period or public transportation during rush hours. Clearly, this is not an inviolable rule. There are times when human beings unexpectedly select the crowded over an equally convenient less crowded area. Winkel and Hayward (1971), observing the use of subway platforms, found a tendency toward clustering in the vicinity of the entrance points even when more space was available a slight distance away. It was unclear why people would not move, even when there was time to do so. Was it habit, lack of energy, enjoyment of crowds, protection from others? It was impossible to tell. What was clear in this situation was the willingness of people to tolerate the presence of many others.

It seems apparent, then, that crowding as a psychological phenomenon is only indirectly related to mere numbers or densities. The significant element appears to be in the fact that the presence of others frustrates the individual in the achievement of some purpose. In some cases there appears to be a depersonalization. The individual loses his sense of identity, and the many others take on the characteristics of objects. It should be recognized that the crowding in itself may be necessary to the purpose or in some way related to it. Under such conditions, frustration is less likely. People prefer a packed to a sparsely populated grandstand at athletic events because the presence of others adds to the excitement. The roar of the crowd is part of the fun.

Experimental Studies

A number of investigators have sought to uncover the possible effects of crowding on such factors as task performance, judgment, and psychological reaction. One must bear in mind the variety of definitions employed and the range of concentrations of people labeled "crowding."

In an experiment dealing with the effects of hot and crowded conditions, Griffitt and Veitch (1971) concluded that a stranger entering a room in which both density and temperature were high was likely to be met with more hostility than would be the case where crowding alone was the variable. Less conclusive results were found in a series of experiments by Freedman (n.d.). In one study, males in a confined, high-density environment showed distinct signs of aggressiveness whereas females did not. Women actually seemed to like being crowded. When asked to render "verdicts" based on taped courtroom cases, the men in a small, crowded room gave more severe sentences than those in a larger and less crowded room. However, the women's verdicts under these same experimental conditions did not differ. More recently Freedman, Klevansky, and Ehrlich (1971) tested subjects for simple and complex task performances and found no appreciable difference between "crowded" and "uncrowded" conditions.

Individuals sometimes react to the stresses of crowding by withdrawing into themselves or into a "private" space. Whether it is the temporary escape from a crowded apartment or party, the nursery school child to his cubby, or Esser's patients territorializing their ward space to relieve the conditions of institutional life, all seem directed toward controlling the range of person-stimuli inputs. This was shown in a study by Hutt and Vaizey (1966) of the effects of group size on children's behavior. Normal, autistic, and brain-damaged children were observed in a playroom setting. Although the numbers in this study did not reach high levels of crowding (the groups consisting of six or seven, to eleven or twelve children) very specific reactions were seen. As the group size increased, brain-damaged children became more aggressive; the normal children tended to reduce their social encounters and autistic children spent more time at the boundaries of the room. Normal children increased in aggressiveness in the largest group. The autistic children seemed to react with negligible aggression as the group size increased, but in the largest group their encounters with the adults increased. A wide range of stress reactions appeared with behaviors that were specific to the size and composition of the group.

In a series of studies, similar but not completely comparable to the Hutt and Vaizey approach, McGrew (1972) considered two issues relevant to density effects, the number of children and the available space. This research, based on observations of free play in a variety of nursery school settings, described a series of changes in play as the conditions were varied. Most interesting was the finding that social density, that is, increases in group size, had a greater disruptive effect than spatial density. At high group density levels this research supported the Hutt and Vaizey finding of a reduction in nonaggressive social interactions.

What this suggests is that possible reactions to a crowd will vary widely on the basis of an individual's psychological status as well as his immediate needs and purposes. The overstimulated child, seeking relief from the presence of others, may retreat to his own space, to an adult in his vicinity, or to the periphery of the room in order to find himself. An adult may embed himself in a large group to satisfy his social-emotional needs. Cook (1963) speaks of "productive density"—allowing the individual a variety of choices so that he selects the interactions he prefers. Perhaps density in this sense cannot be called crowding, since it implies options that the involuntary or overwhelming crowd does not. What does seem critical is an understanding of the person's goals at the moment, for the productive density of one moment may be the unbearable crowd of another.

Privacy

On the surface it might appear that privacy is the direct opposite of crowding. However, it is perhaps the more complicated construct. Whether it is Biderman's descriptions of the disregard for "principles of privacy and propriety" in the case of the steerage passengers of immigrant ships (1963), or the need to withdraw, physically or psychically, into some private place to avoid too many others, privacy and crowding are often linked.

Privacy can be defined as an individual's freedom to choose what he will communicate about himself and to whom he will communicate it in a given circumstance (see Proshansky et al. 1970:173–183). Obviously the conditions under which one experiences this freedom to choose vary widely with situation and purpose. As in the case of crowding research, there is an abundance of anecdotal evidence on the importance of privacy in day-to-day existence. Descriptions of lack of privacy and its consequences among ghetto families are reported by Lewis (1959, 1961, 1965) and Schorr (1966).

Kuper's (1953) study of a housing unit near Coventry, England, uncovered much that related to the residents' lack of privacy.

> The Burtons' boy, aged 8, complains that he was seen in his pyjamas by the little girl across the road. . . . [T]here is a feeling among residents that neighbors know when they receive callers. . . . Mr. Dudley tells us: "There is no privacy. . . . You look across at the houses there—they must feel as though you are looking at them. You look out of the bedroom window into their bedrooms. . . . You turn the corner coming home and everybody's eyes are on you. . . . [Pp. 22–24]

Kuper speaks of the "community of the eye." In a society sensitive to its right to privacy he might also have called it the community of the ear. The proximity of the houses studied and poor insulation ensured a breaking of the sound barrier; little was left to the imagination. Notable was the fact that even within this one housing development standards for privacy varied. Some people were bothered more than others and some bothered not at all by the physical setting.

In many situations overcrowding creates social isolation which in turn evokes a sense of loss of privacy. Vischer (1919) reports that the main complaint of French and German prisoners during World War I was the lack of privacy engendered by constant contact with other prisoners. From Vischer's account it is clear that irritability and resentment, revealed in excessive fault-finding and boasting about themselves, was an attempt to maintain personal identity in the face of a complete lack of privacy in day-to-day existence. In a very different setting, the *kibbutz* or communal settlement, Weingarten (1955) reports that some of the smaller settlements did not survive because the same small number of individuals were unable to continue living with each other in an isolated setting. Frustration and tension can be produced in communal life if the continual awareness of other persons and the constant exposure to public opinion result in the loss of the ability to achieve privacy when it is wanted.

Paradoxically, perhaps, physical isolation from others does not always produce a contrasting sense of privacy. In a study of relatively remote communities in the Arctic, Smith (1968) found that there was less "neighboring" than one would expect during the long and dark winters. Somehow, individuals and families did not get deeply involved with each other, and when visiting took place, it tended to be between more remote persons rather than close neighbors. Was this a need to maintain privacy from those within eye's view, a turning away from relationships that might become too intense and intrusive? It is very difficult to say, but there seems to be some connection between relative isolation and privacy, just as there does between absolute isolation and anomie.

Privacy, however, is not the same as isolation. They may seem alike, but they represent different degrees of choice for the individual. A few persons isolated in a room may not enjoy a sense of privacy. The isolation of one person alone may result not in privacy but in anomie or rootlessness.

Altman and Haythorn's (1967) pairs of sailors experienced little privacy except, possibly, as internalized fantasy. In one of their experiments (Taylor, Wheeler, & Altman 1968) a number of variables were added, including that of privacy. In addition to eight actual days of isolation half the group was given a private room. Other variables consisted of providing stimulation measures (documentaries and so forth) versus no stimulations and two conceptions of the length of the mission (being told it was to be four versus twenty days). Without presenting the detailed results, we might focus on the role of the environmental provision for privacy. The authors emphasize that each variable tended to interact with others. The most stressful condition appeared to be the twenty-day mission *with* privacy and no stimulation. The short missions, with stimulation, with or without privacy, were least stressful.

The authors caution against a simplistic conception of the role of physical privacy as a stress-reducing factor, at least in the case of isolated groups. In this study the provision for privacy may have prevented the development of a system for coping with the stress of isolation and confinement.

Theoretical Conceptions of Privacy

The term "privacy" evokes a wide range of conceptions, not all directly relevant to the design and organization of the physical setting. For those relevant conceptions, differences in emphasis and approach still remain. Yet decisions involving the design and use of space are still made as if the meaning of privacy were clear and its implications for individuals and groups were fully understood.

Chermayeff and Alexander (1963) and Westin (1967) have provided definitions of privacy that seem especially useful. Of the two, Westin goes further in attempting a systematic analysis of the various states of privacy and their related functions. It is from his definition that the one presented earlier is derived. Westin (1967) defines privacy as:

> . . . the claim of individuals, groups or institutions to determine for themselves when, how and to what extent information about themselves is communicated to others. Viewed in terms of the relation of the individual to social participation, privacy is the voluntary and temporary withdrawal of a person from the general society through physical or psychological means, either in a state of solitude or small-group intimacy or, when among larger groups, in a condition of anonymity or reserve. [p. 7]

As a political scientist reflecting the changing nature of American sociopolitical structure, Westin states his definition in normative-value terms. To speak of privacy as a right of the individual is meaningful primarily in the context of a democratic society. But this raises a host of related questions: To what extent does the individual actually enjoy this right? What factors in American society facilitate its expression and what factors inhibit it? In terms of the changing character of the urban setting, even if given this right, is it possible to achieve privacy?

For the environmental psychologist an individual's right to make decisions about his privacy is less important than the question of the function of privacy—what it means to him. What are his needs with respect to privacy; and what does he want his physical world to be like in the light of these needs? Day-to-day experience already tells us that cultural and subcultural factors undoubtedly play a role in what individuals want and expect in the way of privacy. Still another task is to specify the conditions under which such needs are aroused and satisfied. Finally, there remains the crucial question of the consequences that follow from the persistent frustration of human needs for privacy; or alternatively, the question of whether there are any conditions under which privacy ceases to be important.

The significance of these questions is revealed by Westin's analysis of the four basic states of privacy and their related functions. These are defined as solitude, intimacy, anonymity, and reserve. Let us review them in turn.

Solitude is a state of privacy in which the person is alone and free from observation by other people. The key words here are *observation by other people.* The individual is still subjected to auditory, olfactory, and tactile stimuli as well as pain, heat, and cold. Solitude, then, is a complete state of visual isolation and is close but not as complete as the definition of privacy given by Chermayeff and Alexander (1963) as ". . . that marvelous compound of withdrawal, self-reliance, solitude, contemplation and concentration"; or Shils' (1966) characterization of privacy as a "zero-relationship between a group and a person."

Intimacy refers to the individual's need for privacy as a member of a pair or larger group that seeks to achieve maximum personal relationships between or among its members, for example, husband and wife, family, or peer group. Here the privacy that is sought goes beyond mere freedom from visual surveillance. There is an attempt to minimize all sensory input from outside the boundaries of an appropriate physical setting.

Anonymity, Westin's third state of privacy, occurs when the individual seeks and is able to achieve freedom from identification and surveillance while in a public setting, for example, walking in the street, sitting in a park, riding the subway, or attending an artistic event. To be self-consciously aware that one is being directly and deliberately observed in public is to lose the sense of ease and relaxation that is often sought in such a setting.

Reserve is Westin's final state of privacy, and in a sense it is not only the most complex of the four states from the point of view of psychological need, but its arousal and satisfaction lie more in the nature of interpersonal relationships than in the nature and organization of the physical setting. Stated simply, even in the most intimate situations each person involved has a need to withhold certain aspects of himself that are either too personal, shameful, or profane. It gives rise to psychological distance, the psychic equivalent of social distance. To achieve reserve individuals in group situations must each claim it for himself and respect it in others.

In discussing these functions, Westin again establishes a fourfold classification. Basic is the need for *personal autonomy*: a sense of individuality and conscious choice in which the person controls his environment in order to have privacy when and if he desires it. Privacy, whether through solitude, intimacy, or anonymity, may also serve the function of *emotional release.* Social and biological factors in everyday life create tension; thus, from the point of view of physical and mental health, periods of privacy are required for the unwinding of emotional states, states that may be the result of conditions and experiences of crowding.

The opportunity for *self-evaluation* is also needed. To take stock of oneself in the light of a continuing stream of information, the person must remove himself from events in order to integrate and assimilate this information. Indeed, in a state of solitude or withdrawal, the individual not only processes information but he also makes plans by interpreting and recasting it, and anticipating his subsequent behaviors.

Finally, Westin sees privacy serving the function of *limited and protected communication,* which in turn serves two important needs for the individual. First, it enables him to share confidences and intimacies with those he trusts; and second, limited communication establishes a psychological distance when the individual desires it or when it is required. Clearly, in many roles, psychological distance or limited communication is required and may be achieved through physical arrangements such as private offices or areas designated "for employees only."

As a preliminary step, Westin's analytical schema for privacy is both provocative and useful, if for no other reason than it seeks out the critical dimensions of the concept. On the other hand, it raises certain questions. For example, the four states of privacy are not always conceptually clear or consistent with each other. "Solitude" describes the state of the individual's relationship to the physical environment rather than his *experience* of solitude. "Intimacy" defines a very close relationship between two people in terms of psychological distance, which is achieved by seclusion from others. Yet this classification overlooks certain kinds of small groups, such as juries, in which members are only formally related to each other because of their involvement with a common task and where privacy is a necessity and intimacy frowned upon.

Still another problem is that relationships among the four states are not considered. Thus, it might be useful to distinguish between individual states of privacy (solitude and anonymity) and group states of privacy (intimacy and reserve). It is also apparent that intimacy and reserve are closely related. Intimacy is achieved by two or more individuals, whereas reserve is a limiting condition placed on that privacy by each of the "intimate" members of the group.

Westin defines privacy as the right of the individual to determine when and what information he should make available about himself to others. These states of privacy specify certain socially prescribed conditions under which various types of behaviors become acceptable. Although these conditions vary widely, they all have the common property of maximizing the individual's choices. The definition also recognizes the paradoxical fact that privacy is essentially a social phenonemon and that it includes the freedom to communicate differently with other individuals and groups. Tasks carry different demand qualities in terms of privacy. Some tasks need or can tolerate communication with others. To make a difficult decision, transmit an important message, or evaluate an employee's work, all imply some state of privacy. Through verbal and nonverbal communication we signal our privacy even if we are in public. The detachment, the intense concentration either of the individual or of the small group are cues to the psychological distance that facilitates privacy. But at times we need clearer signals, physical distance, or perhaps a barrier. The jury needs a room removed from others, and so do lovers in almost all cultures. In our society it is customary for a person who receives news of a tragedy to separate himself from others. Without proper environmental props or supports, the grief may be impossible to work out.

We have earlier discussed Westin's view of privacy in the interests of *personal autonomy,* the perception of ourselves as separate beings. Some psychologists feel that unless men see themselves as individually "self-governing" they cannot realize or experience privacy. In a broad sense privacy is power —power over who shall or shall not control our actions. The child who waits for the adults to turn their backs in order to play with matches or eat the forbidden candy is exercising the power over himself that comes only with privacy; recognizing the areas in which adults exert power over him, he has managed to escape the control of others, no matter how temporary this freedom may be.

This view of privacy is related to the autonomy that comes with territorial control; we use space (our private office, the park bench that we "claim" every morning) to reinforce the sense of self that comes from being in command of a particular place.

Creative privacy is essential for most people who paint, write, compose, or engage in research. This implies a need to control inputs from the outside world. These inputs may be sounds or smells or the potential intrusion of people through telephone or personal contacts. Each of our privacies, moreover, is somewhat different. As the goals vary, the environmental supports may differ as well. For the creator, absolute physical isolation may be needed. For the person in a public setting who withdraws psychologically, the stimuli may surround him, but their demand qualities are not reaching him.

In the past few decades a good deal has been written about the electronic invasion of privacy through the "bugging" of rooms and telephone taps. Allied to this has been a cybernetic intrusion into our private lives via the computer and the data bank. There is little doubt that for modern man, in an industrial society, these forces represent a limitation on his freedom. They make it more difficult for him to choose what he shall or shall not disclose about himself to others. Westin and Baker (1972) have recently completed a study of some fifty-one organizations (including government bureaus) where data banks are widely used. The authors conclude that, in spite of the charges against their use, man is still master of the machine, and, in any case, that the precomputer age is wrongly romanticized as a time of privacy. It is not the machine but what man does with it that makes the difference.

It is difficult to find cultures where privacy is entirely absent, although interestingly, as Sally Higman (1971) notes, the Greek language has no word that corresponds precisely to "privacy" in English. Some societies seem to minimize the need while others, including our own, emphasize privacy. Even communal groups find that despite shared quarters the desire for privacy is never completely lost. A study by Hackett and Sun (1972) noted a shift toward more individual, private dwellings such as tents, trailers, and huts. This is a recent development in many Israeli *kibbutzim* as well. In a study of urban communes by Winkel and O'Mara (1973) similar findings were observed, with privacy needs evidenced in the personalization of living areas and strongly verbalized feelings about the need for privacy.

Work in psychiatric facilities for children and adults, as well as studies now in progress in school and day care settings, have underscored the theme of privacy needs and norms over the developmental continuum. The institutional setting, whether total or partial, seems to increase privacy needs. Observations of bedroom size and use in a psychiatric ward (Ittelson et al. 1970a, b) indicated that the *smaller*, more private rather than the larger room was associated with the greatest variety of behavior. Such behaviors were of a wide range from the more isolated to the very social. Larger bedrooms tended to be used for more isolated and personal functions. Given a chance to select the size of room they would prefer, most patients wanted the double or single rooms.

Children are equally aware of their need for privacy. Unfortunately, in our culture a child's privacy rights are very limited. They are expected to be "on view" during much if not all of their day, and when they are not, there is usually an automatic assumption that some mischief is afoot. Interviews by Laufer and Wolfe (1973) now in progress are documenting the conceptions of privacy held by children, from kindergarten through high school years. There appears to be a developmental sequence in what is regarded as private, as well as where and how to obtain privacy. This apparently begins with the child's realization of the privacy rights of others, generally the parents. These preliminary data suggest that our conceptions of the areas in which we can have privacy, the settings which support it, and the techniques to enforce it are learned through the observation of adults, largely by experiencing exclusion from their lives.

Our interviews in a children's psychiatric hospital have also emphasized the importance of privacy rights for children. The children have expressed the many difficulties they have in finding places where they could be by themselves. In response to a question about suggestions for changes, a common idea was the need for a place away from others; not the seclusion room with its punitive function and meanings, but a place where they could sit. read, or just listen to music when they so desired.

Observations of day care centers and open schools seem to support this view. The open school or classroom is an intriguing example. This is a setting in which varying degrees of physical openness accompany an individualized approach to learning. Children move about the rooms, select their materials and a place to use them, and, to a greater or lesser degree, they program their own days. Rothenberg's (1972) interviews in one of these schools were very revealing. Children yearned to get away from the flux, flow, and stimulation of others, at least for some parts of their day. Many of these open schools have begun to provide private spots in the form of reading areas, raised platforms, or makeshift enclosures within the room. Where they are not provided, the children learn to find them on their own, whether it is a clothes closet, a small recess between equipment, or some other confined space. The message seems to be that for the child's day, as for an adult's, varying degrees and types of both socialization and privacy are needed. But these needs can be met only if the environmental supports are available.

Jourard's (1966) analysis of the psychology of privacy suggests that our architecture makes it very difficult to find "inviolate privacy." Our living areas, he feels, have become much like prisons or dormitories, creating a sense of being condemned to our various roles.

The environment plays a crucial role in supporting privacy needs, whether on the level of the individual dwelling, the neighborhood, or the entire city. Certain contemporary houses are said to lack privacy because of a lack of partitions. A block of tenement buildings compares unfavorably in this respect with a quiet residential street. In large office spaces employees are constrained by the presence of others, including supervisors; to furnish privacy is not the intention of the space.

Few people desire privacy all of the time; indeed, the need to affiliate is equally strong. Private control of one's actions means the ability to decide when and on what basis this social communication will occur, and it is in this sense that environmental props are important. The adage that good fences make good neighbors states the case for privacy in terms of physical boundaries. Although this largely territorial view is simplistic in many ways, it expresses an aspect of the question that is often overlooked. Social interaction is more easily achieved when people's social needs are balanced by the sense of individual autonomy that comes with privacy. It is the ambiguous spaces, which are neither public nor private, that tend to mitigate against interaction, since the individual is less able to control the interaction on his own terms. This may be a drawback of communal living; everybody's space is nobody's space.

In the hospital studies by Ittelson and others (1970a, b), physical privacy was seen as a prerequisite to much socially interactive behavior because it provided patients with a setting that permitted a wider range of personal choices. Michelson (1970) found this to be equally true in a somewhat larger setting. Studying social interaction among residents of a housing development in suburban Toronto, he found that housewives with open spaces that they defined as their own, even though they did not own them, knew more people than women who did not have these spaces. Women whose contacts took place in what Michelson describes as the "no-mansland" of interior hallways were less likely to use these as opportunities for socializing. The families who shared such common spaces were the ones that were more likely to "keep their distance."

We have indicated two dimensions of privacy that are relevant to environmental design: freedom from unwanted intrusion and freedom to determine the time and place of communication. A third dimension concerns the individual's instrumental goals. The open architectural environment, whether a school or an office, often makes fantasy the only possible form of privacy. Yet at times this form of escape may run counter to the occupational or educational goals. We have mentioned that some schools offer the child educationally relevant spaces to which he can physically retreat and where, in terms of goals, privacy becomes meaningful. In large "bull pen" offices, where the activities of workers constantly impinge on each other, a group of employees may arrange filing cabinets and bookcases to make private space. But this means little unless the rearrangement of props allows the individual or the group to achieve privacy in terms of their job performance. Conversely, the man in a private office may experience little privacy if his job permits others to have unrestricted access to him. The "private" cell in a prison is usually reserved for extra punishment. Here, as in many instances, the setting prevents the true privacy that comes when a choice of environments is possible. From the design perspective, which is discussed more fully in Chapter Eleven, the environment offers options; man determines how these will be used to strike the balance between privacy and communication that seems desirable at any given time.

Summary and Conclusions

This chapter has explored the social interaction process in environmental terms. To do so four constructs have been considered at length: personal space, territoriality, crowding, and privacy. These are not to be thought of in themselves as explanations of behavior. For our purpose they are descriptive and, as such, useful for understanding how certain kinds of individual and group behaviors are affected by the physical properties of the setting and those who occupy it.

Four points may help clarify this relationship: (1) The individual traits and social experiences which the person brings to a setting influence his response to environmental variables. In short, man is socialized to behave appropriately in relation to specific physical environments and the people within them. We have described this behavior in terms of sociocultural norms. (2) The constructs discussed above are broadly interrelated. Each influences, to some extent, how the others will be experienced. (3) To a considerable degree they become habitual, and over time seem "natural" ways of behaving in certain situations. In fact, they are usually learned through prolonged contact with others. (4) One engages in these behaviors not simply for their own sake, but to maximize one's *freedom of choice* in achieving certain goals (see Proshansky et al. 1970). In this sense, spaces, and the objects in an environment, are both a context and a means to an end. The setting that provides alternative ways of satisfying primary and subsidiary purposes is one that gives the individual the greatest freedom of choice. It is in this sense that we can speak of man's ecological or "spatial" behavior in relation to the environment.

Freedom of choice appears to be a helpful unifying concept in organizing and clarifying a wide range of other terms and related behaviors. Thus, the root quality of privacy, whether it is achieved by structuring the physical environment or by virtue of how a person relates to others who are continually present, lies in its capacity to maximize the individual's freedom of choice. This ability is no less evident with respect to territorial behavior. To the degree that an individual can lay claim to and secure a given spatial area or object, he maximizes his choices relevant to that area or object. When he controls the available alternatives, he can achieve privacy and satisfy other relevant needs. Invasion of his territory, for instance, reduces his freedom of choice. Similarly, an increase in the number of individuals in a setting will reach the point where it is experienced as crowding, with what is perhaps less than a conscious realization that one's freedom of choice is thereby reduced. A similar situation exists for isolation. Although we have not systematically dealt with isolation, it too represents a condition of reduced options for the individual experiencing it. Whether it is the sailor placed in an isolated experimental setting or Arctic residents facing a long winter, there is a reduction in freedom of choice.

Such freedom, however, implies more than the qualities of the setting. One can imagine settings that appear to satisfy a wide variety of needs but still evoke rather stereotyped and limited reactions on the part of participants. Other people, however, may perceive the widest range of possibilities. Freedom is thus a function both of the setting and of the attributes of the person that enable him to perceive—or fail to perceive—its potential usefulness in meeting his needs. This does not mean that environmental freedom exists in isolation of other restrictions on behavior—the formal and informal rules and regulations that govern the use of a place. However, it is the environmental component of free choice that has traditionally been ignored.

Our concern here has been with the process by which people position themselves in a setting so that they can accurately cognize and move freely in it to achieve goal satisfactions. A familiar environment, in which the individual routinely satisfies particular needs, is less likely to require continual adaptation. A new setting, on the other hand, or a familiar setting that changes, will result in an attempt to reorganize one's relationship to the environment so that freedom of choice is maximized. When this is not possible, all kinds of problems may arise, problems generally directed toward other people rather than the environment.

Few environments are static. Changes in light, sound, and temperature may either increase or decrease the need for adaptation and correspondingly affect one's freedom of choice. If a meeting room is improperly lighted, the occupants may be unable to read their notes; they may not be able to see the expressions and gestures of others that constitute nonverbal communication. The addition of many people to a room may limit one's ability to carry on a particular activity. At the same time, if the structure of the setting precludes a desired behavior, alterations may be undertaken. In this way the range of available choices is expanded. It should be noted, however, that every expansion of possibilities through environmental manipulation limits the possibility of other choices. Optimum freedom in an existing setting is achieved through the interaction of the individual with other persons, places, and things—interactions which are implicated in the concepts of personal space, territorial preferences, crowding, and the need for privacy. Both social roles and individual differences affect the way in which one experiences this process to attain his goals, and many different types of strategies and devices may be attempted in an effort to maximize choices. The general theme of this chapter has been to review the various social limits on one's freedom in an environmental context.

References

Aiello, J. R., and Jones, S. E. Field study of the proxemic behavior of young school children in three subcultural groups. *Journal of Personality and Social Psychology,* 1971, *19,* 351–356.

Altman, I., and Haythorn, W. The ecology of isolated groups. *Behavioral Science,* 1967, *12,* 169–181. [Reprinted in H. M. Proshansky et al. (Eds.), *Environmental psychology: Man and his physical setting.* New York: Holt, Rinehart and Winston, 1970. Pp. 226–239.]

Ardrey, R. *The territorial imperative.* New York: Atheneum, 1966.

Argyle, M., and Dean, J. Eye contact, distance and affiliation. *Sociometry,* 1965, *28,* 289–304.

Athanasiou, R., and Yoshioka, G. A. The spatial character of friendship formation. *Enviroment and Behavior,* 1973, 5, 43–65.

Biderman, A. D., Louria, M., and Bacchus, J. *Historical incidents of extreme overcrowding.* Washington, D. C.: Bureau of Social Science Research, Inc., 1963.

Brown, R. *Social psychology.* New York: Free Press, 1965.

Calhoun, J. B. Population density and social pathology. *Scientific American,* 1962, *206,* 139–148.

Calhoun, J. B. The role of space in animal sociology. *Journal of Social Issues,* 1966, *22* (4), 46–59. [Reprinted in H. M. Proshansky et al. (Eds.), *Environmental psychology: Man and his physical setting.* New York: Holt, Rinehart and Winston, 1970. Pp. 195–202.]

Calhoun, J. B. Space and the strategy of life. *Ekistics,* 1970, *29*, 425–437.

Canon, L. K., and Mathews, K. E., Jr. The influence of ambient noise level on the body buffer zone. Unpublished manuscript, University of New Hampshire, 1973.

Chermayeff, S., and Alexander, C. *Community and privacy: Toward a new architecture of humanism.* New York: Doubleday, 1963.

Christian, J. J., Flyger, V., and Davis, D. E. Factors in mass mortality of a herd of sika deer (*Cervus nippon*). *Chesapeake Science,* 1960, *1,* 79–95.

Cook, D. A. Cultural innovation and disaster in the American city. In L. J. Duhl (Ed.), *The urban condition: People and policy in the metropolis.* New York: Basic Books, 1963. Pp. 87–93.

Deutsch, M., and Collins, M. E. *Interracial housing: A psychological evaluation of a social experiment.* Minneapolis, Minn.: University of Minnesota Press, 1951.

Esser, A. H., Chamberlain, A. S., Chapple, E. D., and Kline, N. S. Territoriality of patients on a research ward. In J. Wortis (Ed.), *Recent advances in biological psychiatry,* 1965, *7,* 36–44. [Reprinted in H. M. Proshansky et al. (Eds.), *Enviromental psychology: Man and his physical setting.* New York: Holt, Rinehart and Winston, 1970. Pp. 208–214.]

Felipe, N. J., and Sommer, R. Invasion of personal space. *Social Problems,* 1966, *14,* 206–214.

Feshbach, S. and Feshbach, N. Influence of the stimulus object upon the complementary and supplementary projection of fear. *Journal of Abnormal and Social Psychology,* 1963, *66,* 498–502.

Festinger, L., Schacter, S., and Back, K. *Social pressures in informal groups: A study of human factors in housing.* Stanford, Calif.: Stanford University Press, 1950.

Freedman, J. L. The effect of crowding on human behavior. New York: Unpublished manuscript, Columbia University, n. d.

Freedman, J. L., Klevansky, S., and Erlich, P. R. The effect of crowding on human task performance. *Journal of Applied Social Psychology,* 1971, *1,* 7–25.

Fry, A. M., and Willis, F. N. Invasion of personal space as a function of the age of the invader. *The Psychological Record,* 1971, *21,* 385–389.

Gans, H. The balanced community. *Journal of the American Institute of Planners,* 1961, *27,* 176–184.

Garfinkel, H. Studies of the routine grounds of everyday activities. *Social Problems,* 1964, *11,* 225–250.

Grant, S. S. Spatial behavior and caste membership in some North Indian villages. Unpublished doctoral dissertation, City University of New York, 1971.

Griffitt, W., and Veitch, R. Hot and crowded: Influences of population density and temperatures on interpersonal affective behavior. *Journal of Personality and Social Psychology,* 1971, *17,* 92–98.

Hackett, B., and Sun, A. Communal architecture and social structure. In W. J. Mitchell (Ed.), *Environmental design: Research and practice–Proceedings of the EDRA 3/AR 8 Conference.* Los Angeles: University of California Press, 1972.

Hall, E. T. *The hidden dimension.* Garden City, N. Y.: Doubleday, 1966.

Hearn, G. Leadership and the spatial factor in small groups. *Journal of Abnormal and Social Psychology,* 1957, *54,* 269–272.

Hediger, H. *Wild animals in captivity.* New York: Dover, 1964.
Hediger, H. *The psychology and behavior of animals in zoos and circuses.* New York: Dover, 1968.
Higman, S. Level of living indexes: Five metropolitan case studies. *Ekistics,* 1971, *32,* 32–40.
Horowitz, M. J., Duff, D. F., and Stratton, L. O. Body buffer zone: Exploration of personal space. *Archives of General Psychiatry,* 1964, *11,* 651–656. [Reprinted as Personal space and the body-buffer zone. In H. M. Proshansky et al. (Eds.), *Environmental psychology: Man and his physical setting.* New York: Holt, Rinehart and Winston, 1970. Pp. 214–220.]
Howard, H. E. *Territory in bird life.* London: J. Murray, 1920.
Hutt, C. and Vaizey, M. J. Differential effects of group density on social behavior. *Nature,* 1966, *209,* 1371–1372.
Ittelson, W. H., Proshansky, H. M., and Rivlin, L. G. A study of bedroom use on two psychiatric wards. *Hospital and Community Psychiatry,* 1970a, *21,* 177–180.
Ittelson, W. H., Proshansky, H. M., and Rivlin, L. G. Bedroom size and social interaction of the psychiatric ward. *Environment and Behavior,* 1970b, *2,* 255–270.
Jones, S. E., and Aiello, J. R. Proxemic behavior of black and white first, third and fifth grade children. *Journal of Personality and Social Psychology,* 1973, *25,* 21–27.
Jourard, S. M. Some psychological aspects of privacy. *Law and Contemporary Problems,* 1966, *31,* 307–318.
Kleck, R. Physical stigma and task oriented interactions. *Human Relations,* 1969, *22,* 53–60.
Kuper, L. Neighbour on the hearth. In L. Kuper (Ed.), *Living in towns.* London: The Cresset Press, 1953.
Laufer, R. S., and Wolfe, M. Privacy as an age-related concept. Paper presented at the meeting of the American Psychological Association, Montreal, August, 1973.
Leavitt, H. J. Some effects of certain communication patterns on group performance. *Journal of Abnormal Social Psychology,* 1951, *46,* 38–50.
Leibman, M. The effects of sex and race norms on personal space. *Environment and Behavior,* 1970, *2,* 208–246.
Lewis, O. *Five families.* New York: Basic Books, 1959.
Lewis, O. *The children of Sanchez.* New York: Random House, 1961.
Lewis, O. *La vida.* New York: Random House, 1965.
Leyhausen, P. The communal organization of solitary mammals. In *Symposium of the Zoological Society of London,* 1965, No. 14, 249–263. [Reprinted in H. M. Proshansky et al. (Eds.), *Environmental psychology: Man and his physical setting.* New York: Holt, Rinehart and Winston, 1970. Pp. 183–195.]
Lorenz, K. *On aggression.* New York: Harcourt, 1966.
Lott, D., and Sommer, R. Seating arrangements and status. *Journal of Personality and Social Psychology,* 1967, *7,* 90–95.
Lucas, R. C. User concepts of wilderness and their implications for resource management. In *Western Resources Conference Book—New horizons for resources research: Issues and methodology.* Boulder, Colo.: University of Colorado Press, 1964. [Reprinted in H. M. Proshansky et al. (Eds.), *Environ-*

mental psychology: Man and his physical setting. New York: Holt, Rinehart and Winston, 1970. Pp. 297–303.]

Lyman, S. M., and Scott, M. B. Territoriality: A neglected sociological dimension. *Social Problems,* 1967, *15,* 236–249. [Reprinted in R. Gutman (Ed.), *People and buildings.* New York: Basic Books, 1972. Pp. 65–82.]

McGrew, W. C. *An ethological study of children's behavior.* New York: Academic Press, 1972.

Michelson, W. *Man and his urban environment: A sociological approach.* Reading, Mass.: Addison-Wesley, 1970.

Osmond, H. Function as the basis of psychiatric ward design. *Mental Hospitals* (Architectural Supplement), 1957, *8,* 23–29. [Reprinted in H. M. Proshansky et al. (Eds.), *Environmental psychology: Man and his physical setting.* New York: Holt, Rinehart and Winston, 1970. Pp. 560–569.]

Proshansky, H. M., Ittelson, W. H., and Rivlin, L. G. Freedom of choice and behavior in a physical setting. In H. M. Proshansky, W. H. Ittelson and L. G. Rivlin (Eds.), *Environmental psychology: Man and his physical setting.* New York: Holt, Rinehart and Winston, 1970. Pp. 173–183.

Proshansky, H. M. Visual and spatial aspects of social interaction and group process. Paper presented to Society for Human Factors, New York, 1971.

Roos, P. D. Jurisdiction: An ecological concept. *Human Relations,* 1968, *21,* 75–84. [Reprinted in H. M. Proshansky et al. (Eds.), *Environmental psychology: Man and his physical setting.* New York: Holt, Rinehart and Winston, 1970. Pp. 239–246.]

Rothenberg, M., and the children of P.S. 3. Planning at P.S. 3. Unpublished manuscript, City University of New York, 1972.

Scheflen, A. E. Living space in an urban ghetto. *Family Process,* 1971, *10,* 429–450.

Schmitt, R. C. Implications of density in Hong Kong. *Journal of the American Institute of Planners,* 1963, *24,* 210–217.

Schorr, A. L. *Slums and social insecurity.* Washington, D. C.: U. S. Department of H.E.W., Social Security Administration, 1966.

Shils, E. Privacy: Its constitution and vicissitudes. *Law and Contemporary Problems,* 1966, *31,* 281–306.

Smith, W. M. Interaction characteristics of an isolated community. Paper presented at the meeting of the Western Psychological Association, 1968.

Sommer, R., and Becker, F. D. Territorial defense and the good neighbor. *Journal of Personality and Social Psychology,* 1969, *11,* 85–92.

Steinzor, B. The spatial factor in face-to-face discussion groups. *Journal of Abnormal Social Psychology,* 1950, *45,* 552–555.

Strodtbeck, F. L., James, R. M., and Hawkins, C. Social status in jury deliberations. In E. E. Maccoby, T. M. Newcomb and E. L. Hartley (Eds.), *Readings in social psychology.* (3d ed.) New York: Holt, Rinehart and Winston, 1958.

Strodtbeck, F. L., and Hook, L. H. The social dimensions of a twelve man jury table. *Sociometry,* 1961, *24,* 397–415.

Suttles, G. *The social order of the slum: Ethnicity and territory in the inner city.* Chicago: University of Chicago Press, 1968.

Taylor, D. A., Wheeler, L., and Altman, I. Stress relations in socially isolated groups. *Journal of Personality and Social Psychology,* 1968, *9,* 369–376.

Thomas, P. *Down these mean streets.* New York: Knopf, 1967.

Vischer, A. L. *Barbed wire disease.* London: John Bale and Davidson, 1919.
Weingarten, M. *Life in a kibbutz.* New York: Reconstructionist Press, 1955.
Westin, A. F. *Privacy and freedom.* New York: Atheneum, 1967.
Westin, A. J., and Baker, M. A. *Databanks in a free society: Computers, record-keeping and privacy.* New York: Quadrangle Books, 1972.
Willis, F. Initial speaking distance as a function of the speakers' relationship. *Psychonomic Science,* 1966, 5, 221–222.
Winkel, G. H., and Hayward, D. G. Some major causes of congestion in subway stations. Unpublished manuscript, City University of New York, 1971.
Winkel, G. H., and O'Mara, E. Personal communication, 1973.
Wolff, K. H. (Ed.) *The sociology of Georg Simmel.* New York: Free Press, 1950.

Suggested Readings

Argyle, M. *Social interaction.* New York: Atherton, 1969.
Birdwhistell, R. L. *Kinesics and context: Essays on body communication.* Philadelphia: University of Pennsylvania Press, 1970.
Brown, R. *Social psychology.* New York: Free Press, 1965.
Goffman, E. *Behavior in public places: Notes on the social organization of gatherings.* New York: Free Press, 1963.
Goffman, E. *Strategic interaction.* Philadelphia: University of Pennsylvania Press, 1969.
Hall, E. T. *The silent language.* New York: Doubleday, 1959.
McBride, G. Theories of animal spacing: The role of flight, fight and social distance. In A. H. Esser (Ed.), *Behavior and environment: The use of space by animals and man.* New York: Plenum, 1971.
Ruesch, J., and Kees, W. *Nonverbal communication.* Berkeley and Los Angeles: University of California Press, 1964.
Sommer, R. *Personal space: The behavioral basis of design.* Englewood Cliffs, N. J.: Prentice-Hall, 1969.

Seven

Individual Development and the Environment

Our discussion to this point has focused on the behavior and experience of the individual and groups of individuals in given contexts. The question has been: What factors in the physical environment relate to the way a person thinks, feels, or acts in specific situations at specific times? In Chapter Four we took the position that the behavior and experience of the person were rooted in the interaction of a host of inner and outer factors. Some of these factors may be social, as we saw in Chapter Six, based on socializing experiences within specific groups.

Our attention now shifts from explaining behaviors in given physical settings at given times in specific cultures to considering how these behaviors became possible in the first place. The crucial ingredients for answering this question are the internal and external influences interacting over time that mold behavior and experiences into a unique identity. Chapter Four stressed that many of the factors that influence behavior in a given situation are the enduring tendencies—interests, values, attitudes, and temperamental traits—that the person brings with him to that situation. At this point we ask how and to what extent these enduring tendencies are formed by man's continual interaction with the environment.

Thus, even the "behavior setting," which may regulate our

actions in accordance with the demands of a particular milieu, does not account for individual differences within the setting—why some pupils learn more rapidly or are more cooperative than others; why Bill drinks too much at the country club dance whereas Bob is a model of sobriety; in brief, why different persons use the same setting in quite different ways, still conforming to the setting's indicated behavior pattern. Quite obviously, such differences may be accounted for in a number of ways. Perhaps Bob is simply not feeling well; on the other hand, he may be abstemious as a matter of principle. If so, this may be due to his upbringing in a strict family setting in which drinking is considered sinful. Behavior in any situation reflects the type of person we are, and this, in turn, involves our parental upbringing, the socioeconomic class to which we belong, the values of our society, our religious and ethnic background, the influence of significant figures on our lives, accidents of fate, our short- and long-range goals, the education we have achieved, the norms of the society in which we live, and so on. All these factors, in the very broad sense, are part of our environment. They constitute the world we know.

Such influences are long in the making, beginning at birth and, in many cases, enduring throughout our lives. We term these influences *developmental* in the sense that they continue over time and contribute to the development of the total person, both as an individual who has a unique genetic endowment as well as acquired skills and attributes, and also as a social being who must live and work with others. Whether they are part of an organized or institutional environment (as in the home and school) or in the form of generally accepted mores that we come to recognize simply because they are pervasive in our particular culture, their existence is critical in shaping our personality, our character, and our identity as individuals.

Our interest here, however, is not in the development of the individual per se. Unlike most discussions of development, we will move the lens of analysis to the more specific and usually neglected influences of the properties of physical settings, and away from a direct concern with biological, social, cultural, and unique personal influences. The latter of course will necessarily be involved in our discussions because, as we have already assumed, physical settings are defined by social and cultural systems that establish their meaning, significance, and purposes for the individuals whose existences are circumscribed by them. Yet these systems will not be of direct concern nor will they be treated in any elaborate fashion. We are not likely to ask how various types of parental discipline influence the development of the child. We are likely to ask how parents use environments to discipline children and the role the environment plays in the process. Does a family household whose dwelling structure makes punishment of the child a public event have different consequences than one that allows it to be a private event? Is the environment used by parents to exert control, by banishing the child to his room as punishment or invading his privacy as a form of surveillance?

The discussion in previous chapters leads us to group the effects of physical settings on the successive stages of individual development under three types of influences. First, physical settings, their spatial properties, organizational configurations, and other related attributes (objects, color, on-going activities) influence the space-related behavior and experience of the person. In short, these properties bear on the kinds of dispositions and tendencies he develops in knowing, using, and experiencing particular physical settings. For example, the young child living in a very crowded apartment, sharing his bedroom with his brothers or sisters, may respond differently to the restrictive and shared space of a very crowded classroom when compared with the child from a more spacious household.

Experiences with physical settings in the socialization process have consequences for more than the spatial tendencies and characteristics of a person. They also influence social, intellectual, and temperamental dispositions that go beyond his use of a particular environment. Our illustration of the house as a factor in parental discipline, on how the child responds, and on the way the child might act in school, is a case in point.

Finally, there is a third kind of influence. One of our assumptions about the nature of environment, stated earlier, viewed the individual as a component of the environment that acts upon and is acted on by all other components that comprise it. In influencing their settings, by altering them, for instance, they feed back possible developmental consequences. For example, if early life experiences establish special privacy needs in the individual as an enduring tendency, it is very likely that there will be a carry-over to the home and play settings he selects or creates in later life. As a neighbor of one of the authors stated: "I came from a home where even for the children, having some privacy was a right and not a privilege. Now you can see why tall hedges around my house are so important to me."

A Framework

To ask questions about the nature and process of individual development is to be confronted by the panorama and complexity of human existence. Thus far we have narrowed our task to a concern on the environmental side with the influence of physical settings and their characteristic properties; and on the person side to both physically oriented tendencies and socially oriented attitudes, feelings, and needs with respect to self and others. It is helpful to circumscribe the discussion of human development in still other ways.

Human development is a continuous process. It is customary to think of this development as a series of successive stages, usually labeled in terms of significant culturally rooted periods in the existence of each individual. For our purpose, we will emphasize periods that are relevant to our primary emphasis on the physical setting. In this respect it becomes clear that two periods in the normal life span of a person are especially significant because of the more restricted capacity of the individual to respond to and use his physical setting: infancy-childhood and the period sometimes referred to as "old age" or the "declining years." These two periods are also ones in which individuals have somewhat limited power in controlling their settings. Thus, infancy-childhood and old-age settings will receive major attention in this chapter. These separations are used primarily for analytical purposes. Even during late adolescence and early adulthood the individual is still developing physical capacities that enable him to cope with physical settings and impose his demands on them; similarly, it is very likely that except for those who make special attempts to overcome the first signs of the declining years, the person just past forty may have somewhat more difficulty climbing the stairs or working in a smoke-filled room or smog-filled city than he had in earlier years.

In the discussion that follows we will deal then with four periods in the chronology of human life: infancy-childhood; adolescence; the mature years; and the declining years, although the emphasis will be on those periods for which environmental evidence and data are available. Before we turn our attention to this task, one more elaboration in our developmental framework remains. On the individual or response side of our framework we have already specified our interest in the development of two types of enduring human tendencies: needs, attitudes, values, and behavioral predispositions directly related to the nature and use of physical settings; and corresponding tendencies related to the self and others, that is, to people rather than places. Let us consider the environment side for a moment. Throughout this volume we have reversed figure and ground in the usual discussion of man and his environment. For our purposes, figure is the physical environment; its backdrop consists of the cultural, social, and psychological systems that establish, define, and maintain this environment.

In our analysis the physical setting in relation to human development can be conceived on at least two levels. For want of better terms we distinguish between the *design* attributes of the setting and its *meaning* attributes. By design attributes we mean such physical properties as length, size, shape, distance, objects, relationships among these properties, and still others. Meaning attributes include the names, roles, people, activities, events, percepts, purposes, feelings, beliefs, values, and attitudes that are generally associated with a setting of given design attributes. In a sense the design attributes represent the "geographical environment," those aspects of the setting that exist apart from the perceiving person as distinguished from those that exist because of the meanings imposed on them by man. Of course, all attributes of a setting, design as well as meaning, are necessarily processed by man as a perceiving organism. As was suggested earlier, however, what is processed and what is "out there" are closely if not exactly matched because of the clarity, integrity, and objective nature of many of the dimensions of physical settings. By the same token, particular physical settings with specified design attributes often evoke meaning attributes that seem to be rooted in measurable or objective characteristics of the setting. Common experiences, purposes, and uses lead us to perceive a six-inch piece of wood with equidistant numbers and marks on it as a ruler, as if this "meaning" property were inherent in it in the same way that a six-inch piece of wood that is thin and half an inch in width is seen as long rather than round.

The interrelationship between design and meaning attributes is axiomatic. Yet both exert an independent power and influence of their own. If meanings—interpretations, attitudes, and the inner life—can influence the behavior and experience of the person apart from the "real" or design properties of a setting, not only are there limits to this, but the design properties, in turn, do have consequences on the experience and behavior of the person both with and without his awareness. It is one thing to imagine walking through the wall of a room and another thing to do it; and where, how, and with whom we sit in a room may in part be determined by a host of design properties of which we are unaware.

Such a perspective is useful in understanding the broad influences that impinge on people who grow up in radically different kinds of environments —for example, the remote rural setting as compared with the urban metropolis. The farm child obviously does not experience the same world as the city child; each acquires a distinct place identity, a sense of belonging to a certain kind of locality on the basis of what the land- or city-scape communicates. The growing child learns from the culture of the world around. Examples range from the extreme simplicity of the rural Amish with their ethos of hard work, self-denial, and frugality to the ostentation of the suburban wealthy. Here we realize that the physical setting does not create such values so much as reinforce them. People in the environment—parents, grandparents, teachers, community leaders—determine what particular value system will be stressed, and a good measure of this value system is about aspects of the physical environment. Yet there is a point at which this environment becomes its own teacher, and for most children opportunities provided by (or lacking in) the setting play an important role in their social and intellectual development.

We see this demonstrated in the numerous studies made of school achievement among slum children. In most cases, it is very difficult, if not impossible, to separate the social and physical effects of the setting. Although it has not been established that the physical elements of the slum are the primary causes of underachievement or failure, it seems quite possible that growing up amid decaying buildings and garbage-strewn streets communicates a message of failure to the child. The constant view of such conditions, day after day, and the social pathologies that often accompany them, may very well lead a child to evaluate himself in much the same way as his setting. The consequence may be to limit expectations of what he can achieve (Schorr 1966; Irelan 1967). Failure becomes contagious; the physical setting both reflects and reinforces the social environment, defining one's socioeconomic status and providing a ghetto identity with, generally speaking, unfortunate consequences.

The immediate or home environment is also critical in the kinds of opportunities it provides or denies the developing child. A survey (*New York Times*, September 13, 1970) of 16,000 children in England, Scotland, and Wales linked poor school performance—especially in reading and arithmetic—to overcrowded housing conditions. Sociologists Peter Wedge and Jane Petzing concluded that lack of amenities in the home, particularly hot water and indoor toilets, contributed to "feelings of malaise or alienation among parents and children" which discouraged academic achievement.

To the extent that any environment provides or denies enrichment or stimulation, it plays a crucial role in the maturation of the individual. Physical aspects of the setting are not the least of the factors at work, although the intangible cultural aspects are more commonly given credit—the intellectual stimulation, for example, provided by parents. Culture is also distilled into the setting. It is supported by the environment. It represents books and a quiet and well-lit place to read them, paintings and places where they can be seen, records, a record player, and a place to listen to music. Thus, cultural deprivation and enrichment are relative qualities manifested in physical, as well as interpersonal, terms. Beyond the home, enrichment may mean a variety of places to experience: camps, schools, settlement houses, museums, lively streets or accessible open spaces.

Throughout there is a subtle comparison going on. As the child moves through various settings, both inside and outside his home, he learns from being excluded from some settings and experiences as much as he does from those that are open to him. He may learn that the living room is his parents' domain, the local playground the territory of a gang, the tennis court an area for those who can afford to pay.

Within this encompassing environment the child seeks to structure his own experiences; the kind of setting he lives in sets limits on certain interactions and provides opportunities for others. We need only compare the experiences of Huck Finn and a modern counterpart, *Manchild in the Promised Land* (Brown 1965), to see how the combined geographical-social environment shapes behavior in vastly different ways. The differences cannot be explained solely along racial lines. In *Born Black* the black photographer and filmmaker Gordon Parks (1971), who grew up in a small Kansas town, writes of experiences much closer to Huck Finn's than "Manchild's."

Fried and Gleicher (1961) describe the way in which an urban slum studied by them provides a distinct social identity based on close kinship ties, well-defined neighbor relationships, and the way that physical space is structured around the residential unit. They found that inhabitants feel a stronger commitment or sense of "belonging" to their area than do members of the more mobile urban middle class, which are likely to exhibit less localism toward their neighborhood. Here, the use of space becomes a major norm for the development of attitudes within the group.

In summary, the kinds of environments that influence development are: family and home, social class, ethnic subgroups, schools and institutions, the peer group and the community. *All of these are embedded in and reflect a physical setting.* Through interaction with these environments, the child grows cognitively, socially, and emotionally. To his sense of "who he is" by virtue of his roles as "pupil," "eldest son," "Boy Scout," and so on, he acquires place identities suggested by the kind of house he lives in, his neighborhood, the nature and size of his community, and his socioeconomic class. All of these forces contribute to the kind of person he becomes.

Infancy and Early Childhood

Properly speaking, the first environment is the mother's womb. The developing child's relationship to the mother is almost wholly spatial in the sense that the womb houses an organism that is already a living, although hardly a human, entity, with a neural organization and blood supply independent of the mother's. Essentially, the womb is a space capsule that supplies a genetically coded organism with food and lodging, so to speak, until it is physically able to enter the world on its own. It is easy, and perhaps dangerous, to endow this relatively unknown environment with all manner of qualities. One hardly needs to add that all of this is speculation from the outside. Freud conceived of the womb as the primal sanctuary and held that we all have a desire to return to it in later life. Whether we agree or not, it is apparent that the womb has come to symbolize a place of refuge from the external world, the only completely human environment we will ever know.

To the newborn, his environment becomes the first source of learning about objects and people. For most children in the United States (although not in many other countries) this new, external world is institutional—usually the hospital. This fact immediately limits and orders the available stimulation. The infant goes from the womb into the hand of nonfamilial professionals, generally from the doctor in attendance to the nurses who bathe and care for it, treated as one of many in an impersonal setting where individual differences are minimally considered.

The nursery offers identical accommodations and a regular schedule of feeding and bathing; generally only those babies with special problems or unusually small size are separated and given modified conditions. What is critical at this point is not so much the emotional climate of an institution, but rather that it provides a similar setting for all babies. Fathers usually see their children through the plate glass window of the nursery, mothers at feeding time.

We can only conjecture what long-range effect this early regimentation has on the newborn—perhaps relatively little; in fact, the effect may be more pronounced for the members of the family who have to delay their opportunity to learn about their newborn as an individual. It is noteworthy that some maternity wards today have various forms of rooming-in arrangements.

Whatever the circumstances of this period, the infant soon moves into the family context that shapes his development over the next several years. He is not, however, an empty vessel. Children are born with a wide range of reflexive actions and individual differences, including considerable responsiveness to external stimuli.

Infants severely deprived of the chance to explore their world or to structure sensorimotor experience by manipulating the objects ordinarily present in a child's environment may suffer affectively, cognitively, and socially. We shall discuss this in greater detail later. At present, we stress the "wholeness" or "oneness" of this early child/environment relationship. In manipulating his world, in his movements through space, the infant is learning to organize his environment "as a sphere of meanings and relationships, and not merely as a collection of things" (Stone & Church 1968:89), but it is still a world in which the child is very much at the center, and from which, too, he only gradually learns to think of himself as separate. Piaget called this behavior egocentrism. As Stone and Church indicate (1968:90) ". . . the child's universe is centered upon himself," without his being aware that he is, indeed, at the center.

Nor, up to age five, does he distinguish among different levels of environmental reality. *Everything* is real, and real in the same way—dreams, feelings, material objects, words, pictures, rules, people. During the earliest weeks of a baby's life, human beings are simply other objects in the world of objects and spaces, although humans are capable of a responsiveness that does differ from the inanimate world. More personal relationships develop over time and through close contacts.

Beyond passively receiving sensory data and responding to them, the baby actively seeks stimulation. Many such stimulus objects center about feeding and bodily comforts, so that responsiveness is associated with the infant's basic needs; but beyond this, he seeks stimulation for its own sake. As objects pass before him, there is an effort to see, touch, taste, and move them. Experiences are rewarding, although not necessarily in terms of mere physical gratification. It has been shown, for example, that children at about one year of age will attempt to change the position of their playpen in order to bring into view objects that are partially hidden (Smith & Smith 1962).

Such pursuits are seemingly unrelated to the alleviation of primary drives, such as hunger and thirst. Nor are they motivated by the actions of another person who consciously stimulates curiosity by manipulating the environment himself (as is often the case when parents play with children). As active explorers of their environment, children are pleased simply by their accomplishments. Kessen and his associates (1970) have cited research on a number of factors critical to early cognitive development. Surprise (see, for example, Charlesworth 1969) and complexity (see Berlyne 1960) are both related to early learning efforts and attracting the infant's attention. As Kessen and his associates suggest, the "emerging picture is one of an infant who gives high priority" to novel events (1970:340). The infant will enact behaviors that are rewarding in themselves, often in the presence of obstacles.

The Sense of Self

Only gradually does the infant come to realize that he and the world around him are somehow not the same. In a very limited way, and because he is beginning to learn to rely on and, in Erikson's (1950) term, to "trust" his world, he achieves the first move toward independence. This in itself, coinciding with his ability to crawl and later to take a few precarious steps, is a measure of his growing self-identity. He seeks to create his own experiences by going to the environment—an environment which seems to be there simply to be crawled over, climbed on, pounded. The range of experiences, stimulations, and places is expanded. He learns to identify and utilize space, and objects in space—in brief, to exercise some control over his surroundings.

The details of these modes of accommodation are by no means universal. Even across and within social classes there are wide differences in what an infant is encouraged or allowed to do, and what is forbidden. In our own culture the setting tends to be a "given"; manipulation of it is discouraged. "Don't touch that!" "Don't move that!" "Stay away from there!" are common warnings in many if not most homes, and not always for the child's safety. The vase must not be broken, nor the living room disturbed. The fact that in later life we become reluctant to alter what is, may well be the result of a basic norm laid down in the early years.

An important component of the child's early experience is the stability of the environment during the period of learning various social roles. The stable setting that permits the child to associate specific physical attributes of the world with specific sets of expectations of behaviors very likely facilitates role learning. It also facilitates the development of a sense of place, so crucial in the acquisition of a sense of place identity.

In sum, the opportunity to explore space, objects, and their qualities and relationships is cardinal to the development of both autonomy and early cognition. The toddler pays close attention to the world in its tiniest details; above all, he is curious. He notices and is able to pick up the stray pins and lost nails, but he is just as likely to get at the valued breakable item supposedly placed out of his reach. He learns to identify and "name" objects. His early language development—the result of his communication with other people—will also reflect his freedom to explore this continually expanding universe.

For most infants this happens in the family context, in itself located within a well-defined spatial dimension. They learn through the child-rearing practices of the parents. Such practices can be loving or rejecting, dictatorial or permissive, indulgent or neglectful (or, as is often the case, somewhere in between these extremes). Madge (1950) notes that until the child is old enough to explore on his own, the house represents a "parental body" that intervenes between himself and the outside world—"a boundary between what is familiar and what is strange." [p. 193] Let us look briefly at the effect on early development when such a family context is missing.

Effects of Maternal and Stimulus Deprivation

Many studies have been made in past years concerning the influence on babies of the withdrawal or absence of maternal care. These are the so-called "maternal-deprivation" babies who have been reared by nurses or constantly changing surrogate mothers in routinized and often bleak orphanages or hospitals. A consequence of these studies has been the elimination of most such institutions for healthy babies, at least in this country and many others. An effort has been made to provide foster families for infants who lack natural ones and to do so as quickly as possible. Whether it was the lack of mothering, the lack of stimulation, or both, children in bland institutional settings suffered from a wide range of affective and intellectual impairments that are not seen when children are placed under foster care. The classic work of Bowlby (1953), Goldfarb (1945), and Spitz (1945) as well as later work documented the lack of affect, retardation in language development, and other intellective impairments in these children. Some of the problems in interpreting the early Spitz findings rested in the suspected chronic health and nutritional problems of the children he studied. It was very difficult to separate the specific effects of maternal or stimulus deprivation from the child's physiological conditions. Later work by Provence and Lipton (1962) in institutions where health and nutritional standards were adequate but stimulation minimal still revealed severe retardation of those behaviors where adult interaction was needed. However, it has been shown that "extra" mothering, that is, stimulation from a surrogate, ameliorates the effects of institutional life and in cases where the child is returned to a normal home after a period of institutionalization, the more severe symptoms of deprivation disappear.

This would seem to suggest that an environment characterized by social attentiveness and stimulation is necessary for the healthy early development of the child. Such a view is buttressed by psychoanalytic findings concerning the effects of the mother-child relationship on the later years. Recently, however, more attention has been paid to other factors in the environment, which suggest that variety of physical stimuli, as well as opportunities for play and social interaction, may be equally if not more important.

The foundling home of the past has been notoriously regimented and "stimulus poor." Whatever emotional deprivation this may cause, the effect on intellectual development is equally striking. Goldfarb (1945) compared the mental development of children who were moved into foster homes after three years in institutions with children who had lived in foster homes since early infancy. Although the natural mothers of the former group were superior in intelligence to those of the latter, it was found that, by the time of puberty and early adolescence, the institution-raised children lagged far behind their foster-home peers in intellectual ability. Goldfarb attributed the difference to the opportunities for normal social stimulation and perceptual experiences present in the foster home but lacking in the institution.

Piaget has demonstrated that intellectual development is heavily dependent upon the kinds and quality of stimulus properties in the child's early environment insofar as these provide the experiences necessary for the structuring of intellectual growth. "It is not necessarily the maternal element as affectively specialized (in the Freudian sense) that plays the principal role but the lack of stimulating interactions . . . ." [Piaget & Inhelder 1969: 27] Escalona (1959, 1968) notes that investigations into the detrimental effects of early institutionalization reveal the importance of rich perceptual experiences—toys, interesting sights and sounds, and opportunities to engage in activities—appropriate to the child's age in overcoming the deprivation syndrome. She reports that in countries where institutionalized children receive highly personalized care and where the environment is rich in perceptual stimulation, no significant difference is found in comparison with family-raised children.

Kagan (cited in *New York Times* December 27, 1972) comparing the intellectual development of middle-class American children with youngsters brought up in poverty in rural Guatemala, found that the early lag apparent among the latter children disappeared by the time they were eleven years old. This was true in spite of the fact that as a result of the village custom and fear of illness, the Guatemalan children were not permitted to leave the huts in which they lived during their first year. In addition, they had no toys, and although babies had considerable physical contact with the mothers, they did not play or talk with them. By United States standards, by the end of their infancy these children were severely retarded. Older children, presumably reared in the same way, proved to be active, alert, and seemingly intelligent.

The picture that emerges from these studies is that "maternal deprivation" is more than simply the absence of a mother figure (indeed, it can occur when the mother is present—as in cases of severe neglect) and that more than just affection for and care of the child is involved. The surrounding environment plays an important role. The fundamentals of learning—drive, cue, response, and reward—are intricately tied in with the opportunities (or lack of them) provided by the setting. A rich perceptual environment in infancy prepares the child for the perceptual complexities he will meet later on. The child conceptualizes his environment not only by "taking it apart" (differentiating its parts) but by "putting it together" and making mental wholes out of related parts. The instruments with which he learns to do this, whether the act is "real" or simply perceptual, become critical elements in his cognitive growth.

The Socialization Process

From the moment of birth the world is mediated through the significant people in the child's setting. With the possible exception of the periods of sleep, the environment is made up of the combined effects of people and setting, affecting the expression of and satisfaction of physical drives and needs as well as the integration of the individual into the group into which he is born. Over many years, in the course of interaction with significant persons, the child learns the appropriate social behaviors for his or her group. Thus, the need for nourishment, the hunger drive, is experienced on the one hand as a physiological stress, an imbalance that requires satiation, and on the other as a social one. The feeding process teaches the child a vast number of lessons about his closest institution, his family, as well as the larger group from which they come. In the process of having one's need for nourishment met, the child takes in or internalizes a great deal about the form of eating behavior, the types of foods that are appropriate, the manner of eating, the posture to be maintained, the utensils to be mastered—that is, a vast amount of social and technological information. In some cases the setting is conducive and helpful, the people are encouraging and supportive. In other cases the setting, usually designed for adults, may provide considerable obstacles to overcome, having been constructed or arranged for the convenience of fully grown persons. The adults in the setting may not always be aware of or concerned with these difficulties. The process of eating provides a clear example of the interaction of physiological needs, institutional forces, and the degree of environmental supports. Eating may seem to be passive for an infant, yet along with the breast or bottle a number of other stimuli are presented. First, the degree to which the expression of a need for food is met by those on the outside communicates a powerful message. Then the manner in which the food is presented, the accompanying sounds and touches are enfused with the food itself and say much about the outside world. The process of eating may be rushed or relaxed, on a hard surface or a soft one, easy to initiate or difficult.

The setting will vary in complexity and symbolic meanings. Consider, for example, the child in a society where the meal is cooked over an open fire, who sees the person preparing the raw material, placing it in a vessel, and then starting a fire. It all may be quite difficult to comprehend, especially the concept of heat and the fire, but not so complex and unclear as the process by which the child's meal comes out of a jar of baby food, mysteriously heated in an electric baby plate. The first example is technologically closer to the food-preparation process, and the many steps involved in the meal may communicate a sense of various roles in the eating ritual, as well as the customs of handling and processing food in the society.

Preschool Period through Childhood

Childhood commonly begins when the infant leaves the stage of complete dependence and propels himself into the world on his own two feet. What are the environmental implications of this radical change in the child's way of life? On the most obvious level, he is no longer limited to exploring his immediate setting. He searches out new objects and areas, gradually increasing his range of contacts and stimulation. This "brave new world" of childhood is enhanced if the child is enrolled in a day care or nursery program, but even without such a formal setting, the expanded friendships and social experiences enable him to become more separate and autonomous, to be exposed to values from outside the home.

Much of the child's day in the new environments, as well as in the home, is spent in some form of play. In fact, the play experience makes up a good part of the expanded stimulation which is necessary to his development at this age. It will be helpful to see just what this process consists of and why it is important.

Play and Play Settings

Many theories have been advanced to explain the nature of play—why children (and both animals and adults, for that matter) engage in such behavior. Quite obviously, it does not fit in with the need-reduction theories of hunger, thirst, and so on, which see the organism's goal as one of quiescence. On the contrary, play is an arousal-seeking behavior. In reviewing various theories on the meaning of play, Lowenfeld (1967) cites the philosopher Herbert Spencer, who saw play simply as an expenditure of surplus energy. The American psychologist G. Stanley Hall posited the idea that play "recapitulated" the earlier development of the species; thus, boys like to climb trees because their mammalian ancestors lived in them. The Swiss philosopher Karl Goos believed that play enabled the individual to practice the skills necessary for survival in adult life. These, and other theories, are no longer seriously regarded by modern-day psychologists, although individual elements in them may shed light on play behavior. Our use of the catch-all term "play" will simply refer to those behaviors and activities that are not completely structured or circumscribed by the demands of an assigned or obligatory task. For example, homework or a chore in itself would not be considered play, but the interpolated behaviors, either in the form of free play or games, would fit the definition. The doodling during homework, the adventure on the way home from an errand—that is, the interstitial activities —would qualify as well.

The truth is that we are not really sure why people play; what we do know is that play is an essential experience in childhood development and that it obviously takes place within an environment. This environment may support the play, obstruct it, challenge it, or perhaps be a neutral backdrop. In any case, the context is as much a part of the play behavior as any objects, toys, or people that may participate. The design of so-called play environments, whether in the nursery school or the playground, is a critical issue which we will look at later.

At the preschool level, play occupies most of a child's waking hours; this is a universal phenomenon and would seem to indicate that it is a necessary developmental step between the complete helplessness of the infant and the relative independence of the school-aged child. But even the infant does things that are frequently identified as play, whether it is exploration of his body, his crib, or the objects placed around him. It appears that these behaviors are most likely to occur when basic needs are satisfied and in the absence of anxiety (White 1959). The infant, unlike the older child, is still much at the mercy of the setting given to him and the objects within it. When he begins to crawl and later to walk, the child can exert some power over the world that surrounds him, moving across environmental settings instead of being placed within them. Since much play is stimulated by curiosity, it is also a way of learning about the environment and one's place within it. The imitative nature of many activities ("playing house," "playing doctor," and so forth) conspires to bring the adult world into manageable, if imaginary, dimensions where the child can deal with it on his own terms. In some cases the child may work out problems through fantasy play, translating them into action and possibly resolving his fears, conflicts, and difficulties with the world of people. Play becomes a means whereby he can practice his autonomy. And because his separation from the world is still incomplete, "make believe" is easy for him.

Piaget (1970) regarded play as a necessary step in the growth of intelligence; in this sense, of course, it is hardly "useless." We will deal with Piaget's theory of logical thinking later on; it is necessary to anticipate, however, one of the major propositions on which his theories are based: ". . . in order to know objects, the subject must act upon them, and therefore transform them: he must displace, connect, combine, take apart, and reassemble them." [Piaget 1970: 704]

Piaget regarded learning as an interactive process between the individual and his environment that involved three distinct phases. By assimilating information the organism makes it part of himself, very much in the way that food is digested; in accommodating himself to the external world the individual adjusts his actions to fit reality; but this is done in order to better assimilate the world. When the two processes are balanced, or in equilibrium, the organism has adapted to his environment. Such adaptations are constantly shifting, according to the nature of the activities engaged in.

In Piaget's view play is assimilation without accommodation; the environment is used simply to satisfy the child's momentary needs. Reality is seen as a foil to which one need not seriously adjust; it is there "to be played with," although we should emphasize again that such seemingly childish behavior serves an important function in learning (of which the child is quite unaware). In the period we are dealing with here, play is largely make-believe or, in Piaget's term, *symbolic.*

In infancy the child uses (and plays with) his environment largely as a form of sensorimotor practice. After age two, as the environment becomes more and more representational—that is, as it begins to exist as images in the child's mind quite apart from its immediate presence—play helps to organize his thinking. Reality is very much distorted in play because the child has no very clear notion of what "reality" is, much less a need to adapt to it. This aspect of play gradually disappears as the child grows older and is superceded by more elaborately organized "games" that are characterized by rules and competition. Individual fantasy gives way to group reality (which may still be "unreal" in adult terms). There is less need to distort reality or employ symbolic substitutes because the child himself is becoming adjusted to the real nature of the social and physical world.

Piaget's theory focuses on the role of play in cognitive development and views it as the child's reaction to an absence of stimulation. Easily bored, children seek means of bringing stimulation about. In play they are creating opportunities to deal with their environment and, in so doing, to exercise power over it. Out of this may come learning (Piaget) or competence (White 1959). Ellis (1972) writes: "Men cannot tolerate the absence of stimulation, and may be considered to play when they maintain their interactions with the environment after insuring their immediate survival. Play can be seen, then, as a type of arousal-seeking behavior. It prevents boredom and generates a base of information about the environment from which to operate." [p. 5-4-2]

Whatever the reasons for play, its environmental implications for development of the child are many. It affords sensory pleasure (as in swinging), improves certain skills (as in handling physical objects), and encourages creativity (as in painting and modeling). The child, of course, does not break down the play experience into such didactic categories; for him it is a continuous process with different goals or consequences, some emotional, others cognitive, one often flowing into the other. Although he may not realize it, the child is also learning his sex role in the world, encouraged, rightly or not, by the play materials provided, the activities approved, and by the degree of freedom he is allowed to explore the environment. In the examples given here, play is learning in a much more inclusive sense than Piaget described it, integral to the child's total (not simply his cognitive) development.

Clearly, play environments cannot be limited to the organized settings provided for child and adult recreation, although most current research in this field deals with planned play areas, especially those for very young children. The current awareness of the inadequacy of many existing play facilities, the fear that urban sprawl may eliminate many play areas, the tendency to include designed recreational areas in new housing and renovation of old has brought about a new play consciousness, and a growing body of research. Most planners and researchers are aware that prepared settings contribute to but a small sample of the child's total play experience. A more comprehensive view of play includes walking to and from school, the "horseplay" in the schoolyard or on the steps, running up the back alley while doing errands, and the play sandwiched into school and home responsibilities. One of the few comprehensive analyses of children's play behavior, now in progress, is Hart's (1973) study of a small New England town, where he is following children during their day, recording play behaviors and settings.

The question of unplanned and planned play settings raises the issue of the difference between urban and rural environments mentioned earlier. Obviously, the opportunities available to children will vary widely, a function of age, family background, socioeconomic status, and—significantly—geographic location. The ghetto child will have one set of play locations, different, in turn, from the youngster in a middle- or upper-class high-rise apartment, and still different from the suburban or rural setting. Each area provides its own set of limitations and opportunities.

From an environmental view there are at least two important attributes of play settings and their equipment. These are availability and responsiveness. Many settings, such as traditional playgrounds (with slides, swings, seesaws, and the like) may be available and relatively close to home. Parents often consider them a good safe place to play, and most children enjoy being in them (Housing Development Directorate 1973). However, their responsiveness might be questioned. Responsiveness in this sense is the ability to engage the child in a personal and reactive manner, the capability of giving the child a sense of discovery. Sand or dirt may enhance this responsiveness, but in most cases the nearest lot or the street itself may provide available areas that are more responsive. It should not be assumed, however, that all play areas outside the playground or the city are necessarily responsive in this sense. Hart's (1973) study suggests that suburban middle-class children are often encouraged to remain in their landscaped yards, well supplied with elaborate but unresponsive equipment and toys, thus discouraging the exploration and use of more challenging areas.

Recognition of the limitations of available play spaces, especially in urban areas, has led to the construction of "adventure" or junk playgrounds, after a form devised in Denmark in the 1940s. These provide a more interactive setting than the traditional ready-made playground of swings, junglegyms, and so on. Utilizing raw materials such as sand, wood, scrap metal, bricks, and rubber tires, adventure or junk playgrounds encourage the child to deal with the degree of environmental complexity he is ready for. This is not to imply that adventure and junk are necessarily synonymous. Rather, adventure seems to come from, in Nicholson's term, "loose parts" (Nicholson 1971), that is, variables within the environment that lead to inventive-

Fig. 7-1 *Top*: Contemporary design playground, Paris. Conventional equipment is styled to provide esthetic as well as functional interest. *Bottom:* Adventure, or "junk," playground, London. Informal design of the setting is marked by use of do-it-yourself building materials. Photographs by Leanne Rivlin.

ness, creativity, and discovery. These qualities seem inherent in the adventure playground, although they clearly are not limited to it. Many of these settings simulate some of the elements of street play experienced by the ghetto youngster and the "vacant lot" conditions of the small town. By isolating the child, the playground gives him somewhat greater privacy and freedom, but it also removes him from the play opportunities available in the natural environment. Studies of playgrounds of all types indicate that they are grossly underused (see Bangs & Mahler 1970; Dee & Liebman 1970; Gold 1972). Given a choice, most children from the age of six or seven on prefer the complexity of the "real world," even though social regulations and physical obstacles may make this a less convenient outlet.

It would be unfortunate to give the impression that there is sufficient understanding of children's play requirements to posit an ideal play setting. We might suggest that the qualities of availability and responsiveness seem critical, but this does not imply a specific design solution. We do know from observation of children playing in many settings that specific playground types seem to differ in their effects on aggressive behaviors, social interaction, interest, isolation, and so on. The design parameters of these qualities have yet to be uncovered.

One group concerned with these issues, the Motor Performance and Play Research Laboratory at the Children's Research Center of the University of Illinois, has begun to accumulate empirical data. Ellis (1972), for example, reports studies on children's preferences for encapsulated spaces, indicating that visual separation is an intrinsic component of the spaces desired by children. Thus, translucent and opaque boxes were preferred over transparent ones.

A recent study (Hayward et al. 1973) of three types of playgrounds in New York City (described more fully in Chapter Eight) compared a contemporary design playground, a traditional, and an adventure playground. Observations of the three facilities and interviews with users revealed that they differed in the activities that took place and the types of users they attracted. The researchers stress that their results suggest complex interactions between the users and the setting, and between the setting and the surrounding community. One result for the adventure playground was its emergence as a kind of "neighborhood lot" with which children in the immediate vicinity strongly identified. In contrast, the other playgrounds drew on inhabitants of the immediate area, and transients, for users.

Another comprehensive study of orthodox and unorthodox play areas in England has also pointed up the localized needs of children (Housing Development Directorate 1973). Children from afar rarely visited the adventure playgrounds. Availability, which also includes adult management or supervision of areas, either formally or informally, becomes a critical component of the freedom that children bring to play settings.

The Role of the School

It is rather arbitrarily assumed that children in the United States begin their formal education at about age six. In fact, for an increasing proportion, "school" begins perhaps as early as their first year with enrollment in some form of day care program, and later in a nursery school, often followed by a year in kindergarten. Such schooling, although not as regimented as in later years, has its own parameters of formality. Activities are structured, rules are taught (and enforced), and the child, for perhaps the first time, begins to play an institutional role that will continue in one form or another throughout his life. Interestingly, too, as one looks at the physical form of day care and nursery facilities, one realizes that they tend to resemble schools, presenting the child with the first physical and social model of what school is like. We might recall the earlier conception of the role of space and its design and meaning attributes in assessing the implication of school form on the child, especially since there is a recent trend toward experimenting with various physical forms for classrooms.

We tend to think of the first grade as the point when the child is given systematic instruction in the skills that we refer to when we speak of education, although most day care programs include the foundations for the formal instruction of later years. Two broad implications follow from this: The pupil's cognitive powers are being directed (by instruction, learning to read and write, and so on) while he assumes the institutional role of student. This latter development implies a type of social accommodation quite different from what the child has known at home, in a setting where he gains recognition surrounded by age-mates against whom he can be compared. In environmental terms he must accommodate himself to a group setting where he may not have a stable place of his own. He must learn to relate in a very personal way to a new authority figure, the teacher, whose personality, values, and system of discipline and their expression through the use of the environment may differ from those of his family. Punishment, for example, which might have been a sharp word at home, may now be banishment from the class—or the reverse may be true, with verbal control now substituted for environmental control.

Apart from this, school supplies an institutional identity that reinforces the social identity of neighborhood and community. An attempt to alter this is seen in the construction of new and rather elaborate facilities in ghetto areas. This is an environmental intervention that not only may provide (hopefully) "quality" education, but a radically different physical setting which encourages a more positive self-image and signals the pupil that others care about his future. Busing, however controversial, is another method of intervening environmentally for an educational end.

Finally, the school, no matter what its nature, exposes the individual to sets of expectations as part of a group. In terms of time schedules, physical location, activities, and the necessity of sharing the facilities with others, one's freedom of choice becomes increasingly limited. Both the physical setting and the program or curriculum constrain certain behaviors and encourage others. But of course this is important only in terms of the school's objectives—to teach, or "educate," the student. Attempts by modern educators to give the child more options, including greater freedom to use his environment spatially, are based on the notion that most normal children learn better when they are allowed, at least to some extent, to structure their own experiences, largely on the basis of their individual interests and at their own pace.

Significant here is the interaction among the program, the setting, and the participants. In no place is this as clear as in the open classroom movement with its deemphasis on a structured setting. Brunetti (1972) claims, for example, that there can actually be more privacy of a sort in a large open classroom than in the standard "four wall" room. Some of these instructional areas are equal to thirty classrooms in size; visual and acoustical separations between different classes are limited or nonexistent. Yet the results (in the areas studied) revealed that there is less noise and distraction than when pupils are lined up in rows, facing the teacher, in a smaller room. In addition, the conventional room seems to provide fewer choices for the students to separate themselves from others. On the other hand, some open classroom efforts, using traditionally built rooms, have found that students have a difficult time finding a quiet and/or private area.

To what extent the open classroom is good or bad in meeting educational objectives is difficult to say. Modern educational theory presupposes the former, at least to the extent that the open classroom movement is increasingly in favor. In any case, the physical setting is recognized as facilitative to learning rather than as merely a neutral "container" wherein learning takes place. An extensive, ongoing study throughout the metropolitan Toronto school system where the open plan is being introduced revealed some interesting findings. Observations made in twelve schools, both conventional and open, indicated that activity patterns of open plan schools were different from those in traditional schools. In the experimental open classes there was less structuring of spaces, with teachers more personal and informal with the students, students working more frequently in small groups or alone, and using a greater variety of tools (Durlak et al. 1972, 1973). A telling analysis was by level of activity; that is, an index of the number of focal points within the room, the movement within the room, the number of student clusters, and the variety of tools used. This, more than the mere designation of open or traditional, seemed to be a better discriminator of many differences within the schools (Durlak et al. 1973). We know that behavior has been affected, but whether in the direction of greater creativity, initiative, and improved learning is another question. How much is related to the spe-

Fig. 7-2 Two views of an open classroom. *Top*: Area accommodates free-choice multipurpose activities. *Bottom*: Nook shows possibility of achieving privacy in the larger setting. Photographs by Frances Buschke.

cial effects of operating an experimental program is also unclear. A follow-up study in the Toronto schools will provide at least some of the answers.

A previously cited study by Barker and others (1969) suggested the importance of size in eliciting participation in student activities. In brief, although there are more things to do and more facilities for doing them in a very large school, more actually goes on in a small school. This is because the latter settings are generally "undermanned"; almost everyone gets a chance to take part in something. In larger institutions a good percentage of the student body is sidelined or "vetoed out" in favor of the few who can perform expertly.

This is an observation that applies as well to the community as a whole. In *Midwest and Its Children* (1955), Barker noted that the great variety of settings available to a small population brought pressure on everyone to take part in many activities. School-aged children, especially, were frequently drafted into adult roles. But he also pointed out such children tended to perform at a level lower than their capabilities. Because of the pressure to do so much, the chance to attain maximum competence in any one activity was limited.

Like any setting the school is a complex system for delivering certain services to those who enter it. These services are influenced by the quality of the staff, budgetary considerations, administrative policies, educational philosophy, type of student body, community desires, and physical configuration. In addition, the combination of these elements creates a psychological setting or institutional style. In the development of the child this can have important consequences. The youngster attending a school where pupils are encouraged to program their own days might be expected to acquire a vastly different attitude toward his role as a developing person from that of the boy or girl in a school that emphasizes strict discipline and adherence to certain established norms. Environmentally, each responds to and uses his setting in a different manner.

Cognitive Growth

During the years from six to twelve, the child learns to deal with ideas, concepts, and, to a limited extent, abstractions. His development of language and verbal skills accelerates. As a social person he learns as much or more from his playmates and fellow pupils as from his teachers and family.

Is this progressively greater ability to think, to read and write, and to "do" things simply a result of the educational process itself? This seems unlikely. There are other factors at work. Temperament and personality traits are certainly among them; drive or ambition—which usually stem from personality—are important factors. One's social environment may restrict one's ability to "live up to his potential." (Or, conversely, give him a privileged position.) All of these influences affect our cognitive growth, although the extent to which they determine cognitive ability is a matter of dispute.

In our comments on behaviorism (Chapter Three) we outlined a learning theory based on the individual's ability to discriminate among various stimuli and respond to those which gratify some immediate or longer-range need. This reinforcement approach holds that we seek out those experiences, and repeat the responses they elicit, that offer the greatest satisfactions; at the same time, we avoid stimuli (aversive) that cause pain or dissatisfaction. These negative reinforcers help us learn because they tell us what not to do. Classical behaviorism sees the newborn baby as an empty vessel to be filled by environmental experiences; cognition is a product of the nature and progression of these experiences. Context is all.

Another view is a genetic one, expressed perhaps most comprehensively in the writings of Piaget. It is beyond our intention here to deal with Piaget's theories in detail; what we can do is sketch in the salient features as they apply to two of the major concepts we are discussing in this chapter: (1) the role of the environment in the development of cognitive processes; and (2) how the child learns to perceive and relate himself to objects and spaces.

Like the behaviorists, Piaget (1970) sees cognition as the product of "continuous interaction between subject and external world." [p. 703] But here the comparison ends. For Piaget, learning depends as much on what he calls "progressive internal coordinations" as on "information acquired through experience." Learning to think is not simply the result of an accumulation of information, but the ability to process this information along ever-increasing modes of complexity.

To put it in more general language, all of us are born with the ability to organize experience in certain logical ways; the extent to which we do this, however, depends upon our interaction with the external world. "Biological maturation does nothing more than open the way to possible constructions. . . . It remains for the subject to actualize them. . . ." [Piaget 1970: 712] But this actualization can only take place in accordance with the individual's stage of readiness. The infant, for example, has no conception of the "conservation of objects"; a toy that is taken from him is gone forever. Repeated return (and removal) of the toy will not change his belief that the object has ceased to exist. Only at a certain age (about twelve months) does this experience become translated into a very rudimentary form of thought so that the infant understands that the toy has simply been put away or moved to another location. Piaget called this sudden illumination, which occurs with increasingly complex situations as we get older, the "capacity to respond."

Such capacity is not automatic, but rather is based on previous experiences with the environment. Experience alone, however, does not create capacity, which increases as we move up the developmental timetable. A quotation will help us understand this concept: "The main point of our theory is that knowledge results from *interactions* between the subject and the object, which are *richer* than what the objects can provide by themselves." [Piaget 1970: 713–714] Piaget is saying here that thinking is a creative process, initiated by the organism, and not simply a "response to stimulus." We structure experience and are not mere passive receivers of it.

He cautions, however, that ideas themselves are not "innate." Nor is logic innate. In hundreds of experiments Piaget has shown that until a certain developmental stage is reached, the child is unable to grasp the true "meaning" of objects and their relationships. The same quantity of water poured into a thin glass and a wide glass, for instance, will appear unequal in amount, the thin (taller) level seeming to be greater. Logic is another characteristic which develops by stages. So is the child's understanding of movement, velocity, space, and time. In the case of time, the "bigger" something is, the "older" it is.

From about one-and-one-half years to six or seven the child develops a "preoperational" form of intelligence according to which he must "act out" his thinking; it is not yet possible for him to conceive of things apart from his participate in them. During the elementary school years he will be able to reason independently of his own actions, but only in terms of "concrete" operations, of specific objects, situations, and persons. (He learns to add and subtract, for example, by actually handling and counting physical objects.) As an adolescent he is able to think more abstractly. Concepts are added to things and relationships among things are quite capable of being dealt with "in the abstract." Yet this does not mean that the adolescent's formal thought is as good as that of the adult. It may not be under specific circumstances.

The importance of these emergent stages is simply this: our perception of the world changes as we learn to substitute "signifiers" and symbols for concrete "things." As our perception changes, so does our behavior. The world that we assimilate (and accommodate to) formally or conceptually is not the same world that we perceived as self-centered children. As infants we lack a clear differentiation of the self from the space around us; our knowledge *of* it is essentially derived from our actions *in* it. As adults we "know" the world more abstractly, in terms of its formal and logical properties.

This is an important distinction and it is at the heart of Piaget's theory of a developing intelligence. We are able to do this—we cease to be children—because the adult mind is capable of apprehending the world on a higher level. Objects are replaced by concepts. This new order of reality is only possible because of a capacity of the mind to assimilate it at a certain stage of the developmental continuum, but of course it will come about only to the extent that environmental objects are present to make it possible. Children who are not taught mathematics, or logic, do not become mathematicians or logicians. On the other hand, to introduce "ideas" or experiences before the child is ready for them can, in Piaget's view, have a blunting effect, preventing complete understanding. The implications of this in planning facilities for children as well as educational programs is apparent.

Space and Spatial Relations

The development of cognitive representations of space emerges from a history of manipulations of objects, not from perception alone. Moreover, not all of the spatial-geometric properties are achieved at the same time. Flavell (1970: 1016) notes their order of development as topological (proximity, order, and so on), projective (perspectives, and so on), and Euclidean (rectilinear coordinates, and so on). Thus, from the age of seven or eight the child develops an idea of conceptual space as distinct from perceptual or representational space that begins at about age two.

Representational space is not simply a mirror image of what the child sees, a picture recorded on the mind, but a child's picture of the world produced by the view he has of it *if he were actually acting in relation to it,* although in fact he is not. The action is simply implicit. This "imitative" representation is a displacement of motor activity (in sensorimotor perception) by motor expectations. The child "acts out" his perceptions mentally.

Such representation of the environment gradually leads to the construction of what Piaget calls "conceptual space." Objects and their relations are no longer perceived solely in terms of "internalized imitations" but acquire a quality of total representation. The system is seen as working independently of the observer. This is possible, Piaget tells us, because by the time he is seven or eight years old the child has become "decentered"; he is capable of perceiving objects in a coordinated way, capable of exploring all their aspects. At the same time settings may have very different meanings for him at different ages in terms of the design and meaning attributes described at the beginning of the chapter. How the child learns to move through and use settings, especially enduring long-range ones, quite obviously relates to the opportunities these setttings provide him. As he gets older, an understanding of measurement, perspective, and proportions helps him realize that the visible world exists for others pretty much as it exists for him. When this happens, space becomes an abstract concept, or idea, capable of being understood apart from one's experience. However, it is not until adolescence or beyond that the child wholly grasps this notion of formal operational space.

A central interest in Piaget's work for environmental psychology is the child's conceptualization of the larger world. Piaget feels that an understanding of this world must precede the information about it conveyed by mental images. Imitation creates the resemblance between imagery and perception—the acting out of what we see. The process of coming and going in space results in a framework for memory images of districts and landscapes (Piaget, Inhelder, & Szemenska 1960).

Using an experiment in which children between the ages of four and ten were asked to make a sand box model of their school and its environs, Piaget and his associates (1960) found that in the preoperational stage children used an action-centered reference system. Unable to organize details into a whole, they had to think out routes in terms of their own movements. The child, for example, thinks out its way to school and adds on landmarks later.

Evidence that environmental experiences of children influence their spatial abilities is revealed in a series of studies of the Gusu and Logoli children in Kenya (Munroe & Munroe 1971; Nerlove et al. 1971). They found a relationship between the distance from the home that the child ranged and his ability on selected spatial tasks. The children observed roaming farthest from home (generally males who are given freedom to range afar) showed greater skill on a block-copying task. After considering many explanations, the authors suggest that exploration of the environment is one of the learning experiences that contribute to the development of spatial abilities.

Learning the larger world is also related to aspects of the child's psychosocial development; his growing independence and autonomy, for instance. As the physical space within which he operates becomes larger, new sources of potential learning experiences present themselves. But these are not simply "there for the asking." Space is controlled. In the home it is under the dominion of parents, but the opportunities available are also important. Discussing housing developments in England, Madge (1950) writes that:

> It seems probable that the relationship between the house and neighboring houses has a lot to do with early social development. Under living conditions where a child is able to move freely into other people's houses and gardens, and where other children visit its own house and garden, the parental body will be extended, by a series of analogies, to include a whole group of houses and perhaps even a neighborhood, village or town. Early restriction on this freedom of movement would tend to produce a generation that keeps itself to itself. [p. 193]

Outside of the home, various private and public personages determine the accessibility and use of space. A significant component of the learning process, then, must be sought in the direct and vicarious contact the child has with those people who make use of and control the spaces and objects outside the child's home. In a word, environmental learning is heavily saturated with social learning. One of the authors (Winkel) has termed these controllers of space "gatekeepers." The doorman of an apartment building, the supervisor of a playground, a homeowner, the plant guard, and the policeman all regulate and define spatial accessibility for a variety of different areas. The implication of this view is that the range of a child's learning possibilities is strongly influenced by the social definitions of space as well as the stimulations available in the space itself.

If we conceive of the environment as an important source of learning opportunities in the broadest sense of the term, then more consideration must be given to the social factors involved in spatial perception. A child's behavior away from home may be very much controlled by parental space norms;

he is told where he may or may not go to play. Peers and older children also provide cues as to what spaces can be invaded, and in this sense, they can be termed surrogate gatekeepers. Needless to say, conflict between the actual and surrogate gatekeepers is not uncommon; witness the street gang leader who urges his followers into forbidden territory.

Finally, the role which socioeconomic and ethnic factors play in environmental learning needs to be considered. We might think that middle-class children, especially in cities, enjoy a larger living environment with a broader range of activities than poor children. Yet we know little about this, especially in terms of restrictions set by gatekeepers and parental rules and regulations. Ethnic groups, moreover, may feel constrained to keep their children within certain cultural boundaries, so that environmental experience remains largely parochial. In addition parents offer models for the child's behavior. The way in which they use space and the frequency of use subsequently influence the child's spatial behavior. Factors unique to the individual may also be a major determinant. Girls are generally encouraged to be less venturesome than boys. Previous environmental experiences likewise influence both perception and use of various kinds of external space. The youngster who has been set upon by gangs in another neighborhood is not apt to return—at least until he is older or has a gang of his own.

What do we know about children's abilities to cognize complex large-scale spaces? There is considerable research evidence suggesting that at an early age children are capable of rather extraordinary mapping abilities, however action-centered their reference system might be. A basic problem in determining what and how children cognize is the selection of appropriate measurement techniques. The limitations of a young child's coordination, drawing powers, and reading ability make the selection of devices difficult indeed. Many of the tools which will be discussed in connection with cognitive mapping in adults are not appropriate for use with children.

One study (Blaut et al. 1970) of five, six and seven-year-old first graders in North American and Puerto Rican schools tested their map reading and map use on the assumption that a cognitive map was employed in these tasks. Two types of procedures were used. In the first the children were shown oblique and vertical aerial photographs and asked to identify features on them. The second condition involved preidentification of features in the vertical photograph, preparation of a tracing from the photo, interpretation of a traced pattern after removal of the photograph, and use of the tracing in the solving of a "navigation problem." The photograph was either that of the child's school area or one similar to it. In general the results revealed that in both cultures the first graders were capable of interpreting the vertical aerial photographs, abstracting from them to a "system of highly iconic map signs," using the presentation to solve a route-planning problem, and generally engaging in a very real form of map reading, map making, and map use.

In attempting to explain the origin of this capability in children the authors attribute much of it to the child's early play behavior—games, drawings, gestures, and so on. But most basic, they feel, is toy-play. Studies of five-year-old children capable of arranging toys to represent landscape features (Stea & Blaut 1970) are cited to support this view.

We need only review what toy-play is like in these early years to comprehend the rich source of stimulation it provides for the child's mapping abilities. For one, the child generally looms over his minature world, that is, he gets an aerial view of it. His aerial experiences accumulate, probably beginning with being held and looking down and around at the world of objects and areas, continuing as he moves his toys—blocks, cars, and dolls. Thus, most normal early years provide a varied series of spatial experiences for children in which toy-play participates as a concrete opportunity to learn and store experiences about the world.

It is interesting that we often underestimate children's conceptual abilities. In a study of a new children's psychiatric facility (Rivlin & Wolfe 1972), both the architect and the newly appointed director were concerned that the rather complex design of the building, with a mirror-image arrangement of living areas, would create problems for the disturbed young children who would be patients, especially those with orientation problems. A later study of the functioning of the building revealed that these fears were unfounded. Children appeared to make their way about the facility with ease. Attempts to check their knowledge of the building by having newcomers give a researcher a tour revealed that they quickly acquired sufficient conception of the overall space to take an adult almost anywhere.

In sum, children learn their environment in two ways. One of these is simply orientational. The individual learns to get around, first by relating himself to certain objects or fixed reference points, then by relating objects to each other, and finally by conceptualizing space as a coordinated system of reference in which the town or city is seen as a kind of geometric abstraction. Secondly, the child learns his environment socially, in terms of what spaces are accessible to him and what kinds of activities are permitted in them.

Adolescence

Adolescence represents a stage in life that has an uncertain onset (although technically it is often said to begin at puberty) and even less clear ending, depending in part on society's definition of who is an adult. As recently as sixty years ago, the classification of teenager was unknown (Goldberg 1969). As a social phenomenon it is a time often linked with continued dependence, and the terms "transition" and "search for identity" are commonly included in a description of it.

What is the significance of this period from an environmental view? Any generalization is likely to be incorrect in some details, but a view of the cognitive, social, and physical demands at this stage, provides a picture of the environment's contribution. Piaget points out that the concept of "native land" does not develop until twelve or over (Piaget & Inhelder 1969). Similarly, social consciousness and social ideals do not appear until this period. We are looking at a cognitive stage in which the individual is capable of thinking that is quite symbolic and abstract, but as Piaget has indicated (see Wadsworth 1971: 111–112), this does not mean that the adolescent's formal thought is always on an adult level. The tendency to base judgments on logical thought rather than realistic thought may often create crises of ideals. These crises will be most intense in relation to the adolescent's immediate settings, friends, and family, whose values and judgments may not always live up to his expectations.

What place does the environment have in this conflict? Space can exacerbate or smooth over disputes. Available and accessible settings may enable the adolescent to separate himself and work out these problems as well as those related to the physical, emotional, and social changes that accompany this stage. A room of one's own—a place to retreat—can provide a context for meeting crises. On the other hand, in crowded conditions, where space is limited, the conflicts may intensify. The adolescent's retreat to and monopoly of the bathroom may be an additional source of irritation and dispute. As Stone and Church (1968) suggest:

> The adolescent's own room, if he has one, or the privacy of a hotly contested bathroom, serves as a refuge where he can study and register his own growth, where before the mirror he can experiment with, practice and perfect the masks he wears, the styles and images he wants to project. [p. 445]

The issue of privacy is an especially salient one during this period. Faced with a changing physiology, uncertainty over the future and questions regarding family values, privacy needs become especially powerful. Yet within the home the adolescent is still the child in a family, with limited rights over space. Often he must seek his privacy outside the home, for even possession of a room may not keep it and objects within it from the view of siblings or parents. In fact, parental concerns over the adolescent, concerns that include experimentation with sex and drugs, may very well increase surveillance. however secretly this may be achieved. A quick survey of the "Dear Abby" type of newspaper column will reveal the kinds of invasions adolescents face —parents who search their children's private belongings or read their mail, all in the interests of the children.

Earlier we spoke of the socializing functions of eating. Mealtime and its setting continue to be the source of much social learning during the later years of growth. However, the family dinner time can also become a kind of arena (Stone & Church 1968) in which to air all manner of grievances, depending on the composition of the family group, and perhaps too the available space for family eating. Interaction can help resolve problems, but it can also kindle them.

We often think of the adolescent period as one in which increasing freedom is given to explore the environment. The boundaries or home range of the adolescent do, indeed, progressively expand from those of childhood, accompanied by the tendency to spend less and less time at home. Yet the gatekeepers described earlier still exist at this stage. They continue to censor and set limits, although perhaps in a more subtle manner than in earlier years, especially since adults, whether out of real concern or envy of their freedom, tend to be decidedly suspicious of adolescents.

Adolescent behavior in the United States is far from uniform, varying widely across both socioeconomic and ethnic lines. We see this in the street corner society of the city where status is often achieved through gang affiliation. Gangs operate via the spatial component of hangouts, corners, and vacant lots that mark a group's territory. Leonard Bernstein's *West Side Story* dramatizes the importance of "turf" as a mediatory factor between different ethnic groups (with, of course, different shared values). Needless to say, this is not the environment familiar to the small-town or small-city youth, who tends to mirror himself not so much in physical places as in things. He, too, may have his hangouts—the drive-in hamburger stand or bowling alley—but these are more likely to be seen as places for meeting and interacting with others than as turfs to be defended.

Above all, he has the automobile. Outside the largest cities, almost all adolescent youths—upper class, middle, and lower—are inherently mobile (for those few who are not, there is always the telephone; among teenage girls especially, the separately listed telephone number has become the status symbol that cars represent for older boys), a fact which dissolves most of the old spatial boundaries, substituting freedom of movement, a social egalitarianism, and a global environment for the fixed and stratified universe of the pool hall and ice cream parlor of an earlier generation. That much of this movement is ritual ("cruising") hardly diminishes the value of the car as the great unifier of adolescent culture.

Writing on the automobile as a social institution, Goldberg (1969) points out that its importance has grown not so much as an instrument for getting places, but because in many communities there are so few places for the adolescent qua adolescent to get *to*. The rock festival has since come along to supply this needed "full-blown social arena"—at least for a few days at a time—but even the festival must meet a criterion of meaningfulness. One such, held at a race track in a New York City suburb, failed spectacularly to draw an audience. In the words of a veteran festival goer, it was "too easy to get to." And once there, it offered no "adventure"—sitting in the grandstand is simply not the same thing as sleeping in the mud at Woodstock.

According to Goldberg (1969), "cruising" in the car serves a strong need for social gathering. The slow parade becomes a device for meeting members of the opposite sex. It also becomes a source of conflicts with adults as congestion interferes with both traffic and business. What represents a search for a place on the part of the young becomes an irritation to the adult community.

We provide few settings that adequately meet adolescent needs. To some extent the school must function as a focus of social life, a "hangout" for peer activity, although its space is largely taken over by formal purposes. The importance of school size in the opportunities provided for participation in student activities has already been cited. Much could be written about the high school as a central experience in the development of the adolescent. We can do no more here than ask the reader to identify from his own high school days those cardinal influences which helped shape his maturity. He may discover that the classroom and formal instruction were less instrumental in his growth as a person than the social environment which absorbed his extracurricular self.

The Mature Years

If we live a normal span of years, most of our life will be spent as adults. Yet there is a sense that, having come of age, the "formative" if not the best years are behind us. In reality no normal adult stops growing in some respect until he dies. These are also the years of our greatest productivity and generally our greatest power. This power is reflected on many levels— physical, social, political, economic—and all of these affect one's use of the environment in some way.

Unfortunately, we know a great deal less about adulthood than we do about childhood and the later years, both of which have been more intensively studied by psychologists and others. Neugarten (1968) suggests that our ignorance of this stage rests in the paucity of systematic data over the life cycle and the lack of a useful theory around which the central issues can be studied. Two of these issues deserve mention: (1) the need for adults to establish close long-term relationships with others; and (2) the need to find a direction in life, a set of values, and some way of acting upon one's own interests and talents. In a sense, this is what life is about, although such psychological needs may be clouded by the persistent economic need to make a living.

In a very real sense the world is largely designed to function at an adult level. Even though we acknowledge individual differences among age groups, much of the built environment is geared to an adult size and level of competence. Environments are usually controlled by adults who, as space managers, decide how they are to be used, by whom, and for what purpose. In many ways this is simply an extension of the political, economic, and social power that already rests in adult hands. It is the teacher who determines how the classroom will be used, the park department and its agents control the use of parks. Several writers have noted that in many institutions and office buildings it is really the maintenance personnel who set the norms of space usage by their power to regulate pedestrian traffic and seating patterns and control over the use of certain areas.

Adults are also the most active gatekeepers for the young, mediating their passage from space to space. The neighbor at the window eyeing the cluster of adolescents below, the shopkeeper with his view of the children outside, enforce definite limits on the child's spatial freedom. Such power, of course, is not equally shared—status and role differences bring about degrees of authority. The adult, in brief, not only builds and arranges the environment but is responsible for how it shall be used. Such power brings its own problems, and resolving them is at the heart of the environmental movement.

If one of the central issues of the adult years is establishing close long-term relationships, in what ways can space be used to achieve this objective? The setting can foster closeness or alienation; in family life, as we know, inadequate or poorly arranged space can be a source of conflict. The fine balance between opportunities for privacy and aloneness, communication with others, closeness without crowding—all this has a spatial component. A very crowded apartment or house may be as devastating for interpersonal relations as geographical isolation. Social workers frequently note the relationship between troubled families and lack of adequate living space, although the latter is by no means the whole story.

Housewives who are trapped in multistory housing seem especially vulnerable to the effects of forced isolation. A study by Fanning (cited by Michelson 1970) of the wives and children of British occupation forces in Germany following World War II revealed a startling difference between those who lived in separate houses and those in apartment bulidings. The illness rate for the latter group was 57 percent higher, with respiratory ailments predominating. The psychoneuroses also showed a greater incidence and within the buildings the rates of neuroses varied directly with the distance from the ground floor. Higher apartments seemingly created more social isolation (see Michelson 1970: 161–162). Another result of such verticality is the difficulty of supervising small children at play; it is impossible for mothers to observe them. This, too, seems to contribute to stress. In short, mass housing, especially in "projects," contributes to feelings of impersonality in dealing with other tenants. Neighbors are kept at arm's length, and the effect of such housing developments is not so much to create a sense of crowding as of loneliness.

One other factor that discourages the making of close and enduring human relationships has been discussed in Toffler's (1970) popular study, *Future Shock*. Cultural changes that once took generations to achieve are now telescoped into a single lifetime. The stabilizing influence of a given, or a slowly changing, environment is lost through an accelerating technology that makes each day truly "new" in some respect. And because the tempo of life is increased, we ourselves run faster to catch up. In Toffler's phrase, is there ever a "now"? More mobile than ever before, we seek out new jobs, travel widely, change locales for climatic or esthetic reasons. For many people such movement has very positive values, but it can also be culturally disorienting. One must learn a succession of environments with no strong loyalties, perhaps, to any one of them. This is essentially however, a middle-class phenomenon; the poor experience a different kind of mobility and impermanence with decidedly limited freedom of choice.

Marc Fried (1963) has described the effects on long-term residents of a neighborhood when they are forcibly uprooted as part of an urban renewal program. Chapter Nine discusses the "grief syndrome" that ensued and other examples of the loss of place identity. The phenomenon, of course, has much to do with the dissolution of social networks, but environmentally it also reflects the importance of places in which networks operate—the front stoop, local shops, the street corner, the living room in which family and friends are entertained. The functions of these places distill themselves into symbolic meanings as well and become interwoven with the person and the place relationships sustained over the years. Significant objects in one's life, a stable home and neighborhood, as well as enduring personal relations, contribute not only to the sense of "who I am" but to a meaningful direction. "I know where I'm going" means, to most of us, "I know where I've been." This is difficult in an era of mobility, where permanent aspects of one's life are decidedly limited.

Involved in this sense of direction are two other factors. To what extent does the setting provide the person with opportunities to personalize his immediate environment in a way that is uniquely his? And to what extent does he enjoy freedom of choice in the use of his environment? Perceived freedom must be considered in terms of individual personality traits and potential interactions with a setting. We realize our goals in an environment, in the long-range sense of the term, only if the environment supports them. Environmental tradition can be, for some, a dead end. In the relocation studies, of which Fried's was one, it was found that the younger, better educated, upwardly mobile residents preferred relocation—indeed, relocated themselves, usually in the suburbs. For them the old environment had failed to support the meanings and directions they sought in their lives.

Implicit in these studies of urban neighborhoods is the question of life styles: that is, the combined effects of socioeconomic status, ethnic or group background, stage in the life cycle, religious or philosophical outlook, among other elements. Life style, as a generalization, implies a set of attitudes, needs, and values that will vary with different persons and perhaps with one person over his lifetime. These relate to the housing he selects, its location, and the arrangement of objects and furnishings within, the use of the house and its environs, as well as a broad array of goals. The "proper Bostonian" prefers Beacon Hill, or its equivalent, because it is environmentally appropriate to his mode of living and social status. This is essentially based on adult choices—options we have only after we are old enough to determine for ourselves what these choices shall be. Yet there is little evidence that environments in themselves effectively change life styles. Gans (1967) has noted that people who move to the suburbs do not become suburbanites in the life-style sense simply because of a change in locale. The move is made to realize already acquired values which other environments deny. Berger (1960) cites the obverse side of this coin in challenging the notion that suburban housing by itself will transform a non-middle–class person into a homogenized middle–class suburbanite. In his study of the working class residents of a Los Angeles suburb, he found that even with obvious improvements in economic condition this group retained life styles which were quite similar to those they had experienced prior to moving.

The Declining Years

Environmental failure is often common for the elderly. Declining health, insecurity, and decreasing productivity make them a class apart, although it would be a mistake to consider them as a monolithic group. The later years are "later" in terms of an ambiguous point in life and generally extend for many years thereafter. But whatever the individual differences among the aged—we all know of the ninety-year-old who still does a day's work—critical problems arise for the older person, not least the fact that the environment is clearly organized in favor of the young adult and the middle-aged. Fewer resources, morc narrowly defined social roles, and poorer health limit one's power and adaptability. On the physical level this is seen in the constraints imposed by such things as steep bus and subway steps, speedy traffic lights, insufficient illumination. To a considerable extent the aged along with children and the handicapped have been "vetoed out" of society by designers and space managers. A symptom of the difficulties is the increase in home accidents with increasing age (Birren 1964) which, in part, reflects the inadequacy of settings to meet physical needs as one's power declines and as one is confined more and more to home.

In spite of this the breakdown of the extended family has made it necessary for the elderly to remain "independent" financially, socially, and environmentally for longer than ever before. Lack of transportation for the aged in many large cities and their dependence on being taken places restricts the life space as well as the life style of many (Nahemow & Kogan 1971). With the poor especially, isolation becomes the curse of old age, and inflation has moved many elderly on fixed incomes into an economic status that precludes supportive aids at a time when they are needed most.

Psychologically, the elderly become separated from the environment as their affective ties weaken. Cumming and Henry (1961) speak of this as "disengagement." There is a withdrawal from the immediate world as more of life is lived in the past, or at best vicariously, through the lives of others in the family. Congruently, society itself withdraws from the older person. One result of this may be a decline in self-concept, a feeling that one is no longer the person he used to be. But to be separated from the larger society is not necessarily to be totally alienated. Retirement colonies, the burgeoning Senior Citizens movement, and the hotel porches along Collins Avenue in Miami

Beach all testify to some of the ways in which the elderly are isolated in behavior settings of their own with varying degrees of success or satisfaction.

In looking at the many special facilities for an aging population, from nursing homes to store ramps, from low cost housing to reduced fares on subways and buses, they seem to be meeting a variety of needs, some more effectively than others. First, there is increased recognition that the spatial needs of the elderly are somewhat different from the needs of earlier years. This has led to what Lindsley (1964) has termed a "prosthetic environment" for maintaining function in the face of old-age disability. Prosthetic substitutes are made for a wide spectrum of ages and strengths, and range from a simple ramp to a geriatric institution full of compensatory equipment. Lawton (1968) breaks down the prosthetic environment into five functional categories:

1. *Life-maintenance activity.* This involves basic physical safety, from secure housing to nonskid floors.
2. *Perceptual behavior.* Failing eyesight on the part of many elderly people necessitates large-faced clocks, for example. Beyond this, the esthetic barrenness of institutional environments can be depressing. Brighter decor, the addition of paintings, and the use of attractive "noninstitutional" furnishings offer more visual pleasure.
3. *Cognitive behavior.* "Mapping" one's environment can be made easier for the older person by the use of color-coded room doors and floors to mark out important routes.
4. *Self-maintenance skills.* Bathroom facilities can be arranged to anticipate the physical limits of old age. Kitchen facilities (in individual apartments) are designed for easy and nontaxing use.
5. *Effectance behavior.* Lawton cites hobbies, recreation, and "unprogrammed thinking" as activities important to the morale of the elderly. But stress on too-active participation is not necessarily desired. A good deal of effectance behavior is vicarious—"sitting and watching" more active people.

He warns, too, against a "caricature image" of a prosthetic environment filled with strange-shaped objects, "animated furniture," and all manner of odd and exotic mechanical devices.

The spatial implications of aging are both perceptual and functional. Testing individuals over sixty with the experimental technique used by Piaget on children, Sanders, Laurendeau, and Bergeron (1960) found that subjects reacted to a model landscape much as Piaget's children did before the age of six and seven; that is to say, nonanalytically. Moving a "house" into different positions in the model was seen as somehow increasing or decreasing the amount of land available for cultivation. If these findings can be generalized, there is evidence that the elderly perceive their environment in more concrete and less conceptual terms than adults of middle age.

On a functional level older people undergo an increasing degree of spatial isolation (a possible explanation for the above results). In part, this is due to decreased mobility, but it is also both socially and self-imposed. In brief, "home range" shrinks to an ever smaller area, often culminating in the institution with a concomitant reduction of social relationships. Efforts to create more "interactive" space are a prime concern of the space managers in retirement homes and geriatric centers, although sometimes the effort misfires; Lawton (1970) notes that in remodeling a home for the elderly in Philadelphia to provide easier access among inmates and staff, structural changes that made the various areas more visible resulted in fewer staff-patient interactions—quite the opposite of what was intended." Our *ex post facto* reasoning leads us to feel that the easier surveillance gained by the increased visual communication between the three types of areas actually made it easier for the staff to avoid interacting while still checking on the status of the patient." [p. 48]

For their part, the elderly inmates may strongly desire the opportunity to watch others—a place that permits visual accessiblity to stimulation without too much involvement in the noise and bustle of ongoing activity. It is not uncommon in nursing homes or residences for older people to find that protected seating areas behind the buildings remain unoccupied as the residents move chairs to a less desirable front area where "outside" activity can be viewed. Lawton (1970) has described this in a housing project where the social room, equipped with a television, was underused in favor of a room with a view of the lobby.

The elderly often experience both a constriction of their home range and changes in their residences. As home range diminishes, the proximal environment takes on added importance, both in terms of people and objects. Belongings become a source of psychological support (Gelwicks 1970). Keepsakes and photographs serve as mirrors of the past which help personalize new surroundings and preserve the continuity of self. Yet, while space may be restricted for the elderly, if properly managed, it may also provide for more social interaction, especially in planned housing. Carp (1966) noted that interaction was increased among a population of older persons who moved from dispersed to age-segregated housing, and Lawton (1970) observes that a higher level of within-building social activity takes place in buildings that have more open doors. Projects for the elderly, however dismal they may appear to the outsider, may offer their occupants a better choice of when and with whom they will interact, although the high-rise propect may not be the only way to achieve this. As a social phenomenon, the "open door" symbolizes the readiness of the tenant to receive visitors; tight security in better-managed housing makes this practical. Thus, while high-rise apartments seem to isolate tenants among a mixed population, the confining nature of such buildings tends to draw the elderly closer together, although this takes place almost exclusively on a floor-by-floor basis (Lawton 1970).

Not everyone wants to live in a "project," and indeed, many elderly persons maintain a high degree of identification, both physically and psychologically, with younger people. But in our society with its compulsory retirement age and family mobility, this is becoming increasingly difficult. Special environments for the elderly may be ways of maintaining dignity and well-being that were formerly left to chance or to families. In a sense these have become symbolic as well as physical environments—the "niche" that everyone seeks but which, until recently, was almost nonexistent for the aged. Lawton (1970) reports that his varied studies with the elderly reveal a capacity on their part to match their own competence with the environmental possibilities. In their ecological theory of aging, Nahemow and Lawton (1973) suggest that the individual operates best in a "moderately challenging" environment. It seems logical that providing an array of environmental choices is probably the most realistic solution to the search for appropriate settings in the later years.

That this does not always happen is evident from the literature dealing with alienation among this group (see, for example Granick & Nahemow 1961; Burrows & Lapides 1969). The elderly are often isolated from activity, community, and family; but rather than enjoying a state of privacy, they are relegated to feeling alone, detached, with anomie and often illness as the result. Especially for those in some form of institutional care, privacy is frequently lost along with their change in status. The consequences of this can be a less effective person, especially in an institutional context. In the absence of physical areas in which to obtain privacy, psychological withdrawal may be the only possible retreat from invasions. Yet, as Pastalan (1970) points out, privacy facilitates the maintenance of personal autonomy, so vital to a sense of individuality. The social control imposed by institutions undermines the individual's autonomy and thereby limits his capacity to exert power over his life, over the spaces he inhabits, and the persons who have access to him.

There is a readiness, on the part of the outside world, to discount and ignore the privacy needs of the elderly, much as those of children. Our institutional architecture tends to lump older people together in spite of the fact that we know little of their needs. Lawton (1970) checked the preferences for private rooms of a broad group which included older persons in institutions, a range of ages of noninstitutionalized persons, and professionals in geriatrics. Assuming they were to live in an old-age home, they were asked to select the form of housing they would prefer: a room by themselves, with another person, or more than one. For noninstitutionalized persons, the preferences for private rooms was roughly a function of their ages, from late adolescence to middle life, remaining high through the later years. Professionals in geriatrics expressed a high preference for the private arrangement at all ages. In the case of the institutionalized elderly, there was a tendency to choose what they already had. In institutions with few private rooms, 62 percent chose to be with one or more persons; 49 percent of those living in settings which had primarily single rooms preferred that arrangement. Lawton suggests that the results need to be examined in terms of other variables (for example, health, cultural factors), but cites the readiness to prescribe a multiple arrangement for others while eschewing this for oneself.

Many questions still remain regarding physical settings in later years, not the least of which is a clearer understanding of the attributes of this varied stage in life. Before one can generalize about settings, it is essential to clarify the specific physical, social, and economic changes that characterize this period.

Summary

In this chapter we have traced the role of the environment in the continuing development of the individual. Our lives, at any given time, reflect a history of interactions with the environment. This environment includes people as well as things and places. Indeed, the significant persons with whom we are in contact in early life clearly influence the kind of person we become, our values, and to some extent our personality, aspirations, and intellectual growth. Such influences are the staple of developmental psychology; we have said little about them here since our emphasis is on the physical setting. Brown (1965) has made the point that although the core of one's personality is formed very early and remains stable throughout life, behavior as such changes under different environmental conditions. Slum and suburb will act on personality development in quite different ways as the individual adapts to the necessities of the setting.

Given the importance of the social milieu, there remains the question of how this milieu interacts with the physical environment; beyond this, how the individual gets to know his environment, and how "space" and "objects" enter into his affective and cognitive development. These factors embrace a broad range of behavioral influences, beginning with the earliest stimulations that an infant receives and ending with the "managed" environments of old age. Between infancy and old age is a continually shifting set of environmental experiences; as we depend less on direct perception and more on conceptual understanding, the environment of man becomes increasingly complex, taking on new meanings at each stage of life. The apprehension of these meanings is a measure of how successfully we adapt to a continually changing world.

References

Bangs, H. P., & Mahler, S. Users of local parks. *Journal of the American Institute of Planners*, 1970, 36, 330–334.

Barker, R. G., & Gump. P. *Big school, small school.* Stanford, Calif.: Stanford University Press, 1964.

Barker, R. G., & Wright, H. F. *Midwest and its children.* New York: Harper & Row, 1955.

Berger, B. *Working class suburbs: A study of auto workers in suburbia.* Berkeley, Calif.: University of California Press, 1960.

Berlyne, D. L. *Conflict, arousal and curiosity.* New York: McGraw-Hill, 1960.

Birren, J. E. *The psychology of aging.* Englewood Cliffs, N.J.: Prentice-Hall, 1964.

Blaut, J. M., McCleary, G. S. Jr., & Blaut, A. S. Environmental mapping in young children. *Environment and Behavior*, 1970, *2*, 335–349.

Bowlby, J. *Child care and the growth of love.* Baltimore: Pelican, 1953.

Brown, C. *Manchild in the promised land.* New York: Macmillan, 1965.

Brown, R. *Social psychology.* New York: Free Press, 1965.

Brunetti, F. A. Noise, distraction and privacy in conventional and open school environments. In W. J. Mitchell (Ed.), *Environmental design: Research and practice,* Proceedings of EDRA 3/AR 8 Conference. Los Angeles: University of California Press, 1972.

Burrows, D., & Lapides, F. R. (Eds.) *Alienation: A casebook.* New York: Crowell, 1969.

Carp, F. M. *A future for the aged.* Austin, Texas: University of Texas Press, 1966.

Charlesworth, W. R. The role of surprise in cognitive development. In D. Elkind & J. H. Flavell (Eds.), *Studies in cognitive development.* New York: Oxford University Press, 1969. Pp. 257–314.

Cumming, E., & Henry, W. H. *Growing old: The process of disengagement.* New York: Basic Books, 1961.

Dee, N., & Liebman, J. C. A statistical study of attendance at urban playgrounds. *Journal of Leisure Research*, 1970, *2*, 145–159.

Durlak, J. T., Beardsley, B. E., & Murray, J. S. Observation of user activity patterns in open and traditional plan school environments. In W. J. Mitchell (Ed.), *Environmental design: Research and practice,* Proceedings of EDRA 3/AR 8 Conference. Los Angeles: University of California Press, 1972.

Durlak, J. T., Lehman, J., & McClain, J. *The school environment: A study of user patterns.* A report prepared for the Ministry of Education, Ontario, April 1973.

Ellis, M. J. Play: Theory and research. In W. J. Mitchell (Ed.), *Environmental design: Research and practice*, Proceedings of EDRA 3/AR 8 Conference. Los Angeles: University of California Press, 1972.

Erikson, E. H. *Childhood and society.* New York: Norton, 1950.

Escalona, S. K. *The roots of individuality: Normal patterns of development in infancy.* Chicago: Aldine, 1968.

Escalona, S. K., & Heider, G. *Prediction and outcome.* New York: Basic Books, 1959.

Flavell, J. H. Concept development. In P. H. Mussen (Ed.), *Carmichael's manual of child psychology.* (3rd ed.) New York: Wiley, 1970. Pp. 893–1059.

Fried, M. Grieving for a lost home. In L. Duhl (Ed.), *The urban condition.* New York: Basic Books, 1963. Pp. 151–171.

Fried, M., & Gleicher, P. Some sources of residential satisfaction in an urban slum. *Journal of the American Institute of Planners*, 1961, *27*, 305–315.

Gans, H. *The Levittowners: Ways of life and politics in a new suburban community.* New York: Pantheon, 1967.

Gelwicks, L. E. Home range and the use of space by an aging population. In L. A. Pastalan & D. H. Carson (Eds.), *Spatial behavior of older people.* Ann Arbor, Mich.: University of Michigan Press, 1970. Pp. 148–161.

Gold, S. Nonuse of neighborhood parks. *Journal of the American Institute of Planners,* 1972, *38*, 369–378.

Goldberg, T. The automobile: A social institution for adolescents. *Environment and Behavior,* 1969, *1,* 157–185.

Goldfarb, W. Psychological privation in infancy and subsequent adjustment. *American Journal of Orthopsychiatry*, 1945, *15*, 247–255.

Granick, R., & Nahemow, L. Preadmission isolation as a factor in adjustment to an old age home. In P. H. Hock & J. Zubin (Eds.), *Psychopathology of Aging Proceedings.* Vol. 17. New York: Grune & Stratton, 1961.

Hart, R. A. Personal communication, 1973.

Hayward, D. G., Rothenberg, M., & Beasley, R. School-aged children in three urban playgrounds. Final report to the National Science Foundation, Grant No. GZ–2562. City Unversity of New York, Environmental Psychology Program, 1973.

Housing Development Directorate. *Children at play.* London: Her Majesty's Stationery Office, 1973.

Irelan, L. M. (Ed.) *Low-income life styles.* Washington, D.C.: U.S. Department of Health, Education and Welfare, 1967.

Kessen, W., Haith, M. M., & Salapatek, P. H. Human infancy: A bibliography and guide. In P. H. Mussen (Ed.), *Carmichael's manual of child psychology.* (3rd ed.) New York: Wiley, 1970. Pp. 287–445.

Lawton, M. P. Social and structural aspects of prosthetic environments for older people. Paper presented at the Third Annual Institute on Man's Adjustment in a Complex Environment, Veterans Administration Hospital. Brechsville, Ohio, June, 1968.

Lawton, M. P. Ecology and aging. In L. A. Pastalan & D. H. Carson (Eds.), *Spatial behavior of older people.* Ann Arbor, Mich.: University of Michigan Press, 1970. Pp. 40–67.

Lindsley, O. R. Geriatric behavioral prosthesis. In R. Kastenbaum (Ed.), *New thoughts on old age.* New York: Springer, 1964.

Lowenfeld, M. *Play in childhood.* New York: Wiley, 1967.

Madge, C. Public and private spaces. *Human Relations*, 1950, *3*, 187–199.

Michelson, W. *Man and his urban environment: A sociological approach.* Reading, Mass.: Addison-Wesley, 1970.

Munroe, R. L., & Munroe, R. H. Effect of environmental experience on spatial ability in an East African society. *Journal of Social Psychology*, 1971, *83*, 15–22.

Nahemow, L., & Kogan, L. Reduced fare for the elderly. Report submitted to Office for the Aging, Mayor's Office, City of New York. City University of New York, Center for Social Research and Ph.D. Program in Environmental Psychology, 1971.

Nahemow, L., & Lawton, M. P. Toward an ecological theory of adaptation and aging. In W. F. E. Preiser (Ed.), *Environmental design research,* Proceedings of the EDRA 4 Conference. Stroudsberg, Pa.: Dowden, Hutchinson and Ross, 1973.

Nerlove, S. B., Munroe, R. H., & Munroe, R. L. Effect of environmental experience on spatial ability: A replication. *Journal of Social Psychology*, 1971, *84*, 3–10.

Neugarten, B. L. *Middle age and aging.* Chicago: University of Chicago Press, 1968.

New York Times. Report on survey by P. Wedge & J. Petzing. September 13, 1970.

New York Times. Report on work of J. Kagan. December 27, 1972.

Nicholson, S. How not to cheat children: The theory of loose parts. *Landscape Architecture*, 1971, *62*, 30–34.

Parks, G. *Born black.* Philadelphia: Lippincott, 1971.
Pastalan, L. A. Privacy as an expression of human territoriality. In L. A. Pastalan & D. H. Carson (Eds.), *Spatial behavior of older people.* Ann Arbor, Mich.: University of Michigan Press, 1970. Pp. 88–101.
Piaget, J. Piaget's theory. In P. H. Mussen (Ed.), *Carmichael's manual of child psychology.* (3rd ed.) New York: Wiley, 1970. Pp. 703–732.
Piaget, J., & Inhelder, B. *The psychology of the child.* New York: Basic Books, 1969.
Piaget, J., Inhelder, B., & Szeminska, A. *The child's conception of geometry.* New York: Basic Books, 1960.
Provence, S., & Lipton, R. C. *Infants in institutions.* New York: International Universities Press, 1962.
Rivlin, L. G., & Wolfe, M. The early history of a psychiatric hospital for children: Expectations and reality. *Environment and Behavior*, 1972, *4*, 33–72.
Sanders, S., Laurendeau, M., & Bergeron, J. Aging and the concept of space: The conservation of surfaces. *Gerontologist*, 1960, *1*, 281–286.
Schorr, A. L. *Slums and social insecurity.* Washington, D.C.: U.S. Department of Health, Education and Welfare, 1966.
Smith, K. V., & Smith, W. M. *Perception and motion.* Philadelphia: Saunders, 1962.
Spitz, R. Hospitalism: An inquiry into the genesis of psychiatric conditions in early childhood. *Psychoanalytic Study of the Child*, 1945, *1*, 53–74.
Stea, D., & Blaut, J. M. Notes toward a developmental theory of spatial learning. In J. Archea & C. Eastman (Eds.), *EDRA Two: Proceedings of 2nd annual environmental design research association.* Pittsburgh: EDRA, 1970.
Stone, L. J., & Church, J. *Childhood and adolescence: A psychology of the growing person.* (2nd ed.) New York: Random House, 1968.
Toffler, A. *Future shock.* New York: Random House, 1970.
Wadsworth, B. J. *Piaget's theory of cognitive development.* New York: McKay, 1971.
White, R. W. Motivation reconsidered: The concept of competence. *Psychological Review*, 1959, *66*, 313–324. [Excerpts reprinted in H. M. Proshansky et al. (Eds.), *Environmental psychology: Man and his physical setting.* New York: Holt, Rinehart and Winston, 1970. Pp. 125–134.]

Suggested Readings

Aries, P. *Centuries of childhood.* New York: Random House, 1962.
Erikson, E. *Childhood and society.* New York: Norton, 1950.
Pastalan, L. A., & Carson, D. H. (Eds.) *Spatial behavior of older people.* Ann Arbor, Mich.: University of Michigan Press, 1970.
Piaget, J. & Inhelder, B. *The child's conception of space.* New York: Norton, 1967.
Piaget, J. & Inhelder, B. *The psychology of the child.* New York: Basic Books. 1969.
Stone, L. J., & Church, J. *Childhood and adolescene: A psychology of the growing person* (2nd ed.) New York: Random House, 1968.

Eight

Research Methods in Environmental Psychology

Approaches to Environmental Psychology

One of the central problems in environmental psychology is that of selecting a suitable strategy for studying human behavior in various settings. This search for methods grows out of our contention in Chapter Five and elsewhere in this book that the investigator should concentrate on understanding behavior in the large-scale environment rather than confine himself to the piecemeal approach that results from examining limited behaviors in highly contrived settings such as the laboratory. Because of the complex nature of the physical settings within which human activity occurs, our task is the development of research techniques which are sensitive to this complexity. At the same time our search is complicated by the fact that it is difficult to alter the physical environment for experimental purposes. Most environments are simply not subject to the kinds of experimental changes and controls that the research psychologist typically demands. This fact poses a different set of methodological challenges for the environmental psychologist.

Such challenges focus on the manner in which we approach behavior. Barker (1963) and Brunswik (1956) have both argued persuasively that techniques are needed which allow us to capture behavior as it is lived rather than confine ourselves only to that which is observable in the laboratory. We know that human behavior is extremely sensitive to the conditions under which it is investigated. There is no guarantee that the regularities of behavior observed in laboratory settings will at all approximate the regularities observed in everyday life. For Barker these regularities can best be studied without the manipulation of the psychologist; he termed this a *transducer* technique, with the investigator serving mainly to "pass along" the observations of behavior without in any way intervening in it. His job is primarily to evaluate what he sees.

Under certain circumstances, however, experimental approaches may be absolutely essential. It has been noted that Pavlov could not have carried out his research on conditioned reflexes if he had to use passing dogs on a street corner. Again, one can successfully study certain discrete behaviors, if this is the indicated approach, only by isolating them from outside contaminating influences. How then does one decide on the most productive methods for comprehending the everyday physical environment and man's behavior in it? What is it about specific environments that suggests particular kinds of research strategies? What are the best techniques for implementing a given strategy? These are some of the questions which will be dealt with in this chapter.

Before discussing this, however, it will be helpful to locate environmental research in the context of the general methodologies employed in the behavioral sciences, to indicate the investigative procedures that are shared with other disciplines and to point out those that seem especially useful in studying the environment. By this time the student will be aware that our knowledge of the environment, and man's role in it, derives from many sources. Sommer (1969) studied spatial behavior, for example, using observation in a natural setting. Altman (1967), pursuing the same general kind of investigation, observed his subjects in controlled, or experimental, environments. Or one might ask people to describe or evaluate their own reactions to a given environmental situation, either by means of a questionnaire, a simulation of the environment, or psychological tests that reveal attitudes which a person may not be aware of.

Indeed, more than one procedure can and should be used to study a specific phenomenon, but no matter which is selected, the appropriate data must be forthcoming if the study is to reveal what is sought. A good research design is one that (1) identifies the nature of the variables most relevant to the behavior under investigation; (2) utilizes the most fruitful methods for studying this behavior; and (3) yields significant information about the behavior. A little later, studies of a large-scale environment—in each case a community—will illustrate four different research perspectives. At this point, however, it will be helpful to describe the traditional investigative procedures of behavioral research and to say something about their applicability to environmental psychology.

Experimental Research

This is usually conducted within a laboratory setting. Although strictly speaking it need not be carried out in a laboratory, some formal control over the setting and its components is necessary. Experimental design deals with the relationships among selected variables of a system rather than in exploring all the variables of the system operating holistically. It seeks to identify cause and effect among these variables, usually on the basis of an hypothesis about what the relationships might be. Within this research category, the *field experiment* uses existing social structures but attempts to utilize laboratory techniques of control.

Holistic Research

In this procedure the objective is not the study of selected environmental variables, but rather the relationships which exist among these variables as part of a complex situation. Broadly speaking, this design is qualitative, seeking the underlying themes of a situation rather than the relationships existing between isolated variables. "Holistic research takes as its problem the nature of the total system rather than of a particular process within the situation." [Weiss 1968:343] Like experimental research, it also has a set of procedures enabling the researcher to check the validity of his assumptions.

Survey Research

Employing questionnaires, interviews, tests, and simulations, this procedure is widely used in finding out how people think and feel about certain specific issues that can be easily categorized—political candidates, for instance (as in the Gallup poll), or commercial products (as in market research). Survey techniques, in general, explore attitudes rather than behavior. They are also useful in evaluating an individual's reactions to a situation or an environment.

The Field Study

Unlike survey research the field study uses existing data. For this reason it is often called an ex post facto method. Demographic information, such as government statistics, medical records, and the like, comprise the raw material, over which, of course, the investigator has no control. Field studies correlate this social, physical, and psychological data in an effort to find relevant associations that may indicate a causal relationship among specific variables —smoking and lung cancer, for example.

Exploratory Research

Like the holistic model this approach can be used to study complex environments such as cities or ethnic communities. However, the material gathered this way is more likely to be quantified and correlated into possible sets of significant relationships. It says, in effect, "Let's look at the situation and see what characteristics are suggested for further study." Thus, in practice, exploratory research is frequently preliminary to a more precisely formulated and narrowly focused design in which, it is hoped, certain causal relationships can be tested.

All research is simply the gathering and interpretation of information. It is the point of view behind the study—the objectives of the investigation—that determines the most suitable overall procedure. How the data are obtained, however, involves specific techniques, or methods used to implement the design, many of which are applicable to several or all of the various procedures described above.

One might, for example, examine existing archival records. In all the approaches data may be generated through interviews, questionnaires, and attitude scales. Many research procedures rely heavily on the observation of behavior by the investigator. This can occur at various levels of interaction. The researcher may participate in the event he is observing (and to that extent possibly influence it) or he might observe unobtrusively and make an exact record of his observations by using a camera or tape recorder. He may then systematize or map his observations according to predetermined categories of interest or time segments. Sometimes he will use a confederate to stimulate certain kinds of behavior he wants to study.

Additional techniques especially pertinent to environmental research include *simulation* of selected aspects of an environment, *cognitive mapping*, and *gaming*. In simulation one attempts to create a mock environment in order to predict behavior in a comparable real environment. Cognitive mapping indirectly reveals something about an individual's behavior by comparing his mental image of an environment to that which actually exists. Gaming uses simulated situations or processes, as well as environments, in an effort both to elicit behavior traits which the individual may not always be aware of and to acquaint the player with the complexities of the many environments with which he may have contact. Games "create dramatic representations of the real problem being studied." [Abt 1970:13] Later on, these specific techniques will be discussed in greater detail. At this point we want to treat the four major research procedures as they apply to environmental psychology.

Experimental Research—Controlling the Variables

Broadly speaking, when doing research in the behavioral sciences one attempts to identify the variables that bear upon the particular phenomenon under investigation. This is to say, we attempt to separate the essential from the nonessential in observed relationships. Experiments of this sort frequently involve a one-variable model in which a cause-and-effect hypothesis is tested between one component and others that relate to it. Such an approach "insists that experiments should be so designed that all variables but one are controlled.

The effects of that variable can thus be assessed independently of confusing, and possibly contaminating, influences." [Gillis & Schneider in Hammond 1966:204] In an effort to introduce more complexity into experimental approaches, many investigators employ a multivariate design in which a number of independent and dependent variables are studied. Emphasis, however, is still placed upon the identification and control of any contaminating influences which might render the results confusing.

A variable, as we use it here, is anything (such as an object, social condition, behavior pattern, or attitude) which has different values under different conditions. In a word, it varies according to the influences that impinge on it. Variables are either independent (experimental) or dependent. The former are those which the investigator controls, or which can be considered a given. They act as an "effective force." Dependent variables, as the adjective implies, depend upon the independent variable for their values. Because y is found wherever x is found, and if x is altered the nature of y is changed, then the change in x "explains" the change in y. In the sciences we say that such a causal relationship demonstrates the lawful behavior of the organism, or the physical entity, under study. Experiments are generally conducted in highly controlled environments which can be completely manipulated by the experimenter. Specific aspects of behavior rather than the total response of the person are the subject of investigation.

In a great deal of research the investigator hypothesizes a causal relationship among variables and develops a strategy that allows him to test its possible validity. Such a procedure is necessarily either experimental or quasi-experimental—that is, he controls the conditions under which the investigation is made and, to a greater or lesser degree, manipulates the independent variables. In the Freedman et al. (1971) crowding experiment, discussed in Chapter Six, the variables are density, task performance, and the interpersonal reactions of those taking part. Freedman varied the first of these factors and tested the effects of different densities using the latter two.

A somewhat more complex experiment was carried out by Glass and Singer (1972) in investigating the effects of noise on task performance. A group of college students was subjected to both regular and irregular bursts of noise. When a single puzzle task was being performed, the noise had no effect on the ability of the students to work the puzzle, or the time it took them to do so. However, this phenomenon was not the major concern of the test; the failure to find a connection between x (noise) and y_1 (task) led the experimenters to introduce a third variable y_2—a second, more complex task to be performed after the noise had ceased. When this was done, there was a lowering of performance on the second task. In this experiment the investigator's hypothesis was simply that the effects of noise were postadaptive; the finding of a connection between x and y_2 confirmed the hypothesis. ". . . noise can indeed be a stressor with demonstrable effects on behavior, but detection of these effects requires that we look at postnoise and postadaptive behavior." [Glass & Singer 1972:44]

Similarly, an experiment by Maslow and Mintz (1956) studied the effects of esthetic surroundings on a group of college students by placing them in "beautiful," "average," and "ugly" rooms and asking them to judge photographs of people's faces. All students were shown the same set of photographs to control for any differences that might have arisen due to using different photographs in the three rooms. Those in the beautiful room, to a significant degree, rated the faces "zestful" and "content," whereas most students in the ugly room found them "weary" and "irritable." Would the same results apply to "real" faces in "real" rooms? We do not know. The environmentalist would simply conclude that such an experiment is "high on experimental realism but low on mundane" (Aronson & Carlsmith 1968) or real world conditions.

In this connection Campbell and Stanley (1963) draw a distinction between the internal and external validity of an experiment. The former obtains

> . . . if the experimental stimulus has some significant effect within the experimental situation. External validity refers to the generalizability of the effect—to what populations and settings it is applicable. . . . Optimal design is one that maximizes both internal and external validity. [pp. 24–25]

This is not an easy task, since by definition an experiment demands more rigorous controls than most outside settings provide. One means of trying to achieve this representativeness with some degree of investigative control is the field experiment that we mentioned earlier. Here causal relationships are sought through experimental interventions in the real world setting and/or its naturally occurring behaviors. Properly speaking, this kind of methodology is quasi-experimental since it is seldom possible to achieve the tight, all-inclusive control of the laboratory.

Thus, in a housing study conducted in Baltimore, Wilner et al. (1962) surveyed the effects of new housing on former slum residents by comparing their reactions to those of a similar group who remained in the slum. Both groups were randomly selected from the same slum, and the main independent variable (admittedly a complex one) being tested was the new housing. Although nothing was "proved," in the lawful sense, the evidence was strong that good housing, among other things, gives people a greater sense of power over their lives. In this type of research our experimental variable is usually provided by forces outside our control, as is the case in most real world settings.

It was mentioned earlier that the independent variable (new housing) was admittedly complex. If such a study were to become more experimental, careful attention would have to be paid to identifying the components of such a new environment. For example, it would have been desirable to add a control group that moved to different (but not necessarily new) housing to determine whether the move itself might have been responsible for the differences which Wilner and his colleagues found. This control would not be "pure," since the group in question also will be affected by the environment into which it moves as well as the move itself; however, it is seldom possible to meet all the requirements of a classical experimental design when working in field settings. In this case, at least, quality of the new housing for the control group should be similar to that which they left behind.

A similar field experiment was conducted by Fanning (see Michelson 1970:161–162) on the effects of housing differences on the families of British servicemen stationed in West Germany (cited in Chapter Seven). Such quasi-experimental designs have certain advantages over field studies. They permit the manipulation of at least one of the variables (in these cases, types of housing). They are adaptable to a wide variety of problems which reflect ongoing situations. They also improve the capacity to generalize findings to other similar types of environments, thus increasing the external validity of the experiment. The complexity of such environments, however, always creates the problem of possible contamination from uncontrollable or unknown variables.

Limitations of the Laboratory

There are times when a laboratory experiment is the only method, practically speaking, that will yield the information sought. Moreover, the experimentalist recognizes in principle the importance of being able to generalize outside the experimental setting (external validity). Often, however, the degree of control required to investigate a number of variables forces the experimenter into the laboratory. As a consequence studies such as that of Glass and Singer (1972) are often unrepresentative of natural conditions to the extent that the variables (noise and task assignment) are arbitrarily contrived, not to mention the extent to which those taking part tend to behave like subjects of an experiment rather than persons in an everyday environment. Female reaction to crowding (noted in Chapter Six) might have been different if the test had occurred in a living room or subway car. In this case the social, or symbolic, nature of the space was not taken into account.

Objections to experimental procedures, from the point of view of the environmentalist, derive from their emphasis on discrete behaviors rather than the whole man. Ideally, our interest is not in the analysis of isolated psychological functions but in the intact behaviors and experiences of people in relation to relevant physical settings. A methodology for environmental research must evolve out of the nature and characteristics of the phenomena it studies. To the extent that such phenomena are complex, isolated variables cannot (and should not) be specified. Seeking relationships between intact physical settings and the ongoing integrated behaviors of individuals means relating a patterned environment to a sequenced pattern of human activity. Moreover, such relationships must be studied over extended periods of time. Finally, they become meaningful only in the context of the total environment—the social, cultural, and institutional systems that define the existence of modern man.

Holistic Design—The Search for Themes

Holistic research is essentially descriptive in its method. It does not seek to test a set of hypotheses but to discover and interpret the unifying themes that underlie a complex situation. The holistic investigator "will tend to explain particular phenomena in terms of the action of the system rather than in terms of some intersection of causal factors. . . . Taking it all together, he asks, how does the whole thing work?" [Weiss, 1966: 198] Such a procedure can be highly factual in the data it generates, or highly impressionistic; it can include both facts and impressions (and usually does) if these contribute to an explanation of the events being studied. A familiar example is the anthropologist's field report; although many facts are gathered, they do not necessarily "speak for themselves." Variables may be identified and correlated, but of course they are often beyond control. The anthropologist's general observations about the culture he is investigating are equally important.

Margaret Mead's book *Coming of Age in Samoa* is a field study based on the holistic approach. Its method is that of participant observation. The insights which grew out of this extended observation, along with the author's literary skill, give this book its power. It has a good story to tell, but it is a story based on the impressions of a trained observer who was able to interpret what she saw in a meaningful way.

To the extent that Mead's personal orientation operates on her material, however, the data may be replicable only by others who share her orientation. Unlike the experimentalist, the holistic researcher is not entirely neutral; he observes and interprets from a personal point of view. He can be said to intrude his own values into the material he studies although there is often an effort to avoid such intrusions. The theme elicited from *Coming of Age in Samoa* is that adolescent girls on Samoa live a rather carefree and unrepressed sexual life, characterized by a minimum of adolescent adjustment problems and an absence of later neurosis. The author valued this as a good thing.

Many well-known studies of contemporary life in the United States borrow heavily from the methods of cultural anthropology. Indeed, urban anthropology has become a term for describing the approach of social scientists to the problems of cities. Perhaps the prototypical example is Lloyd Warner's *Yankee City* (1963), a series of five studies which dissect the societal organization of a Boston suburb. *Yankee City* represents a high degree of data gathering, but it is also dependent on the classification system and interpretive categories set up by its author to explain his material. The terms relating to gradations in social class such as, "upper-upper," "upper-middle," "middle-middle," and so on have become standard nomenclature, for the satirist if not always for the social scientist. The study is essentially a holistic survey of the urban environment and is concerned largely with the social implications of this environment. One of its primary themes is the importance of status in social relationships.

On the other hand, Herbert Gans' *The Urban Villagers* (1962), a description of life in Boston's West End, was based chiefly on the author's close personal contact with the people he was studying; the accumulation of statistical data was secondary. Gans, moreover, operated as an individual (with informal help from his wife), whereas Warner used research teams, questionnaires, and other survey techniques. Both authors, to some extent, made use of available materials to buttress their findings. Nevertheless, Gans' study is essentially an observation and interpretation of the urban environment. It is concerned with both the physical and social setting.

Despite their differences, these studies share a common characteristic. Their purpose is to discover the broad relationships, both qualitative and quantitative, that exist between the populations studied and the various aspects of their environment. It is the system, not the components or separate variables, that is of interest. Because much of Gans' book deals with the relationship of physical setting to behavior, it is particularly relevant to environmental psychology. Let us look briefly at his methods.

Gans' interest in the West End grew out of the fact that it was the target area for an extensive urban renewal program. He designed his project to discover the relationship of slums and mental illness, one of sociology's particular interests relating to urban renewal. Hypothetically, at least, removal from slum conditions should contribute to better health. That this hypothesis did not obtain—indeed, that urban renewal had the opposite effect—was the major and somewhat unexpected result of the study. Of course, part of the difficulty was that the "slum" was not really a slum.

Like the anthropologists, Gans moved into the area and became a resident, sharing the same general living conditions as his subjects. His technique was that of the participant observer. In *The Urban Villagers* Gans explains what this involved:

1. He used the stores, services, and public facilities of the area as a means of observing people's everyday behavior. This was essentially passive, or unobtrusive, observation.
2. He attended meetings and public gatherings, taking part in them when feasible. In such instances the observer becomes a participant for research purposes—he "may try to steer the conversation to topics in which he is especially interested."
3. In addition, Gans and his wife made friends with their neighbors and formed numerous social contacts. Alone, he spent some time in neighborhood taverns, overhearing (and sometimes taking part in) the barroom conversations, directing them at times into particular channels. It should be added that Gans did not identify himself as a researcher who was studying those with whom he came in contact. He recognized that it was necessary to exploit relationships to gain the information he was seeking.

In addition to direct observation, Gans employed two other techniques in which he explicitly acted as a researcher. He interviewed community leaders, municipal authorities, ministers and priests, settlement house directors, and others who were familiar with neighborhood problems and customs. Finally, he used informants, or confidants, from among people he got to know, to relay significant information to him. From all sources Gans pieced together a comprehensive picture of life in the West End. He kept a diary of field notes which were later sorted and analyzed. These data were then interpreted in the light of the author's original purpose: to correlate the connections, if any, between slum conditions and mental illness.

Gans concluded that the crowded setting was not in itself a major cause of pathology. The uprooting of inhabitants (as part of an urban renewal project) was likely to be more contributory to mental illness. Because of strong family and ethnic ties—the area was largely Italian—any disruption of the social fabric was threatening to the inhabitants' sense of security. He found, too, that neighborhoods which urban planners perceive as a slum are not necessarily so perceived by those who live in them. A decrepit physical environment, in short, does not always mean a pathological social environment.

Thematically, as a result of his general observations, Gans identified a life style similar to that experienced by people in small towns and villages. His book illustrates the relational similarity between the small town and the way in which the West End was organized—hence its title. Its themes concern family ties, feelings about space, neighborhood boundaries, social cohesiveness, and community of interests. The book had wide impact in demonstrating that city planning and urban renewal policies which ignore the behavioral implications of these policies—their effect on the day-to-day lives of the people—are likely to be deficient. "The operation was a success but the patient died." Some of these implications are discussed in our chapter on the urban environment.

Because *The Urban Villagers* is a one-man study, it bears the imprint of a single personality and point of view; in short, it reads like a book rather than a research document. At the same time, because it minimizes objective documentation, it lacks the rigor of *Yankee City* (Warner 1963). Such a highly personal approach, however, can provide intuitive insights that are often missing when the researcher relies wholly on facts to explain his phenomena. The facts are dealt with, but only in the context of a system which is more than the sum of its parts.[1]

Survey Research—The Quest for Self-Disclosure

An approach to data gathering which is probably best known because of the Gallup and Harris polls, survey research is used in a number of cases to determine people's attitudes, beliefs, and feelings about a wide variety of topics. It

[1] John Marquand's *Point of No Return* (1947), among other things, parodies Warner's categorizing approach to society. Marquand's hero, Charles Gray, is unknowingly a better researcher than the professional anthropologist. It is he who tells the "real story" of Clyde, Massachusetts, and it is the "real story" that holistic research is primarily concerned with.

follows the rubric: If you want to know how a person stands on a question, ask him. Of course, he may not be aware of the real nature of his opinions; except for conspicuous deviations from what is usual, for example, new settings may influence the behavior of the person with little or no conscious awareness on his part. What he is unaware of he clearly cannot report, although, in fact, his behavior may have changed. Possibly, he will also be biased; what a person thinks about something is filtered through his prejudices, hopes, and expectations.

This does not mean that self-reporting is always unreliable. A man's prejudices may be the very information we are seeking, although this may be elicited indirectly (as it often is in attitude questionnaires). As a practical matter most research uses some form of survey technique. The social categories in *Yankee City* (Warner 1963) are based, to a great extent, on the self-ranking of its sample population. Gans' conversations with the West Enders were obviously surveys, no matter how informal, of what people thought and felt about their lives.

Survey techniques are neither experimental nor holistic, although they may be incorporated into either of these approaches. In more elaborate surveys attempts are often made to find out how opinions correlate with other indicators of interest. For instance, one may ask, as Costantini and Hanf (1972) did, whether opinions concerning various aspects of environmental problems affecting Lake Tahoe, California, could be related to the respondent's position in the community, his political affiliations, occupation, and so on. A similar survey dealing with attitudes toward environmental concern in the area of Boulder, Colorado, attempts to determine how universal this concern is (Tognacci et al. 1972). By correlating responses to a questionnaire-and-interview technique with various social and economic characteristics of their sample, Tognacci et al. (1972) concluded that the ecology movement, contrary to widely held beliefs, does not unite people of opposing viewpoints.

> At least at this point in time, those persons most concerned about environmental issues appear to reflect the same configuration of social and psychological attributes which have traditionally characterized individuals active in civic, service, and political organizations—e.g., high education and high socioeconomic status. [p. 85]

Conceivably, one might discover these same responses by observing people in relation to the way they use their environment. As a practical matter this would be cumbersome and time-consuming if applied to a significantly large sample. Instead, one assumes that what people say in answer to a given question pretty much reflects how they act out their beliefs when given the opportunity. In any case, we would have to translate our observations into descriptive categories if we want to correlate them into some kind of finding. This is to say that answers by respondents to various questions must be grouped and weighted (usually through multivariate analysis techniques) if they are to be compared and interpreted. A difficulty here is that the survey

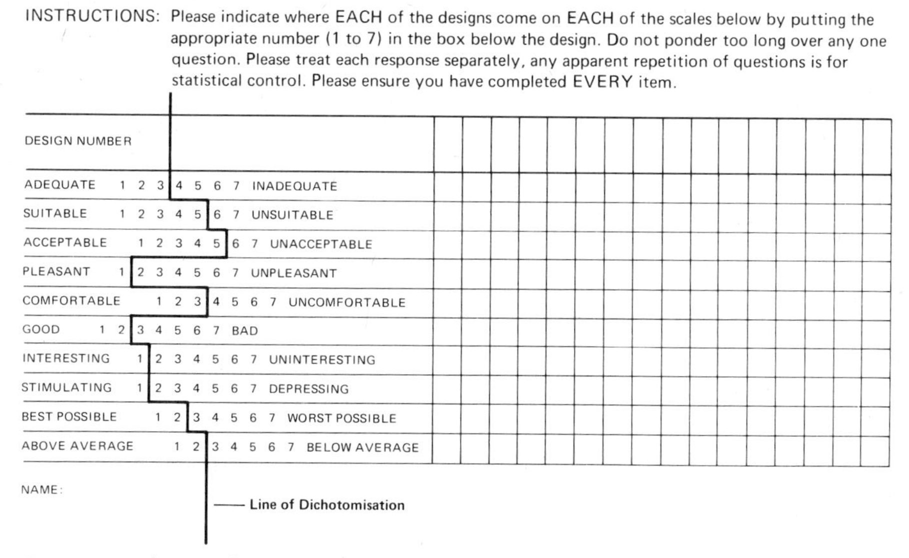

INSTRUCTIONS: Please indicate where EACH of the designs come on EACH of the scales below by putting the appropriate number (1 to 7) in the box below the design. Do not ponder too long over any one question. Please treat each response separately, any apparent repetition of questions is for statistical control. Please ensure you have completed EVERY item.

DESIGN NUMBER

ADEQUATE 1 2 3 4 5 6 7 INADEQUATE

SUITABLE 1 2 3 4 5 6 7 UNSUITABLE

ACCEPTABLE 1 2 3 4 5 6 7 UNACCEPTABLE

PLEASANT 1 2 3 4 5 6 7 UNPLEASANT

COMFORTABLE 1 2 3 4 5 6 7 UNCOMFORTABLE

GOOD 1 2 3 4 5 6 7 BAD

INTERESTING 1 2 3 4 5 6 7 UNINTERESTING

STIMULATING 1 2 3 4 5 6 7 DEPRESSING

BEST POSSIBLE 1 2 3 4 5 6 7 WORST POSSIBLE

ABOVE AVERAGE 1 2 3 4 5 6 7 BELOW AVERAGE

NAME:

—— Line of Dichotomisation

Fig. 8-1 Scalogram based on ten semantic differential items. (Reproduced by permission from Canter and Thorne 1972.)

researcher does not generally have any control over the variables which lead to certain responses on the test instrument. In many cases he does not even know what the relevant variables are. One purpose of a survey might be to discover them. Correlations are an effort to at least identify those variables which might be causally implicated in certain situations. If one learns which occupational groups show high ecological concerns, one knows whom to look to for help in improving the quality of the environment.

Where the variables are known or controlled by the investigator, it is possible to carry out a survey that is at least quasi-experimental. For example, in a cross-cultural survey the attitudes of first-year students of the undergraduate schools of architecture at the University of Strathclyde, Glasgow, were compared with those of a similar group of students at the University of Sydney, Australia. The question posed was: "Do different groups of people living in different countries, but of similar education, age and social status, have different preferences for house types?" [Canter & Thorne 1972:5]

Students were shown sixteen colored slides of house types from Scotland and Australia, and one each from Italy, the United States, and England. A scalogram was provided with ten dichotomies, each rated one through seven (Figure 8–1). The students were asked to give their subjective reactions to living in each type of dwelling and the results were plotted on an attitude scale (Figure 8–2). In addition, students were asked to complete three open-ended sentences describing their reactions to the houses. Nine of the sixteen illustrations produced significantly different responses for the two groups, seven did not.

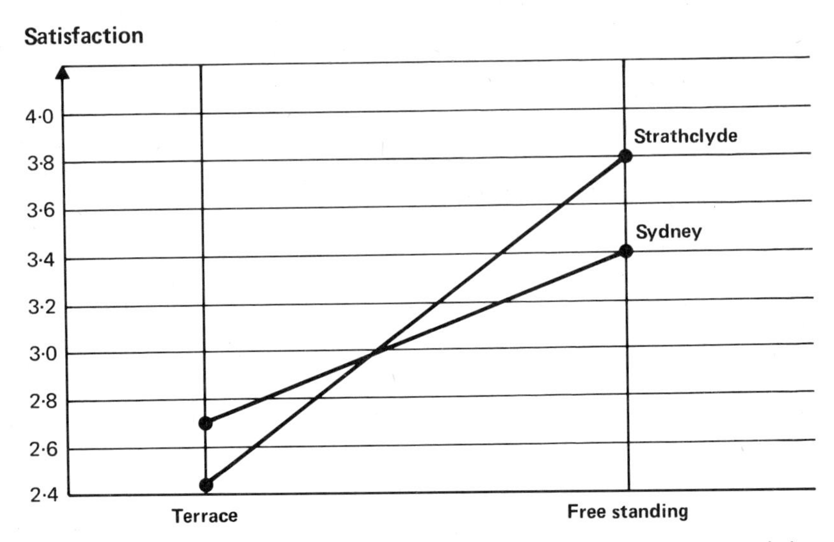

Fig. 8-2 The combined attitude-scale means for all terrace houses and for all free-standing houses presented separately for the sample from Strathclyde and Sydney. (Reproduced by permission from Canter and Thorne 1972)

The conclusions are interesting. In brief, familiarity with house types did not produce preferences for those types. Indeed, the opposite was the case. Sydney students had a preference for old terrace-row housing (as found in Scotland) and one particular nontraditional house. In comparison, Glasgow students preferred the traditional individual bungalow style of house as it existed in Australia (Canter & Thorne 1972:25).

As a research approach, the study combined two methods: attitude measurements (the completion of sentences and the use of a Semantic Differential scale) and visual simulation (photographic slides). Basically, of course, it was a survey of attitudes and not behavior. The Semantic Differential (Snider & Osgood 1969) scale as employed by Canter and Thorne is one way of categorizing attitudes. This technique can be further illustrated in a survey by Lowenthal and Riel (1972) dealing with the observation of environmental characteristics in four urban settings.

The authors employed twenty-five bipolar attributes to describe these environments. Some examples are:

ugly—beautiful
ordered—chaotic
smooth—rough
old—new
clean—dirty
quiet—noisy

The reader will note that these pairs represent opposites. The observer must choose which of the two words in each set best describes his personal reaction to the setting. (In addition, he was asked to write down what he "considered 'important' constituents of outdoor environmental experience." Different types of observers (Boy Scouts, secretaries, nurses, housewives, and the like) and different localities (Boston, New York, Cambridge, Massachusetts, and Columbus, Ohio) were observed. This resulted in a matrix of 300 paired relationships; from these, it was found that 59 correlated "among all groups of observers in each of the four cities." [Lowenthal & Riel 1972:197] The 59 relationships, in turn, were dominated by ten attributes and their bipolar opposites. Cities were judged to be ugly *or* beautiful; clean *or* dirty, and so forth. These attributes were linked with other characteristics of cities—"newness," for example was associated with fresh, ordered, and rich environments. "Quiet" was associated with fresh, ordered, and clean. What we are saying is that the bipolar descriptions, when factored, fell into clusters from which a meaningful pattern could be drawn. The overall conclusion of the study was that different urban milieus, observed by different groups of people, share a common set of response attributes. "Neither past environmental experience nor any background differences in age, sex, education, or occupation significantly affects the strength of these associations." [Lowenthal & Riel 1972: 197]

This survey is an example of a rather sophisticated use of the Semantic Differential scale. It illustrates one approach to evaluating an environment from the user's point of view. Like the questionnaire survey, it is subjective; unlike the interview, however, it limits choices and thus does not allow a wholly free response. Behavior in an environment, as we noted earlier, may not be consistent with a verbal evaluation of an environment; that is, a person's verbal response may differ from his behavioral response. Because people are not always aware of the effect a setting has on their actions, the survey approach, in some instances, may be quite inappropriate. In general, however, where the attitudes of large numbers of people are sought, it is a useful method of extrapolating from representative samples into the general population.

Exploratory Research—Looking for the Questions

The exploratory approach begins by seeking out problems to be dealt with rather than answers to questions already agreed upon. In this sense it is the least scientific of procedures, although frequently more appropriate than others in studying complex situations. The reason is apparent. "But if [experimental] paradigms guide, they also limit. . . . A paradigm can even insulate the community from those socially important problems that are not reducible to the puzzle form, because they cannot be stated in terms of the conceptual and instrumental tools the paradigm supplies." [Kuhn 1962:37] Rather than impose a hypothetical set of relationships on an environment, to be tested by experiment or survey, exploratory research explores these relationships in naturally occurring situations. The exploratory researcher is not afraid to use hunches and suppositions, although he will have a general notion, based on his particular interests, of the direction he wants to follow.

It is when the problems relevant to his interests have been identified that his suppositions require further elaboration; his research techniques are then "zeroed in" on the material at hand. This may be by the holistic route, or it may involve making certain quantitative measurements. Infrequently, it means applying experimental interventions "in the field." What is important is that the techniques must grow out of, or be adapted to, the nature and characteristics of the phenomena that are being explored.

This approach does not ask whether the existing measuring instruments are reliable and valid in themselves, but whether they have "phenomenon legitimacy" for the problem studied: Do they depend on that type of human response system that is empirically consistent with the nature of the phenomenon being studied? To investigate reactions to stress by applying mild electric shocks in a laboratory (as is often done) does not tell us very much about the ambiguous stressors that exist in the real world. We say, simply, that the laboratory, used in this way, lacks psychological reality. We repeat a point that has been made frequently in this book: Our primary task is to define and study the phenomena of man-environment relations in the ongoing context in which they occur.

The Interpretation of Data

Once the investigator has gathered his information there remains the problem of interpretation. What conclusions can be extracted from the data? How can the raw material of the study (the experimental data) be reduced to a meaningful or possibly a "lawful" pattern?

In holistic and exploratory research such material is evaluated largely on the basis of personal judgment, with statistical formulations playing a secondary role. Although there are criteria for judging the adequacy of holistic research (Filstead, 1970), these criteria do not overlap completely with those required for an experimental study. In experimental research the investigator's concern for the establishment of lawful relationships among variables generally requires that they be quantified in as rigorous a manner as possible. This quantification renders the variables capable of mathematical or statistical manipulation to determine whether they are related to one another. When physical objects are the components of an experiment this is relatively easy. Distance, weight, size of object, and the time necessary for a given event to take place can be expressed in quantitative terms; interaction among the variables—which is the purpose of the experiment—is measured empirically and described statistically.

When human subjects are used (as in highly controlled psychological experiments) empirical measurements are also sought, but they tend to be less reliable since living organisms are seldom closed systems and are subject to a wide variety of influences which could be reflected in their experimental performance. The experimenter, of course, rarely knows what these influences might be and he attempts to control for them by randomly assigning subjects to various experimental treatments. The effect of random assignment is to insure against the inclusion of systematic sources of error in the study.

Experimental studies allow us to make causal statements concerning the relationships among the variables. It has already been noted, however, that much environmental research is not subject to the controls demanded by experimental design. As a consequence, the investigator must often rely upon statements of the degree of relationship which exists among variables. In effect, he is dealing with correlations among variables, which do not, of course, always imply causation. How, then, does he arrive at conclusions; or assuming that he began with an hypothesis, how does he test it?

The answer is that he attempts to identify, from the information developed, those variables of interest which seem to form a relational pattern. In effect, they "co-relate," that is, they share something in common which does not appear to be shared with other variables. This correlation may be one of cause-and-effect, although in field research (because of the other variables that may be implicated) he cannot be sure. All that can be done is to analyze the data in statistical form and see what they suggest. Schoor (1966), as will be noted in a discussion of the urban environment, correlated inferior housing conditions with respiratory illness (Chapter Nine). He did not "prove" this to be the case in any scientific sense, but rather marshalled impressive statistical evidence in favor of this hypothesis. Likewise, the HEW report cited in the same chapter correlated certain types of crime with low income, high population density, and other aspects of slum life. Faris and Dunham's (1939) study of mental disorders hypothesized an association between the incidence of such disorders and the kinds of neighborhoods in which they were most frequently found. All of these field studies formulated their conclusions through statistical, rather than empirical, methods.

Unlike the laboratory investigator, who exercises rigorous control over his *material* (as well as the resultant data), the field researcher must generally content himself with a rigorous analysis of the *data*, since he has little or no control over the conditions that gave rise to them. The survey researcher also correlates his data but with no assurance that this correlation represents a demonstrable cause-and-effect relationship. We find the phrases "strongly correlated" and "strongly associated with" commonly used to express the results of this kind of research. Statistics are thought of as evidence rather than absolute proof.

In this respect a problem faces the researcher if the number of variables is large. The classical experiment involves a one-on-one relationship: We control x to see what happens to y; or, if we want to be a bit more daring, we measure the influence of x on w, y, and z. But field research usually deals with a wide spectrum of behaviors and attitudes. In the Lowenthal and Riel (1972) study, for instance, the responses of almost three hundred observers in four different environments were scaled against twenty-five sets of bipolar adjectives. The resulting data, necessarily unwieldy in their raw state, do not lend themselves to simple analysis. How, then, do we make sense out of them; more specifically, how do we discover a pattern of relationships among the observers, the different settings, and the environmental attributes that are being evaluated?

A number of techniques are used to make such information more clearly interpretable. The most commonly employed, and the one discussed here, is *factor analysis.* In essence, factor analysis identifies those items or attributes that can be grouped (hence studied) together, rather than separately, because of a particular property or "factor," they share in common. Ideally, it limits the number of variables which must be dealt with and in this sense simplifies data analysis. This affinity grouping is done statistically by ascertaining the nature of the correlations among the items included in the study. Since factor analysis often deals with scores, or even hundreds, of variables, the exact procedure is somewhat complicated. The student should simply bear in mind that it is a mathematically exact way of grouping these items so that they may be studied more easily. An illustration from the wilderness study by Hendee et al. (1968) cited in Chapter Ten will help us understand how this is done.

The purpose of the study was to determine the patterns of response to various items that comprise the wilderness experience. The authors were in essence saying: There are a wide number of experiences one can have when entering a wilderness area. Different people take a wilderness trip for different reasons, and we wish to know whether various experiences tend to be related to one another. By means of a 60-item questionnaire it was hoped to discover which aspects of the wilderness contributed to the wilderness experience and which did not; in addition, the relative importance, or "strength," of these aspects was sought. The questionnaire was completed by 1,348 campers.

Here we have a problem of assessing 80,880 answers. The questions themselves were diverse, reflecting such items as physical exercise, tranquility, drinking mountain water, looking at scenery, the chance to stumble onto wealth, the absence of people, and low cost. By tabulating the answers to each of the questions in terms of their strength ("strongly dislike," "neutral," "strongly favor") it was determined that half of the total, or 30 items, did not figure significantly in the experience of the respondents. Scores from these items were dropped and the remaining 30 items were used to calculate the final "wildernism" scores. This was done by correlating the responses to the remaining 30 items and subjecting these correlations to factor analysis. The authors wished to know whether there was a smaller set of dimensions (factors) into which the 30 items could be collapsed. Their factor analysis indicated that the 30 items were clustered into 7 broad categories, or factors, which varied in their importance in contributing to the wilderness experience. Thus, "improve physical health," "adventure," and "the simple life" were among those items making up the factor of "spartanism." The presence of "alpine meadows" and "rugged topography" was associated with "primevalism." These, of course, were arbitrary terms chosen by the investigators. The camper himself may not have defined his experience in these same terms.

The effect of this analytical procedure was to make the interpretation of the data easier by having to examine only 7 factors rather than 30 individual items. It is important to stress the fact that these factors can now serve as hypotheses for further research. For example, a person who receives a high score on the "primevalism" factor might be expected to behave differently in the wilderness compared to someone who receives a low score on this factor. The validity of these factors must be tested in more extended research designed to yield additional information about the variables the factor is measuring.

Choosing the Appropriate Method

In the preceding pages the various approaches and procedures used in environmental research have been described, with some indication of how the resultant data are analyzed and presented. Which method is adopted depends, in part, on the nature of the problem to be studied. Choice will also be influenced by the researcher's training, his biases, and, above all, his values. Ultimately, it is one's orientation to the question of theory itself which may dictate how the data will be approached. If the investigator is oriented toward the notion that separate researches dealing with a limited number of variables under controlled conditions can be finally combined together (inductionism), then it is probable that an experimental design will be preferred. If he believes that the search for broad themes and relations is the best way to avoid the artificiality of the laboratory, then holistic or exploratory research will be preferable.

The holistic researcher may be able to give yes-no answers to certain questions about the probable effects of an input into a social system. He may not, however, be in any position to tell us what specific variables are operating to produce an effect, nor will he generally be in a position to make precise quantitative statements. On the other hand, the experimentalist is often bound to those factors over which he has some measure of control but without being able to extrapolate beyond them. Nor, indeed, can he say much of anything if there is no control over other variables which might be implicated in any social setting. He is most at home studying isolated behaviors in limited settings.

We want to discuss now certain methods that function as modules, so to speak, which theoretically can be plugged into or taken out of any type of investigation. Their use will be dictated by the empirical opportunities of the situation. Some may be more appropriate to an experimental approach while others can be used by holistic or survey researchers. An idea of the scope of these methods is suggested by Craik (1970) in what he terms a "basic research paradigm" of environmental psychology. We paraphrase briefly the general outline of this paradigm. Craik states:

> When an environmental psychologist sets out to study the comprehension of any environmental display, he must deal with four issues. How shall he present the environmental display to the observer (Media of Presentation)? What behavioral reactions of the observer is he going to elicit and record (Response Format)? What are the pertinent characteristics of the environmental display (Environmental Dimensions)? And whose comprehensions is he to study (Observers)?

The media of presentation consist of three kinds.

1. Direct presentation refers to the immediate experience of places—the person's direct sensory reactions.
2. *Representation.* This includes sketches, maps, drawings, models, and replicas, as well as such usual media as cinema, television, and still photography.
3. *Imaginal* presentations employ simply the name or other designation of an environmental entity or place to evoke the individual's enduring memories or image of it. The environment that is "remembered" or "visualized" from familiarity with the empirical environment.

To these, Craik sees six possible response formats:

1. *Free description.* The observer may simply describe what he sees in his own words.
2. *Standardized description.* For example, he may indicate his reactions by selecting appropriate items from an adjective check list or other environmental descriptor.
3. *Global response.* In general, this measures the observer's overall reactions. He might ask: What goes on in this environment? What symbolic meaning does it possess? How graphically does it impress itself on me? What role does this environment offer me?
4. Inferential. What personal theories about the structure and functioning of an environment are suggested? What kinds of people are likely to be associated with it? What would happen if flood control works were constructed along a river?
5. *Attitudinal.* The observer reacts positively or negatively to certain features of the environment on the basis of previously acquired attitudes. These may have little to do with the environment's "real" qualities.
6. *Preferential.* An observer's preferences are a measure of the intensity of his attitudes. These may involve a favorable response, not only to certain types of environments, but for the amount of complexity or simplicity in any environment.

Taking the media of presentation and the response formats together, Craik works out four categories, or *dimensions*, by which an observer records his experience of an environment.

1. *Classification in everyday language.* The observer uses "plain English" in either free or standard form. "This is one means of ordering the population of environmental displays." [Craik 1970:79]
2. *Objective physical and geographical measures.* The topological attributes of a setting, both as entities and in relation to one another, are subject to measurement. They have size, weight, shape, color, and temperature, and are separated from other entities by exact distances. These are the verifiable physical qualities of an environment.
3. *Sequential notational systems.* (Thiel 1970). These describe reactions to an environment as experienced by an observer moving through it. Certain objects and surfaces constitute "space-establishing elements" which orient one's movements through a setting. The architect's elevations, plans, and perspectives together constitute a form of notational system. Thiel (forthcoming) has expanded his notational system to include sensory and psychological factors.
4. *Modal behavior attributes.* These focus on the qualities most frequently ascribed to environmental displays, the images evoked, the themes that are stimulated, and the moods induced. Such a dimension is descriptive of the setting itself rather than of what the response to it reveals about the observer.

The significance of any response to the environment, of course, is partly dependent upon who is doing the observing. No two persons "see things alike" because they do not necessarily make the same use of a setting. Craik squares off his paradigm by classifying observers into four general groups:

1. *Special competence groups.* These include persons who have a professional interest in the environment—architects, planners, real estate appraisers, and so on.
2. *Special user-client groups.* Elderly persons, migrant workers, and college students are examples.
3. *Personality types.* One perceives, and uses, his environment on the basis of psychological traits. The introvert may be less "sensitive" to a setting than the extrovert.
4. *Everyman.* This includes the general public, the average person whose observations are not affected by special considerations. [Craik 1970:66–85]

Craik models environmental research along user-evaluation lines. He is more concerned with the individual's own perceptual and cognitive response to an environment than with others' interpretation of that response. By using various kinds of tests (such as adjective checklists or the Thematic Apperception Test) Craik does achieve some quasi-objective status for his descriptive responses. On the whole, however, he depends upon the observer to make his own assessments of the "display." Table 8–1 summarizes the paradigm in outline form.

There are both advantages and disadvantages to this approach. On the plus side, behavior is uninfluenced—hence less in danger of contamination—by the research situation. On the other hand, it is seldom possible to predict what might happen if certain changes are introduced into the system under observation. As the stimuli become more complex and varied, response be-

TABLE 8–1 A Process Model for the Comprehension of Environmental Displays

Observers 1	*Presentation of environmental displays* 2	*Nature and format of judgments* 3	*Validational criteria* 4
Special competence groups: architects planners real estate appraisers stage designers "space" managers, i.e., hotel, theatre, resort managers, building superintendents, etc.	Direct experience: looking at walking around and through driving around and through aerial views living in	Free descriptions	Measures of objective characteristics of environmental displays
Special user-client groups: elderly persons migrant workers college students	Simulative exploration	Adjective checklists	Judgments by experts
Groups formed on the basis of relevant personality measures	Cinematic and photographic studies	Activity and mood checklists	Any judgment-form in Column 3 based upon more extensive acquaintance with the environmental display
Everyman, general public	Sketches and drawings	Q-sort descriptions	
	Models and replicas	Ratings	
	Tachistoscopic views	Thematic potential analysis	
	Laser beam presentations	Symbolic equivalents	
	No presentation	Multisensory equivalents	
		Emphatic interpretations: "role" enactments "role" improvisations	
		Social stereotypic cues	
		Beliefs about human consequences	
		Viewing time	
		"Notatonal" systems	

From K. H. Craik, "The comprehension of the everyday physical environment." Reprinted by permission of the Journal of the American Institute of Planners, *Vol. 34, No. 1, January 1968, and the author.*

comes more contingent upon the total field, which is difficult to control methodologically. Oftentimes, what we seek are measures for observing behavior from an objective point of view, in a natural setting, by an observer who uses certain systematic techniques for evaluating and recording what he sees.

Direct Observation—An Ecological Approach

Probably the best known research project using observational techniques is carried on at the Midwest Psychological Field Station in Oskaloosa, Kansas, under the direction of Roger Barker. Barker's theory of the "behavior setting" has been discussed in Chapter Three. We are interested here in his methodology—how he observes the behavior of those (mostly young people) who comprise his samples.

It will be recalled that Barker with his colleagues Wright (1954) and Gump (1964) advanced the hypothesis that behavior is best studied in its everyday, "natural" environment; they call this approach "ecological psychology." Obviously, however, one cannot observe all people in action at once. In fact, most of our activities occur in well-defined physical settings—a classroom, a bus, a playground, a park, a restaurant. Each of these environments becomes the context for a social setting that imposes a specific type of behavior (studying, riding, playing, relaxing, eating) on those who enter it. This is to say that the setting is defined by its social as well as its physical properties. Within the "environment/behavior milieu" there is a "stream of behavior," and it is this stream that Barker and his associates measure through a detailed system of observation.

Important to an ecological approach is the notion of the *representativeness of locales.* In his work on perception and "probable" cue validities, Brunswik (see Hammond 1966) stressed the "ecological sampling" of the environment. This means simply that if one wishes to develop an understanding of perception it is essential to sample different environments rather than limit oneself to a single setting. You would not expect to infer, from observing people listening to a concert, how they might behave in a supermarket. Classroom behavior is not that of a card party. Above all, the laboratory setting, in Barker's words, fails to provide the "frequency, duration, scope, complexity and magnitude of some important human conditions." [1968:3] Ecological psychology studies people in drugstores, at choir practice, in the courthouse square, at Boy Scout meetings, playing bridge—in general, going about their daily lives. The significant thing about Barker's method, therefore, is the inclusiveness of the phenomena that are studied.[2]

Over a period of some twenty-four years, Barker's (1968) researchers have made detailed observations of life in the Kansas community dubbed "Midwest." The procedure is to station trained observers in various locales and ask them to write extended commentaries on the stimuli with which the subjects come in contact and to note their responses. These are based on notes made during thirty-minute observation periods. This (thirty-minute) "stream of behavior" is broken into "behavior episodes"—incidents that are distinct from what precedes and follows them. Here is a brief example of one such observation, made in a school class that is about to take its daily music lesson.

2:10. The children seated themselves in a semicircle across the front of the music room.

[2] Not every locale, physically speaking, constitutes a behavior setting. A high school gym, in itself, cannot be so defined; it becomes a setting only when certain behavior patterns—a basketball game, dance, or PTA meeting—are enacted in the gym.

Anne sat with Opal Bennett directly on her right and Rex Graw on her left. Alvin Stone was one seat over from Rex.
Miss Madison said briskly, "All right, let's open our books to page 27."
Anne watched Miss Madison solemnly.
Anne licked her finger.
She turned to the correct page.
Miss Madison asked the class, "How would you conduct this song?"
Immediately Anne raised her hand urgently, eager to be called on.
2:11. Miss Madison called on Ellen Thomas to show how she would conduct this song.
Ellen waved her right arm in three-four rhythm.
Miss Madison watched Ellen critically.
With her hand still partway in the air, Anne watched earnestly.
Someone in the class objected that Ellen's beat wasn't quite right.
Persistently, Anne put her hand up higher wishing to be called on.
Miss Madison called on Stella Townsend.
Anne put her hand down with disappointment showing in her facial expression.
Intently she watched Stella demonstrate the pattern for conducting the song.
Miss Madison called on Opal Bennett.[3]

The student may well ask: What does this prove? In fact, it is not proof of anything that is sought but, in Barker's words, constitutes the identification of those "discriminable phenomena external to any individual's behavior" [1968:13] which have a bearing on it.

You will note that Anne's behavior is dictated by the fact of the music lesson. Within that activity she engages in numerous individual behavior variations—showing disappointment, raising her hand, licking her finger—most of which derive from the lesson context. Technically we can call these episodes sequential dependencies. Through thousands of such observations, Barker's staff has been able to describe the "standing patterns of behavior" which make up the 220 "settings" of Midwest. Each has its own regulatory, even coercive (although by no means total), power to compel behavior to an appropriate pattern.

Ecological psychology, as we noted, is what Barker terms a "transducer science": that is, the research psychologist is simply a transmitter of data which are observed on the scene. Barker distinguishes such "T" data from experimental, or "O," data that are "arranged in accordance with the curiosities of the psychologist." To this extent a "T" approach is more "typical" of ongoing behavior, since the results of an experiment are never free of "the system that generates the data." The strength of the Barker-Wright (1954) approach is its naturalism. Behavior "speaks for itself." Analysis of the behavior has led to several significant conclusions useful to planners and educators—the "undermanned setting," for instance, which was discussed in

[3] From R. G. Barker, *Ecological Psychology.* Stanford, Calif.: Stanford University Press, 1968. Reprinted by permission of publishers and author.

Chapter Seven. Like *Yankee City* and *The Urban Villagers, Midwest and Its Children* identifies the behavioral characteristics of a number of people living in a given community. It does not, however, draw any inferences that are not the result of direct observation.

In this connection it is interesting to compare the methodology of these three books. *Yankee City* is based on the quantitative analysis of existing data and a survey of attitudes; *The Urban Villagers* is partly observational, relying upon interviews as well; it depends upon the interpretive skill of one man—the author. In *Midwest and Its Children*, Barker and Wright (1954) use objective, detailed observations made by many people and classify its data into behavioral categories. The three studies, of course, were written from different perspectives; their authors were seeking different kinds of information about their communities. It was this that dictated the research procedures used.

Measurement Techniques of Direct Observation

One criticism made of Barker's method is that it relies too strongly on the personal judgments of the observers. Even well-trained observers will perceive behavior episodes subjectively, hence differently. Inferring moods, states of mind, and motivations from looking at gestures or facial expressions can be unreliable. Such expressions in our sample from Midwest as "solemnly," "critically," "earnestly," "wishing to be called," and "disappointment" imply a knowledge of what is felt or thought by the subject that may be erroneous. Moreover, where observation is obtrusive, there is the E. B. White problem[4]: The observed is tempted to watch the observer.

In contrast many psychologists, especially those in the field of child development, attempt a more objective and unobtrusive measurement of behavior. Gesell and Ilg (1943, 1946) in their work at Yale used motion pictures as a basis for detailed analysis of infant behavior. Hutt and Hutt (1970), whose work has been largely with brain-damaged and autistic children, make their observations from an adjoining room through a one-way mirror. In this instance observers, working simultaneously, dictate their "behavior commentary" into a tape recorder. A "behavioral repertoire," dealing with visual fixations, postures, locomotion, manipulation, and gestures is refined into "behavior categories," and these in turn are separated into specific actions which are identified on a check list. The duration of each activity is timed with a stop watch.

Observation of an ongoing series of activities made at specific intervals is known as time-sampling. By shifting the emphasis one can also measure the various occurrences irrespective of their time span. This is known as event-sampling. Sophisticated equipment makes it possible to record such events

[4] Humorist White, when asked if he watched birds, replied: "Yes, and they watch me."

quickly and accurately—in some cases, automatically. Many such instruments are able to record the duration as well as the nature of the event.

The usefulness of these methods is obvious. Precise measurements can be obtained which would not be possible with the more loosely structured procedures employed by Barker and Wright. There is less estimation and more evidence of what is really happening. At the same time the techniques have some apparent limitations. It would be impractical, for instance, to apply them to the "ecological" environments sampled by Barker—the drug stores, churches, tax offices, and ball fields of Midwest. Finally, one suspects that the scientific rigor which characterizes such observation is sometimes redundant. One counts the trees at the risk of missing the forest.

Behavioral Mapping—A Spatial Approach to Observation

A form of direct observation that does fit into real-world environments is behavioral mapping. Here, we track the movements of people through existing physical settings and observe the kinds of behavior that occur in relation to these settings. Where ecological psychology stresses the social activity of a locale, mapping seeks to identify the uses of space as a factor in ongoing behavior. The two methods are complementary rather than incompatible, for the behavioral stream is always subject to the contingencies of its physical setting.

By making an accurate record of what activities take place where, mapping helps us study behavior in its functional relation to a particular environment. Behavior will be enacted in accordance with the opportunities or limitations of the milieu in which it occurs. By using mapping one avoids the difficulty of asking people to describe their reactions to an environment, which is frequently inadequate; many people do not verbalize their experiences satisfactorily and they may also be unaware that any change in behavior is taking place. The technique is a reliable one and rigorous enough so that the categories of behavior can be used as dependent variables within an experimental framework, yet without cluttering this framework by control interferences.

The standard procedure for behavioral mapping involves the following steps:

1. Identification of observational categories. This is done by continuously observing the areas to be mapped and recording in narrative style the observed behaviors. These narratives are then analyzed for the major behavior categories relevant to the particular study. Emphasis is on overt, easily identifiable behaviors, requiring a minimum of inference by the observer.
2. Identifying the physical area to be mapped—the room, playground, or street that is under observation.
3. Preparation of observer instructions and observational forms, permitting easy recording of who is doing which of the behavior categories in what locations.

4. Preparation of an observation schedule. In most common schedules the entire physical space to be mapped on a time sampling basis is covered typically every fifteen minutes. Variations include continuous observation of smaller areas and sampling of spaces as well as times.

Table 8–2 shows the results of the authors' mapping of patient behavior in a psychiatric ward of a large city hospital. In this instance all areas of the ward were observed every fifteen minutes in three- to four-minute intervals. Unlike the method used by Hutt and Hutt, however, observation was obtrusive. Observers spent considerable time getting to know the ward occupants, both staff and patients. (Ward personnel reported no differences in the behavior of patients between periods with the observers present and periods without them.) All physical spaces on the ward were covered and observations were recorded on a data sheet. These permitted direct coding of the data for statistical analysis.

TABLE 8–2 Comparison of Behavior on Three Different Days: Average Ward

	Traffic	*Visiting*	*Social*	*Mixed Active*	*Isolated Active*	*Isolated Passive*	*Total*
Monday	3.2	3.4	20.6	11.2	10.1	14.0	62.5
Wednesday	3.2	7.8	21.6	11.2	10.4	14.4	68.6
Friday	3.4	8.0	20.2	9.8	14.0	12.0	67.4

From W. H. Ittelson, L. G. Rivlin, and H. M. Proshansky, The use of behavioral maps in environmental psychology. In H. M. Proshansky, W. H. Ittelson, and L. G. Rivlin (Eds.), Environmental psychology: Man and his physical setting. *New York: Holt, Rinehart and Winston, 1970. Reproduced by permission.*

Behavioral maps can be used in four ways. They provide a shorthand description of the distribution of behaviors throughout a given space. They can also be used to compare behaviors—between men and women, for example. As a research tool mapping provides data which lead to the development of general principles about the use of space in a variety of settings. Finally, the maps enable the prediction of behavior, vis-à-vis certain kinds of space, and thus make it possible to design specific facilities more effectively in advance of occupancy. A more complete description of behavioral mapping is found in an article by Ittelson, Rivlin, and Proshansky (1970).

Simulation Techniques for Evaluating the Environment

Quite obviously, there are practical limits to the kinds of areas that can be mapped. Oftentimes it is not possible for an observer to be present. Perhaps the real setting does not yet exist, and we are interested in discovering how people will respond to it when it is built. One way around this problem is to reproduce a simulated or mock environment and then observe the individual's response to it. A scale model of a house or a school—or for that matter a whole community—is one such method. By looking at the model and evaluating our reactions to it, we decide, for example, whether or not we think it is attractive or whether it will suit our needs. In studying the effects of close, long-term confinement on flight personnel, NASA observed the behavior of four crewmen on a simulated space flight (by means of closed circuit TV) for a ninety-day period (Collins et al. 1971). This is one method of finding out how people react to a situation where it is impractical to use the real environment. It has the further advantage that it can precede and therefore act as a guide to changing the real environment. If we do not like the scale model of the house, we ask the architect to design another.

The above examples are rather crude and depend for their effectiveness upon reproducing a section of the environment in toto. This can be difficult and expensive. Recently techniques have been devised in which the relationships generated by the environment are used rather than a realistic reproduction of it. In other words, our model need not resemble the real object; it is important, however, that its components operate as though in a real-life situation. "Successful simulation requires only that one be able to reproduce the system under study as accurately as possible without actually employing the system itself." (See Winkel & Sasanoff 1966:623.) In a sense the laboratory is a simulation. It abstracts what are believed to be the salient aspects of the real-world system and replicates them for purposes of study. However, we can also simulate analytically by using a mathematical model descriptive of the system. In this case the computer becomes a simulator. Systems theory is essentially a simulation technique for studying the environment in terms of the data generated by it. It represents the highest degree of abstraction from the real world.

An Example of Laboratory Simulation

Most simulation falls midway between the "realistic" (scale model; mock-up) and the analytic. A concern of environmental psychology is how people use given types of space. In discussing behavioral mapping it was observed that this was done on location. To find out if this kind of user-behavior could be predicted in a simulated environment, Winkel and Sasanoff (1966) conducted a study at the Museum of History and Industry in Seattle, Washington. In this instance the main gallery and its exhibits were reproduced on colored slides. These were shown to "visitors" seated in a projection room; the amount of time spent viewing the exhibits, as well as the preferences and the order in which they were viewed, was recorded. These data were then compared with the experience of actual visitors to the gallery whose movements were tracked by observers.

Results indicated that similarities in the real and simulated worlds produce similar behaviors, although not, of course, in minute detail. The value of such an experiment lies in its being a shortcut to an understanding of visual behavior as it is affected, for instance, by movement—driving along a highway. Moreover, if we can predict how people will use a real environment on the basis of their response to a simulated one, the designer has a practical tool in planning new structures, especially those in which large numbers of people must be accommodated.

Simulation is limited by the types of behaviors one wishes to study. To ask people to look at pictures of a housing project and estimate how well it meets their needs would be of little value: Need satisfaction comes largely through use. The problem can be illustrated as follows: Suppose one is interested in a new kitchen design. People could view a picture and estimate how well it might work. This type of simulation—well known to everyone who has ever been handed a manufacturer's brochure—is limited by the degree to which it abstracts (or fails to abstract) the salient features of the situation. The really salient features have to do with ease of movement, accessibility to materials, and so on, and these can only be tested by trying them out. Where this is not possible (as it seldom is) simulation might be better achieved by the use of packing boxes arranged like the kitchen. The mock-up need not resemble the actual setting. What is tested is the use of the setting.

Gaming as a Simulation Technique

Simulation is useful in finding out how people respond to the physical attributes of a given environment when a selected part of that environment is modeled in terms of its operational whole. But this does not always give us the true complexity of the setting when others participate in it. Gaming attempts to surmount this difficulty by introducing roles into the model. As Abt (1970) expresses it, games "create dramatic representations of the real problem being studied. The players assume realistic roles, face problems, formulate strategies, make decisions, and get fast feedback on the consequences of their action." [p. 13]

A well-known, if somewhat simplified, example is Monopoly. This board game is played for pleasure; unlike more serious teaching and research games, it involves the element of luck (the roll of the dice). However, the principles of risk and reward which are paramount typify most gaming situations, but to this is added the knowledge that the players are projecting their roles into larger and more "real" social situations. The serious game endeavors to simulate existing problems—for instance, the problems of urban ecology, land use, services, cost, and the like—without losing the intuitive freedom and imaginative play that is characteristic of "fun" games.

A widely used game among students of urban planning and design was developed by Allen G. Feldt (see Taylor 1971). Known as CLUG (for Community Land Use Game) it has been compared to a combination of chess and Monopoly (Taylor 1971:36). Play money supplied to the teams is available for buying and selling property. However, this must be done in terms of community as well as personal interest—community interest being determined by the administrator of the game. "With prudent management, teams can maximize their investments and also make a positive contribution to the growth of the community." [Taylor 1971:36] Several variations of CLUG have appeared in different teaching contexts.

The value of gaming is that it allows the players to pit not only their skills and daring against one another but also their respective value systems. Although reward is involved, winning is secondary to learning. What is sought are the consequences of decisions if they were to be executed in real-life situations.

Cognitive Mapping

Evaluation of behavior through observations in either real or simulated environments is a relatively objective method. Since it is not practical to observe behavior on any global scale—for an entire city, for instance—we are up against the problem of representativeness. Barker approaches this problem through the continuous observation of behavior in a wide variety of settings. He has been able to define the behaviors that accord with specific settings and predict, with a fair amount of accuracy, that like settings elsewhere will produce similar behavior patterns. Brunswik, working more experimentally, pleads for a representative design—"the suitable samplings of . . . experimental situations [that] reflect the environments to which we wish to generalize our findings." [See Hochberg 1966:366] In fact, no such design has been forthcoming. The best that one is able to do is make predictions about probable behavior on the basis of past experience with an environment.

One way this is done—although not in the way Brunswik foresaw—is by conceptualizing the global environment in terms of its images, or molar objects—the streets, buildings, roads, hills, parks, and the like, that form the map of an area that everyone carries around in his mind. As a research method cognitive mapping can reveal something about how people use their environment (in the sense of finding their way around in it) as well as what it means to them symbolically. It derives from the fact that it is impossible to perceive, say, the city of Boston, Massachusetts, or Middlesex County, New Jersey. One can experience only that part of it within his immediate range of perception at any given moment. As a result we "visualize" what we cannot perceive. Everyone carries many such "imaged" models in his mind simultaneously. At the same time these cognitive maps are almost never replicas of the actual land- or city-scape; rather, they arise from useful distortions of the environment based on previous experiences with it.

As another strategy for coping with the environment, cognitive mapping has been explored most frequently in the urban setting and will be discussed more fully in Chapter Nine. Essentially, it deals with how the inhabitants of cities read the physical world as a "generalized mental picture." [Lynch 1960] In this sense it provides an additional research perspective to our study of cities, limiting its concern to the immediate physical environment and the ways in which it is ordered cognitively.

In his book *The Image of the City*, Lynch (1960) employs a user-evaluation approach. Because of the admittedly small samples selected, his investigations of inhabitant reaction to the central areas of Boston, Jersey City, and Los Angeles are in the nature of pilot projects rather than fully developed studies. Nevertheless, they indicate the potential value of such an approach for city planners and architects. Lynch and his colleagues first conducted a "systematic field reconnaissance" of the areas to be studied, mapping the most visible and easily imaged elements—landmarks and prominent buildings, for example—along with such other salient features as parks, important streets, hills, and waterways. Lengthy interviews were held with a sample of city residents to elicit their own images of the same environment; maps based on these images were then drawn and compared with the originals.

In this type of research we learn what people think their environment looks like in terms of the images that have become significant to them over a period of time—in Lynch's words, how they "extract structure and identity out of the material at hand." [1960:43] This, in turn, gives them a sense of security and orientation—they know "how to get around." We abstract from space a coherent pattern and, whether accurate or not, this pattern helps us to organize our activity. Finally, images provide the group with a common memory of the environment in question, and to this extent enhance its meaning. The character of a city is to a large degree its memorability manifested in the images it impresses on our minds.

We conclude this chapter with a research design that illustrates many of the things we have been discussing. This relatively simple design seeks to provide an empirical base for the planning of successful play areas for urban youngsters. It is quasi-experimental in the sense that there was possible control, as an independent variable, of three different types of play environments: (1) the traditional type—slides, swings, seesaws, and so on; (2) the designed type, which joins discrete swinging and sliding elements into a continuous sculpture based on sand; and (3) the so-called adventure or "junk" playground in which children create their own equipment out of old tires, discarded lumber, packing crates, and so forth. The major objectives of the project were to determine whether there were differences in *frequency* of use of the different areas; to analyze the play in the areas in terms of the children's behavior and the relationship between the *time* a child spends in settings and *level of mastery* developed from those settings; and to study the *specific apparatus* in all three playgrounds to determine their proportional use by the child and the opportunities they afforded for play. In addition it was hoped to discover which of several factors, such as convenience and the facilities available, governed the child's selection of a play area.

To gather this information, two observation techniques were used, in addition to interviews with the children. The first involved behavioral mapping, with a trained observer moving from place to place in each setting at regular time intervals (every twenty minutes), recording the age, sex, and number of participants engaged in particular activities at specific locations. To this was added a "behavior" or "settings" observation, in which the investigator followed the sequence of a randomly selected child's activity during his length of stay at a particular playground. A small tape recorder was used to describe ongoing activity, as well as such pertinent data as the number of other children involved with that child, the duration of involvement, and the equipment used. Interviews were then obtained from a sample of approximately thirty children (randomly selected) in each area as they left the playground. These interviews elicited the reasons why the child came to a certain playground, whose decision it was to come, how often he came, the activities he engaged in, the equipment he used, and his opinion of the advantages and disadvantages of the playground.

The research team consisted of a psychologist, an architect, and an educator working with a group of trained observers. A computer program was developed to analyze the behavioral mapping data and a factor analysis was conducted on the settings records by the investigators. In effect, a profile of each play area was compiled based on the frequency, duration, and kinds of activities engaged in by the children, along with the extent and form of their interactions. The multimethod approach was especially important as data analysis progressed. The mapping, settings records, and interviews each provided a kind of information which could be viewed in perspective with the other two methods. Thus, distribution of ages, use of specific areas or apparatus, and kinds of activities engaged in by school-age children could be assessed in several ways. The time sampling of behavior from the mapping was clarified by interpretation of data from the settings records and by the preferences and playground usage reported during the interviews.

The general conclusions of this study were that, contrary to a common belief that children are inventive in any play environment and that the environment itself is of secondary importance, it was the opportunities available in playgrounds that largely determined what went on there. That is, the kinds of activities engaged in stemmed directly from the available equipment and materials. Loose parts such as dirt, sand, water, boards, and crafts materials were important to school-aged children and allowed for stimulating and involved interaction with the world around them. Further, the creative potential of a place was seen to be important in fostering social as well as environmental interaction. Where there were more materials that could be combined or changed, there was also more peer-group interaction and more responsive communication.

Our concern here is that the practical consequences of the study derive from the validity of its methods. These investigators approached the problem on a comparative basis. Each playground constituted a different level of the independent variable. Had it been possible to rotate the same children over all three areas on a regular basis, a more controlled and experimental study would have resulted. But this would have necessitated concern about the novelty of different playgrounds to the children and would have invalidated one aspect of the study: why children chose the playgrounds they did, and how often. Thus, in terms of the objectives, a quasi-experimental design was more suitable (Hayward et al. 1973).

Summary and Conclusion

This chapter has sketched the major approaches to behavioral research, emphasizing those that seem most applicable to a study of the environment. These range from highly controlled laboratory experiments to loosely structured exploratory investigations. The student should keep in mind the extent to which an approach to a problem reflects the broad orientation of the researcher; whether he is experimentalist or holistic, a survey man or an explorer, depends on how he assesses the implications of his research material in relation to his own interests, biases, and values. He might ask: What methods does the problem call for and how can I reconcile these methods with my convictions as a researcher? As a practical matter, different methods are often used to attack a single project; within our general design, we utilize the techniques that promise the best results.

In illustrating the various techniques of data gathering and interpretation, attention has necessarily been focused on more commonly used examples. Thus, numerous scaling techniques have been omitted as beyond the scope of our present concern. The sociometric approach has been referred to only briefly in our discussion of *Yankee City*. It is concerned primarily with social interaction among groups and only incidentally with the physical environment. Recent innovations such as concealed cameras, hidden microphones, and time-lapse photography have not been discussed, partly because they are mainly variations of what has already been learned about observation in general and partly because they raise certain ethical questions with respect to the invasion of privacy. No attempt has been made to describe techniques for replicating and verifying research findings once an investigation has been completed. The interested student may wish to consult the general texts on methodology listed at the end of the chapter for a fuller description of these aspects of research.

If there is a single point that needs to be emphasized in researching the everyday physical environment, it is simply that our strategy is usually flexible and pragmatic—from the full repertoire of methods, we borrow those that seem most likely to uncover the data that are sought. But in making such choices, priority should be given to those methods that leave the events and settings intact. These methods must evolve out of and be adapted to the nature and characteristics of the phenomena that are being studied. We are asking, in effect, what things or aspects about the physical settings should we measure in that they have psychological reality for the persons involved, and they serve as the focus of his desires and feelings and therefore have consequences for his behavior? It is in this sense that environmental psychology as a field of inquiry relies relatively little on the laboratory and rather more heavily on exploratory and descriptive investigations.

References

Abt, C. C. *Serious games.* New York: Viking, 1970.

Altman, I. The ecology of isolated groups. *Behavioral Science,* 1967, *12,* 169–182. [Reprinted in H. M. Proshansky, W. H. Ittelson, & L. G. Rivlin (Eds.), *Environmental psychology: Man and his physical setting.* New York: Holt, Rinehart and Winston, 1970. Pp. 226–239.]

Aronson, E., & Carlsmith, J. M. Experimentation in social psychology. In G. Lindzey & E. Aronson (Eds.), *The handbook of social psychology.* Vol. 2. 2d ed. Reading, Mass.: Addison-Wesley, 1968.

Barker, R. G., & Wright, H. F. *Midwest and its children: The psychological ecology of an American town.* Hamden, Conn.: Shoe String Press, 1954.

Barker, R. G. *The stream of behavior.* New York: Appleton, 1963.

Barker, R. G. *Ecological psychology.* Stanford, Calif.: Stanford University Press, 1968.

Barker, R. G., & Gump, P. *Big school, small school.* Stanford: Stanford University Press, 1964.

Brunswik, E. *Perception and the representative design of psychological experiments.* Berkeley, Calif.: University of California Press, 1956.

Campbell, D., & Stanley, J. *Experimental and quasi-experimental designs for research.* Chicago: Rand McNally, 1963.

Canter, D., & Thorne, R. Attitudes to housing: A cross-cultural comparison. *Environment and Behavior,* 1972, *4,* 3–32.

Collins, B. E., Ranere, J., & Rosenthal, A. Psychological assessment of confined crews. In A. D. Pearson & D. C. Grana (Eds.), *Preliminary results from an operational 90-day manned test of a regenerative life support system.* Washington, D.C.: NASA, 1971.

Costantini, E., & Hanf, K. Environmental concern and Lake Tahoe: A study of elite perceptions, backgrounds and attitudes. *Environment and Behavior,* 1972, *4,* 209–242.

Craik, K. H. The comprehension of the everyday physical environment. *Journal of the American Institute of Planners,* 1968, *34,* 29–37. [Reprinted in H. M. Proshansky et al. (Eds.), *Environmental psychology: Man and his physical setting.* New York: Holt, Rinehart and Winston, 1970. Pp. 646–658.]

Craik, K. H. Environment psychology. In K. H. Craik, B. Kleinmuntz, R. L. Rosnow, R. Rosenthal, J. A. Cheyne, & R. H. Walters, *New directions in psychology, 4.* New York: Holt, Rinehart and Winston, 1970.

Faris, R. E. L., & Dunham, H. W. *Mental disorders in urban areas.* Chicago: University of Chicago Press, 1939.

Filstead, W. (Ed.) *Qualitative methodology: Firsthand involvement with the social world.* Chicago: Markham, 1970.

Freedman, J. L., Klevansky, S., & Erlich, P. R. The effect of crowding on human task performance. *Journal of Applied Social Psychology,* 1971, *1,* 7–25.

Gans, H. *The urban villagers.* New York: Free Press, 1962.

Gesell, A. L., & Ilg, F. L. *Infant and child in the culture of today: The guidance of development in home and nursery school.* New York: Harper & Row, 1943.

Gesell, A. L., & Ilg, F. L. *The child from five to ten.* New York: Harper & Row, 1946.

Gillis, J., & Schneider, C. The historical preconditions of representative design. In K. R. Hammond (Ed.), *The psychology of Egon Brunswik.* New York: Holt, Rinehart and Winston, 1966.

Glass, D. C., & Singer, J. E. *Urban stress: Experiments on noise and social stressors.* New York: Academic Press, 1972.

Hammond, K. R. (Ed.) *The psychology of Egon Brunswik.* New York: Holt, Rinehart and Winston, 1966.

Hayward, D. G., Rothenberg, M., & Beasley, R. School-aged children in three urban playgrounds. Final report to National Science Foundation, Grant No. GZ–2562. City University of New York, Environmental Psychology Program, 1973.

Hendee, J. C., Catton, W. R., Jr., Marlow, L. D., & Brockman, C. F. *Wilderness users in the Pacific Northwest—Their characteristics, values and management preferences.* U.S.D.A. Forest Service Research Paper PNW–61. Portland, Ore.: Pacific Northwest Forest and Range Experiment Station, U.S. Department of Agriculture, 1968.

Hochberg, J. Representative sampling and the purpose of perceptual research: Pictures of the world, and the world of pictures. In K. R. Hammond (Ed.), *The psychology of Egon Brunswik.* New York: Holt, Rinehart and Winston, 1966.

Hutt, S. J., & Hutt, C. H. *Direct observation and measurement of behavior.* Springfield, Ill.: Charles C Thomas, 1970.

Ittelson, W. H., Rivlin, L. G., & Proshansky, H. M. The use of behavioral maps in environmental psychology. In H. M. Proshansky, W. H. Ittelson, & L. G. Rivlin (Eds.), *Environmental psychology: Man and his physical setting.* New York: Holt, Rinehart and Winston, 1970.

Kuhn, T. *The structure of scientific revolutions.* Chicago: University of Chicago Press, 1962.

Lowenthal, D., & Riel, M. The nature of perceived and imagined environments. *Environment and Behavior,* 1972, *4,* 189–207.

Lynch, K. *The image of the city.* Cambridge, Mass.: The M.I.T. Press, 1960.

Marquand, J. *Point of no return.* Boston: Little, Brown, 1947.

Maslow, A. H., & Mintz, N. L. Effects of esthetic surroundings: I. Initial short-term effects of three esthetic conditions upon perceiving "energy" and "well-being" in faces. *Journal of Psychology,* 1956, *41,* 247–254.

Mead, M. *Coming of age in Samoa: A psychological study of primitive youth for Western civilization.* New York: Morrow, 1929.

Michelson, W. *Man and his urban environment: A sociological approach.* Reading, Mass.: Addison-Wesley, 1970.

Schoor, A. L. *Slums and social insecurity.* Washington, D.C.: U.S. Government Printing Office, 1966.

Snider, J. G., & Osgood, C. E. (Eds.) *Semantic differential technique: A sourcebook.* Chicago: Aldine, 1969.

Sommers, R. *Personal space: The behavioral basis of design.* Englewood Cliffs, N.J.: Prentice-Hall, 1969.

Taylor, J. L. *Instructional planning systems.* Cambridge, England: Cambridge University Press, 1971.

Thiel, P. Notes on the description, scaling, notation and scoring of some perceptual and cognitive attributes of the physical environment. In H. M. Proshansky, W. H. Ittelson, & L. G. Rivlin (Eds.), *Environmental psychology: Man and his physical setting.* New York: Holt, Rinehart and Winston, 1970. Pp. 593–619.

Thiel, P. *Towards an experiential envirotecture.* College of Architecture. University of Washington, Seattle (forthcoming).

Tognacci, L. N., Weigel, R. H., Wideen, M. F., & Vernon, D. T. A. Environmental quality: How universal is public concern? *Environment and Behavior,* 1972, *4,* 73–86.

Warner, W. L. (Ed.) *Yankee city.* New Haven, Conn.: Yale University Press, 1963.

Weiss, R. S. Alternative approaches in the study of complex situations. *Human Organization,* 1966, *25,* 198–206.

Weiss, R. S. Issues in holistic research. In H. S. Becker, B. Geer, D. Reisman, & R. S. Weiss (Eds.), *Institutions and the person.* Chicago: Aldine, 1968.

Wilner, D. M., Walkley, R. P., Pinkerton, T. C., & Tayback, M. *The housing environment and family life: A longitudinal study of the effects of housing on morbidity and mental health.* Baltimore: Johns Hopkins Press, 1962.

Winkel, G. H., & Sasanoff, R. *An approach to an objective analysis of behavior in architectural space.* Architecture/Development, Series No. 5. Seattle, Wash.: University of Washington, 1966. [Reprinted in H. M. Proshansky, W. H. Ittelson, & L. G. Rivlin (Eds.), *Environmental psychology: Man and his Physical Setting.* New York: Holt, Rinehart and Winston, 1970. Pp. 619–631.]
research. Chicago: Rand McNally, 1963.

Suggested Readings

Campbell, D., & Stanley, J. *Experimental and quasi-experimental design for research.* Chicago: Rand-McNally, 1963.

Filstead, W. (Ed.) *Qualitative methodology: Firsthand involvement with the social world.* Chicago: Markham, 1970.

Selltiz, C., Jahoda, M., Deutsch, M., & Cook, S. W. *Research methods in social relations.* New York: Holt, Rinehart and Winston, 1959.

Underwood, B. J. *Psychological research.* New York: Appleton, 1957.

Webb, E., Campbell, D., Schwartz, R., & Sechrist, L. *Unobtrusive measures.* Chicago: Rand McNally, 1966.

Nine

The City as an Unnatural Habitat

> Many people actually like the city—we have authenticated pictures of people smiling—and if they come together in the crowded areas it is often because they want to. Complain as they will how horrible it all is, they enjoy the hustle and bustle. They like to watch the parade go by; they like being part of it; they like to shmooze, to girl-watch, and whenever any sort of decent open space is provided, they will quickly make it into a very sociable place.
> —William H. Whyte in the *New York Times,* Dec. 3, 1972.

Any approach to a study of the urban environment is complicated by the different frames of reference within which the city is placed by students from various disciplines. The political scientist sees it as a complex of governing units. To the economist it is a generator of commerce and industry. Geographers and population experts study the city in terms of its growth, the movement of its people, and the specialized functions of its zones and neighborhoods. Planners often see the city in terms of its physical characteristics, although this orientation is slowly changing. Urban designers view it from the standpoint of the physical relationships among buildings, streets, plazas, parks, and playgrounds. And nearly everyone, of course, is interested in the cultural and occupational opportunities available in the city.

The city has also been studied by sociologists and others whose major interest is in the pathology, morbidity, and deviancy associated with urban conditions. In the United States, especially, crime, dirt and noise, pollution, high population density, and the deterioration of central areas ("urban blight") contrast with economic and cultural advantages, conveniences, enhanced privacy, vitality, and diversity. Whatever else they may be, cities are stimulating places. Economic factors play an important role; the easy contact and stimulating exchange among many spheres of human creativity (Mead 1957) clearly contribute to the urbanizing trend. Quoting Spengler, Park (1952) noted "Nations, governments, politics, and religions—all rest on the basic phenomenon of human existence, the city." [p. 15]

It is difficult and perhaps impossible to weld these different images of the city into a coherent and unified picture. Our purpose in this chapter is to approach the city in a somewhat different manner, focusing on the psychological inputs that affect the behavior of its inhabitants. How do people perceive and conceptualize their urban surroundings? What are the psychological sources of their satisfactions and dissatisfactions? In what ways is the city physically and emotionally stressful? How does the urban resident learn to orient himself in a highly complex environment? To what extent must he adapt and what is the cost of this adaptation? What social and symbolic meanings are important in man's urban habitat? What opportunities exist for psychological development? These are some of the questions we will be dealing with.

Such a task is made difficult because the city, like the natural environment, has had a history of rather negative associations. Intellectuals in general and urban researchers in particular have demonstrated a bias toward country over city values. In past times this bias reflected a conception of the natural environment as conducive to a moral and upright way of life. Nature was seen as somehow transcendent to the mundane experience of the city. Thoreau expressed this attitude in quasi-spiritual terms, Thomas Jefferson from a concern for civic virtues, and Theodore Roosevelt by arguing that the outdoor life was essential to the building of national character and virility. Green makes the point that because of the nation's agrarian and pioneering past, Americans are predisposed to put a higher value on the rural rather than on the urban setting (see Catton et al. 1969). Today, the antipathy toward cities is often a reaction to the superior "quality of life" that is believed to exist in the suburbs and smaller communities. But whatever its source, it is clear that the modern city is likely to be viewed from a perspective that is antiurban in orientation. Investigators look for the faults of the city rather than its virtues. And not surprisingly, they often find what they look for.

During the last few years urban sociology has moved away from the ecological and fact-gathering method toward a finer-grained and more directly experiential view of the city. The result of these parallel lines of investigation —one relying chiefly on census-type, routinely collected statistical correlations, the other on observation and interviews—has been to create a new and largely ambivalent image of the city. On the one hand it is described as impersonal and anonymous, a source of psychic stress and "overload," overwhelming its poorer inhabitants with a disproportionate share of illness, fostering bad housing, and acting as a breeding ground for delinquency and crime. At the same time, even the city's worst neighborhoods, in the sense of physical environment, may be warm, human, culturally vital, self-sustaining and cohesive areas that reinforce social identity. These two ways of viewing the city might be characterized as the pathological versus the romantic. It is not unreasonable to assume that the real city lies somewhere in between.

Whatever the significance of this ambivalent attitude, it is clear that America is becoming increasingly urbanized, although the greater part of this growth is in the suburban portions of the metropolis. This in itself has created new problems for the urban dweller as the central city loses population to its surrounding area. This urban-suburbanizing trend, moreover, is characteristic of most all Western societies and is a direct result of the industrial revolution. Davis (1965) has pointed out that prior to 1800 there were no urban societies as we know them today, and that only one had come into existence by 1900 (Great Britain). Whereas 7 cities in the world numbered half a million inhabitants or more in 1800, 42 had achieved this size by 1900, and today there are more than 200 (see Gottman 1966).

Here are some other figures that illustrate the extent to which the demographic character of western countries is being altered as cities get bigger and more numerous, and the countryside thins out. Today, more than 70 percent of the population of the United States lives in cities or suburbs (compared to 6 percent in 1800). In Europe, including the Soviet Union, the urban population grew two and a half times between 1900 and 1950. One-fifth of the American nation—40 million people—now live on 1.8 percent of the land of the continental United States and "in most countries 15 to 30 percent of the total population is now gathered on less than 5 percent of the land area." [Gottman 1966: 14] This trend, also characteristic of developing nations, creates stresses among the population that make the problem of urbanization ever more cogent.

The most obvious conclusion that we can draw from this worldwide trend is that man is changing his habitat significantly, and he may be changing himself as well. An environment governed by "natural" and more-or-less ecological forces is giving way to an "unnatural" or man-made environment with wholly new implications for human behavior. To call the city an "unnatural" habitat, however, is not to deny its viability or its value; there have always been cities and it is in cities that history has been made. The term *urbane*, by which we mean civilized and knowledgeable, represents qualities of life associated with the *urban* person. Nevertheless, the civilizations built around ancient Athens, Rome, and Alexandria were the product of a different kind of urbanization than that which characterizes the modern metropolis.

This is true in at least two respects: (1) The city today is an industrial-technological complex that is quite different environmentally from the mercantile-trading city that existed prior to the nineteenth century; as a result, much of the stimuli that impinge on present-day inhabitants were unknown to our ancestors. (2) Both the scale of the modern metropolis and its rate of growth have introduced qualitative changes in urban living which require new modes of adaptation.

It is from this perspective that the environmental psychologist seeks the general requirements which must be considered when thinking of people's creative use of the city. Although the requirements outlined below apply to a number of different environments, they are especially salient in an urban context. Their function is to identify psychological linkages between the environmental properties of the city and the responses of its inhabitants.

1. *Stress.* Before the urban resident can realize his potentialities for psychological and social development, he must remove or control the noxious, stressful stimulus information stemming from his environment. The city is, so to speak, contaminated by noise, polluted air, and the multitude of congestions occasioned by the presence of "too many people." The urban environment has been said to demand too much psychological energy in simply learning to cope with the multiple and often conflicting stimuli which the urban resident encounters (Milgram 1970; Meier 1962). The density of city living is blamed for creating special conditions which, taken together, make the city an unpleasant and/or unhealthy place to live.

2. *Orientation and Ease of Movement.* A special kind of stress of interest to urban designers and urban geographers has been that associated with difficulties in learning to find one's way through the city. In a limited sense the readability of the city is an essential aspect of the urban resident's adaptation. More broadly, however, we not only need to be able to "image" the city (Lynch 1960) but to have access to those aspects of urban living which help a person to use the city creatively to further his or her goals. In this respect we are concerned not only with transportation systems but the way in which the things required by city dwellers can be knowable or known. Ease of movement is as much psychological as physical.

3. *Sociability and Community.* We view the city here not merely as an aggregate of people but as a complex entity organized to achieve specific goals. This entity is a composite of neighborhoods, districts, and areas which fit together into a variegated "social mosaic" differentiated by function, physical character, and social structure. The term *community* has been loosely applied to the city as a whole and to the sub-divisions which comprise the urban structure. Sections of the city are said to provide people with an identity based on territory or with a sense of place. This view stands in contrast to typical characterizations of urban residents as preoccupied with a desire for anonymity. In fact, however, people are concerned with the intangibles which are often associated with the term community. Many of the satisfactions identified with urban life are strongly linked to one's perception and use of the social and physical spaces provided by his neighborhood or district. The environmental psychologist must be concerned with the variables which create community and the balance that must be struck between socialization and privacy necessary to a satisfying life in the city.

4. *Cultural-recreational Opportunities.* The city is traditionally a center for theaters, concert halls, museums, sports stadia, and leisure-time activities. Yet, as with ease of transportation, the satisfactions derived from these amenities must be measured not by what exists, but by the city dweller's perception of what is available to him. Education, income, and social class are factors that contribute to this perception and, ultimately, to the experienced benefits. We must also consider the ways in which the physical environment contributes to the quality of these experiences.

5. *Enrichment of Experience.* Beyond the opportunities noted above, the city also provides an ambience, a sentient environment of colors, textures, and sights. In the physical sense, vitality, novelty, and movement; variegated spatial and building forms; a rich assortment of sounds and smells; contrasting architectural styles; a vivifying street life—all combine to make this aspect of the urban experience a stimulating one. The city is alive. Perceptually, Carr and Lynch (1968) see it as a context for learning. This enrichment can also be conceptual. We give meanings to the city that are mirrored in its physical form. It is environmentally permissive; a place to get ahead; a setting for the good life; a symbol of civilization itself. For many, at least, the city is intellectually exciting.

6. *The Decision Process.* The city is political, not only for those who seek to control the decisions which allow them to achieve the preceding five requirements. Every urban resident, directly or indirectly, experiences the power struggles that center on how the city shall be governed. In the environmental sense, these struggles may take the forms of community control, provision of local services, zoning regulations, urban renewal, noise levels, safe streets, or transportation routes. In general we see the development of a participatory strategy among community groups that is often at odds with conventional planning. As urban problems intensify, the population seeks to decentralize power in favor of more local control. Technologically, this may be difficult; behaviorally, it is a response to remote and insensitive decision-making at higher levels. The urbanite is more than a statistic. He wants to relate decisions to his own environmental needs.

Such an approach to the city as outlined here is not the traditional view developed by city planners and design professionals, who, in Appleyard's (1970) phrase, structure their communities "so that they read well at an altitude of 30,000 feet." [p. 116]

This emphasis on the economics of land use, physical forms and spaces, transportation networks, and traffic circulation often predominated over the inhabitant's personal activities, his sentient or existential experience of the city. Fortunately, urban planning today is somewhat more aware of the man on the ground and of the immediacy of his setting. It is from this perspective that we will examine the city here. Since some of our material is drawn from the literature of urban sociology, especially with respect to its stressful and pathological aspects, it will be helpful to trace the roots of this sociological approach and indicate its relevance to our theme.

Historical Background of Urban Studies

In the United States the city as a social setting began to attract systematic academic interest in the second decade of the present century. Scholars such as Burgess (1926), Wirth (1938), and Park (1952) of the University of Chicago studied the city in terms of social and physical pathologies that could be correlated with various geographical sections and social classes. The result was a large body of literature developed mainly from correlational studies of deviancy and slums. The problems and difficulties inherent in city life, as expressed in crime, poverty, disease, mental illness, alcoholism, and so on, were emphasized, often at the expense of the city's positive features.

These men saw the city as a system (although not a closed one) made viable by the interaction of a number of specialized economic and social functions. In another sense, it was an organization of well-delineated spaces or sections which served as integral parts to the whole. People live together not because they are alike, Park (1952) noted, but "because they are useful to one another." [p. 80] For Wirth (1938) the size, density, and heterogeneity of the large city inevitably resulted in spatial differentiation.

One result of this approach was that, for Park in particular, the city was modeled along classical ecological lines. Park believed that ecological concepts served not only as analogies but as having direct reference to the changes that occur in the city. As a system the city illustrated both the interdependent, cooperative working of nature and its predatory and competitive aspects as well. The concepts of "invasion" and "succession" were introduced to explain the demographic changes that took place as lower socioeconomic groups "invaded" sections of the metropolis and "succeeded" the upwardly mobile groups who sought their niches elsewhere. The invading group might itself be succeeded in time. The consolidation of ghetto areas is essentially the end result of this process. In brief, borrowing from ecology, the Chicago school attempted to explain the city with techniques and concepts taken from the natural sciences.

At the same time, these sociologists were just as much influenced by critics who viewed the city as a potential source of pathology. How else can we explain their preoccupation with the problems of mental health which seemed to characterize the central city? This concern did not necessarily imply an acceptance of the pathological features of urban life, however; on the contrary, by showing that the central city was indeed a repository for all sorts of pathologies, social critics had a strong case for remedial action, whether this took the form of slum clearance or the settlement house approach of Jane Addams and Hull House.

More recent writers, such as Timms (1971), echoing Park, describe the city as a "mosaic of social worlds." In this view, zones or sections of a city are identified with the functions enacted in them (business, manufacturing) or the socioeconomic status of their residents. These zones, in turn, embrace subunits, or districts, which may be quite homogeneous ("Little Italy") and well demarcated. The problems of such communities in the face of physical change is well documented in urban renewal literature (Wilson 1962). In general, the more a community is tied to a specific place, the more likely are its residents to suffer from large-scale and disruptive physical changes in that place.

To some extent every neighborhood is a setting in which certain types of behavior are associated with (and sometimes attributed to) the local environment, a rubric exemplified when we speak of the "character of the neighborhood." Even larger areas exist, psychologically as well as geographically, as the place where one "belongs," although as Fried and Gleicher (1961) point out, this is demonstrably truer for the lower- than the middle-class urbanite.

In brief, for the urban ecologist much of the city's influence on behavior is spelled out along demographic lines. The "mosaic" concept sorts people out into well-defined socioeconomic classes that coincide, although not rigidly, with geographical areas. It is assumed that these areas will undergo changes, and as they do, the character of the city will be better understood. The difficulty with this approach is twofold: (1) Variables which are significant at an aggregated scale are not predictive of individual behavior; and (2) Much of the data employed by urban ecologists are correlative rather than causal, so that if changes occur, it is not clear why they took place.

Quite a few years ago Robinson (1950) pointed out that attempts to explain the city in terms of large-scale demographic variables fail to account for much of the individual and small-group phenomena that are characteristic of urban life. Figuratively speaking, what is needed is not a telescope but a microscope. Knowing that a certain district in a city is characterized by upper-middle-income people with at least a college education will not allow us to predict how any individual or even small group in that district will respond to a wide range of possible changes that might affect that section. To understand how individuals and small groups (for example, families, friendship groups, or neighbors) behave requires analytical techniques which are more appropriate to psychology than to demography.

This does not mean that the aggregated data of the urban ecologist are useless. On the contrary, it is possible to imagine a combination of socioeconomic indicators of urban areas with other statistical data (such as the physical condition of the housing, number of complaints to the police, and rate of hospitalization) that would make possible an early warning system which alerts us to the possible decline of specific neighborhoods. Such a system would make possible remedial actions in an area before it becomes so pathological that the only solution would be massive demolition and reconstruction. We cannot, however, rely on such a system exclusively. Gans (1962) and others have pointed out that a much finer-grained analysis of neighborhoods is required before policy decisions are made. This analysis must concentrate on the lives of the individuals who comprise the area under study.

Urban ecology must also develop models which describe how urban subareas change over time and how they interrelate to one another. One example of a project that points to a more psychologically oriented investigation of the relationships among districts of a city deals principally with Seattle, Washington (Grey et al. 1970). The study focuses on the contrasting appeals of the Central Business District and an outlying shopping center, with emphasis on factors that account for the declining use of the former. The authors surveyed a variety of available materials (land-use surveys, and so on), conducted questionnaires and group interviews, photographed people walking through the downtown areas, and tracked them from one point to another, "relating the results to and recording a variety of, personal and behavioral characteristics." [p. xiii] The result of this study was a comprehensive evaluation of the subdistricts of the Central Business District, showing how people actually used these areas, the behavioral linkages which existed among the areas, and the kinds of images which urban residents had of the Central Business District. This represents a major departure from the traditional urban planning approach with its essentially static approach to subareas based on similarities or differences of physical function and condition, socioeconomic standing, ethnicity, and family status. Such an orientation seldom indicates how the people characterized by these demographic variables interact or how the identifiable subdistricts interrelate to one another on a behavioral level. By comparison, the Seattle study presumes a much more dynamic model of these interrelationships and it is in this direction that urban research is moving.

Such an approach is still in the pilot stage and most of what we know about the city is based on more aggregated studies. This is particularly true of the so-called pathological indicators—social disorganization, physical and mental illness, and the predisposition toward (or absence of) delinquent and criminal behavior. Here, the sociomedical literature is replete with evidence that cities are, indeed, seemingly unhealthy and unsafe places in which to live. Our task here is not simply to review this evidence for its own sake, but to ask how reliable it is.

The Pathological City

That cities present health hazards beyond that which obtains in smaller communities, and that they are also associated with high rates of social pathology, is indicated by numerous studies correlating these variables. According to a report by the U.S. Department of Health, Education and Welfare (1969), although an estimated 2 percent of the country's population suffers from a major mental illness, "estimates for concentrated urban populations run as high as 10 percent." [p. 3] Taking the year 1966, the Department noted that 98 percent of the drug addicts treated at the Lexington, Kentucky, and Fort Worth, Texas, Public Health Service hospitals were urban residents.

Figures for crime and delinquency are likewise disproportionately heavy for cities. The Department notes:

> Twenty-six cities containing less than 18 percent of the total population account for more than half of all reported serious crimes against the person and more than 30 percent of all reported serious property crimes. One of every three robberies and nearly one of every five rapes occurs in cities of more than 1 million. The average rate in these cities for most serious crimes is about twice as great (and more often) as in the suburbs or rural areas. . . .
>
> The findings have been remarkably consistent. Burglary, robbery, and serious assaults occur in areas characterized by low income, high population density, physical deterioration, overcrowded and substandard housing, concentrations of ethnic minorities, broken homes, working mothers, etc. [p. 32]

With certain notable exceptions, this correlation between pathology and population density is a worldwide phenomenon. The Swedish sociologists Carlestam and Levi (1971) report that although Greater Stockholm accounts for only 16 percent of Sweden's total population, "these 16 percent commit 39 percent of all robberies. . . ." [p. 4] They add that Stockholm residents "call in sick" at a rate 30 percent higher than that for the whole of Sweden and that the death rate for certain types of cancer, hypertension, and suicide is significantly higher, although for diabetes mellitus the rate is considerably lower. In his study of Luton, a London working-class suburb, Timms (1971) found that the rooming house area, with approximately 5 percent of the adult population and 3 percent of its juveniles, accounted for "30 percent of [Luton's] adult criminals, 13 percent of its juvenile delinquents and 12 percent of its mental hospital first admissions." [p. 29]

Numerous studies of hospitalized mental patients indicate that their residential location is an important factor in such illnesses, although it is not a proven cause of them. This approach can be termed a location hypothesis. One of the earliest and most ambitious studies made along these lines is Faris and Dunham's *Mental Disorders in Urban Areas* (1939). Taking Chicago and Providence as their samples, the authors found high rates of psychotic illness associated with the rooming house areas around the central business district —neighborhoods characterized by a rapid turnover of population and low socioeconomic status. The rates declined in the more settled residential areas at the periphery of the cities. Faris and Dunham explain the differences in terms of the social isolation experienced by the residents of rooming house neighborhoods. A more recent study in New York City, the Mid-Manhattan Project (see Srole et al. 1961), supports earlier findings that "mental disorder" is high (in relation to the overall population of the city) in a central area characterized by a large population of working wives, unmarrieds, and/or small families. This survey by Srole and his associates differs from others in that it uses self-reported symptoms rather than hospitalizations as indices of illness. Thus, perhaps, it more accurately reflects the less severe, neurotic, and more common types of mental disorder widely found in the general population.

Another interesting statistical finding is that as city size increases, the differences in male/female mortality rates decline. The longer life-expectancy of women, Lewit (1971) believes, may be the result of environmental rather than biological factors. Noting earlier research that the wage differential between men and women also narrows as the size of a city increases, Lewit hypothesized that urban women perform more male-type activities and therefore die at a similar age.

What is it about the city, the student may ask, that accounts for these rather striking features? More importantly, why has so much urban research focused on the city as a breeding ground of social pathology and morbidity? Does sheer concentration of people—population density—create such pathology, or does it simply make the pathology easier to tabulate and study? Are illness, crime, and social disorganization more visible in cities—more reliably reported and more available to treatment and correction? Looking at it another way, is the city a haven rather than an agent—a setting in which certain behaviors flourish because afflicted and antisocial types find the city a more permissive environment?

These are important questions because they involve such aspects of the urban crisis as deterioration of housing stock, crime, blighted neighborhoods, and ghettoization of the races. Urban renewal, better health facilities, and decentralization—or at least improvement of—municipal services may not be possible if the basic causes of the crisis cannot be documented. In short, if cities are to be saved, this can only be done by finding answers to the kinds of questions the urban sociologist is asking.

But in reviewing this material, the student is confronted with a bewildering array of arguments and statistics, many of which contradict each other. What seems to be true for some large metropolitan areas does not prove to be true for others. The extremely complex nature of the city makes it difficult to give accurate weights to the variables in question. Thus, the researcher has generally depended upon correlational studies of existing records; these demonstrate associative rather than causative relationships. Very little research has been conducted on attempting to understand what it is about certain areas of the city that may be implicated in the presence or persistence of pathology.

The problems encountered in using the correlational method are illustrated by the abundant studies on mental illness. Thus, the hypothesis put forth by Faris and Dunham (1939) and others has been challenged by Hollingshead and Redlich (1958). Their New Haven, Connecticut, study suggests that socioeconomic class is a more reliable index for predicting hospitalizations than place of residence. The lowest socioeconomic group (Class V) was found to have the highest incidence of hospitalized illness. Of course, such low-status groups might be expected to inhabit slum or rooming house areas—the "zones in transition"—areas changing from middle-class housing to slums (Timms 1971). An interesting finding in the New Haven project reveals how dangerous it can be to jump to conclusions. The investigators found that Class V patients showed better mental and emotional adjustment after their release from the hospital than middle-class patients. On the face of it, one might assume that whereas the lower-class individual was more likely to have a breakdown of some sort, he also, seemingly, enjoyed greater recuperative powers than persons higher on the socioeconomic scale. Is this the case? Not at all. By refining their investigation further, the researchers learned that compared with others, hospitalized patients in Class V were not as likely to be taken back to their families until they had made a satisfactory recovery.

Likewise, in their study of crime and cities Swedish researchers speculated that it was not the urban environment as such that influenced lawbreaking but social factors attendant on migration into the city. For asocial types the city might be called an "attractive nuisance." There are fewer controls in the city as compared with smaller communities, for, as Wirth (1938) contended, primary groups such as the family play a less prominent role in urban than in nonurban environments, whereas secondary groups—friends, voluntary groups, and so on—assume greater importance for city residents. Finally, all urban-rural comparisons are suspect to the extent that cities tend to keep better records than small communities. Indeed, Cappon (1971) suggests that only as unincorporated (or "inchoate") rural areas become organized into larger governing units are rates of mental illness, crime, and disease fully reflected in statistics. Such "communities in transition," although they show a rise in these "rates of malaise," may actually be healthier than before, since identifying the extent and nature of the pathology is the first step to remedial action.

Moreover, recent statistics on disease rates challenge the notion that the city is, ipso facto, an unhealthier place in which to live. Dohrenwend and Dohrenwend (1972) state that in the clear majority of the studies comparing urban and rural mental health which they reviewed, psychoses were found to be more prevalent in rural areas, whereas both neuroses and personality disorders were found to be more prevalent in urban areas. Recent studies by the National Center for Health Statistics used self-reports of twelve psychiatric symptoms in comparing five communities of different sizes, from "giant metropolitan areas" (3 million and over) down to rural areas. For men, the giant cities showed a lower incidence of the self-reported symptoms than any other; for women, only the 50,000 to 500,000 city size was higher, and this by a small degree. Concerning physical disease, hypertension rates are but slightly higher in New York City than in the country at large and the estimated rates of arthritis, rheumatism, and heart condition are lower (Srole 1972).

Here again, figures do not necessarily tell the whole story. Srole points out that many people bring their illnesses with them to the city from other places. For most of us, the type of community occupied in adulthood is self-selected. In his Mid-Manhattan study, Srole found that a large number of "functionally impaired" people were escapees from smaller cities or towns; for them the metropolis was a hiding place whose tolerance for deviance either stabilized the pathology or relieved it. In this view the city is seen as an outlet for certain behaviors that have little if any causal linkage to urban stresses. If we may mix our metaphors, the city is both a hiding place and a safety valve.

These are some of the problems inherent in trying to disentangle the causal fabric of urban life by resorting to statistical correlations. If there are no differences between urban and rural residents with respect to illness and crime, then the search for the cause of pathology cannot be confined to the city but must be sought elsewhere. In any case, the difficulty of knowing where rural areas stop and cities begin makes these attempts to compare rural and urban rates of pathology somewhat less than productive. A more fruitful approach might be to take a much closer look at what is happening in various parts of cities themselves—those characterized by high degrees and by low degrees of pathology respectively. To aid in this process it is necessary to generate some hypotheses about the possible reasons.

One variable that has been consistently implicated in a wide variety of urban ills is density. Before examining the density issue in detail, however, it is necessary to add that as yet we do not know whether density does in fact cause the effects that are attributed to it, and how it works if, indeed, it is responsible for them. Work in this field nevertheless represents a step forward, since a variable is specified and can be experimentally tested. But more significantly for environmental psychology, if density is an important factor it may lead to a number of implications for the design of the built environment.

Effects of Crowding and Density

As defined by public health experts "crowding" refers to the number of persons occupying a unit of living space—1.5 persons per room is frequently considered the threshold in America. Density is the distribution of units over a given area—a neighborhood or census tract. As was noted in Chapter Six, crowding may well be a perceptual concept. "Dense" environments, moreover, are not necessarily crowded: An area of forty-story, luxury apartment houses will very likely provide quite adequate living space for its occupants. In areas of the city characterized by housing with less than adequate space per family, crowding does appear to be an important variable in explaining certain kinds of pathology and deviant behavior. The extent to which this is generally the case, however, is by no means established.

On the level of residential dwelling space, Schorr (1963) concluded that overcrowding was the most significant factor in such ill effects as stress, poor

Fig. 9-1 High density is characteristic of urban living. (Photograph, Shelly Katz, from Black Star)

health, cynicism about people and organizations, sexual frustration, and feelings of dissatisfaction. He points to the respiratory infections associated with "multiple use of toilet and water facilities, inadequate heating or ventilation, inadequate and crowded sleeping arrangements." [p. 14] Loring (1956) found that socially disorganized families tended to have less dwelling space and live in more crowded areas than the control families who were roughly matched on cultural and economic variables. The much-studied West End renewal project of Boston, however, indicates that social structure rather than density per se mediates mental health and satisfaction (Fried & Gleicher 1961; Gans 1962).

Another approach to this question was taken in Schmitt's (1966) study of Honolulu. Schmitt compared the density of twenty-nine census tracts in the city with that of the constituent households in relation to social pathology and physical health. His object was to discover which was more relevant—high density or overcrowding. With the density of persons-per-acre held constant, the degree of crowding within living quarters showed virtually no relation to the incidence of pathology. Degree of density, however, did. Population per acre rather than crowding per se correlated strongly with such measures as family disorganization, juvenile delinquency, adult crime, high rates of physical illness, and mental breakdown.

Why this should be so is not easy to explain. We might speculate that high-density neighborhoods invite the kinds of social interaction or "contagion" that lead to antisocial behavior. Then, again, ghettos in particular represent a source of frustration to their residents that may find expression in various unacceptable behaviors. One of the elements of density in such a setting is the lack of community services in relation to the demands made upon them, services frequently more in evidence in affluent neighborhoods. Finally, in cities, densely populated settings are usually inhabited by the poor, the undereducated, the migratory, and, to some extent, the unskilled. It is possible that these social factors, rather than living conditions as such, explain the high ratio of pathology to density.

There is at least some indication that this is the case. When Schmitt (1966) statistically controlled measures of income and education for his Honolulu study, he found that the suicide rate and infant mortality no longer correlated positively. However, other measures that related density and pathology retained a positive correlation. A similar study by Winsborough (1965) correlated infant mortality, death rate, public assistance, and the tuberculosis rate with density-per-acre in Chicago. Using partial correlations for educational, economic, and migration levels, he discovered that density is actually associated with less morbidity, disease, and the need for public assistance (Cited in Freedman et al. 1971). When Winsborough studied living quarters rather than people-per-acre, however, he found that seven persons per room correlated with pathology. In Schmitt's study such a correlation did not obtain.

The difficulty of attributing the social and physical ills of the city to density and overcrowding is indicated by another study made by Schmitt (1963), this one of Hong Kong, the most densely populated city in the world. In Boston and New York high-density areas seldom exceed 450 persons per acre of ground space. In Hong Kong more than 2000 persons per acre were found in some 13 census tracts. Yet, except for tuberculosis, disease rates are relatively low. Basing his information on census figures for 1961, Schmitt notes that a mortality rate of 5.9 per 1000 inhabitants in Hong Kong compares with 9.3 for the United States. Hospitalization for mental illness, at 0.3 per 1000 population, was less than 10 percent of the U.S. rate. Six times as many cases of murder and manslaughter were reported in America as in Hong Kong, and the rate for all serious crimes combined was less than half the American rate.

This disparity is something of an enigma to the urban sociologist; lack of space, in itself, would not seem to be perceived as a disadvantage by the Hong Kong Chinese nor does it express itself behaviorally. When new housing was made available to some families, many of them sublet space in their apartments to others. The highly organized nature of Chinese family life, with its tight controls, may account for lower crime rates. More importantly, the study points up the difficulty of explaining such complex dependent variables as various types of crime and disease on the basis of density alone. In Hong Kong the cultural setting is perhaps the more significant factor; certainly numbers, density, and amount of land may mean very different things to the inhabitants of Hong Kong than they do to urban residents in New York or Los Angeles. Ethnic characteristics may also account for an ability to adapt to crowded conditions. Mitchell (1972), in a comprehensive survey of several Far Eastern cities, suggests that compared with other groups the Chinese are able to withstand crowded living conditions because of their low level of affect and emotion, which protects them "from the excessive stresses to which they are often brutally exposed." [p. 5]

Tokyo is another city in which high density seems not to be associated with high rates of antisocial behavior, yet here again the explanation for this behavior must be sought in the nature of the total environment. More than 20,000 persons per square mile live in Tokyo, over ten times the average for many American cities. Yet, according to David and Sandra Canter (1971), "Violence and vandalism are rare, streets are alive until late at night, and community participation is an integral part of local decision making." [p. 61] The Canters attribute this happy state of affairs, at least in part, to the fact that Tokyo is not so much a city as a collection of "vibrant urban neighborhoods," an "agglomeration of towns and villages." [p. 60] Michelson (1970) believes that the Japanese have adjusted to very high densities by "turning inward," although this is possibly a matter of reverse cause-and-effect; "inward turning" people desire intimate environments. In any case, private open space is minimal, dwellings are small and scantily furnished, and space is used intensively. A common, although by no means proven, explanation for the well-known politeness of the Japanese people is that the extremely crowded conditions under which they live compel such behavior as a means of getting along with one another. However, newspaper accounts (1973) of a rampage of Tokyo commuters in the subway suggest that a critical threshold of crowding can be reached, that even in Japan there are indeed limits to the ability to adapt. In this instance the subway cars were literally "overloaded" and cultural norms did not prevent the riders from "blowing their stacks."

The kind of cross-cultural research described here is a helpful tool in measuring crowding effects, but it also presents difficulties. We must know, in brief, not only that different cultures tolerate different degrees of crowding, but more specifically how a given culture works to ameliorate the effects. Such a cultural explanation is important in another respect in that it points to the limitations of a purely physical-factors approach. It suggests that people work out strategies for dealing with environmental stressors, so that if we are to reconcile contradictory data, we must search more carefully for an adequate explanation of the underlying chain of events linking density to social and physical health.

In any event we do have a measurable variable. In the Winsborough study (Freedman et al. 1971), for example, the finding that crowding in the house apparently does have an influence on health could lead to a series of investigations to determine if, because of the weather, Chicago residents spend more time inside than outside. It also suggests that we could examine alternative internal spatial layouts of the apartments while, at the same time, varying the number of people living in a space. These kinds of studies are especially germane to the environmental psychologist who looks for relationships between density, crowding, and indicators of social pathology and physical health.

What is needed at this point, then, is a theoretical statement that could deal with this question in a more inclusive framework. One such statement, or hypothesis, is that of *overload,* which has received increasing attention from various environmental researchers.

The Overloaded Environment

Earlier in this chapter the city was called a stimulating place in which to live. The question is: What price does one pay for this stimulation? Even "desirable" stimuli may be of such range and frequency that they produce undesirable side effects. The city is continually in a state of environmental and social flux, or at least our experience makes it seem so as we move through it. When this stimulus-information from the physical environment, including the presence of other people, exceeds our capacity to scan and process it, a possible consequence is cognitive overload. The environment makes too many demands on the individual to allow him to perform at his behavioral norm. As Miller (1961) has indicated, increasing levels of stimuli require new sets of adaptational strategies. They force the individual to utilize responses which simplify the information. Difficulties, however, may arise if these modes of adaptation result in a loss of significant data from the environment. Should the amount of stimulus information become too overpowering, it may appear to an outside observer that the individual becomes increasingly withdrawn and his behavior very routinized and simplified.

Historically, the notion of the overloaded environment can be traced to the sociologist Simmel (1950), who argued in 1903 that the urban setting tends to prevent people from responding "normally" to new stimulations because their energy is dissipated in coping with an excess of environmental information. The individual is encouraged to maintain distance from rather than make contact with others to counteract the pressures of the multitude. To conserve psychic energy, one avoids all but superficial relationships. One result of this "people overload," then, is that the person filters out contact with all but the necessary minimum of "others." The architect Alexander (1966) has summed up much of the foregoing by pointing out that it is not stress as such that accounts for the ills attributed to urban life, but rather the avoidance of stress in an effort to protect oneself from it. Such "turning off," he believes, fosters a withdrawal from normal social behavior and creates a kind of "autonomous" man. This "autonomy withdrawal syndrome . . . creates more people who believe in self-sufficiency as an ideal, it makes intimate contact seem less necessary. . . ." [p. 32]

The theory of cognitive or sensory overload was most elegantly stated by J. G. Miller (1961), who identified eight sets of adaptational strategies which individuals use in coping with increasing levels of stimulation. In general, the individual is likely to screen out inputs which seem (but may not be) less important to him; there is less time available to evaluate environmental information; dealing with the environment becomes more impersonal as the individual gives less time to each input and attempts to find surrogates in the form of other individuals or institutions to handle the overload.

Although these strategies are not completely explanatory, they do serve a heuristic role in organizing material which may very well have implications for research. Milgram's (1970) work applies Miller's conceptual approach to a series of mundane urban situations. In an equally broad vein, Meier (1962) had adapted Miller's theory to social institutions. Emphasizing the systems approach to information overload, Meier applies it to the increasing complexity of the city in terms of communication among its members: ". . . the proliferation of communications technique is a fundamental property of urbanism. By spelling out what machine-interposed communication is, how it works, and what it is becoming we add to our understanding of the dynamics of cities." [p. 14]

Meier concentrates on the role of organizations in handling transactions or "bits" of information among "senders" and "receivers." Stress results when information begins to overlap and accumulated backlogs result in poorer service, more errors, and lower morale among those taking part. The "back office" crisis of some stock exchange brokerage firms during periods of peak activity results from an inability to keep up with the paper work. The present dissatisfaction with the United States Postal Service can be traced, among other things, to an overloaded system. When this happens, Meier notes, more work is automated. While this may help solve the problem, it also results in less face-to-face contact. People are "more and more free to transfer their attention from knowledge about things to techniques for solving problems . . ." [p. 140]—chiefly via computer. In overloaded environments stress begins on the institutional level and is measured by a failure to perform "up to expectations." As the load intensifies (and if the problem is not solved) institutional stress is eventually transmitted to the individual members or working units in the form of lower morale and lessened efficiency. Institutional failure thus produces adaptational strategies on the part of individuals which may be stressful. But for the city as a whole, Meier observes, cognitive stress becomes a problem only for those who accept responsibility.

The city's vulnerability to information overload suggests a number of consequences for individual behavior. Foa (1971), for instance, believes that the specialization of the city and its high density make for an efficient exchange of what he calls "universalistic" goods, such as money, jobs, and information, while decreasing the opportunity for exchanging the "particularistic" ones of service, love, and personal face-to-face communication. The city, in brief, emphasizes the common denominators of day-to-day existence at the cost of a long-range and more humane involvement in living.

An extensive discussion of the effects of environmental overload on the individual is presented by Milgram (1970). Among the various strategies for dealing with overload, Milgram emphasizes these in particular: (1) Less time is given to each input; (2) Low-priority inputs are disregarded; (3) The burden of responsibility in many situations is shifted to others—"It's none of my business"; (4) Social screening devices are interposed between the individual and the environment ("Get in touch with my secretary"); and (5) Specialized institutions are created to absorb inputs. There is a general diminution of social responsibility among city dwellers because the ". . . moral and social involvement with individuals is necessarily restricted. This is a direct and necessary function of excess of 'input over capacity to process.'" [p. 1462] It is commonly believed that people in cities are less likely to be friendly to strangers than people in smaller communities; that they are less polite; more distrustful and frightened of others. Several studies cited by Milgram have tested this popular assumption. In brief, an overloaded social and physical environment tends to depersonalize human relationships. Milgram summarizes:

> . . . the concept of overload helps to explain a wide variety of contrasts between city and town behavior: (1) the differences in *role enactment* (the urban tendency to deal with one another in highly segmented, functional terms; the constricted time and services offered customers by sales personnel); (2) the evolution of *urban norms* quite different from traditional town values (such as the acceptance of non-involvement, impersonality and aloofness in urban life); (3) the adaptation of the urban-dweller's *cognitive processes* (his inability to identify most of the people seen daily; his screening of sensory stimuli; his development of blasé attitudes toward deviant or bizarre behavior; and his selectivity in responding to human demand); and (4) the far greater competition for scarce *facilities* in the city (the subway rush; the fight for taxis; traffic jams; standing in line to await services). I would suggest that contrasts between city and rural behavior probably

> reflect the responses of similar people to very different situations, rather than intrinsic differences between rural personalities and city personalities. The city is a situation to which individuals respond adaptively. [p. 1465]

This view may also help explain the city dweller's reluctance to help strangers in an emergency. In their study on helping behavior, Latané and Darley (1970) point to several field experiments in New York that tend to confirm what many of us have observed: Witnesses to someone in distress are likely to ignore the incident and pass by. Testing this hypothesis in a number of situations, ranging from minor requests for assistance (time of day) to emergencies (a man falling on the sidewalk), the authors found that although the former situation is usually complied with, incidents that require a major intervention on the part of the bystander are not. Moreover, the more bystanders present, the less likely that any one of them will come to the victim's assistance.

Is this a uniquely urban phenomenon? A case can be made that it is. City people are more likely to be strangers to one another than people in smaller communities; there is less solidarity among them. The setting is not as likely to be familiar to them, with a resultant sense of insecurity affecting the situation. This notion was borne out by an experiment comparing the response of people on a crowded subway platform with travelers waiting in an airport lounge. In both locales a test subject, walking on crutches and wearing a bandage on his leg, stumbled and fell in the presence of one man sufficiently isolated from others so that he and he alone might be expected to help. The incident was staged sixty times in both settings. Results: 83 percent of the subway riders helped the man to his feet while only 41 percent of the airport people did.

Latané and Darley speculated on the reasons for this wide difference in response. One possible explanation was that because subway riders as a group comprise a lower socioeconomic class than airline travelers, they are more acquainted with "trouble" and are accustomed to helping out in emergencies. The middle and upper classes find such action socially embarrassing. Interviews with the bystanders, however, did not bear this out. A more cogent argument, in the authors' view, is that people who ride subways are more familiar with their surroundings than the traveler in an airport lounge. "In both airport . . . and the subway . . . there was a significant correlation between familiarity and responding to the emergency. In neither case was there a significant correlation between social class and helping behavior." [p. 119]

Why should familiarity make a difference? ". . . [A] person who is more familiar with his environment is more aware of the way in which the environment works. He is not overloaded with stimuli. . . . He may have a greater stake in keeping that environment safe. He is in control. Thus he is more likely to help." [p. 119]

People in cities are not necessarily lacking in humanity, the authors conclude, but are more likely to be exposed to distracting situational factors—

the presence of many others, the strangeness of the locale, confusing extraneous stimuli. All contribute to an "it's none of my business" attitude which inhibits whatever humanitarian impulses they may have. To the extent that the city supplies these social and environmental pressures, it discourages helping others where intervention requires positive action on the part of the individual.

At the same time, helping behavior in the city is not totally absent. The student should test his own experiences empirically in everyday situations. One of the authors, for example, after writing the above paragraphs, walked three blocks through the heart of Manhattan, just off Times Square. In this brief journey he was apologized to twice for such minor social infractions as cutting across his line of march and unavoidable physical contact. Neither apologist was well dressed. It is the experience of some, at least, that urban civility has not disappeared, especially if one takes the initiative in difficult situations.

Another possible difficulty with Milgram's approach is the danger of assuming that a crowded environment is necessarily an overloaded one or that it turns people away from social interaction. Edward T. Hall (1966) has described the "involvement ratio" of different ethnic groups, noting that blacks, and whites of southern European stock, have a long history of close contact with one another so that crowding, psychologically at least, is not regarded as necessarily undesirable. Anglo-Saxons and northern Europeans, on the other hand, prefer a less dense environment. Both types maintain distance according to cultural norms, but it is more difficult for the latter to do this in large cities.

Again, what are the empirical measures of stimulus overload? Although this may be ascertained for institutions or systems, as Meier notes, on the basis of impaired functioning, cities are not closed systems and individuals even less so. People have different tolerances for stress and handle "inputs" from the environment with different degrees of responsiveness. Age, time, and purpose all contribute to one's management of stimulus overload. Some people do, indeed, "turn off" from the overloaded environment, but for others—especially the young—a high degree of stimulation is an attraction. For still others the anonymity of city life may be the background for establishing good interpersonal relationships. Finally, this quality of the urban environment is an advantage for the culturally different and for those who seek a high degree of privacy in their personal lives. The impersonal city is more tolerant of social deviants and permits a greater variety of life styles.

What this suggests is that future research on overload should be oriented to more discrete studies on a much less global scale than that conducted by the investigators discussed here. These studies will be more psychologically oriented, which means smaller groupings and more clearly defined dependent measures. In sum, we need to take a closer look at what goes on in specific crowded situations. How do children behave in playgrounds under various degrees of crowding? Are there changes in people's capacity to solve problems under different degrees of crowding? One would expect more errors to be made under conditions of high density compared to low density situations. Although the controlled experiments of Freedman et al. (1971) did not show this to be the case, such a hypothesis can only be tested satisfactorily under naturally occurring conditions. Finally, if we take the enrichment criterion of city life as a test of crowding, it is possible that there would be less chance to appreciate and remember a perceptually interesting area of the city if a great many people were present. Even if the overall organization of the area is the same for high- and low-density conditions we would expect fewer details to be remembered, for much of our attention would necessarily be diverted to coping with others. Those of us who have been members of conducted sight-seeing tours are well aware that the usual crowdedness of such groups interferes with what we are supposed to be looking at.

Stress in Urban Living

Up to this point we have dealt with attempts to differentiate various subareas of the city and one factor (density) which might contribute to man's adaptational strategies to the problem of overload. Perhaps a more general concept which can help us tie some of these orientations together is the notion of stress. Our problem here is to specify which aspects of an environmental situation are indeed stressful. Since a bewildering variety of conditions associated with urban living seemingly do cause stress, one of the tasks of the environmental psychologist is to isolate the stressors and relate them to the sociophysical configuration of environmental settings. First, however, it is necessary to know just what stress is.

Stress in general can be defined as the unpleasant physiological and psychological reactions of the person to new, demanding, and often persistent stimuli. The Canadian physician Selye (1956) sees stress as a nonspecific response by the body to the demands made upon it. Because man has outgrown his early adaptation pattern of "fight or flight," many of today's responses to stressful situations are phylogenetically inappropriate; response behavior "programmed" centuries ago is out of touch with the newer threats and choices that confront us. Social learning and adaptive behavior have closed the gap to some extent, but our biological equipment lags. The rapid growth of an industrialized urban society has brought about a whole new class of stimuli to which man must adapt. The attempt to do this creates certain stress reactions.

Selye dealt primarily with man's biological responses to stress. Many students of behavior, however, emphasize the psychological aspects of dealing with stress. This is an important distinction because it interposes cognitive mediation between the stressful stimuli and the individual's adaptation to them. We learn to appraise the "threat cues" and deal with them accordingly. If the stress is perceived as harmful, some form of coping strategy will be adopted (for example, some of the strategies devised by Miller and Meier). If benign, we may simply shrug it off. Whether or not, and how, we do one or the other will depend on our psychological make-up and the nature of the situation. Soldiers in battle are trained to handle conditions of extreme—indeed, life-threatening—stress. But a timid man may become panicky while being interviewed for a job.

Our ability to handle stress is a highly individual matter. Moreover, it is usually affected by repeated exposure to similar types of stress. As the stimuli become familiar, we deal with them less consciously and more effortlessly. Psychologists term this adaptive process *habituation.* Harris (1943) defines habituation as "response decrement as a result of repeated stimulation." [Quoted in Glass & Singer 1972:8] Paraphrased, we devote less time and effort to adapting to a situation as the stimulus becomes more familiar. This phenomenon probably explains why the city dweller of long standing can seemingly ignore the noise, dirt, crowding, and frenetic pace that visitors find unpleasant and ennervating. "The most remarkable feature of current urban existence is not how stressful the city has become, but how unaffected day-to-day functioning of the city dweller is despite the indignities heaped upon him." [Glass & Singer 1972:9]

It should be remembered in this connection that stress is intrinsic to the nature of life. Stress warns us against danger and stimulates new ways of dealing with difficult situations. Moderate amounts of psychological stress encourage self-evaluation and a reappraisal of our relationships with others. These are some of the beneficial aspects of aversive stimuli; indeed, life is a continual processing of such stimuli in the search of a balanced or "homeostatic" state between the individual and his physical and social environment.

In considering man's ability to adapt, however, it is easy to lose sight of the possible biological and psychic costs of adaptation. Many psychologists today are concerned less with the immediate effects of stress than its hidden or long-range consequences. In some situations at least, one adapts at a price. There is evidence that much of modern man's mental and emotional maladjustments, his feelings of alienation, even his physical disorders, are the aftereffects of his adaptation to stress. Carlestam and Levi (1971) cite studies indicating that certain forms of high blood pressure and coronary disease show a higher incidence among individuals who have adjusted to the tensions of modern living than among those for whom such adjustments have not been necessary. Moreover, the accelerating pace at which adaptation is made necessary by technical and social innovation may tax the system's ability to keep up. In the long run the psychic cost of coping with a stressful environment may show up in an individual's decreased ability to perform in the face of subsequent demands.

It may be questioned whether this phenomenon is exclusively an urban one; nevertheless, it is in cities that the more noxious environmental stressors are concentrated. Physiological measures—an altered heartbeat, for example—are often used to indicate the presence of stress. Nonphysical reaction to stress is perhaps more difficult to measure. Nevertheless, its hypothesized effects range from irritability and diminished efficiency to feelings of alienation and anonymity, antisocial behavior, a distrust of others, and a lessened "community spirit." A common, although not wholly accurate, criticism of cities is that it's "every man for himself."

The Miller and Meier model referred to earlier indicates some of the ways that people cope with stress that is attributed to an overloaded environment. Other stressors are more directly physical. Air pollution, for instance, is suspected of causing cardiovascular, glandular, and respiratory changes. Some evidence exists to substantiate this belief. Dr. Wilbert S. Aronow (see *The New York Times*, November 19, 1972) of the Long Beach (California) Veterans Administration Hospital tested the effects of automobile exhaust on the Los Angeles freeway on ten male drivers with heart disease. "When these patients breathed the polluted freeway air they developed raised blood levels of carbon monoxide, slower heart rates, lower blood pressure, decreased lung functions, and poorer exercise performances." When the same volunteers breathed pure air through a mask, however, their condition did not worsen.

Probably the most common urban stressor is noise. The automobile—in particular the automobile horn—construction work, sound trucks, wailing sirens, factory whistles, all contribute to the characteristic din of the downtown city. The phrase "noise pollution" has crept into the urban lexicon and the recent proliferation of municipal codes and task forces to control the decibel level attest to the fact that noise has become a concern of the city resident and a possible damaging factor in health. The intensity, frequency, and intermittency of noise all figure in its perceived effects. The loss of sleep from ordinary street noises may be more stressful than an occasional sonic boom, the effects of which may go deeper than a resultant physical fatigue. For some, noise may be simply the "last straw." Added to a general stimulus overload, it becomes another (and useless) input that interferes with efforts to deal with complexity. It is in this area that noise pollution is most often experienced by city residents.

Nevertheless, noise appears to be a stress to which man adapts quite easily. The air-hammer down the block is somehow tolerated and in time forgotten. It may be annoying, but is it harmful? Psychologically, we know relatively little about how noise affects us in the everyday environment, although there is considerable conjecture that it contributes to the tension of modern life. Experimental research does suggest that high-intensity noise adversely affects the working of complex tasks. In *Urban Stress* Glass and Singer (1972) report on a number of studies in which noise is the variable. Several experiments have shown, for example, that intermittent and unpredictable noise "has a greater tendency to impair performance than does steady noise." [p. 16] The authors cite Kryter (1970) to the effect that "the context in which noise occurs is a principal determinant of its effects on task performance." [p. 16] If noise is viewed as punishment, those subjected to it will "perform better" in an attempt to reduce it. Conversely, if noise is part of a man's job (that is, the proverbial boiler factory), he will "put up with it" for the implicated reward (that is, paycheck), even though the long-term effects may be the loss of auditory sensitivity to certain frequencies.

To a large extent tolerance of noise is subjective. Neurotics are said to suffer more from noisy conditions than normals. The source of noise may determine the degree of annoyance, as when the neighbor's children rather than our own are causing the disturbance. It is worth noting too that an absence of noise can also produce discomfort, especially when one is accustomed to living with it. The razing of the old Third Avenue El in New York City in 1955 is said to have resulted in the decision of some nearby residents to move to the vicinity of other Els still standing.

In their laboratory experiments, Glass and Singer (1972) have shown that the postadaptive effect of noise, when it is intermittent and unpredictable, is to reduce efficiency and accuracy. These effects, however, were measured within a relatively short period after the noise had ceased—twenty minutes to half an hour. Long-term effects were measured by Cohen, Glass, and Singer (in press) using fifty-four children of elementary school age whose apartment house complex was subjected to heavy expressway traffic and noise. The purpose of this field experiment was "to test the notion that prolonged exposure to noise may be related to delayed aftereffects in the form of impaired reading performance." [p. 3] This in turn might account for poor school performance.

The study is interesting from several viewpoints. It was found, for example, that auditory discrimination is related to reading ability and that discrimination, in turn, is related to the noisiness of the home environment. Children living on the higher floors of the thirty-two–story buildings achieved higher reading scores in school tests; these higher floors were considerably quieter. Inversely, children living on the lower floors where noise was much more prevalent scored relatively worse. It was hypothesized that these pupils were unable to make the kinds of auditory discriminations necessary to learn verbal skills. Moreover, length of residence also affected the magnitude of the correlation. The finding that children who had lived in the building less than four years showed much less impairment of reading ability than those who had lived there more than four years suggests that the effect of noise is long-term and, incidentally, quite subtle. Partialling out the social and economic class of the subjects had little effect on results.

Another by-product of noise to which little attention has been paid is its effect on social relations. In an interesting pilot study of three residential streets in San Francisco, Appleyard and Lintell (1972) compared the differential effects of traffic noises on various aspects of human behavior. On a "heavy street," where traffic was dense and noise levels high, they found little social interaction among neighbors, an absence of "peace and seclusion," very little local responsibility for the appearance of the street, and the feeling of living in a restricted environment. The level of satisfaction was low; stress and withdrawal on the part of the residents was common. As a result, those who could do so tended to move, leaving behind the old and the poor.

On a "moderate" street, although traffic noise was considerably lighter, residents were actually more dissatisfied than the people on the "heavy" street. This seeming paradox is explained by the psychological expectations which these residents brought to their environment. A "moderate" street was in a state of transition from "light" to "heavy"—"an in-between street with no real sense of community." People had expected more of it, and their disappointment was greater. Dissatisfaction was perceived in terms of previous expectations rather than present discomfort; nevertheless, it was no less real.

A "light" street enjoyed relative quiet. One apparent result was that families with children tended to move onto the street and to remain longer. There was a sense of pride in how the street looked; inhabitants formed a lively, close-knit community, had twice as many friends, and three times as many acquaintances as the people on the "heavy" street. Instead of withdrawal there was interaction. Residents also experienced a much richer and more discriminating awareness of their environment.

Noise per se, of course, is only one of the variables involved in the three settings. One would have to take into account the traffic hazards and the congestion on each of the streets. Differences in responses are perhaps also due to a self-selection process by which the most desirable conditions attract those who can and will pay the most to live in them and who are most strongly committed to a family and the neighborhood way of life. Nevertheless, the noise-related variables constitute an overriding feature in how residents perceived and used their streets. The need (real or fancied) to isolate oneself from excessive traffic with its consequent restrictions on human contact is probably more significant than the continued exposure to the noise itself in limiting social interaction, just as the absence of traffic is only one factor in establishing friendships and a sense of community.

Housing and the Urban Environment

Streets and neighborhoods are examples of specific environmental settings which relate to the issues we have discussed earlier. Another of the factors bearing on residential satisfaction, stress, and the like is the kind and quality of the urban housing stock. Historically, housing quality was seen as somehow related to the pathologies allegedly characteristic of the city. For example, Schorr (1963) believes that the kind and quality of housing can have an important influence in three areas: (1) the occupant's self-perception, or image of himself; (2) subjective stress; and (3) physical health: " . . . *extremely poor* housing conditions perceptibly influence behavior and attitudes." [p. 8] Schlorr's generalization is borne out by Wilner et al. (1962) in a review of fifty studies which investigated the relationship of housing to physical and social factors. Sixteen of these studies involved European, and thirty-four dealt with American cities. Twenty-six of the studies showed a positive association between housing and health, or housing and social adjustment.

An individual's self-perception is intimately related to the immediate environment in which he spends most of his time. If a man's home is his castle, the condition of that castle, whether or not he owns it, and the kind of neighborhood it stands in all contribute to his sense of personal evaluation. The house is a symbolic extension of oneself; as such, its character (slum or mansion) may be the result of personal qualities (inadequacy or skill) as well as a reinforcer of these qualities. With many poor families the housing-poverty cycle is, indeed, a vicious one. The low esteem induced by economic circumstances is invoked again by the constant reminder that one inhabits an appropriately mean dwelling. Although there are apparently some compensating values in slum life, it is generally agreed that for many of these people low morale is partly reflected by the quality of the housing.

Such factors, of course, may also result from the purely physical conditions of the dwelling. The amount of space available, the state of repair, sanitary facilities, and the like affect the ease with which the occupants are able to carry on housekeeping chores, raise children, entertain, and provide the privacy needed for school work or simply for occasional periods of seclusion. These elements of daily living account for a good deal of stress associated with slum life. Schorr points out that it is the secondary effect of coping with these inadequacies that causes the fatigue, irritability, and passivity seen among the poorly housed. However, it might be added that these behaviors are by no means strangers to the suburban household; too many appliances to look after and three bathrooms to scrub can be as fatigue-producing as none at all. In general, the middle-class home is "overloaded" with what the low-income home lacks.

Housing is a factor in stress, but since people exhibit different levels of tolerance for it, a dilapidated dwelling is not necessarily more stressful than an expensive one. The latter may be uncomfortable and the former quite habitable; the layout of the space may be more important to its efficient use than the number of square feet; likewise, the number of occupants will affect liveability, as will their ages, economic status, and their scheme of personal values. Housing as a factor in stress shows up most dramatically when conditions reach a point of intolerability, when the individual, whatever his personal characteristics, can no longer cope with conditions.

Beyond this, the physical state of the dwelling represents only one factor in housing satisfaction. Symbolic associations ("These places are not slums. These are our homes, our shrines."), whether one owns or rents the property, its value, the kinds of neighbors one has, and the friendship ties that have been developed in the area—these subjective elements may outweigh physical inconveniences or even hardships. Rossi (1955), in his study of Philadelphia housing patterns, found marked differences in attitudes toward one's dwelling according to socioeconomic class. In general, the lower socioeconomic groups were more subjectively satisfied than objective housing condition indicators (number of rooms, degree of dilapidation, and so on) would suggest should be the case. Moreover, the physical dilapidation of low-income neighborhoods did not always correlate with "social dilapidation." People in slum areas tend to have many friends in the immediate neighborhood and to depend upon the neighborhood for their social life. Of the four areas studied, that which rated next to lowest on a scale of objective physical quality (Kensington) had the highest positive subjective satisfaction ratings by its residents. They were not as likely to move as residents of West Philadelphia, where the socioeconomic level was high.

The reader should bear in mind, however, that the deprived city dweller often stays put simply because he has little freedom of choice. Habituation to a slum, moreover, is more characteristic of the older generation; the young couple, if they are ambitious and economically successful, frequently "head for the suburbs," assuming that there are no overriding reasons to stay. A further problem in interpreting these surveys is seen when one studies the effects of relocation on the behavior of the rehoused. In general, public housing in the United States has a bad institutional image. (Such is not the case in England where half of all housing is public.) Low-income developments have been called instant slums, blamed for concentrating into one set of buildings the pathology that was formerly spread out over many blocks. An exhaustive study, correlating aspects of social behavior and public housing, recently completed by Newman (1972), concluded that much of the success or failure in public housing can be traced to the design of the buildings, site layout, and the orientation of the project to the surrounding community. This was especially applicable to crime and vandalism—the taller the building, the higher the crime rate. Given the same densities and types of tenants, low-rise projects also showed greater tenant satisfaction. Newman identifies four reasons for these differences, which he describes as territoriality, natural surveillance, image, and milieu.

Low-rise tenants have a greater *territorial* sense, essentially because they are adjacent to one another rather than "piled up." They are more likely to know their neighbors and to exercise a proprietary attitude toward their living space. *Surveillance* is achieved through easy visibility of all sections of the project. Newman notes that many high-rise structures lack "defensible space." Lobbies, blind elevators, long corridors, enclosed firestairs, and rooftops give easy access to intruders whose actions go unobserved. The *image* of the low- to mid-rise project creates a better response on the part of tenants to the physical ordering of their lives; these more humanly scaled developments are less regimented than the massive complex, as well as more susceptible to personal involvement—in the symbolic, if not always in the actual, sense. The mere idea that one's environment can be engaged in in some meaningful way, whether one actually does so or not, is important. The *milieu* of the project is its total setting; how does it relate to the neighbor-

Fig. 9-2 One of the apartment complexes of the Pruitt-Igoe Project in St. Louis being dynamited. Most of the remaining buildings of this low-income housing project are empty. This project was a social disaster for its residents. (United Press International)

hood of which it is a part? Fenced-off developments in unsympathetic areas create visible segregation. Newman would integrate public housing in compatible neighborhoods, using the principle of scattering sites over all parts of the city rather than concentrating them in one area; he would also build more walk-ups, which in most cities are still economically feasible.

The disastrous consequences of the Pruitt-Igoe project in St. Louis, Missouri, some buildings of which were demolished after only nineteen to twenty years of occupancy, is often cited as a prime example of the failure of large-scale public housing. This mammoth complex of units was built at a time when slum clearance and relocation were the magic words in the lexicon of urban renewal. Efficient, modern buildings, subsidized by cities, would take the place of the dilapidated structures of the ghetto. A benign housing authority would replace the slumlord. Rents were scaled primarily for low- to moderate-income families.

In 1972 a good part of the project, much of which had by then been abandoned by its tenants, was dynamited by the city authorities (see Figure 9–2). Dreams as well as mortar came crashing. Postmortems by urbanologists suggest the following reasons for Pruitt-Igoe's demise: (1) Almost entirely black in racial composition, it was no less a ghetto than the housing it replaced. (2) Environmentally, the site plan failed to provide the proper kind of space for the development of social networks—the spontaneous interactions of people along lines of shared interest. There were few places where tenants could meet and form friendships. Living was vertical and institutional. (3) The Public Housing Authority was shown to be poorly administered. Projects, in short, do not run themselves. (4) In contrast to a lack of semi-private, sociopetal space, an extensive "no man's land" of public hallways and grounds became an arena for vandalism and misbehavior on the part of the young. These stairways, rooftops, and parking areas were largely unsupervised by authorities and were difficult to supervise by parents. (5) The sheer scale of the project, minimal landscaping, and general isolation from the surrounding neighborhood withheld from tenants a sense of "belonging to" the project on any personal level. People from low-rise slums, where boundaries are permeable, may find the enclosed, vertical proximity of a high-rise building too confining. The social contacts that are easily made on the neighborhood level are more difficult to achieve. For the tenant, there is no real "home ground." Hall (1966) has noted that in the case of blacks on Chicago's South Side a switch to high-rise living destroyed the cultural infrastructure by which block life was maintained, or at least influenced, by the dominant persons under the old system.

Newer developments attempt to avoid the mistakes of Pruitt-Igoe. In San Francisco a recent low-cost project (Patri 1971), primarily for blacks, consists of two-story, two-family attached "town houses." These are attractively designed and emphasize privacy for the individual families while encouraging social contact by means of gardens and other semiprivate spaces. The institutional image is missing. A unique feature of this development was participation by prospective tenants in the design and decor of the houses. Construction was preceded by a series of "encounter sessions" in which the architects sensitized themselves to the needs and desires of a racial group about whose life style they knew little. At the same time, tenants were made aware of the practical and economic problems involved in a low-cost project.

Not all conventional projects are failures. In comparing a test group of 300 Baltimore families who moved into new public housing with a control group of 300 who remained in the slum, Wilner et al. (1962) found a number of advantages for the former group. Accidents were one-third lower in the housing project; tenants enjoyed better relations with neighbors, took part in more mutually supporting activities, made more new friends, and took more pride in the immediate neighborhood and community. The investigators found more "personal satisfaction" with life. In school, daily attendance of children from the families was considerably higher than that of control children.

Research on the effects of the housing environment demonstrates one of our contentions in Chapter Four: It is impossible to look at the physical setting without considering the social setting and vice-versa. This does not mean that we cannot ask whether social or physical factors are not more or less important in a given situation; we must simply remember that our conclusions will be limited by the success with which we have identified and controlled other factors which could have influenced the outcomes of the study.

Fig. 9-3 Low-rise "townhouse" style public housing project on San Francisco's Marcus Garvey Square. A total of 101 unit projects allows for a mixture of elderly, young couples and single families. Photographs by Jeremiah O. Bragstad; courtesy Whisler-Patri.

Fig. 9-4 (opposite page) Site plan for Marcus Garvey Square, San Francisco. Courtesy, Whisler-Patri.

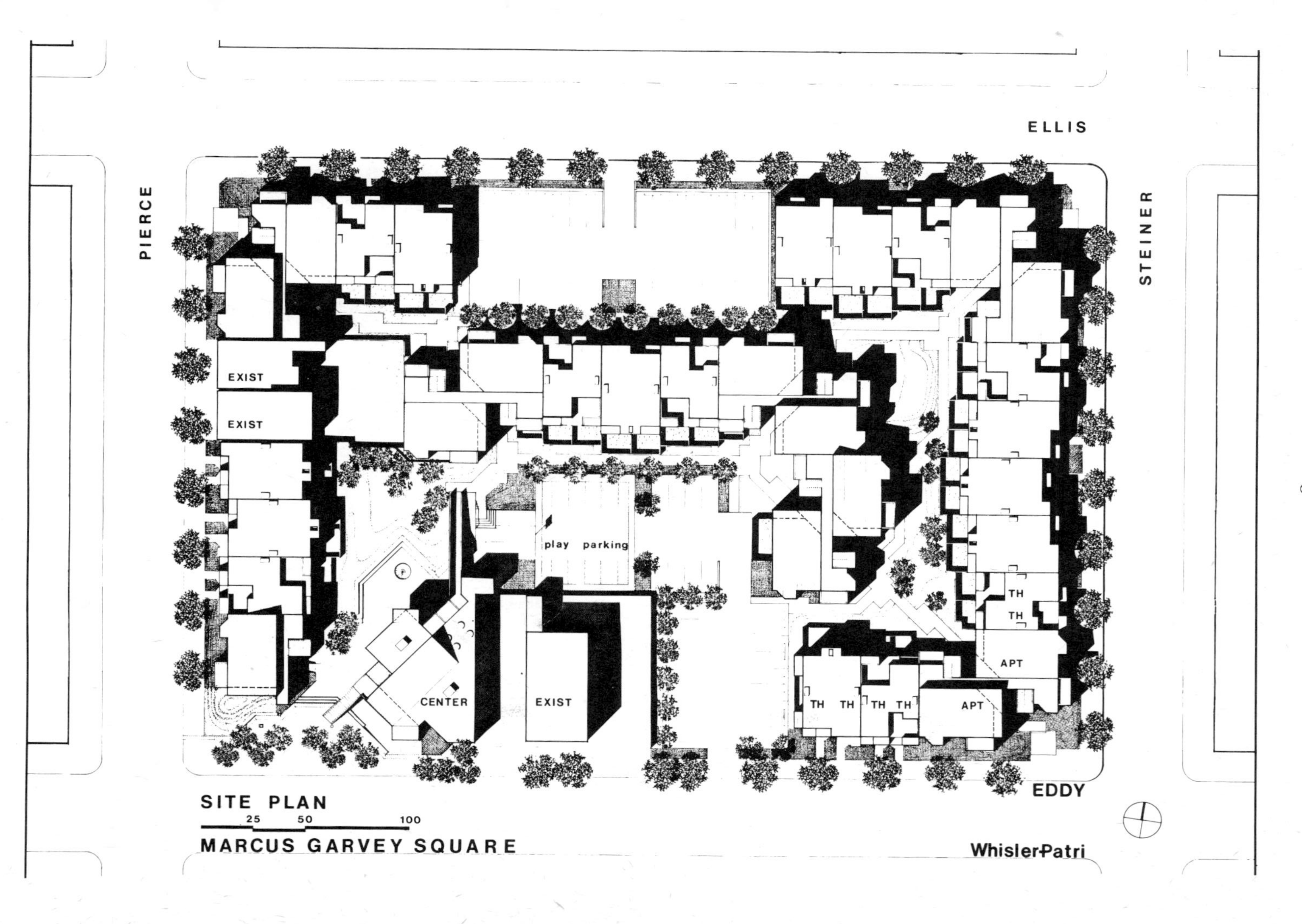
ELLIS
PIERCE
STEINER
EXIST
EXIST
play
parking
TH
TH
APT
CENTER
EXIST
TH
TH
TH
TH
APT
EDDY
SITE PLAN
25
50
100
MARCUS GARVEY SQUARE
WhislerPatri

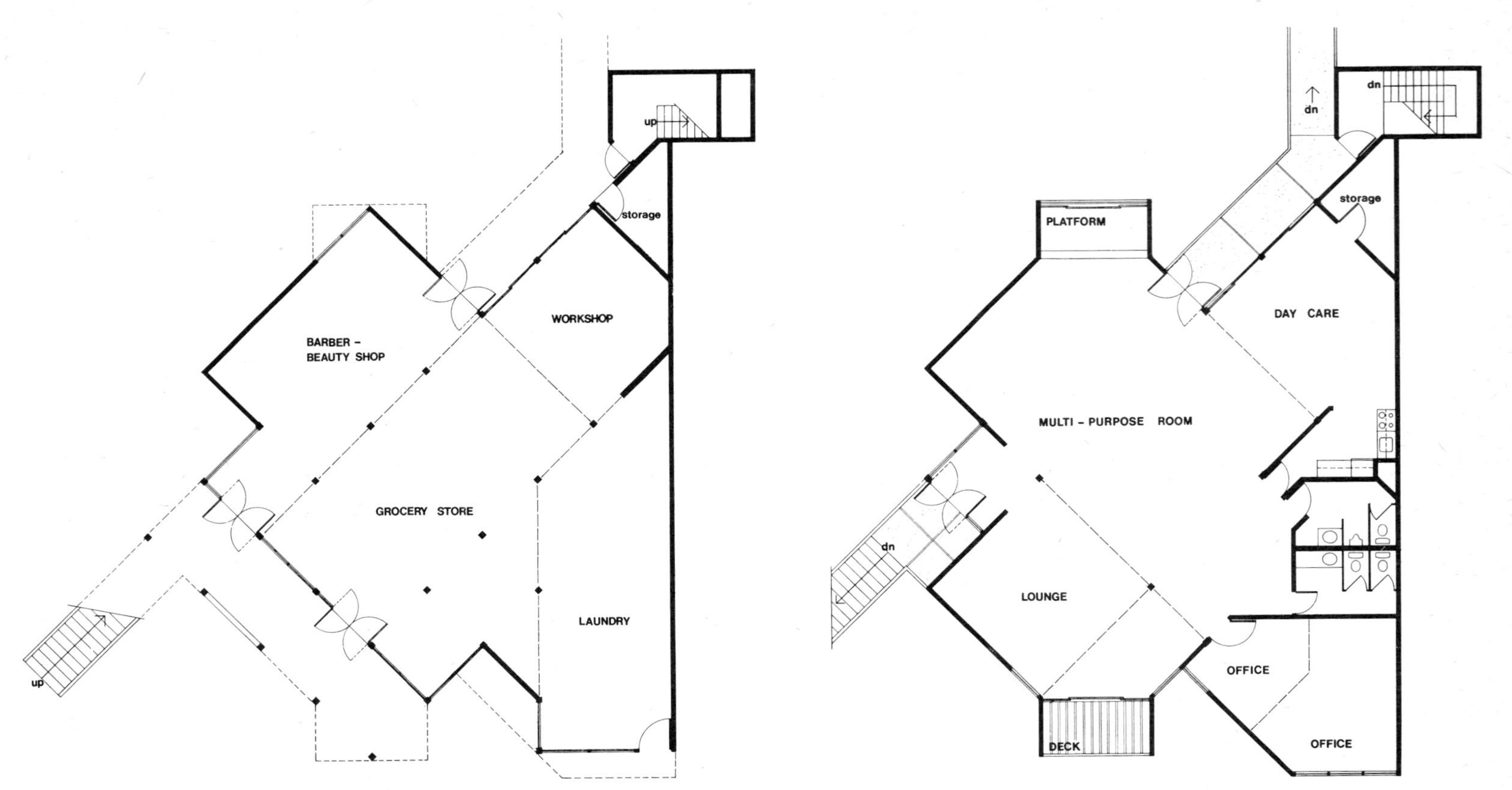

Fig. 9-5 Plan of Marcus Garvey's commercial and neighborhood center, San Francisco. Courtesy, Whisler-Patri.

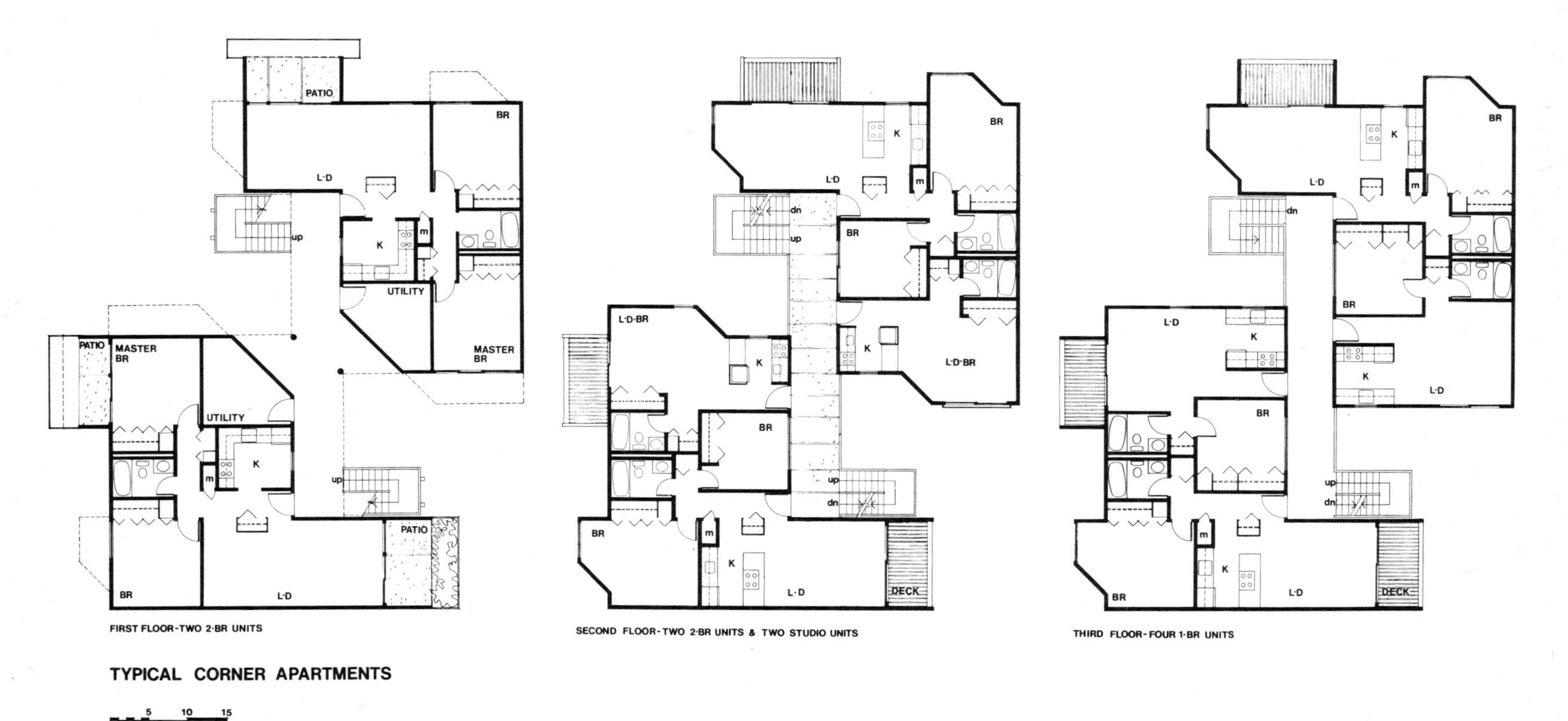

Fig. 9.6 Plans of typical corner apartments, Marcus Garvey Square, San Francisco. Courtesy, Whisler-Patri.

Open-ended studies are frequently deficient in this respect. There often seem to be too many variables included, and it is difficult to know how these variables relate to one another. A better experimental model would employ some defined dependent variables such as decision to move or stay, amount and rate of social interaction, home maintenance activities, complaints to management, or resistance to being forced to move. These variables could then be related to one another where appropriate and to the sociophysical characteristics of the areas within which the study was conducted.

We turn now to another aspect of the urban environment which influences people's evaluations of their housing situation—the neighborhood. In this respect it will be helpful to look at some of the ways in which the city resident perceives his environment in terms of the more positive values outlined at the beginning of this chapter: the amenities available, the sense of community engendered, the meanings it has, and the enrichment provided by the sensory qualities of the environment.

The Neighborhood and Forced Urban Change

In looking at this other side of the coin of urban life, it is not surprising that investigators have found a quite different and occasionally conflicting picture from that which has occupied our attention so far. The data of the "pathological" school and those of the romantics do not, in themselves, vary greatly; what differs are the values attributed to these findings by the individual researcher, and these can occasionally be traced to his ideological bias. One way of reducing this discrepancy is by taking a closer look at what is happening, or supposed to be happening, in neighborhoods. Here, the dependent variables that were stressed in connection with housing can be quite useful, although researchers have tended to neglect them while concentrating almost exclusively on the neighborhood's capacity for social interaction. The physical design quality of the neighborhood or district is also important. Does the relatively homogeneous character of New York's Greenwich Village provide a greater sense of community than, say, the amorphous Washington Heights section? In Gans's (1962) view the city is not an undifferentiated mass of streets and buildings but a collection of urban villages. Anyone who has lived in a city knows the importance of the corner grocery, the local pharmacy, the neighborhood bar. He knows the people who run these establishments, often on a first name basis. Through his neighborhood, one circumscribes the metropolis to manageable proportions.

There are other ways, too, in which the city presents a positive face. It permits a wide variety of individual, and often idiosyncratic, behaviors. It provides for the troubled and the social misfits a haven that allows alternative and often constructive activities not possible in smaller communities. As Izumi (1968) has written: "One of the important reasons why 'ghettos' are popular is because this environment is permissive and [provides] a more conducive psycho-social environment for the necessary distraction and emotional outlets within easy reach of any person. . . ." [p. 7] The residents themselves, far from feeling "anonymous," enjoy warm social and kinship ties and a strong sense of personal identity. This identity, in comparison with that of the more mobile and occupationally oriented middle class, is basically rooted in the local environment.

The new emphasis on cultural pluralism in the United States, on alternative life styles and ethnic identity, is congruent with a view of the city as a hospitable environment that is lived in for its own sake rather than partly out of economic necessity.

In almost all instances this hospitality is related to specific areas or neighborhoods. The hippie in San Francisco chooses North Beach; for the Boston Brahmin it is Beacon Hill; and for the ethnically rooted in that city the West End has long been their home. It is instructive to see what happens, both to the people and the area itself, when physical demolition changes this environment and uproots many of its inhabitants. In this sense Boston's West End has become a classic case history in the effects of forced urban change.

The significance of this forced change can best be understood within the context of urban renewal in the United States since World War II. It was assumed that the future of deteriorating cities rested heavily upon physical renewal of the downtown areas. If cities could be made attractive they would increase in population or at least stem the flow to the suburbs; opportunities for new business enterprises would be created. To accomplish these objectives it was believed necessary to renew—and in some cases level—rather large tracts of land. Existing structures would have to be either destroyed or renovated and many of their inhabitants relocated in other, and supposedly better, housing.

Throughout the country these settings served as excellent study sites for an investigation into the human consequences of large-scale urban change, something which the planners had neglected in their concentration on physical change. Through a series of fortuitous events, the West End of Boston has become probably the most intensively studied of these renewal areas. Between 1958 and 1960 the 48-acre central section was razed by the Boston Housing Authority, based upon evidence indicating that this area was characterized by physically deteriorating houses interspersed with light industries, corner markets, and small businesses. In short, the area was considered to be a slum.

Ethnically, the population of the West End consisted of 47 percent Italian stock, with the remainder of the people divided mostly among the Irish, Jews, and other non-WASP groups. The Boston Housing Authority intended that the land be converted into new apartments and high-rise office buildings; those who had been relocated could then return and live in the new housing.

Did events work out this way? This was the question that Gans and his colleagues (1962) posed. We can summarize the main conclusions resulting from their research as follows:

> Inhabitants of the area saw the West End as quite distinct from other parts of Boston, not only in the physical sense but in the social sense as well. It had its own environmental character and "flavor." Residents felt at home and secure there. One either "belonged" in the West End or he didn't. Territorial identity was strong. People knew their way around. This "localism" represented a traditional way of life for West Enders, giving them a continuity between past and present. The environment presented few uncertainties to them.
>
> Residents of the West End were family-centered, with strong friendship ties in the immediate area. Two or three generations of the same family lived together and close relatives were within easy visiting distance, a factor that is especially important to ethnic groups of working class origin. And because the population was drawn mainly from a single socioeconomic class, there was a homogeneity of cultural values. People "got along" because they shared the same general interests.

The external dilapidation of streets and buildings did not mirror a disorganized social environment. Residents were interdependent and cooperative. A good social network had been developed and the West End was self-maintaining in terms of services. Neighborhood relations were interactive, but they also tended to be casual and without intimacy or depth.

Physical boundaries within the area were permeable. The kind of privacy cherished by suburbanites, for instance, was not sought after. Residents "spilled out" in the streets as public spaces became an extension of the home; street life itself was an important element in dealing with one's neighbors and friends. Formal visiting was at a minimum. Internal space, although perhaps crowded by objective standards, was seemingly adequate and well arranged for the needs of these working-class residents.

For the sizeable number of inhabitants who were either housed locally or relocated elsewhere, urban renewal was a social disaster. People felt cut off from many of the things that had given meaning to their lives. An improved physical environment (in "better" neighborhoods) did not compensate for the loss of personal and social relations attendant on life in a familiar setting which had served them well. And for those who moved back to the West End, the changes had destroyed much of what had made possible a particular life style.

Much of the present tolerant attitude toward the so-called "slum" can be traced to the Boston school of urbanologists. They have drawn an important distinction between a physical and a social slum. The West End may have been physically run down, but "sociologically" it showed few negative effects on its inhabitants. Studies of relocation efforts in other cities indicate that in general the Boston findings are valid for similar types of populations: To uproot people is to destroy a way of life. At the same time, it should be noted that there are vast differences among slums. The West End was virtually all-white; although its population consisted largely of minorities, racial discrimination, as blacks experience it, did not enter into the lives of the people.

The trouble began when it was decided that Boston should become a "model city" (although this occurred before the official Model Cities program was inaugurated). As federal funds were pumped into the West End, via the Boston Housing Authority, the "urban village" was destroyed and many of its inhabitants uprooted. However inadvisable this approach may have been in retrospect, the action was not capricious. Physically deteriorated, the West End harbored the kinds of illnesses that are attributed to crowding and poor housing. Although compared with other Bostonians West Enders might be friendly, they were supposedly not healthy. Evidence gathered later, however, did not indicate that the West Enders were as unhealthy as officials in the Boston Housing Authority believed (Gans 1962).

Gans's *The Urban Villagers* (1962) was the most extensive of the West End studies. Gans found, for instance, that the number of new housing units constructed did not equal the number of units destroyed. Many residents could not afford the new rents. And for those who moved elsewhere, the psychological cost of relocation proved difficult. In "renewing" the area planners unwittingly shattered the social cohesion that made life satisfying to the residents. In Fried's (1963) suggestive phrase, they were "grieving for a lost home."[1]

Why this should be true was explored by Fried and Gleicher (1961) in another study that grew out of the West End project. These authors stress the concept of "home ground" which dominates the lives of the working-class poor. Because neighborhoods are the focus of social relationships, which for higher socioeconomic groups are selectively developed throughout the city as a whole, a sense of "local spatial identity" is fostered. Physical space around the home becomes a "territorial" space to which one belongs and is emotionally committed. Ryan (1963) contrasts this "corner friendship" source of identity with the occupational roles which are salient in the "dominant middle class configuration of 'identity.' " Life in the West End, he notes, was focused upon more immediate events rather than future goals. Status in work as a source of pride and self-worth is less important than control over the home and the surrounding environment.

That the West End was not an isolated situation is shown by Reynolds (1966) in a survey of housing relocation preferences in forty-one U. S. cities. Reynolds reported that twelve city blocks was the maximum distance from their old addresses selected by a majority of all relocated families.

The reluctance of people to move even from the worst slum areas was documented by a U. S. Department of Commerce study (1964) which found

[1] Fried's survey of West Enders after relocation found that 46 percent of the women and 38 percent of the men "give evidence of a fairly severe grief reaction or worse," a condition that persisted among 76 percent of the women two years afterward.

that the black ghettos, for all their well-advertised problems, are still preferred by the majority of those living in them. "Negroes . . . seem to have stronger emotional and family ties to their current place of residence than the white population." [p. 15] Ghettos also permit the building of black institutions and the exercise of political power and economic leverage. Racial separatism, as such, however, does not appear to be a significant factor in the blacks' assessment of the ghetto. In its study of the devastating ghetto riots of 1967, the Kerner Commission (National Advisory Commission on Civil Disorders 1968) found that no more than 18 percent of ghetto residents took a separatist position.

We cannot generalize that everyone who moves from these close-knit neighborhoods is necessarily unable to recreate something of the old social structure and life style in a new environment. Obviously, some people are more adaptable than others, just as some settings lend themselves to the building of new social networks. Walter (1972) deals with this question in terms of a public housing project in a Boston suburb. He found that far from constituting an instant slum, the project in question preserved a lower-class life style consistent with the neighborhood that had been abandoned.

> Our research experience supports none of the stereotypes about public housing or about the so-called culture of poverty. . . . We found not simple victims destroyed by poverty, but a rich social life full of vitality, conflict, problems and hope—interesting lives full of resourcefulness, courage, dignity and humanity. (Walter, personal communication, 1972).

In expounding this point of view, Walter challenges the idea that high-density settings necessarily have negative effects. It is not density per se, he believes, but "network density" that matters in urban environments. Network density is the "actual number of links between people [in a given enclosure] and the total number of relationships possible in that space." The type of project and its design may influence network density; but no less important, of course, is the type of people and the conditions under which they move into the project. Did they come by choice? Was it economically advantageous for them to move? What were their social aspirations? Most importantly, did the respondents in this study see their lives in the same way that Walter's did? It might be argued, too, that he was fortunate in the project he chose to investigate. How typical of projects in general was this example, and how representative of public housing occupants were its tenants? A more serious matter is the set of values the researcher may have brought to the situation in terms of his sympathies (perhaps unconscious) for this particular socioeconomic group. Nevertheless, Walter's study, like Gans's, was based on extensive participant observation (he and his research staff lived in the project for some time) and constitutes a provocative challenge to two concepts dear to the hearts of urban planners in their explanations of public housing failures—the "culture of poverty" and "the tangle of pathology." Walter concludes that the troubles experienced by housing projects are not the result of poverty or the "life style" of their residents, but the willy-nilly way in which people are selected for occupancy, without regard to previous affiliation or compatibility. With little control over their environment, excluded from "power, resources and honor," their "pathology," as we noted earlier, is at least partly a revolt against an inappropriate setting.

Other Neighborhood Effects

Emphasis on slum areas in urban research has tended to overshadow investigations of "gold coasts," middle-class and suburban neighborhoods. Moreover, working-class areas in many cities are by no means necessarily dilapidated. Vast working-class tracts in Chicago and Cleveland—to mention two heavily industrialized cities—are characterized by neat, owner-occupied homes. It should also be remembered that neighborhood populations are not frozen into permanent status; even among the poor there is considerable mobility (in changing jobs, or seeking a better environment). The young in particular abandon slums if they have a choice.

Whatever the type of neighborhood, behavior is broadly congruent with the area, although there may be isolated deviances. Such deviances, even if tolerated, will usually seem inappropriate to the majority of residents—or at least an object of curiosity. When the poet William Butler Yeats lived in a run-down neighborhood near London's Russell Square he was distinguished from others in the area as "that bloke down the street who gets mail."

Specific interaction patterns based on housing placement has been observed in residential neighborhoods where the population is relatively homogeneous. Studies of such areas suggest a special influence on friendship formation and social relations. In the United States the initial, and still classic, study of proximity and friendship is Festinger, Schachter, and Back's (1950) investigation of housing for married war veterans at M.I.T., discussed in Chapter Six. The authors concluded that ". . . those people who reside closest to each other in terms of distance, physical orientation, or accessibility tend to become friends or form closely knit social units." [Schorr 1963:26] Gans (1967) found this to be true also for Levittown, New Jersey, in its early stages, but noted that the "proximity principle" is usually reinforced by the homogeneity and youthfulness of the population and that for sustained social interaction, social compatibility is necessary. Thus proximity became less important as a factor in friendship formation as the community grew older. In a comparable study Merton (1947) investigated families who lived on opposite sides of a street. Corner locations were found to be the most focal, and of all the residents those whose doors faced the street were much more likely to make contact with their across-the-street neighbors than residents whose houses did not—by an impressive 75 to 4 percent margin.

If physical placement influences friendships, it also facilitates enmities; to make contact is not necessarily to make friends. Moreover, as neighborhoods mature, the selective interests of the individual play an increasingly important role in his choice of social contacts. To this might be added ethnic and religious factors. This was suggested in a Detroit-based study by Lauman (1973) comparing the friendship patterns among Jews, Catholics, and Protestants. It was found, for example, that the interlocking, or closed, friendship networks that were more likely to characterize Jews and Catholics were largely a result of the strong ethnic ties of these groups rather than mere physical proximity, although proximity seemed to reinforce these ties. Protestants, on the other hand, exhibited a "radial" or open network that depended little on proximity or ethnic background. These people seemed to make friends along shared sociocultural interests and economic lines.

In any neighborhood, regardless of demographic composition, there is a strong tendency for the establishment of a behavioral norm to which individual families conform—often against their better judgment. In the suburbs, spatial norms are codified in various zoning ordinances that determine, among other things, the minimum space that a family must live in. Other ordinances specify where the laundry shall be hung and on what days. One of the most ambitious attempts to study behavior in relation to the neighborhood environment is based on a survey by Terence Lee (1968) of 219 housewives in Cambridge, England. Lee used three behavioral criteria—friends in the locality, local club members, and the use of local shops. His argument was that the "duality of physical and social neighborhoods" could be unified only in terms of the individual's perception, his "mental representation of physical-social space." Social contact and community participation are related to a person's image of the kind of neighborhood he lives in. The image may or may not conform to actuality.

Although Cambridge is known best as a university town, its population (104,000) is primarily middle and working class. Lee's findings call into question some of the American studies' conclusions concerning both the "proximity principles" and the factor of homogeneity. For example, he found no relationships between housing density and local friendships. "The level of each one's social interaction is presumably set by herself rather than by the density or proximity of potential friends." [p. 359] Homogeneous neighborhoods, which he calls the "our sort" locality, provided many acquaintances but few friends and a low level of commitment to the neighborhood. A sense of belonging did not imply participation. Residents tended to "stick to themselves," and Lee suggests that accurate description of such localities would be not "people like us" but rather "people who live in houses like ours."

It was in the heterogeneous neighborhoods that the highest levels of participation occurred. Lee attributes this to the presence in such neighborhoods of professionals and others from upper-socioeconomic groups. He also found that subjects living in terraced houses had the greatest number of local friends, followed by those in detached houses, and then semidetached. This, again, is probably a function of economic status, with its implied cultural involvement, rather than of spatial location.

Planners are traditionally interested in identifying those aspects of the physical design of neighborhoods which make for residential satisfaction, but the problem obviously goes deeper than the physical. Lansing and Marans (1969), for instance, surveying 1042 residents in 99 neighborhoods in the Detroit area, found that only a moderate degree of correlation existed between planners' and residents' evaluations of the neighborhoods. For example; In neighborhoods rated as "unpleasant" by planners, 88 percent of the residents liked their settings moderately well. The authors offer two explanations for this discrepancy. Planners tend to concentrate on the physical design of the neighborhood whereas residents take both the physical and social environment into account. Such variables as building setback, land coverage (density), proximity to adjacent structures, and land-use character—stressed by the planner—are seen as less relevant to residents than the general upkeep of the neighborhood, the noise level, and degree of separation from neighbors. Proximity itself was not regarded as important, suggesting that the cluster development type of housing would be quite acceptable to the urban and suburban dweller since it is compensated for by additional, and usable, open space (Whyte 1968).

A second explanation for these findings concerns relative differences in social class among the residents. College-educated people were more likely to agree with the planners' evaluations of a neighborhood than the noncollege group. Perhaps college people not only have higher expectations for their environment, but are more sensitive to variations in architectural style, landscaping, and spatial character—the physical elements of a neighborhood. In any case, the respondents in the study had no other choice, and this absence of alternatives may account for a satisfaction rating that would not have been obtained were other choices available. Adaptation and satisfaction are not necessarily the same.

Another and quite different approach to residential satisfaction, also from Detroit, is Kasl and Harburg's (1972) study of neighborhood stress. A cross-sectional sample of 1000 married adults equally divided geographically into "high-stress" and "low-stress" areas was also equally divided by sex and race. Thus, both black and white groups were sampled from each area. "High stress" was measured on the basis of demographic data showing a high level of social disorganization (crime and slum conditions) and a low socioeconomic level.

It is not surprising that the whites and blacks living in "high-stress" tracts perceived their neighborhoods more negatively than those living in "low-stress" areas or that the perceptions of blacks were more negative than those of whites. What emerges from this study, however, is the importance of a social indicator often overlooked by planners—safety. People will tolerate a number of inadequacies in their neighborhood if they feel it is at least safe. Indeed, familiarity with events of crime and violence was the most frequently cited reason for disliking it. Paradoxically, when questioned as to whether they were happy in their neighborhood, ". . . the associations were about the same for high and low stress residents, and the level of reported unhappiness in the high stress areas was only slightly higher than in the low stress areas." [p. 324] Again, people adapt but often at a considerable cost.

A sense of "belonging" to one's immediate environs has been found to indicate satisfaction with an area. Cooper (1971) noted this in her study comparing the attitudes of residents in St. Francis Square (a middle-income co-op project) with the attitudes of tenants in two twenty-story slab buildings. When asked where they felt they "belonged," three-fifths of the latter group replied "in my apartment" and the remainder said "nowhere." In St. Francis Square, two-fifths identified with the development as an entity, about a third with their particular section of the development, and about a fourth with their own building or apartment. These differences reflect a number of variables. Because residents of the co-op owned their apartments, they were somewhat permanently attached to the area and had a proprietary attitude toward it. The careful siting of the buildings provided a feeling of community; this was further enhanced by attractive landscaping, private gardens for first-floor residents, and playgrounds. The project was designed in cooperation with the expected owner-tenants. As a result of these factors, most residents saw themselves as part of a total setting, both socially and physically.

Perhaps the lesson to be drawn from this research is that what is true for a Detroit ghetto need not apply to Boston's West End and may be even further removed from the working class area of Cambridge, England. Neighborhoods are settings for behavior that is already rooted in tradition, class position, economic circumstances, and one's personal aspirations. The effect of such settings on people, therefore, is relative to well-established and extra-environmental values. The conclusion to be reached is not whether physical factors are more important than social ones in the matter of friendship formation. Rather, for those who expect to interact with their neighbors and wish to do so the form of the physical environment may very well inhibit or facilitate such interaction. For the people on "light"- versus "heavy"-trafficked streets, physical conditions proved a significant factor. For the Detroiters in the Lansing and Marans (1969) study, physical form was important chiefly to the group that appreciated certain esthetic and "educated" values in their environment. For the residents of St. Francis Square, it was the sense of ownership and personal involvement. Our discussion of the Athanasiou and Yoshioka (1973) study in Chapter Six also illustrates the importance of space and form as a mediating rather than a determining factor.

The Flight to the Suburbs

Even though there have been examples of successful efforts to develop housing in the city, and the city is a repository of potentially rich experiences, cities have been losing their populations rather consistently.

Aside from economic reasons, such as getting a new job, why do people move away? And why do they frequently select the satellite suburb? The comparatively few empirical studies that have explored behavioral changes brought about by a move to the suburbs can be roughly divided along two opposing lines: (1) Suburban living simply brings out the latent, usually middle-class, life styles that many city people aspire to ("suburbs are good"); and (2) It does indeed produce new and perhaps unrealized behaviors that are often tension-producing and stressful, that is, social striving ("suburbs are bad"). It is the contention of this latter argument that people act differently in the suburbs not because of some inherent characteristic but because the new environment imposes specific norms of behavior not present in the city. A city-dweller friend of one of the authors states bluntly: "I don't want to enter the competition for the best lawn on the block." A third position that might be examined is the attitude of the suburbanite to the city once he has moved. What does the metropolis as a whole mean to him from the vantage point of "Crestwood Acres"?

The first of these two positions is expressed by Gans (1967), who sees the behavior expressed by suburban residents as "reasons for moving in the first place." We might call this the pursuit of the suburban ideal. Changes that are directly attributable to the move are mostly positive and follow from the satisfactions of home ownership, more living space, increased social life, and community participation. The suburbs are "safer" than the city and the schools are "better." Negative effects are seen in adolescents and cultural deviants for whom the suburb lacks opportunities for expressing individual, that is, nonconforming behaviors.

This view was reinforced by Berger (1960) in his study of the semirural community of Milpitas, near San Jose, California. Berger surveyed one hundred families of Ford Motor Company workers who were transferred there when the Ford plant moved from Richmond, California, a drab industrial city whose physical amenities and social style were vastly different from Milpitas. His initial assumption that the Ford workers "would be learning middle-class behavior, beliefs, and aspirations as a result of the suburbanization process" [p. v] was not borne out. Although home ownership increased to 99 percent, from 31 percent before the move; and although the families were in general more satisfied with their new surroundings, the physical character of these surroundings brought few if any changes in their way of life or their aspirations. Class-bound, they simply transplanted an existing life mode to a new milieu, much as Whyte's (1957) "organization man" is transplanted, like a potted plant, from one country-club–oriented setting to another. Berger writes: "Membership and activity in formal associations are rare; so is semiformal mutual visiting between couples. There is little evidence of pronounced striving, status anxiety, or orientations to the future. . . . Their tastes and preferences seem untouched by the images of "suburbia" portrayed in the mass media." [p. 92] Berger concludes that the fears expressed by some that the suburbs produce a drab uniformity of behavior in its residents rather dramatically overstates the actual situation.

With its industrial cast, and considering the homogeneous group that

Berger studied, Milpitas, however, cannot be considered a typical suburb, if any such exists. Gans (1967), for example, also challenges the stereotyped view of suburban life as a bland mixture of social conformity, community busywork, and nonstop cocktail parties. But to some observers, this attitude is too sanguine. Studies by Hollingshead and Redlich (1958) and Meyer and Roberts (1959; see Moller 1968) found suburbanites of the white-collar class (whom the authors designated Class III) to be as tension-ridden and alienated as the lowest socioeconomic group in the city (Class V). They attribute this finding in part to the fact that Class III individuals were preoccupied with maintaining or improving their status.

> They had always to be conscious of their role performance; the tension never let up. . . . Accepting values such as respectability and responsibility, Class III members were less likely than Class V to express their frustrations in aggressive, hostile or violent behavior. Instead they were more likely to turn it inward into psychological conflict. They displayed more intense feelings of shame, guilt, and inner conflict. . . ." [Quoted by Moller, 1968]

No doubt the suburbs cannot be held wholly responsible for behaviors that are motivated by status seeking or the desire for economic improvement. Nevertheless, to the extent that communities intensify such feelings because they demand emblematic proof of success or inhibit cathartic behavior in the face of conflict, they are clearly implicated. "Keeping up with the Jones's" is a well-known suburban syndrome, not to be discounted as a factor in behavioral dynamics. Moller (1968) believes that this can be as damaging to the mental health of the privileged classes as is the alienation brought about by segregating the low-income and ghetto groups. People do tend to assume the protective coloration of their social environment, often at psychological cost. While the authors know of no empirical studies that bear out the point, it is widely reported that residents who are Democrats in the city frequently register Republican when they move to the suburbs. But once having registered, they use the privacy of the polling booth to express their real (Democratic) sentiments. Indeed, every suburban community contains a sizeable mixture of latent, or crypto, city dwellers.

The tone of the suburbs (and many of its norms) is set by the "upwardly mobile." Others (the "townies") must be careful not to offend the image of the community, and to this extent are suburbanized themselves. This is not exclusively an American phenomenon. In their studies of suburban London, Young and Willmott (1962) noted the clear differences in life styles in comparing the residents of Bethnal Green, a small, tightly knit section of the city proper, with those in outlying districts. At "Greenleigh," a new Council estate (housing project) on the outskirts of London, "We found people cut off from relatives, suspicious of their neighbors, lonely; the atmosphere very different from the warmth and friendliness of Bethnal Green." The more diversified suburb of Woodford revealed seven specific differences between its residents and the Bethnal Greeners. Woodford, for example, was characterized by "house-centered" (rather than neighborhood-centered) couples; there was a distinct generation gap, with fewer extended families and a tendency for parents to have been left behind in the city when the young people moved to Woodford. Residents visited less with relatives and found most of their social life embedded in organized, rather than spontaneous, activities. Contrary to Lee's (1968) Cambridge findings, friendships were strongly influenced by physical orientation of streets and houses. Lastly, social class tensions were much in evidence; "keeping up," a negligible factor in Bethnal Green, was important in Woodford.

Assuming, as Gans does, that people bring their behaviors with them, we may still insist that out of these emerges an environmental identity that is more than the sum of existing behaviors. New attitudes come into play and new interests arise, not least the appearance of one's front lawn. Property values assume major importance. The supraordinate character of the suburb arising from these factors is seen in zoning practices designed to insure the inclusion of like-minded people and the exclusion of the "differents"—the poor, black, and (in certain localities) Jews. To the extent that these conditions still exist in an admittedly changing urban society, suburbia makes very real behavioral demands on its residents, whether they are aware of them or not.

For many suburbanites, of course, the central city remains an economic base. Others see it as a source of easy access to entertainment and culture. In moving to the suburbs people do not necessarily leave the city behind; "Crestwood Acres" simply provides the best of both worlds. This "suburbs are good" viewpoint is reflected in Gans's (1967) assertion that suburbanites return to the city to support the urban culture. They shop, attend the theatre and concerts, go to lectures. In many ways, they are still "city-oriented."

The truth of this rather generally accepted notion, however, is beginning to be challenged. Zikmund (1971), using a Main Line suburb of Philadelphia (Radnor) as his sample, found that use of the central city by its satellite population was much less than might be expected. Of his sample 29 percent reported that they went into Philadelphia more than once a month; 19 percent virtually never did. Both younger and older suburbanites, as well as those in the lowest and highest income brackets, used the city more than the middle-aged and the professional classes. Newcomers to Radnor were much more likely to make the trip than residents who had lived there for longer periods of time. "The city attracts the young and the old, the rich and the 'poor,' and the newcomer; but the middle class family man . . . prefers to stay at home." [p. 195]

How typical Radnor might be of suburbia in general it is hard to say. The implications of this study for urban planning, however, are apparent. The suburbs cannot be counted on to solve the city's problems. Although still part of the metropolis, the suburban resident tends to circumscribe—even to isolate—himself in a subenvironment. Orientation is narrowed and community is achieved in a local setting at the expense of the megacommunity of the city proper. The effect of this on the city inhabitant who stays behind is a question that has yet to be adequately examined.

How the City Is Imaged

Our discussion in the preceding pages has focused on the spatial aspects of the urban environment which aid the resident in creating a livable city. An essential characteristic of this spatial dimension is the ease with which it allows one to orient oneself and easily obtain the goods and services which are among the attractions of urban life. In brief, we do not simply wander around; we must have some conception of where to go and how to get there. Urban designers and architects have long been interested in those elements of the city's physical environment which are instrumental in aiding this orientation process. Psychologists too, in their way, have been concerned with understanding how organisms learn about their environment. Much of this work, however, involves investigating the behavior of rats in mazes. The issue of importance in these studies is whether animals simply learned stimulus-response connections, along the behavioristic model, or whether they possess what Tolman (1948) called "maps" of the mazes. In Tolman's view the maps were overall images of what led to what in the maze.

Lynch's (1960) pioneering work on urban imagery adapts the notion of Tolman's maps to the cognitive representation of areas—principally the city—by humans. Lynch stresses man's need to find order in the environment, his constant effort to reduce physical "chaos" to a meaningful pattern. The essential elements in Lynch's work have been touched upon in Chapters Three and Eight. Here, we will expand on these elements in greater detail.

In his pilot study Lynch (1960) selected three cities which differed in their physical design characteristics—Boston, Los Angeles, and Jersey City. Samples of middle- and upper-middle-class people in these settings were asked to prepare sketch maps of the city and describe trips they took through it. Lynch's analysis of these maps and interviews suggested that five key elements were used by people in an effort to structure their images. These he refers to as paths, edges, landmarks, nodes, and districts. *Paths* provide access from one part of a city to another. They are both vehicular and pedestrian. For example, expressways and freeways turn up repeatedly as devices for gaining orientation, as do main intracity thoroughfares. *Edges* delineate those parts of the city which serve as boundaries. Riverfronts, waterfronts, and roads on the edge of town serve as perceptual boundaries to an urban area. Major and minor landmarks such as buildings, parks, or statues, are often cognitively "mapped." In New York City the Empire State Building, Rockefeller Center, and Central Park all represent landmarks for those who wish to find their way around the city or tell others how to get to where they want to go. *Nodes* serve as points in the city where there are major transitions from one activity to another. Railroad stations, bus and airline terminals, and subway

Fig. 9-7 The compact nature of New York City makes it highly imageable. The edges of the city are defined by the Hudson and East Rivers. Landmarks like the Empire State Building aid orientation. Courtesy, Aero Service.

stops are easily mapped nodes. Intersections of important streets comprise another example. Finally, *districts* are relatively large areas which are recognized as having some common character. Greenwich Village in New York and North Beach in San Francisco are visually familiar "places" even to people who have never visited them.

Lynch's method stresses what people think their environment looks like in terms of the images that have become significant to them over a period of time; in his words, how they "extract structure and identity out of the material at hand." This, in turn, gives them a sense of orientation—they know "how to get around" or, to use Tolman's (1948) term, people have a cognitive map of an area. One abstracts from space a coherent pattern and, whether accurate or not, this pattern helps one to organize his activity. Finally, images provide the group with a common memory of the environment in question and to this extent enhance its meaning. The "character" of a city is to a large degree its memorability manifested in the images it impresses on our minds.

Following Lynch's work, a number of similar approaches to urban imagery have been developed. Lowenthal (1968) stressing perceptual preferences, concludes that people like environments about whose character they disagree; uniformity is uninteresting and limits the ability of the individual to find his own meaning in a setting. Planners are more interested in the legibility of urban environments as essential to ease of orientation and movement. The city should have clarity as well as interest. Two studies by Appleyard (1969,

Fig. 9-8 The horizontal spread of Los Angeles hinders easy orientation. The image is defined largely by the extensive freeway system. Courtesy, Aero Service.

1970) in Ciudad Guayana, Venezuela, dealt with this question on the level of building attributes and overall city structure, or form. In the former study a selected sample of 320 residents were interviewed as to the ways they identified and recalled individual buildings. Five major attributes were found to be important: (1) movement—the amount of activity occurring near the building; (2) imageability—unique features, such as size and design, that made the building stand out; (3) visibility—the role of the structure as a setting for personal activities—its importance in terms of use; (4) the cultural significance of the building to the population at large. Landmarks, a large dam, and statues fell into this category. The country club, although used by few people, was known to all.

Appleyard cites two features of buildings that tended to predominate in recalling them. One of these he calls "shape singularity"; the unusually designed or decorated structure will stand out even though it may be little used. We all know of such buildings in our own localities and they become important points of reference. Beyond this, he notes that the recall of a building "depend[s] as much on its relation to the context as on any absolute qualities." The evidence suggests, he adds, "that the urban vocabulary of architects and urban designers, while it may serve some purpose, is in fact substantially incongruent with the public's urban vocabulary." [p. 155]

Appleyard's follow-up study of Ciudad Guayana dealt with how the inhabitants perceived and mapped the city as a whole. It is interesting that only 15 percent of the sample produced accurate maps; for the majority, a sequential or path system predominated, but this gave a distorted view of areas that were not adjacent to frequently traveled routes. Spatial conceptions of the city were less common, although such elements predominated in the maps of the inhabitants' local areas. Some people drew inferences from previous experience with other cities that did not apply to Ciudad Guayana. Finally, social significance distorted individual perceptions of distance. In short, social distancing encouraged a false sense of physical distance as upper-class groups saw themselves as living farther from slum areas than they actually did and closer to the desirable neighborhoods.

Several studies by others have extended this approach in the United States. Carr and Schissler (1969) emphasized those aspects of city form which were remembered by people moving through the city. Three groups—drivers unfamiliar with the route (an elevated expressway into Boston), their passengers, and regular commuters—shared the same general recall of roadside features although only the commuters were familiar with the route. This overlap in the images of people who might have been expected to differ from one another suggests that the design process can be simplified to the extent that marked individual differences do not have to be accounted for. More important are the character of the features themselves; if they are easily nameable, stand out from the background because of size or uniqueness, and are recognizable by most people who are familiar with the city, they will be remembered. These roadside studies suggest how orientation through the city can be assisted by the selective inclusion of dominant elements which are visible from the road and by the alignment of the road itself.

The problem becomes particularly acute, however, when the entire length of the roadside is a jumbled confusion of objects. Investigating this aspect of response to urban arterials, Winkel et al. (1970) used a visual simulation device in which it was possible to add and subtract design elements at will. They tested for the positive and negative contribution of both specific features and the design context on the total visual picture. By removing (through photo-retouching) billboards, utility poles, overhead wires, and roadside signs in successive stages, they elicited responses from their viewers as to their preference for a "landscaped" versus "commercial" route. In general the removal of billboards and utility poles produced a positive response, but when all the "clutter" was taken away there was a curious tendency to see the roads as extremely monotonous and depressing. The phenomenon of "turnpike hypnosis" is an example of what can happen when at least some of the distracting man-made elements are no longer present. In Texas certain long, flat stretches of road are now decorated with billboard-sized works of art.

Kepes (1960) also reminds us that our image of the city is not a static one, but that it changes constantly as we move through it. "The basic unit of our urban vision . . . is not the fixed spatial location but the transportation-defined pattern of a sequence of vistas." [p. 193] Tall buildings, complex areas, differences in the intensity of light, parks, and open spaces are recurring elements that provide a rhythmic structuring to the environment. Such

Fig. 9-9 A typical limited-access highway in an urban metropolitan area.

Fig. 9-10 The same road with billboards removed.

Fig. 9-11 The same road with utility poles and overhead wires removed.

Fig. 9-12 The same road with utility poles, overhead wires, and billboards removed.

Fig. 9-13 The same road with utility poles, overhead wires, billboards, and store signs removed.

variations are unified by our own movement. Too orderly environments—acres of row houses, for instance—are uninteresting because (among other reasons) they lack the ambiguity which holds the visual field in a state of "perceptual tension." To the extent that design elements are surprising or force us to make decisions, they may be more visible than the grid pattern that offers little or no choice.

Although most research on urban imagery has concentrated on physical form, other factors are equally important. One of the more obvious is the role which psychological response plays in those aspects of the city which are experienced and remembered. Most cities, for example, by virtue of their imageable features, acquire a psychological core, or center—locales which are not necessarily coincident with the central business district. Although the heart of Chicago is its Loop, psychologically the city is oriented toward the lakefront with its impressive juxtaposition of skyscrapers, open parkland, and water. In many cities it is the commons or square which acts as a focus end enables people to orient themselves to less legible surroundings. The City Center (as it is designated in many European capitals), which is frequently based on transportation terminals (nodes), may bear little relation to the cognitive center. At the same time, the cognitive pull of downtown business districts has been shown to exercise considerable influence on the perception of distance. Golledge and Zannaras (1973), in a study of housewives' shopping habits, found that women in Columbus, Ohio, liked to trade in supermarkets that were located in the direction of the downtown business district, even though more easily reached markets existed toward the edge of the city. Like Lee (1968), who noted a similar preference in Cambridge, England, they attribute this to the fact that the values and satisfactions associated with the business district foreshortened the perceived distance in that direction.

Other factors which may influence one's response to the city can be traced to such variables as age, sex, occupation, and race. Cultural subgroups, for example, tend to cognize the city from their own unique perspective. When asked to map Los Angeles from memory, students at UCLA saw it as a whole; in Watts the black residents "imaged" the city chiefly in terms of the county hospital and the jail. Black children in Roxbury, an all-black ghetto in Boston, visualized this area of rundown homes as central to their lives; the white adolescent, it has been suggested, will see his environment as part of a larger context because he has more opportunities for exploration and learning.

All of these elements contribute to a city's image. They add, too, the quality of enrichment that is made possible by the urban environment. In providing cues to orientation, the designer is not only assisting the resident in finding his way around; he wants to make the city more attractive and visually stimulating, more sensuous and interesting. These attempts go beyond simply removing the most obvious sources of conflict and stress in the city; they are positively oriented efforts to provide meaning and fulfillment.

Such an approach, laudable as it may be, is not without its problems. One of these is methodological. As has been noted, the major technique employed in these studies is the so-called cognitive map, details of which are taken as indicators of one's representation of the physical scheme of the city. Yet it is obvious that these maps are subject to a variety of interpretations. They represent, so to speak, subjective cities—in Carr's (1970) phrase, "cities of the mind"—and as such they have different meanings for different people. Among other things, they may simply reflect one's ability at map drawing independent of what his "mental map" tells him. A problem for research, therefore, is to determine how well people orient themselves even if it is not possible for them to represent their knowledge on a map.

If it is proved that there are differences between maps and people's actual use of the city, then we can draw one of two conclusions. Either the map is not a completely adequate means of testing the urban resident's knowledge of the city, or its physical form is so nondescript that people do, indeed, encounter problems of orientation, map or not. Of course, both interpretations may be correct. What we need, therefore, are studies which go beyond those we have discussed, more finely grained approaches which can deal with a number of different dependent measures of urban imageability beyond those now employed. These studies might vary both the imageability of the environment and the measures which are used to tap urban knowledge. At present the subject is heavily weighted in favor of map making as a source of this knowledge.

The Livability of Cities

What makes a city livable? At the beginning of this chapter we framed an approach to this question based on six rather basic requirements. These can be summarized as follows:

Reduction of stress: noise and air pollution; poor housing; crowding; stimulus overload.

Sociability and community: the role of the physical environment in facilitating or inhibiting social and civic interaction; the importance of neighborhood and place in defining residential satisfaction.

Orientation and ease of movement: the use of a city by its inhabitants based on its imageability.

Environmental enrichment: the esthetic and stimulus qualities that contribute to the satisfactions and pleasures of living in the city—its variety, beauty, "aliveness," symbolic meanings.

Culture and recreation: the city's function in providing intellectual stimulation, entertainment, sports facilities, educational opportunities.

The decision process: the urban resident's perception of the environmental decisions which affect his daily life.

In discussing these requirements we have necessarily emphasized those which are most immediately related to the city as a physical environment. Thus, little has been said about the cultural amenities because they fall outside the purview of our study, although they are important to many residents.

Likewise, the decision process may involve comparatively few people, yet it affects many. To this end numerous implications were drawn from neighborhood and area studies in both the United States and England, especially in the realm of forced urban change.

The next chapter will show us some quite precise ways whereby individual environmental preferences can be scaled so that participation in the decision process might be more meaningful than is now generally the case; developed for the natural environment, they have significant implications for the urban setting. Although the political elements which enter into decision-making are perhaps uppermost in people's minds, none of this is of great value if the behavioral consequences of physical changes are not understood. The efficiency sought by the planner does not always mean livability for the user. What matters to people in their daily lives, not what the blueprint or model tells them, determines response. To reconcile professional decisions with the existential experience of those who are affected by them is certainly a conceptual requirement for urban livability.

We conclude this chapter with a discussion of the most elusive of all requirements, environmental enrichment. In one sense this covers almost everything we have talked about, for it is implicated in stress, in one's sense of "place" or neighborhood, in the amenities, and in the legibility of the city. But a livable environment may also include climate, the safety of streets, visual beauty, and even the economic opportunities present. Beyond this is the ambiance or atmosphere that we associate with particular cities, the feeling we have for them. Paris is glittering, London leisurely, New York frenetic, Dublin friendly. Either as traveler or resident we sense their moods. Cognitively, we may be influenced in our perceptions by knowing what a city stands for in history. In Rome we do not so much do as the Romans do as to look for what the Romans did. This symbolic aspect, based on socio-cultural associations, supplies much of the civic pride of cities and helps preserve their character. Unfortunately, it does not always succeed. In Rome, history is at war with an incredibly noisy, traffic-clogged present.

A descriptive profile of New York City, based on interviews conducted by Feldman (1967) as part of his doctoral dissertation, is cited by Milgram (1970). Here are some of the adjectives frequently used:

Sensory	*Pace*	*Behavior*
big	fast	aloof
immense	bustling	anonymous
vast	hurried	impersonal
huge	rushing	cold
monumental	frenetic	rude
tall	active	
towering	teeming	
congested	dynamic	
crowded	spiraling	
sound-filled	intense	
noisy		

Milgram adds:

> A contrasting profile emerges for London, where respondents placed far greater emphasis on their interactions with the inhabitants than on physical surroundings. London elicited such themes as diversity and individuality, but these impressions seem to be drawn far more from the quality of Londoners themselves than from perceptions of the city's institutions or physical layout. On certain themes near unanimity emerged: i.e., those concerned with London's tolerance and courtesy. [p. 1465]

In all large cities the salient environment is usually the immediate setting. Much of the anonymity attributed to urban living is due to the inability of people to localize themselves in environments that carry visual and/or symbolic identity. Ideally, neighborhoods serve this function by making space an extension of the self: this is "my" neighborhood. The larger the metropolis—the less we are able to identify with it as a whole—the more we break it up into phenomenal segments. Speaking of London and Paris, the novelist Lawrence Durrell writes (1972) that "one loves little pieces of them now, not the whole." Affection and intimacy are possible only for cities that are built to human scale. Durrell suggests that "once they grow beyond a certain size, their cohesion gets swallowed up, and it's no longer possible to be haunted by them in quite the same way."

Perhaps this is a subject best left to the novelist and poet. Dickens' descriptions of the physical effect of London on its inhabitants tell us more than all the guidebooks or parliamentary studies of the time. Wordsworth's paean to London, "Earth has not anything to show more fair," is a declaration of love from a man who was not, generally speaking, happy in cities. Indeed, of all the aspects of cities that have been studied by the sociologist, the historian, and the planner, the sentient quality—the tactile, textural, sonic, and ambiant values of the urban environment—has been most neglected. Yet it is this phenomenal city that most of us know best.

An example of how this question can be approached empirically was shown by Southworth (1969), who studied the "sonic environment" of cities and its relationship to visual forms. A city provides both sonic distress (air hammers, screeching brakes, auto horns) and sonic delight (boat whistles, splashing fountains, church bells). Smells, both pleasant and unpleasant, are associated with certain sections of cities. Southworth specifically wished to determine how nonvisual environmental information might be used to improve environmental quality. To what extent can a person identify the sounds of the city, how unique are these sounds, and how much information do they provide concerning the activity and spatial form of the city?

Design students served as observers in the study, and they were divided into three groups: those who could see but not hear; those who could hear but not see; and those who could both see and hear. Each person took a two-and-three-quarter's mile trip through Boston and was asked to describe spontaneously his impressions of the places visited. As might have been expected, most city sounds lacked uniqueness and informativeness. To a large extent, this was because the sounds of automobiles or pedestrian activity tended to mask the informative sounds. They were the least informative themselves even though they demanded the most attention.

The sound districts which were identified most easily were those which contained visible exterior activity. Often they possessed unique spatial characteristics such as tight, narrow streets (Beacon Hill) or tightly confined spaces like alleys and tunnels. At the other end of the spectrum, large open spaces like the Waterfront or the Boston Commons were easily recognized. In general, spaces were more meaningful if the person could hear the echoes of his own sounds. If sounds were unexpected or novel, one's recollection of the area was considerably improved. The most pleasant sounds were those of low frequency and intensity. When sounds were novel, informative to personal action and culturally approved (birds and bells), their perceived pleasantness increased even more markedly.

Based on these preliminary results, Southworth suggested some design techniques which could be used to enhance the sonic environment of the city. In areas which are visually monotonous, informative sounds could heighten their distinctiveness. Many subjects who could see but not hear commented on the dreary nature of the Boston Waterfront while those who could hear but not see thought that the Waterfront was delightful because of the sounds, such as bells, falling water, and ships' horns. In more commercial areas, sonic signs could take the place of visual signs. Those districts which do not have strong visual articulation might be given an identity through sound, while already well-defined areas could be reinforced by congruent sonic information.

Southworth would use symbolic sounds to inform pedestrians of approaching buses, or even changes in the weather. Street criers would make public announcements; animated scruptures in parks and squares would "respond" when people walked past them; and in visually ugly areas specially constructed floor materials would rumble, squish, pop, or squeak to provide variety. Fanciful? Perhaps. But the intention is worthy enough: Sonic design is one way of making the city more varied and interesting, and to that extent, more human.

Summary and Conclusion

City life is complex. No single theoretical model exists which conceptually unifies all aspects of the urban experience, nor is such a model likely. Rather, it is the individual's unique perception of the urban scene that unifies its seeming chaos. Because people perceive various physical, social, and cultural meanings in the environment, the city is experienced differently by each inhabitant.

In the presentation of this view, many facets of city life that make headlines have deliberately been avoided. The financial plight of cities, problems of government, school controversies, law enforcement, and crime are among the factors that affect the livability of the urban environment, although their behavioral results may be largely indirect. Instead, the city has been surveyed as a psychological setting, one that is experienced through the individual's sense of neighborhood, the degree of crowding he experiences, his feelings of social identity, and the physiognomic features of the city which give it orientational and symbolic meaning.

In seeking a structure for the city we reviewed the mosaic concept which sees socioeconomic class and ethnic groupings as the principal dynamics of spatial organization among residents. To this was added a psychological point of view. What behaviors in what settings do or do not go together? The pathology associated with specific areas (notably slums) was cited, and this in turn was related to population density, housing conditions, and forced change of residence. At the same time, the sources of satisfaction perceived by the inhabitants of such environments were pointed out. To these local patterns the more general effects of environmental stress, such as noise, air pollution, and information overload, were added. Finally, the spatial form of the city was seen as important in enabling people to know their city and, more significantly, in providing the symbols which help them endure—or even enjoy—it.

People who live in cities do not rush to statistical year books to find out how they are faring; rather, they know it in their bones. The student might ask himself: How livable is my own city? To what extent are noise, dirt, and traffic congestion outweighed by the cultural advantages, stimulation, and sense of neighborliness of the city? How easy and convenient is it to get around? How good is the climate? What is it about the city that makes me feel at home—or a stranger? What is the ambiance, the style, of the city? How beautiful, or ugly, is it? What are its pleasures? How many of the six basic requirements for livability are positively experienced? It is the psychological city—the city of experienced phenomena—that matters most to us, and in a sense this is the only city we really know.

References

Alexander, C. The city as a mechanism for sustaining human contact. Working paper No. 50. Berkeley, Calif.: Institute of Urban and Regional Development, University of California, 1966.

Appleyard, D. Why buildings are known: A predictive tool for architects and planners. *Environment and Behavior,* 1969, *1,* 131–156.

Appleyard, D. Styles and methods of structuring a city. *Environment and Behavior,* 1970, *2,* 100–118.

Appleyard, D., & Lintell, M. Environmental quality of city streets: The residents' viewpoint. *Journal of the American Institute of Planners,* 1972, *38,* 84–101.

Athanasiou, R., & Yoshioka, G. A. The spatial character of friendship formation. *Environment and Behavior,* 1973, *5,* 43–65.

Berger, B. M. *Working-class suburb.* Berkeley and Los Angeles: University of California Press, 1960.

Burgess, E. W. (Ed.) *The Urban Community.* Chicago: University of Chicago Press, 1926.

Canter, D., & Canter, S. Close together in Tokyo. *Design and Environment,* 1971, *2,* (2), 60–63.

Cappon, D. Health, malaise and the promise of cities. *Ekistics,* 1971, *32,* 48–50.

Carlestam, G., & Levi, L. Urban conglomerates as psychosocial human stressors. Report to Swedish Preparatory Committee for the United Nations Conference on the Human Environment, Stockholm, October, 1971.

Carr, S. The city of the mind. In W. R. Ewald, Jr. (Ed.), *Environment for man: The next fifty years.* Bloomington, Ind.: Indiana University Press, 1967. [Reprinted in H. M. Proshansky, W. H. Ittelson & L. G. Rivlin (Eds.), *Environmental psychology: Man and his physical setting.* New York: Holt, Rinehart and Winston, 1970. Pp. 518–533.]

Carr, S., & Lynch, K. Where learning happens. *Daedalus,* 1968, *97,* 1277–1291.

Carr, S., & Schissler, D. The city as a trip: Perceptual selection and meaning in the view from the road. *Environment and Behavior,* 1969, *1,* 7–36.

Catton, W. R., Jr., Hendee, J. C., & Steinburn, T. W. *Urbanism and the natural environment: An attitude study.* Seattle, Wash.: Institute for Sociological Research, University of Washington, 1969.

Cohen, S., Glass, D. C., & Singer, J. E. Apartment noise, auditory discrimination and reading ability in children. *Journal of Experimental Social Psychology,* in press.

Cooper, C. St. Francis Square: Attitudes of its residents. *A.I.A. Journal,* 1971, *56,* 22–27.

Davis, K. The urbanization of the human population. *Scientific American,* 1965, *213,* 40–53.

Dohrenwend, B. S., & Dohrenwend, B. P. Psychiatric disorder in urban settings. In G. Caplan (Ed.), *American handbook of psychiatry. Vol. III.* Rev. ed. New York: Basic Books, 1972.

Durrell, L. The poetic obsession of Dublin. *Travel and Leisure, 2* (4), 1972, 33–36, 69–70.

Faris, R. E. L., & Dunham, H. W. *Mental disorders in urban areas.* Chicago: University of Chicago Press, 1939.

Festinger, L., Schachter, S., & Back, K. *Social pressures in informal groups.* Stanford, Calif.: Stanford University Press, 1950.

Foa, U. G. Interpersonal and economic resources. *Science,* 1971, *171,* 345–351.

Freedman, J. L., Klevansky, S., & Ehrlich, P. R. The effect of crowding on human task performance. *Journal of Applied Social Psychology,* 1971, *1,* 7–25.

Fried, M. Grieving for a lost home. In L. J. Duhl (Ed.), *The urban condition.* New York: Basic Books, 1963.

Fried, M., & Gleicher, P. Some sources of residential satisfaction in an urban slum. *Journal of the American Institute of Planners,* 1961, *27,* 305–315.

Gans, H. *The urban villagers.* New York: Free Press, 1962.

Gans, H. *The Levittowners.* New York: Pantheon, 1967.

Glass, D. C., & Singer, J. E. *Urban stress.* New York: Academic Press, 1972.

Golledge, R. G., & Zannaras, G. Cognitive approaches to the analysis of human spatial behavior. In W. H. Ittelson (Ed.), *Environment and cognition.* New York: Seminar Press, 1973.

Gottman, J. The growing city as a social and political process. *Transactions of the Bartlett Society,* 1966, *5,* 9–46.

Grey, A., Bonsteel, D., Winkel, G., & Parker, R. People and downtown: Use, attitudes, settings. Seattle, Wash.: College of Architecture and Urban Planning, University of Washington, 1970.

Hall, E. T. *The hidden dimension.* Garden City, N.Y.: Doubleday, 1966.

Harris, J. D. Habituatory response decrement in the intact organism. *Psychological Bulletin,* 1943, *40,* 385–422. [Cited by Glass & Singer, 1972.]

Hollingshead, A. B., & Redlich, F. C. *Social class and mental illness.* New York: Wiley, 1958.

Izumi, K. Draft of brief to Hellyer task force on housing. Unpublished manuscript, University of Saskatchewan, 1968.

Kasl, S. V., & Harburg, E. Perceptions of the neighborhood and the desire to move out. *Journal of the American Institute of Planners,* 1972, *38,* 318–324.

Kepes, C. Notes on expression and communication in the cityscape. In L. Rodwin (Ed.), *The future metropolis.* New York: Braziller, 1960.

Kryter, K. D. *The effects of noise on man.* New York: Academic Press, 1970. [Cited by Glass & Singer, 1972.]

Lansing, J. B., & Marans, R. W. Evaluation of neighborhoods. *Journal of the American Institute of Planners,* 1969, *35,* 195–199.

Latané, B., & Darley, J. *The unresponsive bystander.* New York: Meredith, 1970.

Lauman, E. O. *Bonds of pluralism: The form and substance of urban social networks.* New York: Wiley, 1973.

Lee, T. Urban neighborhoods as a socio-spatial schema. *Human Relations,* 1968, *21,* 241–268. [Reprinted in H. M. Proshansky, W. H. Ittelson, & L. G. Rivlin (Eds.), *Environmental psychology: Man and his physical setting.* New York: Holt, Rinehart and Winston, 1970. Pp. 349–370.]

Lewit, E. Male and female mortality rates in the U.S. *51st annual report: New directions in economic research.* New York: National Bureau of Economic Research, 1971.

Loring, W. C. Housing and social problems. *Social Problems,* 1956, *3,* 160–168.

Lowenthal, D. Environmental perception project: Relevance of research hypotheses for environmental design. *Man and His Environment Newsletter,* 1968, *1* 3–6.

Lynch, K. *The image of the city.* Cambridge, Mass.: The M.I.T. Press, 1960.

Mead, M. Values for urban living. *Annals of the American Academy of Political and Social Science,* 1957, *314,* 10–14.

Meier, R. *A communications theory of urban growth.* Cambridge, Mass.: The M.I.T. Press, 1962.

Merton, R. K. The social psychology of housing. In W. Dennis (Ed.), *Current trends in social psychology.* Pittsburgh, Pa.: University of Pittsburgh Press, 1947.

Michelson, W. *Man and his urban environment: A sociological approach.* Reading, Mass.: Addison-Wesley, 1970.

Milgram, S. The experience of living in cities. *Science,* 1970, *167,* 1461–1468.

Miller, J. G. Sensory overloading. In B. E. Flaherty (Ed.), *Psychophysiological aspects of space flight*. New York: Columbia University Press, 1961.

Mitchell, R. E. Affect among the poor of Hong Kong and other cities. Paper presented at conference: Cognitive and Emotional Aspects of Urban Life, Center for Research in Cognition and Affect, The City University of New York, June, 1972.

Moller, C. B. *Architectural environment and our mental health.* New York: Horizon Press, 1968.

National Advisory Commission on Civil Disorders. *The Kerner report.* New York: Bantam, 1968.

Newman, O. *Defensible space.* New York: Macmillan, 1972.

The New York Times. A study of freeway links exhaust fumes to angina. November 19, 1972.

The New York Times. Article on W. H. Whyte. December 3, 1972.

Park, R. *Human communities.* Chicago: University of Chicago Press, 1952.

Patri, P. Personal communication, 1971.

Reynolds, H. W., Jr. The human element in urban renewal. *Public Welfare,* 1961, *19,* 71–73, 82. Cited by C. Hartman, The housing of relocated families. In J. Q. Wilson (Ed.), *Urban renewal: The record and the controversy.* Cambridge, Mass.: The M.I.T. Press, 1966.

Robinson, W. S. Ecological correlations and the behavior of individuals. *American Sociological Review,* 1950, *15,* 351–356.

Rossi, P. H. *Why families move: A study in the social psychology of urban residential mobility.* New York: Free Press, 1955.

Ryan, E. J. Personality identity in an urban slum. In L. J. Duhl (Ed.), *The urban condition.* New York: Basic Books, 1963.

Schmitt, R. C. Implications of density in Hong Kong. *Journal of the American Institute of Planners,* 1963, *24,* 210–217.

Schmitt, R. C. Density, health and social organization. *Journal of the American Institute of Planners,* 1966, *32,* 38–40.

Schorr, A. L. *Slums and social insecurity.* Washington, D.C.: U.S. Government Printing Office, 1963.

Selye, H. *The stress of life.* New York: McGraw-Hill, 1956.

Simmel, G. *The sociology of Georg Simmel.* Translated by K. H. Wolff. New York: Free Press, 1950.

Southworth, M. The sonic environment of cities. *Environment and Behavior,* 1969, *1,* 49–70.

Srole, L. Urban life and mental health. Paper presented at conference: Cognitive and Emotional Aspects of Urban Life, Center for Research in Cognition and Affect, The City University of New York, June, 1972.

Srole, L., Langner, T. S., Michael, S. T., Opler, M. K., & Rennie, T. A. C. *Mental health in the metropolis.* Vol. 1. New York: McGraw-Hill, 1961.

Timms, D. W. G. *The urban mosaic.* Cambridge, Mass.: Harvard University Press, 1971.

Tolman, E. C. Cognitive maps in rats and men. *Psychological Review,* 1948, *55,* 189–208.

U.S. Department of Commerce. *Negro-white differentials in geographic mobility.* Washington, D.C.: Area Development Administration, 1964.

U.S. Department of Health, Education and Welfare. *The mental health of urban America: The urban programs of the National Institute of Mental Health.*

Public Health Service Publication No. 1906. Washington, D.C.: U.S. Government Printing Office, 1969.

Walter, E. V. Dreadful enclosures: Detoxifying an urban myth. Paper presented at conference: Cognitive and Emotional Aspects of Urban Life, Center for Research in Cognition and Affect, The City University of New York, June, 1972.

Webber, M. M., & Webber, C. C. Culture, territoriality and the elastic mile. In H. W. Eldredge (Ed.), *Taming megalopolis.* Vol. 1. Garden City, N.Y.: Doubleday, 1967.

Whyte, W. H. *The organization man.* Garden City, N.Y.: Doubleday, 1957.

Whyte, W. H. *The last landscape.* Garden City, N.Y.: Doubleday, 1968.

Wilner, D. L., Walkley, R. P., Pinkerton, T. C., & Tayback, M. *The housing environment and family life.* Baltimore, Md.: Johns Hopkins Press, 1962.

Wilson, R. L. Livability of the city: Attitudes and urban development. In F. S. Chapin, Jr., & S. F. Weiss (Eds.), *Urban growth dynamics.* New York: Wiley, 1962.

Winkel, G., Malek, R., & Thiel, P. Community response to the design features of roads: A technique for measurement. *Highway Research Record,* 1970, *305,* 133–145.

Wirth, L. Urbanism and the American way of life. *American Journal of Sociology,* 1938, *44,* 1–24.

Young, M., & Willmott, P. *Family and kinship in East London.* Baltimore, Md.: Penguin, 1962.

Zikmund, J. Do suburbanites use the central city? *Journal of the American Institute of Planners,* 1971, *37,* 192–195.

Suggested Readings

Gans, H. *The urban villagers.* New York: Free Press, 1962.

Gans, H. *The Levittowners.* New York: Pantheon, 1967.

Lynch, K. *The image of the city.* Cambridge, Mass.: The M.I.T. Press, 1960.

Michelson, W. *Man and his urban environment: A sociological approach.* Reading, Mass.: Adison-Wesley, 1970.

Perloff, H. S. *The quality of the urban environment.* Los Angeles: Resources for the Future, Inc., 1969. [Distributed by the Johns Hopkins Press, Baltimore, Md.]

Schorr, A. *Slums and social insecurity.* Washington, D.C.: The U.S. Government Printing Office, 1963.

Ten

The Perception and Use of the Natural Environment

In Chapter Two the natural environment was discussed in terms of attitudes and symbolic meanings which, evolving over the centuries, seemed to fit the particular needs of a given age or place. Thus, the animistic view of nature held by primitive man gave way to later and more sophisticated perceptions of reality, with an increasing tendency to fragment the environment into discriminable bits and to conceive of it as external to the person. This change in orientation laid the basis for a mechanistic science which dealt with the world in terms of parts rather than wholes. Contrasts were drawn between Eastern and Western orientations in this respect, with an idealized Eastern man depicted as closer to nature in the sense that he sees himself as part of an organic whole. Western man, on the other hand, has assumed scientific distance from his environment, putting emphasis on its technical control. Out of this view have come many of the social and economic attitudes that affect his use of the natural world today. It is this question that will be explored here. What will be attempted is a linkage between the very broadly based attitudes discussed earlier and the specific environmental problems that concern us at the present time.

Utility versus Conservation

An expanding population has placed increasing pressure on the natural environment. In part this is due to our apparently insatiable demand for land and to the exploitation of natural resources to support the technology which is characteristic of our society. These factors, added to the rapid decline of our outdoor recreational resources, have created a not unjustified alarm about our environmental future.

As a response to this situation two broad approaches have been taken to the natural environment. One of these can be termed instrumental—nature viewed primarily as a resource for human use and/or subject to technical control. The other and contrasting approach is based on the ethics of conservation, which emphasizes the ecological integrity of nature. The wilderness in particular is the most tangible example of the clash between these different value systems. For example, those oriented to the instrumental use of the environment consider logging or mineral extraction in wilderness areas as absolutely essential to a growing economy. It is, they suggest, a question of priorities, and if the esthetic or recreational qualities of the environment must suffer, then this is the price which must be paid to maintain industrial output and economic independence from other nations.

Conservationists, on the other hand, argue that continued economic growth is meaningless if the result is a depleted and scarred landscape. We will have lost a heritage which in many instances cannot be replaced or regained. We may be rich in a material sense, but we shall have surrendered the spiritual values which are nurtured through direct contact with a nature unspoiled by man. What good are two cars in every garage, a surfeit of electrical gadgets, and an endless supply of money if our air and water are poisoned, our forests turned into wastelands, our wildlife gone because it has no place to live, and our landscape eaten away by strip mining and erosion? This argument on the part of environmentalists is familiar to all of us.

The conservationist ethic, however, embraces more than a concern for protecting the physical resources of nature, its scenic beauty, and the symbolic and recreational values of the outdoor environment. Equally important is the belief that by preserving our natural resources we will be better able to achieve whatever other objectives we may have. These may, in themselves, be partly instrumental. For there are limits to the capacity of the natural environment to support an unending demand for man-made goods. Thus, one conservationist position is that we must sacrifice quantity of production for quality and learn to live within our planetary means, even if this results in some drastic changes in our way of life.

A current example—the "energy crisis"—will illustrate this point. The unavailability of adequate gasoline supplies may result in a loss of mobility insofar as the private automobile is concerned. In addition, a shortage of heating oil has brought rationing of supplies and more cold days to many householders. An instrumental orientation to the environment would suggest that the appropriate response to the energy crisis is an increasing search for new oil supplies, even if this means that the off-shore reserves in the United States be more thoroughly exploited. The disastrous oil spill in Santa Barbara in 1969, however, illustrates the environmental risks which such an undertaking might entail. A conservationist response to the energy crisis would involve a broad-gauged series of steps. These would include attempting to change patterns of automobile use by employing expanded rapid transit systems, driver education to cut down on overuse of the automobile, the development of oil substitutes for energy purposes, and penalizing nonessential car use.

Perhaps the most important lesson the crisis has taught us, however, is that we cannot be at all certain that technological substitutes for the loss of natural resources will be adequate to human needs. In part, the technology may be well enough developed; and, as we shall note later, it may also result in a number of unanticipated and/or undesirable side effects.

We must, in essence, turn to some of the values we discussed in Chapter Two. These can be summarized by saying that we must recognize our interdependence with the environment in which we live, cease assuming that technology will be able to solve all the problems arising from unenlightened environmental exploitation, adopt the approach of a careful steward over our natural resources, and generally refrain from treating the environment as an endlessly exploitable resource, separate and apart from ourselves.

Much of our later discussion relates directly or indirectly to the broad value orientations discussed here. It would be a mistake, however, to assume that these are the only concerns people have vis-à-vis the natural environment, or that they constitute the only reasons for studying the subject. Chapter Two outlined some of man's *symbolic attitudes* toward the out-of-doors which influence his use and conception of it. One such attitude derives from the assumed moral benefits of living close to the land. Thomas Jefferson, who distrusted cities (for their artificiality) much as the early Puritans had distrusted nature, found the countryside a repository of civilized values. For Thoreau and others proximity to nature implied self-reliance and a rejection of machine technology. Such attitudes can be found today in the writings of Lewis Mumford, for whom the rural or small town way of life remains an environmentally "moral" life.

In other hands, the out-of-doors has been seen as leading to a mystical communion with God. The naturalist John Muir (1838–1914) expressed this viewpoint, finding in the glacial formations and botanical wonders of the Yosemite Valley, California, a sense of personal transcendence and a near-pantheistic belief in nature's goodness. Ernest Seton-Thompson (1860–1946), the writer on woodcraft whose studies were adopted by the Boy Scouts of America, regarded contact with nature as a source of youthful character building. Interestingly, however, the idea of wilderness as a place of penance and punishment, or the source of symbolic evil, has largely disappeared—perhaps to the degree that the wilderness itself threatens to become a scarce commodity. Today, wilderness is "good."

Other Perspectives toward the Natural Environment

Symbolic meanings in nature become important to the way in which one deals with his environment behaviorally. This is equally true for outdoor recreation, the problem of natural hazards, and such constructs as environmental quality. It will be helpful to define what is meant by these terms in the context of this chapter.

As a *recreational setting* the natural environment takes on the function of playground. The picnicker, bird watcher, and wilderness camper are all "getting back to nature," although not in equally committed fashion. The popularity of outdoor recreation can be traced to increased leisure, a desire to escape from the city, and the status motivations that equate certain kinds of recreational behavior (skiing, for instance) with social standing. Some psychologists believe that the need for open space is in itself deeply rooted in man; more likely, it is the activity being engaged in, the variation from work routines, rather than contact with nature that does most to satisfy his needs. However, to the extent that play has therapeutic value, the natural environment is frequently an agent in the process. Others (Burch 1965; Klausner 1971) see this setting as an opportunity for role playing, a subject that will be dealt with in more detail in the discussion of wilderness behavior.

Natural hazards deal with the risks, uncertainties, and catastrophies of nature and to this extent present specific problems of adaptation. Involved here is the safety of man's environment, which also implicates its quality and integrity. Generally speaking, hazards are environmental "events" rather than "environments." By controlling them, we not only make possible a more livable environment, in a sense we protect nature from itself. But it is important to know at what point man goes too far; technological intervention may create new problems. The leveeing of rivers in many areas has led to more rapid settlement on flood plains or areas in which the likelihood of flooding is particularly high. Putting out forest fires may prevent nature's way of thinning out natural growth for ecological purposes.

Achieving *environmental quality* along the dimensions outlined above means more than the realization of ecological standards. We must decide what quality costs and who is to pay for it. Implicit too is the higher-level human concern of people's relationship to their world. These questions are at the heart of a psychological approach to the natural environment. For in tampering with nature, we disturb not only an ecosystem but that natural order or environmental given which bears so importantly on how people relate to one another and how, ultimately, they value their place in the universe. In Greek mythology Anteus lost his strength when he lost contact with the earth. For environmental man, however, one's nexus to the earth is less obvious. It is the quality of the natural world that gives significance to one's contact with it.

The question of quality is generally conceptualized in terms of standards on which there is common agreement. Most people agree, for instance, that smog is unpleasant and injurious; or that beauty in the landscape is desirable. It is assumed, too, that agreed standards are thought to be susceptible to political and/or economic control. The conflict arises on two levels: (1) what constitutes a standard, that is, achieving agreement on a subjective level; and (2) what costs and benefits attach to achieving these standards in specific situations. Too often this issue is considered only after desirability is ascertained. Two examples will illustrate this point.

In Los Angeles six million automobiles emit carbon monoxide into a 9200–square-mile area that is especially vulnerable to smog conditions. Because of the California sunshine, car exhaust is transformed into even more harmful photochemical oxidants, the federal limit for which, at 0.08 parts per million, is exceeded more than 200 days of the year in this instance. Air pollution officials in Los Angeles County attribute 90 percent of the area's smog to automobiles; as a result, the administrator for the federal Environmental Protection Agency has proposed gasoline rationing that would reduce auto usage by 80 percent. Only by this method, he suggested, would the clean air standards be met by the legal deadline of 1977.

Such an approach is clearly logical, but is it acceptable? Will people pay for clean air through a drastic change of habits? Former Los Angeles mayor Sam Yorty (1973) doubts it. "I don't think the air is so bad that people would be willing to cut driving by 80 percent, stop the whole economy and throw everyone out of work to make the air better." Right or wrong, Yorty's statement points up the critical question of who pays for quality, and how. While clean air is everybody's business, special interests (the oil and auto industries), entrenched habits, and (in the case of Los Angeles, where there is no subway system and the bus system is inadequate) logistical necessity mitigate against change. The cost, presently at least, is perceived as too high.

Another example of a subjective perception of environmental quality comes from the town of Boron, California, in the Mojave desert a few miles from Edwards Air Force Base. The base is (among other things) a test and development facility for supersonic military aircraft. Although most communities throughout the country are trying to reduce airport noise, residents of Boron have become habituated to, and even enthusiastic about, it. Moreover, theirs is no ordinary noise, but rather a plaster-cracking, ear-shattering sonic boom. Writing in *The New Yorker* (September 16, 1972), William Murray reports that:

> Despite the fact that, on an average, some four hundred flights a day take off from Edwards, and it is not unusual for the town to be rocked by twenty to thirty sonic booms between dawn and dusk, almost no one objects. On the contrary, the town makes a virtue of its affliction. "Air progress and history are made daily in the Boron area," proclaims a brochure put out by the

> Chamber of Commerce. Boron, it continues, ought to be called "The Boom Capital of the World." [p. 89]

"Such enthusiasm, of course," the writer adds, "has strong economic roots."

Environmental quality control is sought in a number of ways. Legislation is a major instrument: We reduce the lead content of gasoline. Taxation is used to penalize the polluter, that is, the gasoline tax is raised. The threat of legislation is sometimes effective. Public opinion has become increasingly important as citizen groups bring legal action against polluters. But here again disagreement about the criteria becomes the sticking point. The decision to use taxation schemes to upgrade quality is dependent upon setting some standard for when and how much to tax. In the following pages these issues will arise again. As we shall see, there are many questions but few answers. One of the tasks for environmental psychology, then, is to extend our understanding of the factors which contribute to these differing conceptions of the natural world. We can only hope that improved knowledge will aid us in solving the dilemmas which face us now and in the immediate future.

Natural Hazard Perception and Response

> As winds of up to 50 m.p.h. brought down trees and more than two inches of rain filled up basements in Westchester Friday, many residents began to realize that they had been through all this last June when Hurricane Agnes caused thousands of dollars of flood damage here.
>
> "These conditions were supposed to have been corrected 20 years ago," raged Mrs. Amy Sullo of 34 Babbit Court, Elmsford. "Where's the tax money going, that's what I'm trying to find out. Every time we get a heavy rain, we get flooded out by the Saw Mill River. How much can a person take?
>
> "During the last flood," Mrs. Sullo continued, "there were three snakes in my basement. I don't know where they came from. I don't like snakes."
>
> [*The Daily Item*, Port Chester, New York, February 3, 1973]

In no realm do the decisions we make regarding the use of the environment have more important consequences than those dealing with natural disasters. Man lives in constant threat of nature's excesses and its parsimony. During the years 1955–1964, loss of life from floods in the United States averaged 70 per year; there was an average of 110 deaths from hurricanes (for the span 1915–1964) and 194 from tornadoes (1916–1964). Table 10–1 gives estimates for property damage from these and other extreme geophysical events. Burton, Kates, and White (1968) put a figure of three billion dollars a year as the cost of these disasters, and Burton (1970) projects a doubling of the number of natural catastrophes annually by the end of the century.

Although we call them natural, many such disasters result from human

TABLE 10-1 Estimates of Average Annual Losses from Selected Geophysical Hazards in the United States[a]

Hazard	Loss of Life		Property Damage	
	Number	Period	Amount	Period
Floods	70	1955–64	1000	1966
			350–1000	1964
			290	1955–64
Hurricanes	110	1915–64	250– 500[b]	1966
			100	1964
			89	1915–64
Tornadoes	194	1916–64	100– 200[b]	1966
			40	1944–64
Hail, Wind, and Thunderstorms			300	1967
			125– 250[b]	1966
			53	1944–53
Lightning Strikes and Fire	160	1953–63	100	1965
Earthquakes	3	1945–64	15	1945–64
Tsunamis	18	1945–64	9	1945–64
Heat and Isolation	238	1955–64		
Cold	313	1955–64		
TOTALS	1106		621–2174	

[a] *Single-year estimates are the level of average losses current to year cited. Property damage figures are in millions of dollars unadjusted.*
[b] *Insured loses only*
From I. Burton, R. Kates, and G. White. The human ecology of extreme geographical events. Natural Hazard Research Working Paper No. 1. Toronto: Department of Geography, University of Toronto, 1968. By permission of the authors.

actions. As man spreads himself and his works over greater areas, as he dams rivers, paves the earth, cuts down forests, and builds bigger cities; both vulnerability to hazard and potential magnitude of loss increase. Approximately 200 cities in the United States lie in flood plains. Between 1940 and 1960, relatively more buildings were constructed below the mean high-water level surrounding our large cities than in the areas above that level. The effect of such action was dramatically pointed up by the disastrous flooding along the Mississippi River in the spring of 1973. Some 11 million acres of land in seven states were inundated, with damages estimated at $322 million and 35,000 persons made homeless. Nature, in such cases, is thought to be out of control. In fact, it is man who has exposed himself to its vagaries. Despite repeated flooding, what geographers call the "pattern of reinvasion" of people onto flood plains is certainly no less than in the past, and probably greater. This phenomenon is observed with similar regularity in areas that have been leveled by earthquakes and hurricanes.

On a theoretical level, people are probably more aware of such risks than ever before; nevertheless, their behavior often belies this awareness. For the past several years, this interesting situation has been studied by a number of geographers, notably at the University of Chicago, Clark University, and the University of Toronto, in a program of natural hazard research. From these studies we can distinguish at least four principal reasons why human reaction to the hazard environment differs markedly from perceptions of the ordinary environment:

1. In most areas disasters occur with relative infrequency; they are not part of our daily lives. Infrequent perception of hazard conditions leads to distortions in conceptualizing the environment. The threat (stimulus) is seen as potential and remote rather than immediate and real.
2. We are dealing with events over which, it is assumed, man has limited control.
3. These events often require major adjustments in our way of life, which people are usually reluctant to make.
4. Information from the hazard environment is frequently ambiguous; it provides us with a paucity of reliable cues. As a result, judgments are less accurate than is ordinarily the case with other environments.

Table 10-2 lists the range of adjustments to these hazards.

In view of this, it is not surprising that the strategies men adopt in dealing with natural hazards vary considerably. We know, for example, that many individuals eliminate the threat from their perceptions altogether ("It won't happen"). Others may recognize the hazard but feel powerless to do anything about it, although such, in fact, may not be the case ("I'll stick it out"). The principal behavior, however, seems to be rooted in uncertainty; disaster is perceived in terms of probability. In this case we gamble with the odds, which, indeed, may be in our favor ("It won't happen to me"). Finally, perception of risk is minimized because of faith in outside solutions; we have become increasingly intolerant of "the vagaries of nature in an age of powerful technology." (Burton et al. 1968:4) Technology suggests that at least some hazards can be controlled ("Let the government do it"). Clearly, this was the attitude of Mrs. Sullo. Twenty years of floods had not dimmed her faith.

We can learn a great deal from people like Mrs. Sullo. From some 2000 in-depth interviews with residents of riverine and tidal flood plains, Burton and his colleagues analyzed the ways in which different individuals perceived flood hazards, chiefly in terms of frequency of occurrence. One conclusion they draw is that the assessments of those who deal with floods as a profession rarely coincide with the assessments of the nonprofessional. The latter, less knowledgeable about the underlying distribution of hazards, are more inclined to exclude themselves from the pattern of risk or to deny it altogether. Table 10–3 shows some of the ways in which people psychologically handle the element of uncertainty in dealing with floods. In general their tendency is to minimize the possibility of environmental control.

This does not mean that people will fail to take action in the face of continued threats; that is, where certainty outweighs uncertainty in the perception of risk or where the magnitude of hazard produces a crisis response. Burton et al, (1968) call this the "It will happen" attitude. In contrast, remedial efforts are few where perceived frequency and low probability

TABLE 10–2 Theoretical Range of Adjustments to Geophysical Events

Class of Adjustment	Event		
	Earthquakes	Floods	Snow
Affect the cause	No known way of altering the earthquake mechanism	Reduce flood flows by: land-use treatment; cloud seeding	Change geographical distribution by cloud seeding
Modify the hazard	Stable site selection: soil and slope stabilization; sea wave barriers; fire protection	Control flood flows by: reservoir storage; levees; channel improvement; flood fighting	Reduce impact by snow fences; snow removal; salting and sanding of highways
Modify loss potential	Warning systems; emergency evacuation and preparation; building design; land-use change; permanent evacuation	Warning systems; emergency evaculation and preparation; building design; land-use change; permanent evacuation	Forecasting; rescheduling; inventory control; building design; seasonal adjustments (snow tires, chains); seasonal migration; designation of snow emergency routes
Adjust to losses:			
Spread the losses	Public relief; subsidized insurance	Public relief; subsidized insurance	Public relief; subsidized insurance
Plan for losses	Insurance and reserve funds	Insurance and reserve funds	Insurance and reserve funds
Bear the losses	Individual loss bearing	Individual loss bearing	Individual loss bearing

From I. Burton, R. Kates, and G. White. The human ecology of extreme geographical events. Natural Hazard Research Working Paper No. 1. Toronto: Department of Geography, University of Toronto, 1968. By permission of the authors.

combine to produce negative certainty; that is, "It will not happen." It is in the intermediate range of these extremes, where probability is uncertain and there is "high variability of perceived frequency [among] the population" [p. 19] that human response is least predictable.

From the interviews it was found that none of the attitudes outlined above bears a significant relationship to age or education. Socioeconomic status does not appear to be a factor except where the cost of meeting the problem is high. In such cases people are more likely to take action if they belong to the middle- and upper-income brackets. Previous experience with a heavily damaged area has only a slight effect on the adoption of new strategies. It is when

TABLE 10–3 Common Responses to the Uncertainty of Natural Hazards

Eliminate the Hazard		*Eliminate the Uncertainty*	
Deny or Denigrate Its Existence	Deny or Denigrate Its Recurrence	Make It Determinate and Knowable	Transfer Uncertainty to a Higher Power
"We have no floods here, only high water."	"Lightning never strikes twice in the same place."	"Seven years of great plenty . . . After them seven years of famine."	"It's in the hands of God."
"It can't happen here."	"It's a freak of nature."	"Floods come every five years."	"The government is taking care of it."

From I. Burton, R. Kates, and G. White. The human ecology of extreme geographical events. Natural Hazard Research Working Paper No. 1. Toronto: Department of Geography, University of Toronto, 1968. By permission of the authors.

the actual frequency of hazards is equated with perceived frequency that action is most likely. The question for psychologists is why actual frequency is not always so perceived or, to put it another way, why the probability of hazard is shifted into the category of uncertainty.

Expanding on this, Kates (1968) suggests, in addition to frequency and magnitude, two other features of natural hazards that affect one's choice of adjustment. One of these is suddenness of onset; a disaster that strikes with little or no warning leaves us few options. A second feature is the relationship of the hazard to a specific environment—is it intrinsic to the ways in which the site is used? Floods are more likely to be seen as a hazard—hence controlled—where flood plain agriculture is practiced, as it frequently is in the Mississippi Valley. On the other hand, drought may be accepted; that is, the hazard is minimized, where farmers depend solely on rainfall, since in these areas there seems to be little that can be done about it.

To these factors Kates adds the element of personal vulnerability. This is influenced, in part, by the nature of the encounter—its recency, frequency, and intensity—as well as the different views that men hold toward nature. The technical feasibility of making changes (to reduce vulnerability) may vary considerably according to the individual. The economic gainfulness involved in such a change will also differ. Not everyone stands to lose by a disaster, this produces different estimates of personal vulnerability. "Similarly, social conformity—to do as my father did—is a basic guide in many areas." [p. 18]

In his work with the dust bowl farmers, Saarinen (1966) noted their optimistic stance in relation to drought frequency. Farmers expect many more good years than drought years, whatever their actual experience, and all but the most extreme droughts tend to be forgotten. Perhaps to admit the possibility of catastrophe would require adjustments that they are not prepared to make. It becomes easier to adjust psychologically. Saarinen did find, however, that perception of the risk increases with age until the elderly years are reached.

In dealing with any hazard area we should remember that many of the inhabitants are a self-selected population. Assuming that they knew the region was hazardous, they have chosen to submit to the risk, to ignore it, to make alterations, or to modify the situation perceptually. Perhaps an equally cogent factor in the decision to live in a hazard area is the faith of risk-takers in the technological "fix." Weather modification (through cloud seeding), barriers such as dams and dikes, and the development of drought-resistant strains of crops give a lessened sense of vulnerability even when such efforts are not successful. The knowledge that such a compromise with nature is possible, even a belief in water dowsing or the efficacy of prayer, in themselves, may reduce one's assessment of the hazard.

It may be surmised that people who have been involved in catastrophes, who "know what to expect," are more willing to accept vulnerability. Such an attitude would undoubtedly depend upon the severity of the experience and is a form of adaptation. Golant and Burton (1969), in a questionnaire survey on "Avoidance-Response to the Risk Environment," found that for a statistically significant number of respondents the greatest avoidance was indicated when there was no previous experience with the hazard. Perhaps this is a way of saying that people are more likely to be afraid of the unknown; in any case, it suggests that experience, particularly that which allows one to come through the disaster, may actually lessen one's perception of vulnerability.

An equally interesting conclusion drawn from this study suggests that there is no relationship between personality factors, such as extroversion-introversion and neuroticism-stability, and a desire to avoid risk. The implication here is that we cannot simply write off differences in response to some fluke of personality, an important insight because of what it says about the nature of human response to hazardous situations in general. In dealing with pollution, for example, people may very well feel that the situation is hopeless because the problem is so pervasive. On the other hand, to the extent that the problem is perceived to be man-made, it may be considered subject to human control. However, Burton, Kates, and White (1968) hypothesize a "natural hazard syndrome" by which men respond to "different natural hazards in somewhat *similar* ways" [p. 27, emphasis added] that nevertheless differ from responses to nonnatural hazards. They cite evidence pointing toward greater anxiety in dealing with such man-made catastrophes as fire and automobile collision, for example, than with floods, tornadoes, and snowstorms.

Finally, in the more severe natural catastrophes, loss is shared, either through insurance or outside assistance. The designation of "disaster areas" by the federal government is a case in point. Although risk is not necessarily lessened, the consequences of not attending to it are. For this reason, the risk itself may be downgraded.

To sum up: Response to hazard environments is based on a global assessment of conditions that have slight counterpart in the environment of everyday living. From this perspective a number of variables influence the decisions that are taken in dealing with hazard situations. Probability of occurrence is certainly an important factor, as are recency and intensity. One's sense of personal vulnerability is another. The technology available and the feasibility of its use affects attitudes. Response will vary according to previous experience and social conditions. These variations are more pronounced among nonprofessionals than professionals. The former tend to "spread the risk" over a wide range of behavioral adjustments and attitudes; the latter seek specific (usually technological) rearrangements in the environment. Policy planning to minimize risk and damage points the way to a change in the perceptions of everyone by making available a more suitable range of adjustments. Such a theoretical range for three types of events is shown in Table 10–3. To the extent that hazards are man-made, that is, the result of enclosing flood plains or surfacing large land areas, they can be considered a form of pollution subject to correction.

Finally, and perhaps most importantly, natural hazards frequently result from a lack of sound ecological planning. The dust storms of the 1930s, vividly described in Steinbeck's *The Grapes of Wrath*, were in part man-made. Excessive cultivation of the prairies and unwise farming methods destroyed the cover for the soil, which blew away under drought conditions. Ecologists such as McHarg (1969) stress the interdependence of nature, with man subject to the same laws as all other components of the biosphere. Anything that interferes with the orderly interaction of the elements within the ecological system is destructive.

In his work as landscape architect and planner McHarg (see Darling & Milton 1966) has shown that it is possible to build homes on the New Jersey dunes, for example, without destroying the shield which makes the dunes a natural protective element in the topography. He has demonstrated similar possibilities for the Brandywine Creek area near Philadelphia, where a plan for the habitation of the area was shown to be consistent with minimal damage to the natural ecology.

Because this is essentially a conceptual approach to nature, only recently has the ecological viewpoint entered into man's perceptions of hazards. But since the consequences of his abuse of nature may be felt mainly by others, or removed from his own experience by a period of time, his perceptions of the cause-and-effect relationship are often attenuated. Moreover, ecological planning is seen as "too big" for the individual; it becomes a government responsibility.

Variations in Individual Response

Much of the emphasis in the preceding section was devoted to the differences that people exhibit in dealing with a common environmental situation. Just as the landscape has physical form (stimulus information qualities) and a social or symbolic meaning, so does one bring to it certain personal qualities that color our perception of it. This point was made at some length in Chapter Five, when we proposed the notion that reality is constructed by the individual, in the sense that the environment represents the raw material out of which he fashions a view of the world.

Such a view is influenced by the values and attitudes an individual holds, and the intentions he brings with him—in what way does he plan to use the environment? But how do we account for the variation among different people in the values and attitudes that are expressed? Why do some men and women prefer hiking to bicycling? To explain such behavior past research in the social sciences has concentrated on the readily measurable aspects of the individual—occupation, income, education, social roles, and so forth. This general approach is characteristic of the way much environmental research is conducted; hence many investigators have attempted to identify personal correlates of environmental action in the hope that these too will suggest the nature of our environmental descriptions, attitudes, and behaviors.

A good many of these measurements can be called demographic. Demographic information is descriptive of the attitudes and behaviors that are likely to be associated with certain things that people have in common. Age and sex are examples; geographical location is another. Occupation may be important; taxi drivers tend to cognize an environment in linear terms, airline pilots spatially (Rand 1969).

In a study of outdoor recreation behaviors among residents of ten communities, Marans (1972), for instance, was able to show that income is strongly related to golfing and boating, and that among men golfing is a "high status" sport while among women it is not. With respect to tennis: sex, concern for status, and educational level were correlates. Shafer (1969) and Lucas (1966) found that people with high education and higher-than-average income have a more benign attitude toward nature and demonstrate a greater concern for its ecological values than do persons of limited education and low income.

Obviously, these demographic characteristics do not account for all the difference in human behavior; not every college graduate, for instance, is a wilderness lover, just as some taxi drivers lose their way. Nor do demographic variables always indicate why they are correlated with other variables of interest. For example, what is it about education that leads to a more benign attitude toward nature? What the researcher seeks, therefore, are deeper levels of analysis that help explain why these differences exist within a demographic group. Given this perspective the investigation shifts from such factors as occupation, age, and status to the less-obvious qualities that describe human behavior.

Motivational drive is one such quality. Intelligence is a factor. Psychological stability plays a part—the insecure person may feel threatened by environments that others find stimulating. The cultural conditioning that shapes one's value system certainly bears a strong relationship to behavior. It should be clear, however, that demographic information and personality traits are intertwined; indeed, the latter may give us the clue to the former. Some people live in cities because they have certain goals; as a city dweller they acquire attitudes characteristic of an urban environment. Demography, therefore, is best viewed against one's personal set of values or general orientation toward the world.

A further distinction has been made between a person's value orientations and his attitudes. Clyde Kluckhohn (1951) has defined the latter as being exclusively referable to the individual. Values, on the other hand, reflect a "generalized and organized conception" of things; they imply a difference between what is desirable and nondesirable. Attitudes are more likely to arise out of the immediate situation and change with circumstances, whereas values relate to personal or cultural standards and are more permanently embedded in our lives. In reality most of our attitudes are manifested within some kind of value-oriented context.

Man's Place in Nature

In Chapter Two the historical changes that have occurred in man's orientation toward the natural world were seen as functions of religious belief, cultural and philosophical differences among peoples, scientific development, and esthetic preferences. The contrast between Eastern and Western modes of looking at the environment was noted. In more specific ecological terms, Florence Kluckhohn (1959) has outlined a typology of value-orientations which is mainly concerned with man's locus of control vis-à-vis the natural environment. This typology is described as (1) man (subjugated to) *under* nature; (2) man (in harmony) *with* nature; and (3) man (dominating) *over* nature.

Kluckhohn (1959) illustrates the first of these types by describing the Spanish-American culture of the southeastern United States where, for the typical sheepraiser, "there is little or nothing which can be done if a storm comes to damage his range lands or destroys his flocks. He simply accepts the inevitable as inevitable. His attitude toward illness and death is the same fatalistic attitude." [p. 347] Saarinen (1966) found similar attitudes among the wheat farmers of the Great Plains, for whom drought was a recurrent hazard. Two-thirds of those interviewed expressed resignation in the face of nature's threats. The environment is felt to have the upper hand. This orientation is frequently called "fate control."

The man-with-nature orientation posits a harmonious relationship between natural forces and man's use of the environment. The value system of China in past centuries can be cited as an example of this orientation. Modern-day environmentalists—the conservationists, for example—adopt a rational rather than mystical approach, although the latter is expressed, to some extent, in the rural commune movement and through such Westernized Zen spokesmen as Alan Watts. In general, man-with-nature is based on a cooperative approach to the environment—an approach that is more likely to result in a better use of the environment. The direction taken by Ian McHarg (1966) and his associates in environmental planning is an example of rational planning which is extremely sensitive to the ecological requirements of the site which is being developed.

The man-over-nature orientation involves the belief that the environment is something to be subjugated. Nature is to be controlled solely for human ends; it is an obstacle to be overcome. Elsewhere, this view has been termed instrumental. It is undoubtedly a reflection of our industrialized Western culture; to a significant extent modern technology has made such a view increasingly veridical, although various environmental interventions have led to all kinds of unanticipated negative outcomes. Still the prevailing view among the developed countries, it is bound up with a philosophy of progress and achievement that is perhaps more important than technological implementation.

One danger with such a typology is that it is subject to easy generalizations. Not everyone fits neatly into one of the "under," "with," or "over" compartments. With relatively "primitive" peoples, such as the Spanish-American sheepraisers, a single orientation may predominate, although anthropological evidence suggests that so-called "primitives" exhibit marked differences among themselves. On the other hand, sophisticated individuals have been known to supplicate nature (by dowsing for water or praying.) Saarinen (1966) found that a fatalistic attitude toward drought among wheat farmers did not lessen their determination to "stick it out." Although recognizing that nature had the upper hand, they apparently did not transfer this resignation to such imponderables as illness or death, still maintaining, as it were, a belief in the possibility of control. An environmentalist who sees his place in the world *with* nature by no means denies the importance of acting on it for certain ends.

The Native-Nonnative Typology

The categories discussed above reflect at best broad orientations that have been formed by sociocultural background. Clearly, what is needed is a finer-grained differentiation among individals, whatever the predisposition of their culture. One such approach, stressing perceptual preferences rather than values, is outlined by Sonnenfeld (1964) on the basis of a person's familiarity with a given environment. In general, a person who is native to a region will respond differently to its physical features than one who is not, regardless of the other qualities the native and nonnative may have in common.

In developing this hypothesis Sonnenfeld displayed pairs of photo slides to Eskimos (natives) and nonnatives in arctic Alaska. "Four environmental elements—vegetation, topography, water features, and temperature—[were] systematically varied." [p. 1] The same slides were also shown to a student population in Delaware. Sonnenfeld reports that "populations native to an area—whether in Alaska or Delaware—seemed generally to prefer landscapes similar to their home environments." [p. 2] On the basis of this observation he proposes the native/nonnative typology as a basis for measuring environmental sensitivities.

Sonnenfeld's dichotomy cuts across other demographic variables that affect responsiveness. It was found, for example, that among his Alaska and Delaware subjects there were measurable differences when sex and age were taken into account. Males preferred the more "subsistence-oriented" or rugged environments, females the more richly variegated and warmer places. Younger age groups favored the exotic inversely to their home location; those from flat country chose mountain scenery in preference to prairies, while those from mountainous regions preferred less rugged terrain.

What all this suggests is that any environment has a connotative dimension formed by, yet going beyond, its visual features. The native may be responding to associations triggered by the place where he grew up, or where life has been particularly good. Craik (1968) calls this attachment "latent affectional responsiveness." [p. 15] For native and nonnative alike, they tell us what we can expect of a given milieu. Prolonged experience with an environment tends to blunt perception of its less obvious qualities; perhaps, more accurately, it changes the whole threshold of sensitivity. One is aware of a shifting threshold but is able to incorporate his perceptions into a broader picture of what is happening and to this extent interpret the setting in a new light.

Thus, we are all nonnatives when we travel or take vacations or change jobs. But environmental distinctions are becoming less sensitive in a fluid and homogeneous society. Easy transportation, mass communications, and the countrywide similarity of social customs and design aspects of the built environment minimize regional differences that formerly required major adaptive effort. In a popular vein, Alvin Toffler (1970) explores nonnative mobility as a symptom of rootlessness; identity becomes subordinated to changing acculturations, a continual readaptation to new places, with the result that men become so accustomed to rapid environmental change as to be unable to make the kinds of discriminations which are required. In this sense the native/nonnative distinction is as much a reflection of social forces as it is an attribute of men's personalities, or the degree of their environmental familiarity.

Esthetic Factors

Sonnenfeld was concerned primarily with the visual and sensory dimensions of the environment—the "display," as represented by topography, vegetation, water, climate, and similar physical features, insofar as these were correlated with familiarity or lack of it on the part of the observer. Other investigators have focused on the landscape for its own sake, its capacity to evoke an esthetic response. Litton (1968) developed a scheme for assessing landscape display based on the extent of the view; topographic variations between foreground, middleground, and background; lighting; degree of enclosure; the presence of isolated forms (such as buildings); and surface contours. This is very much the way we view a landscape painting. It also forms the basis for landscape architecture and allows us to develop a predictive model of a "scenic" environment using empirical standards. If we know which elements, in what arrangements, please an observer, we are better able to design open space that is not merely a reflection of the architect's personal taste. There is, however, some indication that "lay" opinion corresponds only roughly with "expert" judgment in such matters, largely because it has been exposed to the appropriate standards in the media, in educational settings, and through contact with designed landscapes (Craik 1968).

Such interaction theoretically overrides other meanings in an environment and, in this sense, is limited to a single mode of response. We may question whether the landscape is ever perceived "plainly," although there can be little doubt that for most of us a visit to the Grand Canyon (natural) or the Luxembourg Gardens (man-made) is primarily an esthetic experience, at least in its initial stages. This does not mean such settings serve no other purpose; rather, esthetic awareness will be judged on its contribution to a total experience. In this respect Shafer and Mietz (1969), studying wilderness hikers in the Northeast, found that although hiking was the objective of the trip, esthetic-emotional values rated highest in the scale of satisfactions.

Role Enactment

Environmental interactions have also been studied in terms of role theory. In what ways do we give intentions to the setting by the role we hope to play in it? Role enactment deals with socially defined behaviors. One performs in a manner that is appropriate to what others expect. Roles may be inherited (as a title, or fortune) or acquired (through acquisition of a skill). Doctors "act" like doctors; but the role changes to "father" at home and perhaps to "deacon" at the Wednesday night prayer service. Children play adult roles in games. Roles are tied to the sanctions and expectations of a particular culture, and they can be assigned to us by certain settings, as Barker (1968) illustrates in his theory of behavior settings. Roles may be assumed—as when nonstudents adopt student dress and life styles or the traveler "goes native" in a foreign country. To many sociologists, role taxonomy provides a more satisfactory explanation of day-to-day behavior than personality theory. Whether we agree or not, it is clear that roles help define one's identity in the larger society.

Applied to the natural environment role theory can be a useful guide to certain recreational behaviors. The wilderness provides a setting for regenerating roles that have been lost—that of the pioneer, for example—or that are unobtainable elsewhere. In getting "back to nature" the camper drops his routine city behaviors in favor of a "play world," with its "specialized set-apart playing field which clearly demarcates it from everyday life." [Burch 1965:605] Much of this behavior can be called symbolic role enactment—housekeeping ("subsistence play"); hunting, fishing, and rock collecting ("symbolic labor"); and water skiing and tree climbing ("expressive play").

> The campers' predilection for constructing elaborate boat docks, shelves, coolers, lean-tos, etc. is a constant source of dismay to forest managers. . . . My suggestion is that such forest "make dos" have an intrinsic value far beyond their utility value and that part of the satisfaction is the sense of independence from the present and continuity with the resourcefulness imagined to have occurred in the past." [p. 611]

In the wilderness "actors freely choose the games they play." Roles are restructured so that the commuter becomes the woodsman and his wife "the sturdy but gentle pioneer mother." [p. 607]

Klausner (1971) projects a psychodynamic meaning into this kind of activity and notes the association between "ego competence" and the manlier outdoor pursuits. It is his view that an active vacation, say a camping trip into the wilderness, enables one to practice certain campcraft skills that give one a sense of achievement not possible in everyday pursuits, especially since the activity is often traceable to the days of the frontier and "ruggedly individualistic people." Unfortunately, very little empirical investigation into this kind of role enactment has been done.

Speculatively, we might note here the "backpacking" role that has been assumed by many young people in the United States. Originally a badge of hitchhiking and foreign travel, backpacking is now widely practiced even in the largest cities. One senses that there is more to this than mere convenience. Along with the vogue for blue jeans (traditional country and Western garb), backpacking quite possibly represents a protest against urban ways in general and the briefcase (as a symbol of city status) in particular—a protest that requires no escape to the wilderness. On the contrary, this aspect of wilderness behavior is made part of the urban scene.

Nature as a Setting for Group Behavior

Klausner (1971) suggests that natural settings serve as stages on which appropriate social dramas are enacted. Groups associated with "gaiety and sexuality may tend to seek out the seaside setting, while those associated with solemnity and labor have more affinity for the forest glen." [p. 148] Nature becomes a stage for certain ceremonial behaviors (in the way, for instance, that young people use the beach at Fort Lauderdale during Easter vacation), but it can also be a context for working through different social problems.

The typical matriarchal suburban family on a camping expedition may be reorganized around the leadership of the father, Klausner (1971) notes, because of "the types of labors and skills necessary for forest survival. . . . The rebirth through camping is characterized by reassertion of patriarchal control." [p. 158] In a less speculative vein, Burch (1965) emphasizes the self-sufficiency that camping encourages among members of the family. To this we can add the "togetherness" that is fostered at the campsite, the chance to "do things" as a group. For many families the call of the wild is really a call to reaffirm kinship.

One conclusion to be drawn from these studies is that recreational use of the environment is usually related to other factors. Status concern is one example. Personality dynamics is another. For some people, a chance to master certain outdoor skills is paramount; for others, the quest for adventure, as in white-water canoeing or mountain climbing, represents an expressive psychological need which is only incidentally recreational. The wilderness in particular provides an opportunity to change roles or, in Klausner's term, it may become the stage for unique kinds of social dramas. Although untamed nature "yields no personal message" [Yi-Fu Tuan, 1972:248], more than most environments it helps us deliver the message we bring with us. This topic will be treated in greater detail in the following section.

The Wilderness and Recreation Behavior

As a symbol of this country's pioneer past, the wilderness is of compelling historical interest. It is the American counterpart to Europe's reverence for ancient cities and monuments to early cultures. Unlike the city, which is loaded with a varied range of practical meanings, the wilderness lets us recapture, however briefly, a way of life that is denied us by civilization. Our national parks and forests have become vast playgrounds, enjoyed as well for their scenic beauty, their awe-inspiring magnificence, and the sense they give us that we are in contact with some force that is infinitely greater than human life—the natural order of things by which man measures his own place on earth.

Perhaps the real significance of the wilderness today, however, is the fact that it represents a model of ecological integrity that contributes to the maintenance of our entire environmental system. For many people the spiritual meanings previously sensed in the presence of awe-inspiring nature are more appropriately seen as ecological insights. The wilderness in particular has become a setting where the clash of values concerning the use of the natural environment is most sharply focused. The artist-conservationist Alan Gussow (1969) sums up this point of view:

> Open space offers an opportunity for confrontation—not the confrontation of a new politics but a direct look into a system of which man is only a part. Open space—natural open space—offers the settings for the discovery that all things affect each other. As we become ecologically aware, we inevitably become more humble, sensing that man is a part of nature, not versus nature, that we are indeed a part of a vast chain. [p. 36]

Growth of Wilderness Use

The role of the national parks in furthering wilderness values is well known. Dating to 1832, when the Arkansas Hot Springs area was set aside as a national reservation, the idea of protecting areas of unusual beauty, of providing arenas for both recreation and exploration, gained widespread acceptance. The Yosemite Valley in California became a state park in 1864 and was federalized in 1890. The two-million acre Yellowstone National Park was so designated by President Grant in 1872. Less spectacular areas, such as the Adirondack State Park (1885) came into existence as watersheds and forest preserves. Bryce Canyon National Park in Utah is notable for its spectacular geological formations. All the parks serve a number of recreational functions from hiking and camping to sightseeing and picture-taking.

The Wilderness Act of 1964 formalized official policy by setting aside 8.9 million acres that are to remain "forever wild"; another 5.4 million acres are in primitive status awaiting possible reclassification. With an approximately equal area accounted for in our national parks and monuments, the National Wilderness Preservation System is expected to include no less than 40 million acres by approximately 1980 (Stanley 1969). Thus, about one out of every fifty acres in the continental United States will be designated for some type of wilderness use.

The significance of this is seen in the expanded opportunities for wilderness recreation, which is growing faster than any other type of outdoor activity. Cole and Wilkins (1971) calculate that 14 million persons 12 years and over, or 10 percent of the population of that age, camped in 1965. It has been estimated (Stanley 1969) that about "2 percent of the American public visited a wilderness area in 1960." [p. 11] More significant is the rate at which such use is increasing. Visits to U.S. National Parks almost doubled between 1960 and 1970. Based on campground occupancy, wilderness use in general increased from 5 percent of the population in 1946 to more than 15 percent in 1967. The Wildland Research Center (Outdoor Recreation Resources Review Commission 1962) believes that this kind of outdoor activity will quadruple in 1976 (over 1959) and that by the year 2000 it will be ten times greater. By all indications, as more land becomes available for wilderness, more people will use it.

Perhaps the question we should ask, however, is not how many visit the parks or camp in the back country, but whether the values that are found in such visits fulfill the stated beliefs of wilderness proponents, whether such visits coincide with the expectations of the user, and whether the environment can really withstand such use. Beyond these issues is the more inclusive one of quality. To what extent can and should wilderness areas remain protective shields against man's manipulation and pollution of the environment? How effective are they as models of ecological integrity? By knowing the reasons that bring men and women into the wilderness, the policy-maker has at least a partial mandate to maintain a system that is responsive to the variety of uses that contribute to wilderness enjoyment, as well as to maintain the quality necessary to wilderness preservation. Thus, it makes a difference whether the campsite is regarded, for instance, as the setting for a social drama and an opportunity to restructure roles, whether it facilitates individual recreational experiences, or whether all these activities are subsumed under a single function.

Demographic Characteristics of Users

Some interesting facts have been gathered about the kinds of people that are drawn to this type of outdoor vacation. For example, as a group they are highly educated. People with at least some college experience are far more likely to visit the wilderness than are persons who have but a high school education or less. This suggests that the wilderness holds a particular appeal for those with a wider range of intellectual experience, but it may also indicate that rural-based noncollege types are more likely to fish and camp in their own "backyards." At the same time, as Marans (1972) noted, hiking—to cite one activity (although it is not confined to the wilderness)—involves little concern with status. It is probably safe to say that most campers are likewise more interested in enjoying the experience for its own sake than in impressing others.

Based on data compiled by Burch and Wenger (1967), Roenigk and Cole (1968), and others, a profile of camper characteristics shows that a disproportionate share of all campers live in the suburbs; that regardless of present location, people brought up in rural areas are more likely to be "real" or "back-country" campers than others; that campers tend to have higher incomes than the general population, although such trips are among the more economical forms of outdoor recreation; that wilderness recreation is primarily a family activity engaged in by the young to middle-aged (thirty to forty-nine); and that overall, most wilderness use is of the "easy access" rather than the "roughing it" type. Surveying seven different areas, the Outdoor Recreation Resources Review Commission (ORRRC) in 1962 concluded that the "typical" wilderness user was a professional person, with high education and above-average income, who lived in an urban area of 100,000 or more population.

Perhaps these characteristics do not add up to the conventional image of an "outdoorsman" who is committed to the strenuous life, is at home in the forest, a master of woodcraft, and a despiser of civilization. Clearly, for most users, wilderness visits are recreational. Nevertheless, they appear to satisfy certain psychological needs and, to some extent, generate their own norms of behavior. What are the differential aspects of the wilderness that make these activities satisfying?

Why People Visit the Wilderness

What people seek in the woods and what they come away with is often at variance; the range of motives is wide and satisfactions are measured against varying environmental conditions and personal notions of wilderness benefits. Moreover, not every camper enjoys the experience. Women often complain of having to do "too much kitchen work." In the forests, a mischievous bear can spoil a trip. Paddling (and portaging) a canoe may turn out to be more than one bargained for. Nevertheless, the information we do have points to certain values that are shared by a majority of wilderness users.

One of the earliest studies on the subject was conducted by Bultena and Taves (1961) through interviews with 428 campers and canoeists in the Boundary Waters Canoe Area between Minnesota and Ontario, Canada. They were able to identify five clearly distinguishable reasons for making a wilderness trip: (1) sport and play; (2) fascination with the wilderness; (3) the wilderness as sanctuary; (4) the wilderness as heritage; and (5) personal gratification. Significantly, campers who emphasized item (1) reported that the trip gave them a chance to change roles—from that of typical spectator into that of participant. Added to this was the feeling of many respondents that "as a result of a wilderness trip they learned to do things better on their own." [p. 169] It is interesting to note, however, that when the campers were asked about their images of the area before making the trip, only one in seven mentioned "sport and play." By contrast, "wilderness" and "fascination" combined was cited by 40 percent.

In interpreting their results, Bultena and Taves found that a conflict existed in the minds of many campers toward the experience. While cherishing the idea of the primitive life, they missed the amenities of the built environment and expressed a desire for more man-made conveniences.

> Some vacationers . . . will still cling to and cherish their earlier conception of wilderness coexistent with a demand for facilities. . . . At one level of cognition, wilderness is seen as fascination, as appealing and desirable, while at another level the wilderness represents something to be feared or conquered. These opposing positions are not consciously reconciled. . . . [1961: 170]

Whatever the conflict, the authors suggest, "It is psychologically rewarding to feel that one has, in a sense, successfully struggled with the elements and faced the dangers of the wilds. A sense of selfhood results from doing things on one's own." [p. 170] The operative word here is *feel*. Whether the camper actually does "struggle" and "face the dangers" is perhaps not as important as the fact that he thinks he has, or has faced a situation where he might have had to. The setting enables him to play a role whose validity is mainly psychological.

A more ambitious and sophisticated study was conducted by Catton et al.

(1969) from 1345 questionnaires filled out by visitors to three wilderness areas in the Pacific Northwest. The purpose of the study was to discover how people brought up in urban versus rural environments differed in their attitudes toward the wilderness. Taking "wildernism" as a classifying variable, the authors graded respondents on the basis of the importance they attached to such features as rugged topography, waterfalls, virgin forests, remoteness from civilization, absence of people, mountain climbing, and the pioneer spirit. Reflecting more urban-oriented attitudes, they tested for the relative unimportance of campsites with plumbing, private cottages, souvenir stands, power boating, and auto touring—and called this urbanism. Using factor analysis, the scores clustered along seven dimensions on which "wildernist" (or wildnerness-purist) attitudes could be distinguished from "urbanist" (or city-oriented) attitudes.

Leading the list of wildernist preferences was "spartanism"—the idea of the wilderness as a setting for "ablebodiedness, fortitude, and dauntlessness." The second strongest item, "anti-artifactualism," represented a rejection of man-made features or human improvements in the wilderness; it was followed by positive feelings of "primevalism" evoked by seeing the environment in its undisturbed state. The factors of "humility," "outdoorsmanship," "aversion to social interaction," and "escapism" were less frequently registered, in that order.

Conflicting somewhat with other findings that people from rural areas are more likely to be "wilderness-type" rather than "easy-access" campers, in the Catton et al. sample, wildernist value-orientations were found to be more prevalent among the city-raised and better educated. Of 409 such respondents, 67 percent were moderate or strong wildernists. Only 6.3 percent were urbanist or neutralist in their value orientations. It should be pointed out, however, that Catton et al. were studying city people who did go into the wilderness. Probably a majority of city campers are "easy-access," but those who are not tend to have more positive feelings about "real wilderness" than do rural people. In any case, the two groups are not wholly distinct in their attitudes toward nature. Hendee et al., (1968) found that campers as a whole tend to be more "preservationist" in this respect than noncampers.

Hendee's group also explored certain norms of wilderness behavior. For example, they found that campers accept constraints which would be rejected under other circumstances. The presence of radios and unnecessary technical intrusions is frowned upon. A cooperative attitude is fostered and campers are expected to contribute to one another's welfare. Campcraft skills are considered a sign of serious commitment to the wilderness. Finally, maintaining campsite quality is expected. "More than 8 out of 10 persons felt that a good rule to follow in the wilderness is to take only pictures and leave only footprints." [p. 43] In brief, the wilderness imposes an informal code of conduct on its users; it is a place where appropriate and inappropriate behaviors are sharply defined.

Lucas (1966) has suggested that the wilderness simplifies behavior.

Because human relationships (other than with our families) are at a minimum, we are free of the social roles imposed on us by our professional and public lives. The environment, too, is "simple," at least in the symbolic sense. The complexity of the urban scene is one of the things we hope to leave behind when we enter the wilderness. Perhaps it is a new and strange setting, and it may be visually complex, but it is not freighted with obscure or ambiguous meanings, and it is relatively free of social demands.

Problems of Defining Wilderness Behavior

Because the measures differ somewhat in the studies we have cited, it is difficult to extract from them comparable definitions of wilderness use. Moreover, the kinds of users being compared will affect the outcome of our research. Testing camper-motivation in 1960, Glock and Selznick (1962) used five response categories: Exit-civilization (escapism); esthetic-religious; health (to restore health); sociability; and the pioneer spirit (survival ability). The first two of these reasons were found to be the strongest. When respondents were classified according to their social backgrounds, however, there were significant variations. Nonchurch members, for instance, found "exit civilization" a more compelling motive for entering the wilderness than church members. Why this should be so is not clear.

An interesting conflict emerges from this ORRRC study when we compare it with the Hendee et al. study, in which escapism was found to be the least important reason for a wilderness visit. (They note, however, that the idea of escapism is included in most of the other categories, and may be overshadowed by them.) Moreover, the "spartanism" that topped Hendee's list of benefits was rated only moderately important (expressed as a measure of physical use of the environment) in the Shafer and Mietz study, accounting for only half the appeal of the esthetic-emotional factor. And although social values were seen as relatively insignificant, "solitude" in itself was infrequently sought. Only one-tenth as many hikers valued it as highly as the emotional experience—the feelings that were engendered through contact with the environment.

Despite these varied (and sometimes contradictory) results, some general conclusions can be drawn from them. Campers, hikers, and boaters can be divided roughly into two types—the strongly committed and those with weak to moderate commitment. For the former, the experience should involve a degree of hardship or "roughing it." In Hendee's study, 71 percent of the respondents agreed that a road into the wilderness takes most of the fun out of walking there. Nearly 60 percent thought that permanent fireplaces were inconsistent with true wilderness. Hikers with packstock travel farther into the woods than people on horseback; canoeists go deeper into an undeveloped lake region than persons using motorboats; and in general, the greater the distance a visitor travels to get to the wilderness, the more deeply he penetrates it. Whether the experience is described as esthetic-emotional or physical-pioneering is perhaps not as important as the commitment to wilderness values it represents on the part of the camper.

This is one way of measuring use, but it by no means tells us all we want to know about wilderness benefits. For a majority of campers, "wilderness" means developed campsites, which are occupied fifteen times as often as the undeveloped sites. Although the weakly committed camper may have less contact with raw nature than the "purist," the experience can be genuinely rewarding in other respects. The degree to which he has been exposed to wilderness environments will also affect his enjoyment. The man who has never seen a forest may find a grove of trees quite wild, just as, for the socially minded poet, "a Jug of Wine, a Loaf of Bread—and Thou/beside me singing in the Wilderness/Oh, Wilderness is Paradise enow!"

Perception of Wilderness

One of the assumptions of the ORRRC study was that the appeal of the wilderness is only slightly altered by the physical characteristics of designated wilderness areas. One area may be "wilder" than the other, or wild in a different way, but the sense of wildness, measured in its variety, magnitude, and "naturalness," is what is experienced.

Our own assumption is that wilderness features are also scaled psychologically; within a given area, perceptions are relative. The more rugged-appearing the topography, the greater likelihood that it will be considered wild. Except for rugged mountains, a stand of trees will yield a higher rating than a stark setting, no matter how "natural." (The Yorkshire Moors, often described as wild, convey little feeling of actual wildness.) Virgin timber will be perceived as wilder than second growth. Man-made features will subtract from the rating, but the physical presence of people will have minimal effect, provided that no man-made objects are present. Remoteness appears to be another factor; the wilderness should be removed from the settled community.

The area, however, need not be perceived as "spectacular." The Kentucky Appalachians offer no less a varied range of scenic and recreational opportunities than the Rockies, although the features themselves, as well as their magnitude, are obviously different. One explores a region in terms of what is there. Displaying a number of locations in Kentucky by means of slides, Calvin et al. (1972) used a Semantic Differential scale to uncover scenic preferences. It is reasonable to predict that their findings apply to any outdoor environment that is wild by the definitions we have indicated. Viewers rated certain landscape features as "colorful, beautiful, natural, and primitive" at one extreme, and "drab, ugly, artificial, and civilized" at the other. These were seen as passive qualities involving "natural scenic beauty" and accounted for approximately sixty-two percent of the total variation among scenes. This is not an unexpected response, since we usually think of a landscape in terms of its visual appeal.

Less predictable was the finding that observers also perceive an underlying dynamic quality in landscape features. This "natural force" factor accounted for an additional twenty-four percent of the variance between scenes, which were judged as either "turbulent, loud, rugged, and complex" or "tranquil, hushed, delicate, and simple." One could carry this line of investigation even further in defining environmental response. Auditory, olfactory, and tactile sensations are seldom taken into account, yet the wilderness experience is a pleasant mixture—often an ephemeral one—of sounds, smells, and touch as well as sight. To what extent does the splash of a waterfall in the distance, the ripple of a brook, the feel of pine needles beneath one's feet, the smell of woodsmoke, and the echo of footsteps contribute to an enjoyment of the wilderness? Little research has been done to relate such nonvisual elements to the total perceptual experience. Yet on a scale of values most of them would be considered important.

A third area deserving attention is that of perceived recreational opportunities. In a study of Adirondack campers, Shafer and Thompson (1968) used the area of land at developed swimming beaches, the area of water at these beaches, the total number of campsites, and the number of islands accessible by outboard motorboat to show how a combination of variables is "related to use intensity of the total environment." [Shafer 1969:76] But as Shafer (1969) notes, this does not explain "the total range of perceptions that may be involved in a camping experience." [p. 76]

In the Adirondack study Shafer and Thompson (1968) were able to extract from forty variables nine factors that "described" campground environments and, presumably, influenced their use. In addition to swimming and boating opportunities, these included the total expanse of the area, the predominance of white birch trees, accessibility of the sites and their picturesqueness, and "tourist magnetism"—the availability of other attractions. Most of these nine factors are not scenic, yet one may speculate that an overall scenic dimension contributes strongly to the enjoyment of all factors. Equally important is environmental variation. An area that contains lakes and mountain trails; meadows as well as forests, waterfalls, and fishing streams will afford extensive opportunities for both perception and use.

The rather extended review of wilderness studies cited above indicates one way of getting at the "wilderness experience." This is basically a survey-analytic approach; as such, it would seem to contravene much of what we have said about man's holistic perception of the large-scale environment. One weakness of this method is that the investigator rather than the wilderness user defines the terms. To the researcher in these studies, "commitment" generally means a desire for a rugged experience. To the camper, however, it may quite possibly imply a desire to keep the wilderness "wild," regardless of one's use of it. "Anti-artifactualism" is certainly not in the vocabulary of the average visitor to a wilderness area, nor does he think of himself as enacting a "social drama." These ex post facto interpretations suggest something about why people go into the wilderness and what they do there, but by no means everything.

The reader might better recall his own "whole" experience on a camping or hiking trip to see what motivated him and which aspects of the experience provided the major satisfactions. In this respect Burch (1964) suggests an observational approach to wilderness use with free-flow interviewing taking the place of questionnaires. Little of this has been done, but it is possible that a quite different picture would emerge. Comparisons can also be made with the more popular accounts of the wilderness by men and women who write about it professionally. Olson's numerous books (see especially *The Singing Wilderness*, 1959) are useful as well as enjoyable because they deal with the Boundary Waters Canoe Area which served so many of the researchers noted above. Olson extols the values of the wilderness in a mood closer to that of the naturalist John Muir than to the analytic approach of the outside investigator. And it is this reaction which the average person often finds difficult to put into words.

Controlling Wilderness Use

Both behavioral definitions of wilderness and standards of environmental quality are often neglected in setting policy. While some factors are largely ecological (the wilderness as watershed, conservation of resources, and so on) the benefits sought by the user will be personal and intimate. The problem for the decision-maker, therefore, is to accommodate the recreationist within the framework of overall wilderness values. Recreation itself can degrade nature—how "wild" does the wildlife remain if every campsite is filled, or powerboats dominate the waterways? To what extent do we add the urban amenities in order to attract more visitors to the campground? How is the optimal use of a wilderness area measured to determine when the gates must be closed? Safety and supervision are involved: In some New York State campsites the visitor is greeted by the warning: "No camping beyond this sign." This hardly makes for a pioneer experience.

Preserving both the appeal and character of the wilderness while accommodating a steadily growing number of users is a major goal of wilderness management. This can be facilitated along two general lines: Additional research is needed on human use of the natural environment; and control mechanisms must be developed that are more responsive than at present toward the delicately balanced relationship of man and his natural environment. One needs to know how assumed wilderness values correlate with actual activity patterns; how the presence of other people affect these values; to what extent users feel that wilderness values can be found in nonwilderness environments. At the present time definitions are too spotty and lacking in detail to model an accurate "fit" between wilderness and the typical wilderness visitor.

A consideration here is that use must be controlled in the interests of ecological objectives as well as human benefit. We might seek to locate the threshold of acceptability of such control—the point at which regulations become self-defeating. How much control will people accept before they turn to other recreation outlets? Research indicates that reaction to specific areas reflects preference for managerial policy as well as the physical quality of an environment. We also know that "real" wilderness campers will submit to some form of regulation both in the interests of ecology and their own commitment. Lucas (1966) makes the point that "We must choose between unplanned, unintentional, man-made changes or conscious control aimed at maximum naturalness and satisfaction." [p. 122] Only by learning what "naturalness" and "satisfaction" mean to people across a broad range of perceptions can a policy be formulated that serves man while protecting nature.

Decision-Making and the Formation of Public Attitudes

The preservation of wilderness areas, urban land use, control of smoke and exhaust emission, solid waste disposal, and water pollution and treatment are areas in which people make decisions influencing the use and quality of their environment. What are the factors involved in this process? How are attitudes formed that lead to decisions? And who makes these decisions?

As part of the democratic process, environmental policy is established through political channels. Occasionally, policy is the result of pressure on the part of the general public; more often, it comes from special interest or advocate groups such as the highway lobby or the Sierra Club; frequently, it is fostered by an appropriate agency, such as the U.S. Army Corps of Engineers or the Environmental Protection Administration, which is charged with implementing the policy it recommends. In an overview of the process White (1966) defines some of the factors that affect implementation at the managerial level:

> There seems no doubt that an individual manager of a sector of the environment takes into account in some fashion the range of possible uses, the character of the environment itself, the technology available to him for using the environment and the expected gains and losses to himself and others from the possible action. His perception and judgment of each point is bound to occur in a framework of habitual behavior and of social guidance exercised through constraints or incentives. [p. 108]

In some instances decisions will be implemented by a single individual—the warden, let us say, of a state park. Policy administration, however, is usually in the hands of a commission. Such a group will be influenced not only by the nature of the environment that is being managed, but, theoretically at least, by the attitudes of those who use the environment. User's goals, however, will not always coincide with official policy. ". . . standards are often established with little knowledge of public acceptability," Sewell (1971a: 120) writes. "This accounts, of course, for the fact that they are frequently ignored or that they result in behavior which was not intended!" From the user's standpoint, the environment will be judged in terms of experienced satisfactions, which the policy goal may or may not facilitate.

The decision-maker, too, is interested in user-preferences, but he also attempts to discover, in White's phrase, "what others *should* prefer." [1966: 109, emphasis added] He is concerned with efficient use of the environment, resource conservation, and, perhaps, maintaining certain historic and symbolic values associated with a particular place. Many of these goals can be defined by empirical standards up to a certain point; clean air is measured by the amount of particulates and gaseous elements present. Others are more subjective and depend upon feedback from the users. The wilderness surveys cited earlier illustrate this point.

The decision situation is the context in which user-preference and managerial expertise is resolved. White sees three factors affecting this process: the individual's experience with the environment; his perception of his role—how much "managing" he is supposed to do; and his confidence in dealing with its complexity. It is not difficult for farmers to organize an irrigation district. The communications network is simple and the individual's direct experience, his role perception, and his confidence are equal to the task. To clean up Lake Erie is not so easy, for it involves conflicts of interests, a more complex remedial technology, an extended communications network, and a lack of agreed criteria as to what constitutes water quality for this particular lake. In addition, both the United States and Canada must come to a joint decision.

At the center of many of these controversies are the attitudes of users of natural resources such as air and water. People like to believe that such resources are renewable and have treated them as though they were "free" in the economic sense. Parallel with this is a general aversion to controls in an affluent society. With resources seemingly limitless, and historically so considered, why restrict their use? It is at this juncture that the decision-maker becomes an arbiter of rights—hopefully, with the consent of his constituents and an understanding of their preferences, but in practice armed with powers of enforcement. A prohibition in 1972 by a U.S. District Court against further mining of minerals in the Boundary Waters Canoe Area, on a suit brought by the Isaak Walton League (*The New York Times*, January 20, 1973) is an example of decision-making at the judicial level.

Decision-making has been discussed above in general terms and from the perspective of the resource manager. Here are some other factors that contribute to the formation of attitudes on the part of the general public.

The Role of the Expert

In technological societies policy formation is largely institutionalized. From the soil conservationist to the land-use planner, from the forester to the hydrologist, control or modification of the environment is based on information supplied by the expert, who may also define the need for action out of his professional concern with particular environmental problems. This is demonstrated, in a broad sense, by the adoption of the Environmental Quality Control Act of 1964. Given the nature of the problem, issues affecting major areas of degradation will be defined and their solutions proposed at the higher levels of government.

Attempts to democratize this expertise vary in effectiveness, but in theory people are "clued in" at the point of impact through such procedures as public hearings. The purpose of such hearings is to reconcile broad public interest with local preferences. A difficulty, White (1966) notes, is the extent to which the specialist understands the needs and behavior of his clients, and the degree to which the client accepts the need for action. Imposed solutions by a public agency create distrust. The hearing itself may be window dressing for a policy already decided upon. A more serious problem, however, inheres in the fragmented nature of most expertise, with the professionals perceiving environmental quality in terms of their own roles rather than as an integrated, overall problem. Water, air, and soil pollution become discrete targets without reference to their ecological interrelatedness.

The Urban Majority

Many environmental programs require large outlays of money which must be raised through direct taxation or the voting of bond issues. In most states city-dwellers provide most of the tax monies even though state legislatures are dominated by rural interests. Thus, as the ecology movement gains momentum, we can expect less "home rule," especially in issues with a regional impact, and more influence by advocate groups growing out of the urban majority.

From the ecologist's perspective this situation is not necessarily bad. Because most city-dwellers have little to lose (and perhaps a great deal to gain) by environmental interventions, their tendency has been to support such causes as cleaner waterways, mineral licensing, and conservation in general (not to mention the urban problems of smog and noise reduction). An Environmental Improvement Bond Issue on the New York State ballot in 1972 carried handsomely in the cities but failed in the rural areas, where concerns are more locally oriented. In tackling the larger issues, the environmentalist has learned to go where the votes are, not where the problem is.

The Articulate Minorities

O'Riordan (1971) notes that "Resource management is essentially a process of pluralistic group bargaining. . . ." [p. 203] Examples are plentiful: the strip-mining controversy; "save the wetlands"; the Alaska pipeline; the automobile versus clean air; the SST. These widely publicized "impacts" have generated conflicts that are not easily resolved. To ban strip mining is to put a premium on the more hazardous pit mining. A shortage of oil means higher prices for the consumer. To the residents of Boron, California, sonic boom is associated with the ring of the cash register. Trade-offs are inherent in decision-making; increasingly, these are being negotiated by organized advocate groups which vie for public support.*

From the environmentalist's point of view, it is important to know the channels through which such support is forthcoming. People active in political, service, and civic organizations comprise a disproportionate share of membership in conservation and ecology groups. The movement is essentially comprised of educated, middle-class, professionally oriented people (McEvoy 1971; Harry et al. 1969; Tognacci et al. 1972). We have noted elsewhere that the ecology movement does not in itself unite people whose economic interests might be affected by environmental change.

In surveying attitudes concerning the future of the Lake Tahoe Basin in California, Costantini and Hanf (1972) found that businessmen (a high-income but relatively low-education group) fell more readily into a "low-environmental–concern" rather than "high-concern" category by 38 to 21 percent. Even though the Tahoe Basin has been subjected to rapid development as a resort area and water pollution is becoming an increasing problem, the businessmen in this study believed that further development would not impair the scenic qualities of the lake. They also claimed that the water could be considered polluted only if it was a health hazard, whereas conservationists argued that the decreasing clarity of the water indicated pollution and lessened the water's attractiveness.

The question of whether businessmen or conservationists are correct is difficult to answer if we confine ourselves to occupational or income categories. We must know whether the objectives of the two groups are radically different or whether they simply disagree about the means to be used to maintain the Basin as an economically viable resource without destroying its scenic qualities. Because of the problems associated with resolving some of these differences, environmentalists have turned increasingly away from local control over resources. Reasons for this were also identified in the Costantini and Hanf (1972) study. They found that "the larger the scope of geographic jurisdiction, the more environmentally concerned the officials are . . . . within the structure of officialdom it is the local official who appears least likely to be strongly concerned. . . ." [p. 227] The California Coastal Zone Conservation Commission, with veto power over almost all coastal development in the state, was voted over the opposition of many local (coastal) groups by a statewide, largely urban majority. Distance not only lends enchantment but, at times, ecological good sense.

* Environmental Action is not [tax] deductible, we're proud to say," reads a brochure issued by one such organization. "We're a two-fisted political action group, not a charity." (1973)

Social Factors in Attitude Formation

Demographic characteristics of individuals comprise one way to identify sources of environmental concern. Along these lines, Morrison et al. (1972) have proposed a theory of "relative deprivation." For a number of reasons, these authors write, those who are least deprived environmentally are more likely to participate in the decision-making process than are those whose expectations are more or less continually blocked. "[W]ithin this country the main participants in the environmental movement are those persons who presently or potentially live in or have access to the better rather than the poorer environments." [p. 272] The professional elite—scientists, government workers, lawyers, doctors, and teachers—perceive the environment in terms of "abstract desire" and on the basis of their generalized knowledge of what is optimally possible. The deprived individual has no such perspective. Only when a blockage of goals is "sudden and unexpected," according to this theory, do affected groups take action.

Perhaps this is a way of saying that ghetto residents have learned to make the best of a bad environment, no matter what their expectations. It should be noted, too, that the environmentally deprived often lack political power, as well as access to the "communications network." But aside from this, not all affected groups are passive in the face of continuous deprivation. Commercial and recreational fishermen, not professors and scientists, have long formed the backbone of the campaign for clean rivers. Others withhold action, not because they are unaware of the problem, but out of necessity. To the steel mill worker, polluted air is the price one pays for a job; his dependence on the milieu screens out alternative solutions which the outsider is freer to advocate.

Another consideration in the formation of attitudes concerns extraneous factors which impinge on specific environmental issues. In short, many issues are not "socially isolated," but are bound up with other values about which people hold strong convictions. Klausner (1971) notes that when this is the case, group interests crystallize around the social rather than the environmental problem. Rather than dividing across economic, educational, or class lines, the issue is seen as the focal point of a larger social disagreement. Thus, fluoridation of drinking water is opposed by certain groups as a "communist conspiracy." Some environmentalists have used the conservation movement to further the idea of public ownership of natural resources. "Open space" in the suburbs becomes a weapon for excluding the poor and the blacks, opening up latent social cleavages formerly papered over. Everyone agrees that atomic radiation is harmful; for ideological reasons, many disagree on the need for nuclear testing. In such instances the environmental problem is often subordinated to the social conflict, and it is on the basis of the latter that the issue is resolved. In a democracy such conflicts are inherent in the decision-making process. The environment, unhappily, does not always come out ahead.

Attitude Formation among Professionals

Most proposed environmental changes are presented to the public as *faits accomplis*, or in the spirit that "the expert knows best." Lack of familiarity with complex problems among laymen, and the esteem in which the engineer and scientist are held, fosters such an approach if it does not always provide a rationale for it. In the overall decision-making context the question that should be asked, therefore, is not simply how public attitudes are formed, but rather how do the professionals arrive at their attitudes?

In an interesting survey of two groups of professionals in British Columbia whose work is closely related to environmental problems—engineers and public health officials—Sewell (1971b) examined data relating to three factors in the decision situation: perception of problems, perception of solutions, and the attitudes toward both the roles of the public and professionals on the one hand, and the influence of possible "outside" factors on these attitudes. Sewell found a considerable difference between engineers and public health officials on social and environmental questions in general, as well as a significant variation among members of each group based on length of service, seniority, rank and mobility, and general orientation to nature along the lines of the Kluckhohn value hypothesis noted earlier. Decisions evolved, not out of a simple application of knowledge to a specific problem, but through the interaction of a number of social and personal attitudes unrelated to the issue. As in many such situations, how the official saw his role, as well as how he perceived the problem, governed the general direction of his thinking.

A few of Sewell's conclusions will illustrate this point. Whereas public health officials cited environmental deterioration as the most important issue facing the province, for engineers the problem ranked low. (Conversely, engineers' concerns—labor unrest, juvenile delinquency, and unemployment—were subsidiary to environmental problems in the eyes of health officials.) The significance of this distinction is interesting: Health people perceive a close relationship between the problems on which they work and the importance of the problems. Engineers, by and large, do not. Because someone is an expert does not necessarily mean that he is a concerned expert.

Although neither group exhibited a "public be damned" attitude, public awareness of the problem or agitation for change was not regarded as an index of the seriousness of a problem. Physically measurable attributes—the turbidity, smell, and bacteria count of water—rather than public complaints were relied on as measures of importance. In general, experts want quantifiable evidence before they take action.

Solution-approaches likewise differed between the two groups. Health officials are inclined to issue warnings and enforce codes; engineers want to build more facilities. However, neither group suggested ". . . radical departures from existing policies or procedures. . . ." Solutions were perceived "in very conventional terms, reflecting standard practices of the profession . . . and an adherence to established government policy. . . ." [Sewell, 1971b:36] In terms of role-perception, a degree of jealousy exists vis-à-vis the outsider. Expertise implies power, and there was little desire to share it with the public at large. Resource management operates largely as a closed system. This characteristic, however, varies with length of service and seniority; among the health officials, it was the younger men who were more open to outside suggestions, most aware of deteriorating conditions, and least confident in the ability of existing arrangements to cure these conditions. The more senior the official, the more pronounced his tendency to view the social problem with which he is dealing in a very narrow range. ". . . it is clear," Sewell (1971b) comments, "that experts are not in favor of institutional change, especially if it means that their own role will be altered." [p. 58] This gives some idea of the difficulty involved in turning to the expert for solutions. Certainly he cannot be dispensed with. Nevertheless, can he be made more responsive? Will he learn to view a technical problem in its social context?

The Role of Public Opinion

Whatever lack of expertise the public may have in environmental matters—and it is often considerable—a common ground of concern exists in this country that has no historical precedent. This has been called environmental awareness. The environmental crisis in ecology is itself largely responsible for this awareness, fueled by advocate groups, educational campaigns, slogans (Earth Day), and government policy. Like "consumerism," "environmentalism" has become fashionable. Citizens' groups spontaneously spring to life around specific local environmental causes, and even the individual crusade gets results.

> A middle-aged Houston housewife has been the driving force in a movement to save a short wilderness river from being turned into a storm sewer. . . . After months of dogged effort, 2,000 letters and nobody knows how many speeches, Armand Bayou will remain a wild river, and the plans for building a subdivision along the river have been dropped. [*The New York Times*, January 3, 1972]

Klausner (1971) points out that the term "ecology," traditionally a value-free description of a biological schema, "has been distended into a slogan. . . . Current usage carries a warning that the system is becoming imbalanced." [p. 169] Whatever their degree of commitment, people increasingly agree that a problem exists and that measures must be adopted to correct it; and even though a majority of them never participate directly in the decision process, their opinion is felt (at the polls, for instance, or in their support of various advocate groups). Even at the local level, where "town meeting" solutions are feasible, the committed group usually carries the ball for a specific issue and the professional consultant proposes solutions. "The final decision is frequently a compromise . . . to achieve what is desirable rather than what is optimal." [O'Riordan 1971:204] This does not imply that the public is ignored, but rather that it is often deemed incompetent to pass judgment on a technical problem. Frequently the result is alienation from the decision process and a rejection of the resultant policy. It is not the working out of solutions for which one turns to the public, but the discovery of the values they hold to which the solution is important. At present, public opinion is most meaningful as a plebiscite by which efforts to deal with our environmental problems are measured.

Summary and Conclusions

Man's relationship to the natural environment can be classified as instrumental, ecological, and symbolic. Instrumental use of the land involves the conversion of resources for practical benefit. It is largely an economic approach. Ecology focuses on natural disasters, conservation of resources, and a concern for environmental quality. Symbolic responses are elicited primarily by the assumed moral and spiritual benefits of an outdoor setting as well as through a number of recreational, esthetic, and psychological behaviors that are largely unobtainable in the built environment.

Two aspects of the natural environment were seen as particularly critical to the man/nature relationship. One, the phenomenon of *natural hazards*, illustrates the problem of distortion experienced by individuals in perceiving and adjusting to extreme geophysical events and the effect of these perceptions in maintaining a safe or stable environment. The emphasis here was on the highly subjective nature of behavior in a setting whose cues are frequently ambiguous. Another environment, the *wilderness,* was studied for its symbolic and recreational importance and its contribution to standards of ecological integrity. These aspects highlight the contemporary clash of different value systems concerning the use and preservation of the natural environment as an irreplaceable resource. In this respect the problem of defining environmental quality was considered in relation to the varied demands made upon our natural resources by individuals and interest groups.

In looking at man's perception and use of the natural environment, attention was given to factors that determine differences in individual response. Several typologies dealing with man's place in nature were reviewed, including the broad concept of submission–subjugation–harmony. More limited approaches are suggested by one's familiarity with an environment ("native/nonnative") and his use of a natural setting for the enactment of individual roles and "social dramas." Individual response to nature also varies along such parameters as esthetic discrimination, status concern, personality factors, and ecological need. The problem of environmental quality was traced, in part, to a Western cultural tradition that places man wholly outside the natural world.

Final attention was given to the decision-making process in using and managing the natural environment. The role of the professional resource manager was discussed in relation to public attitudes and needs. Demographic, social, and behavioral variables were seen as crucial in reconciling human satisfactions with ecological values. An understanding of this process forms the basis for any attempt to forge an environmental ethic.

References

Barker, R. G. *Ecological psychology.* Stanford, Calif.: Stanford University Press, 1968.

Bultena, G. L., & Taves, M. J. Changing wilderness images and forestry policy. *Journal of Forestry,* 1961, *59,* 167–171.

Burch, W. R., Jr. *Observation as a technique for recreation research.* U. S. Department of Agriculture, Forest Service. Portland, Ore.: Pacific Northwest Forest and Range Experiment Station, 1964.

Burch, W. R., Jr. The play world of camping: Research into the social meaning of outdoor recreation. *American Journal of Sociology,* 1965, *70,* 604–612.

Burch, W. R., Jr., & Wenger, W. D. *The social characteristics of participants in three styles of family camping.* U.S. Department of Agriculture, Forest Service Paper PNW-48. Portland, Ore.: Northwest Forest and Range Experiment Station, 1967.

Burton, I. Cultural and personality variables in the perception of natural hazards. Paper presented at the meeting of the American Psychological Association, Miami, Florida, September, 1970.

Burton, I., Kates, R. W., & White, G. F. *The human ecology of extreme geographical events.* Natural Hazard Research Working Paper No. 1. Toronto: Department of Geography, University of Toronto, 1968.

Calvin, J. S., Dearinger, J. A., & Curtin, M. E. An attempt at assessing preferences for natural landscapes. *Environment and Behavior,* 1972, *4,* 447–470.

Catton, W. R., Jr., Hendee, J. C., & Steinburn, T. W. Urbanism and the natural environment. Unpublished manuscript, Institute for Sociological Research, University of Washington, 1969.

Cole, G. L., & Wilkins, B. T. The camper. In W. T. Doolittle & R. E. Getty (Chairmen), *Recreation symposium proceedings.* Syracuse, N.Y.: College of Forestry, State University of New York, 1971.

Costantini, E., & Hanf, K. Environmental concern and Lake Tahoe: A study of elite perceptions, backgrounds and attitudes. *Environment and Behavior,* 1972, *4,* 209–242.

Craik, K. H. Human responsiveness to landscape: An environmental psychological perspective. *Student Publication of the School of Design* (special issue). Raleigh, N.C.: North Carolina State University, 1968.

The Daily Item. Port Chester, N.Y., February 3, 1973, p. 1.

Darling, F. & Milton, J. P. (Eds.) *Future environments of North America.* Garden City, N.Y.: Natural History Press, 1966.

Environmental Action. *Environmental action now.* Washington, D.C.: Environmental Action, 1973.

Glock, C. Y., & Selznick, G. The wilderness vacationist. In Outdoor Recreation Resources Review Commission Study Report No. 3, *Wilderness and recreation: A report on resources, values and problems.* Washington, D.C.: Government Printing Office, 1962.

Golant, S., & Burton, I. *Avoidance response to the risk environment.* Natural Hazard Research Working Paper No. 6. Toronto: Department of Geography, University of Toronto, 1969.

Gussow, A. Where lifestyle counts, who needs nature? *Open Space Action,* 1969, *1,* 34–36.

Harry, J., Gale, R., & Hendee, J. Conservation: An upper-middle class social movement. *Journal of Leisure Research,* 1969, *3,* 246–254.

Hendee, J. C., Catton, W. R., Jr., Marlow, L. D., & Brockman, C. F. *Wilderness users in the Pacific Northwest: Their characteristics, values and management preferences.* U.S. Department of Agriculture, Forest Service Research Paper PNW–61. Portland, Ore.: Pacific Northwest Forest and Range Experiment Station, 1968.

Kates, R. W. *Natural hazards in human ecological perspective: Hypotheses and models.* Natural Hazard Research Working Paper No. 14. Toronto: Department of Geography, University of Toronto, 1968.

Klausner, S. L. *On man in his environment.* San Francisco: Jossey-Bass, 1971.

Kluckhohn, C. Values and value orientations in the theory of action: An exploration in definition and classification. In T. Parsons & E. Shils (Eds.), *Towards a general theory of action.* Cambridge, Mass.: Harvard University Press, 1951.

Kluckhohn, F. R. Dominant and variant value orientations. In C. Kluckhohn, H. A. Murray, & D. M. Schneider (Eds.), *Personality in nature, culture and society.* New York: Knopf, 1959.

Litton, R. B., Jr. Landscape vocabulary and landscape inventories. Unpublished report, Department of Landscape Architecture, University of California, Berkeley, 1968.

Lucas, R. C. The contributions of environmental research to wilderness policy decisions. *Journal of Social Issues,* 1966, *22,* 116–126.

Marans, R. W. Outdoor recreation behaviors in residential environments. In J. F. Wohlwill & D. H. Carson (Eds.), *Environment and the social sciences: Perspectives and applications.* Washington, D.C.: American Psychological Association, 1972.

McEvoy, J., III. *The American public's concern with the environment.* Environmental Quality Series 4. Davis, Calif.: Institute of Governmental Affairs, University of California, 1971.

McHarg, I. L. *Design with nature.* Garden City, N.Y.: Natural History Press, 1969.

Morrison, D. E., Hornback, K. E., & Warner, W. K. The environmental movement: Some preliminary observations and predictions. In W. R. Burch, Jr., N. H. Cheek, Jr., & L. Taylor (Eds.), *Social behavior, natural resources and the environment.* New York: Harper & Row, 1972.

Murray, W. The sound of the future. *The New Yorker,* September 16, 1972, 85–93.

The New York Times. Report on Armand Bayou. January 3, 1972.

The New York Times. Report on suit. January 20, 1973.

Olson, S. F. *The singing wilderness.* New York: Knopf, 1959.

O'Riordan, T. Public opinion and environmental quality. *Environment and Behavior,* 1971, *3,* 191–214.

Outdoor Recreation Resources Review Commission. *Wilderness and recreation: A report on resources, values and problems.* Report No. 3, The Wildland Research Center, University of California. Washington, D.C.: U.S. Government Printing Office, 1962.

Rand, G. Some Copernican views of the city. *Architectural Forum,* 1969, *9,* 77–81.

Roenigk, W. P., & Cole, G. L. A profile of Delaware campers. *Agriculture Experiment Station Bulletin 370,* 1968.

Saarinen, T. F. *Perception of the drought hazard on the Great Plains.* Chicago: Department of Geography, University of Chicago, 1966.

Sewell, W. R. D. Behavioral responses to changing environmental quality. *Environment and Behavior,* 1971, *3,* 119–122. (a)

Sewell, W. R. D. Environmental perceptions and attitudes of engineers and public health officials. *Environment and Behavior,* 1971, *3,* 23–59. (b)

Shafer, E. L., Jr. Perception of natural environments. *Environment and Behavior,* 1969, *1,* 71–82.

Shafer, E. L., Jr., & Mietz, J. Aesthetic and emotional experiences rate high with northeast wilderness hikers. *Environment and Behavior,* 1969, *1,* 186–197.

Shafer, E. L., Jr., & Thompson, R. C. Models that describe use of Adirondack campgrounds. *Forest Science,* 1968, *14,* 383–391.

Sonnenfeld, J. Variable values in space and landscape: An inquiry into the nature of environmental necessity. Unpublished manuscript, University of Delaware, 1964.

Stanley, G. H. Myths of wilderness use and management. Review draft. Missoula, Mont.: Intermountain Forest and Range Experiment Station, 1969.

Toffler, A. *Future Shock.* New York: Random House, 1970.

Tognacci, L. N., Weigel, R. H., Wideen, M. F., & Vernon, D. T. A. Environmental quality: How universal is public concern? *Environment and Behavior,* 1972, *4,* 73–86.

Tuan, Y.-F. Environmental psychology: A review. *Geographical Review,* 1972, *62,* 245–256.

White, G. F. Formation and role of public attitudes. In H. Jarrett (Ed.), *Environmental quality in a growing economy.* Baltimore: Johns Hopkins Press, 1966.

Yorty, S. Quoted in R. Trubo. United Features Syndicate. *The Daily Item,* Port Chester, New York, May 7, 1973, p. 19.

Suggested Readings

Darling, F., & Milton, J. P. (Eds.) *Future environments of North America.* Garden City, N.Y.: Natural History Press, 1966.

Detwyler, R. (Ed.) *Man's impact on the environment.* New York: McGraw-Hill, 1971.

McHarg, I. *Design with nature.* Garden City, N.Y.: Natural History Press, 1969.

Smith, R. (Ed.) *Ecology of man: An ecosystem approach.* New York: Harper & Row, 1972.

Eleven

The Built Environment

The dominant situation of modern life is individuals living in a setting which was not designed for them.
—*Serge Boutourline*

All environments have a physical basis in some sense; even the natural world, to the extent that we control or modify it, is the product of man's ingenuity and inventiveness. Transforming its resources, man also gives them new meanings and uses, new shapes and appearances. This man-made environment undergoes constant alteration as changes occur in human needs and goals, many of which are themselves the result of earlier changes in the built environment. The use of structural steel, for example, made possible the skyscraper and high-rise apartment, both of which have introduced important changes in the living habits of millions of people, producing, in turn, new demands on the environment, for example, the elevator. The cycle is endless.

Most of us are much closer to, and dependent upon, this built world than on the physical world of nature. Our lives are spent in houses, offices, institutions, factories, and the larger arena of communities. Unlike men in earlier times, who built their world with very limited and primitive tools, modern man has the advantage of sophisticated machine technology. The environment is much more under his control.

This final chapter is concerned with how man consciously designs this environment to accommodate a wide range and diversity of human behaviors. Such design or planning involves a number of factors both obvious and subtle. As Fitch (1972) suggests, this new environment is built to man's specifications and with a purpose; it represents, therefore, a " 'third' environment interposed between himself and the world." [p. 9]

But it is also true that the built environment expresses more than the deliberate intentions of the architect or designer. Planners, as do all others who create, express not only the general values and attitudes of their society, but their own unique personalities and their individual tastes and ways of looking at the world. The architect in this sense is in a position to impose his own views of form, structure, and appearance on the settings that other men live in. Indeed, in a sense that is what he is hired to do.

It is important to remember, however, that even in this instance what emerges as "built to specifications" involves far more than what the architect desires, thinks necessary, and believes essential to the best outcome. The "third environment" is the product of many other forces: clients and consumers, economic specialists, legal codes, building contractors, building material manufacturers, and still other groups. Directly or indirectly, any aspect of the built environment passes through many hands before it emerges and represents the interaction and convergence of a number of influences not directly related to design itself.

Finally, whatever the architect does, unintended as well as intended consequences may result. To design with purpose means to create a physical setting with one or several human specifications as primary, while others are considered secondary, or are taken for granted and not considered at all. Designing in this way means that many assumptions are made about what man is like and how he will react to and feel about given environments. It is frequently the case that the stated purposes of a particular setting are not met because these assumptions turn out to be wrong, or because the design itself could not meet the assumptions; it is also true that settings have unintended consequences in eliciting inappropriate behaviors on the part of the user. This is the case when other human needs and tendencies not involved in the design process are found to be incompatible with the setting that emerges from this process. As will be noted later, the design of "open plan" office space leads to an improvement in work flow and efficiency—the purpose of the planning. But in neglecting people's territorial and privacy needs many of these offices are found behaviorally inadequate by those who work in them. In this respect the designer has not reconciled his client's wishes with certain basic requirements of the employee.

Given this general orientation we plan to examine the built environment on four levels: (1) the person in relation to objects and spaces; (2) the small face-to-face group as a basis for social interaction in its relevant physical setting; (3) interactions among individuals and groups in the context of broader social organizations such as schools, offices, and hospitals; and (4) human interactions involving these institutions and social organizations at an urban and regional level.

All of these environments have been touched upon earlier, largely from the theoretical viewpoint of man's perceptual characteristics, the social norms that affect his use of space, his historical attitudes toward the environment, the roles that he enacts in various settings, and such basic needs as privacy, social contact, and individual development. Here we focus on the architectural and design aspects of these settings as they bear on the social and psychological behaviors that have been discussed. It is precisely this complex set of needs, attitudes, experiences, and choices that the built environment, beyond its obvious function of providing shelter, is intended to serve.

We noted that the modern architect and designer has many more tools and a great deal more knowledge at his disposal than did his predecessors. Three observations grow out of this evolutionary change in technics: First, on a behavioral level, the systematic and interdependent characteristics of this technologically advanced environment constitute an ecology of their own—an ecology of structures, things, and processes with which human behavior has become ever more linked for its survival and development. Unlike natural ecology, this system is largely under man's control, although competition for this control, on a global scale, has led to serious problems that threaten man's survival in another sense.

Second, the ecological implications of our built environment have become increasingly intricate and complex, and largely unknown. For primitives, mystery lay outside the immediate environment, primarily in the natural world. For us, mystery lies more in the dynamic processes that constitute, so to speak, the mechanisms of the environment. Strictly speaking, electricity belongs to the built environment although we never see it. This is equally true of many other forms of power. Television scanners and computers are part of the technological process, and so are radar, satellite communications, and laser beams. Many of these processes touch our lives just as effectively as the houses we live in.

The third point is that the built environment does more than attempt to accommodate existing human needs; it can, with various degrees of success, influence and change behavior. No one would argue that the invention of television has not had profound effects on people's living habits, just as the introduction of the automobile did earlier. More explicitly, prison reformers seeking to remove the punitive stigma associated with the old Bastille-like structures, substitute dormitories for cells and comfortable lounges for barren day rooms in an effort to improve prisoner morale and, hopefully, thereby increase the chances of rehabilitation.

On a larger scale, urban renewal projects—the "slum clearance" of an earlier time—attack both physical and social pathologies through a redesign and restructuring of the built environment. Likewise, the New Town movement invites planners to intervene in a wide variety of social behaviors through the construction of completely new cities like Columbia, Maryland, or Reston, Virginia. Utopias of an earlier era, which emphasized the consensual ideals of their members, have been replaced by a new concept that seeks the attainment of heterogeneous individual and social satisfactions through site planning, the location of service and community facilities, and esthetic enhancement. Much of the rationale of the New Towns is that they foster a better community spirit.

The above discussion suggests something of the complex nature of the built environment. In the most apparent sense this environment is *physical*; the architect builds spatial boundaries around people to satisfy basic needs of the human body. But in another sense this environment is *affective*; beauty, orderliness, and comfort are integrated into the final design. It must also be *functional*—suitable to the task for which it is designed. On a *cognitive* level, this environment provides a continuum of meanings, or messages, as to how it shall be used and interpreted. Finally, it has a integrative, or *social*, function; it supplies cues for social behavior, helping to organize and regulate the activities of groups or, in the case of cities, entire populations. This last aspect of the built environment is of special interest to environmental psychology. It is perhaps most easily comprehended in the case of institutions where behaviors are often highly regulated. In such cases the setting becomes instrumental to the regulative process.

A final observation is important: Developing technologies for the built environment supply new alternatives for man's habitat. On the physical side, shelter and comfort have been enhanced by a host of new amenities: air conditioning, soundproofing, automatic temperature control, new types of building materials, built-in entertainment, mobile homes, and so on. Labor-saving devices make possible a more efficient and productive economy and more leisure for the individual. Man expects more from his environment because it has more to give. Now that his physical needs have been better attended to, emphasis shifts to the social and psychological aspects of buildings and communities. The wider choices available to us technologically make possible a degree of environmental manipulation that is without precedent. Because man controls his environment as never before, to what extent, therefore, does it have greater influence on human behavior?

Determinism and Design

To ask the above question requires us to deal with a central problem in environmental theory—the role of environmental determinism. This notion can be traced historically to early studies by zoologists, plant ecologists, and naturalists, who sought to show how changes in the behavior patterns of living organisms were directly influenced by characteristics of the physical settings within which they lived. In these schemes, alterations in environmental factors such as weather, space, accessible nutrients, and soil conditions were shown to be linked in orderly ways to the types of animal and plant populations representative of any ecosystem. For example, if certain species of animals multiplied faster than the capacity of the environment to provide them with food and space, the size of the population was depleted through either death or migration. In either case, equilibrium was reestablished into the ecological system.

The success with which ecologists were able to formulate laws concerning the changes which might be expected in a natural setting led to the notion of environment as significantly influential to the behavior of living organisms. It should not be surprising, therefore, that such environmental determinism should be invoked to explain why human beings too developed certain patterns of behavior. The geographer Huntington (1915), for example, believed that civilizations rose and fell in accordance with climatic variations in space and over periods of time. Human behavior on a global scale was thought to be shaped by ecological forces that set limits on what men could achieve regardless of their goals. Although they were free to make choices, their geographical habitat put a ceiling on their ability to effect these choices. In Huntington's view, the most productive peoples were found in temperate climates, and the ideal climate was found in New Haven, Connecticut, where Huntington taught. He has few supporters today, and determinism by his definition is no longer taken seriously.

Architectural determinism, so-called, is of quite a different order. In its simplest interpretation, it holds that man can manipulate environments to produce specified behaviors. The theoretical background of this approach can be found in behaviorism and, more recently, in the version of behaviorism known as operant conditioning. In essence this theory (discussed in Chapter Three) holds that objects in the physical environment act as positive and negative reinforcers of innate behavioral tendencies. To the degree, therefore, that we avoid aversive stimuli and are attracted to rewarding stimuli, the nature of the stimulus "determines" the nature of the response. It cannot generally be said, however, that this happens automatically. Usually another agent, such as a human being, makes the judgment and then selectively applies a reward or punishment to the behaving organism.

Only in the most limited sense has this theory been applied to environmental design, the most noteworthy examples being certain teaching situations and the behavior-modification experiments carried on in some prisons and mental hospitals. Even in these instances it is the manipulation of small-scale proximal objects in the environment rather than of the environment as a whole that seeks to "condition" the respondent. Designers of institutions, nevertheless, have used the general idea of determinism to create environments which they believe are conducive to the purpose of the institution; for example, the open plan school. In these settings, however, it is not clear that the physical environment alone operates as a reinforcing "stimulus." Rather, the environment may be considered as a "setting event," that is, it sets the conditions for the response to occur. If the "appropriate" response appears, it may or may not be rewarded, for the decision to reward is usually made by a social agent.

Whether they are determinists or not, architects and planners often proceed on the assumption that empirical linkages exist between psychological events and environmental factors. We assume, for instance, that certain colors are "cheerful," others "gloomy." Frank Lloyd Wright would occasionally have people walk through very confining corridors so that when they entered an open space the openness and light would enhance their experience. In subtle ways these aspects of the designed world do, indeed, affect (if they do not necessarily determine) the way people respond. Parsons (1970) cites the effects of aversiveness in settings by describing the design for a chain of high-volume eating places, where seats were made sufficiently uncomfortable that patrons would not linger.

In this transaction the environment is seen as the independent, and man as the dependent, variable. In larger and more complex settings designed for a wide range of human behaviors—the city for example—such cause-and-effect relationships are harder to find, although it is a mistake to assume that complexity itself is the critical factor. Larger and more complex settings often presume variety but, in fact, set limits that are not found in smaller-scale environments. A hospital or an office is a complex institution that offers a restricted range of choices; one's living room offers many.

In highly engineered settings—the submarine and space ship, for instance—a variety of mechanisms not usually found in free-standing environments limit choices even more and to this extent control behavior. Settings such as these, however, did not create themselves. They are instruments of broader forces that made them necessary or desirable. Ultimately, the environment of the built world must be traced to the economic and social roots from which it springs.

The operant view of design has received considerable theoretical attention by Studer (1970), who sees environments as "learning systems arranged to bring about and maintain specified behavioral topographies."

> What operant findings suggest, among other things, is that events which have traditionally been regarded as the *ends* in the design process, e.g., pleasant, exciting, stimulating, comfortable, the participant's likes and dislikes, should be reclassified. They are not ends at all, but valuable *means*, which should be skillfully ordered to direct a more appropriate over-all behavioral texture. They are members of a class of . . . reinforcers. . . .
>
> A central problem in behavioral accommodation, then, is identifying a class of elements in the designed environment which are likely to have reinforcing potential. [p. 116]

A feature of strict deterministic theory is the notion of unidirectional causality: Stimulus (the environment) acts on the subject to produce a given behavior, mood, or attitude. This is intriguing design but poor psychology, since it ignores the feedback role of the participant—the degree to which his own perceptions of, and reactions to, a situation modify the very stimulus he is responding to. Nor does this position account for the goals which the behaving person brings to any environment. For instance, one does not *necessarily* perceive a cheerfully decorated room as cheerful if his own mood is gloomy; indeed, the decor may be seen as totally inappropriate, or at best neutral. Kasmar et al. (1968), studying waiting-room reactions among psychiatric patients in the office of a Los Angeles psychiatrist, found that most patients were unaware of the attractive surroundings designed to put them at ease. They had more pressing things on their minds.

The Problem of Fit

Studer (1970) is concerned with the ways in which the man/environment interface is kept in equilibrium. Human needs continually change, as do environmental stimuli. Design helps to maintain this behavior-contingent physical system in equilibrium through the proper environmental supports. When equilibrium breaks down, for example, it is often possible to reestablish it by "restructuring and/or relineating certain territorial boundaries. . . ." Men can and do adapt to "dissonant" or dysfunctioning environments, but there are limits to these adaptive powers, and adaptation itself may be made at the cost of physical and mental stress or failure to realize defined goals. A well-fitting physical system, therefore, is essential to human functioning on all levels; the important thing is that it should itself be "adaptive" to the behaviors it supports. In this sense the "open" environment is that which permits the maximum realization of intended behaviors on the part of the user—rather than, let us say, the designer or architect.

In this connection in short, behavior should determine environment. Studer (1970) notes that a problem central to all design is the tendency of human needs to change before physical solutions can be realized; we live, to a great extent, in settings designed to meet the problems of earlier generations. "The design community's mission is not to realize 'timeless' artifacts, or even 'optimal' solutions to man's needs. The real challenge is realization of the technical and conceptual means to maintain equilibrium between behavioral goals and the supporting environment on a *continuing* basis." [p. 120] It is the continually shifting and changing nature of behavior that Studer sees as the challenge to environmental design.

A more socially oriented approach to the problem of determinism is found in the ecological psychology of Barker (1968) and his colleague Gump (1971), both of whom recognize the input of the individual into the environmental situation. The setting is characterized by what Gump has termed the "standing patterns of behavior" that occur in it. The nonhuman context of a setting does not determine the activities that go on within it; it can, however, provide a good or bad environmental "fit." Gump terms this relationship between behavior and milieu "synomorphic," which means similarity of shape. A person sitting in a chair fits the shape he is interacting with; a man pushing a lawnmower must bend to the height of the mower. The available range of postures in bed ("lying behavior") will depend upon the width and length of the bed. As with clothing, environmental "fits" can be good or bad. Much of the work of the design professions is concerned with just such anthropometric relationships between person and object, a topic that will be examined more fully later in the chapter.

Gump (1971) points out that in larger environmental settings, although the designer influences the inhabitants through the effects of his milieu on the standing patterns of behavior, such influence is not direct. He does not, in effect, design a room and say, "This is what is going to happen in it." Rather, the behavior is mediated through the ongoing activities that occur within the setting and it is these, not the physical environment as such, that become the independent variable. "The milieu makes possible or impossible—efficient or inefficient—certain standing patterns of behavior." [p. 50] These patterns are not random or probabilistic, but highly predictable for concrete settings. Thus, a schoolroom "determines" a certain kind of class behavior, but only to the extent that the teacher decrees or allows it. The room may, however, have a "demand quality" suggesting that certain kinds of activities are more appropriate than others. The laboratory and music room are obvious examples.

In specialized or highly controlled settings design is bound to play an influential role, to the extent that the participants subject themselves to the physical nature of the setting; for example, the assembly line that compels regulated actions at specific times. The environment is indeed a "system," although it should be noted that one's submission to it is really a submission to management directives, of which the setting is an instrument. This is much less the case with housing projects, neighborhoods, and communities. In these instances, settings do not determine, but rather are said to be "congruent with" the kinds of people who inhabit them. Michelson (1970) has termed this an "intersystems congruence" approach. Retirement communities, for example, are "congruent" to their inhabitants because the arrangement of facilities and services available to them promote the kind of social relationships and physical supports that people in such communities want. "Thus, the model I suggest is not of determinism or the dominance of one system over another, but rather one of *congruence*—of states of variables in one system coexisting better with states of variables in another system than with other alternative states." [p. 26]

Too often, planners and designers mistakenly adopt a deterministic position. They assume that the physical environment will be sufficiently powerful by itself to overcome the social and cultural characteristics of the users of these environments. However, it cannot be denied that the physical attributes of large-scale environments can indeed modify social behavior over the longer term. Experience with urban renewal and the construction of major highways through central cities has indicated that these activities do fracture and fragment delicate social networks (Gans 1962; Fellman and Brandt 1970, 1971; Wilson 1967). Evidence gathered in England shows that the pub culture of working-class residents of London who were relocated in new housing estates outside the city underwent marked changes, in part because the environmental choices available to them were drastically different from those available in the city (Young and Willmott 1957).

But the effects of such physical changes must be interpreted in the light of the sociocultural characteristics of the users of various environments. Culture stands as a screen through which various environmental experiences are known. Nowhere is this more clearly shown than in the effects which the suburban environment is supposed to have in changing people's behavior. Critics of the suburbs have referred to their cancerous spread over the landscape, the hopeless repetition of housing designs, the deadening uniformity of the landscaping, and so on. Yet evidence developed by Berger (1960) challenges the notion that suburban housing by itself will transform a non-middle-class person into a homogenized middle-class suburbanite. In his study of the working class residents of a San Francisco suburb, Berger found that even with obvious improvements in economic status this group retained life-style practices which were quite similar to those they had experienced prior to moving. Membership in formal organizations was rare and there was very little semiformal visiting between couples. In contrast to the middle- and upper-middle-class residents of Crestwood Heights (Seeley et al. 1956) the working-class residents described by Berger expressed little anxiety about improvements in status position and almost no effort was made to become middle-class.

At this point two further considerations will clarify our general discussion: (1) In evaluating the "success" of a structure, the architect/planner and the user/inhabitant are frequently in conflict; at least their evaluations of the setting are subject to considerable discrepancy. The architect approaches his task objectively (as a technical or esthetic problem); the user evaluates subjectively (the building as experienced). (2) Even when the planner has a clear notion of what is desirable for a setting, he is often insufficiently aware of the limitations of the built environment to modify long-standing patterns of behavior or accommodate a variety of behaviors.

Planners and Users

By training, the architect is primarily concerned with the technical and esthetic considerations of structures. Are the mechanical requirements dealt with efficiently and economically? Has the best use been made of the site? Is the layout "functional"? Has the maximum space been achieved at the lowest practical cost? Does the building fit with its context? These standards are essentially directed at satisfying physical and economic requirements and, to a lesser extent, the esthetic taste of the user. The designer, in brief, is limited to what he knows, and this knowledge seldom encompasses cultural aspects of use that are based, for example, on privacy needs, territoriality, interaction distances, habit, and custom. In Zeisel's (1971) term the *manifest* use of space must be distinguished from its *latent* meaning—the significance it holds for the occupants apart from its practical function. Failure to account for the sociocultural requirements of the users of environments accounts for many of the problems which people experience in using buildings.

Zeisel suggests that among Puerto Rican wives in New York the kitchen has become a status symbol, as a new car is to the men. Both represent to the outsider that these family members do their jobs well. Equally important, perhaps, is the social function of the kitchen. Such a room, with all its glistening appurtenances, is often designed as though it were for robots. Yet we know that it is also a center for many family activities, including the children's homework and the making of model airplanes. Yet how many kitchens are designed beyond the manifest function of preparing food?

An interesting example of the relationship of life style to house design is reported by Patri (1971). Hired to plan a government-sponsored housing project on Guam, he found that the natives of the town in which the project was to be built lived, for the most part, in one-room houses. In the customary sense, they had no real privacy. Yet when the new dwellings were expanded and given additional rooms many families continued to live in the main, or "big," room, leaving the others unused. As a result, the project was completed as a series of "shell" or one-big-room houses (with the exception of a bathroom). The original effort is a clear example of the failure of a different, "Westernized" design to change behavior.

Rapoport (1969) describes the house as "not just a structure [but] an institution . . . created for a complex set of purposes. Because building a house is a cultural phenomenon, its form and organization are greatly influenced by the cultural milieu to which it belongs. . . . If provision of shelter is the passive function of the house, then its positive purpose is the creation of an environment best suited to the way of life of a people—in other words, a social unit of space." [p. 46] Available building materials, technical skills, and climatic conditions are important components of the design process, but sociocultural needs determine how they will be handled.

Differences between the designers and users of space are not just accidental. There is evidence that architects perceive the physical world in ways quite different from the general public (Canter 1961, 1969; Hershberger 1968; Payne 1969). Canter (1969), surveying preferences among architectural versus nonarchitectural students, found that whereas the *friendliness*, *coherence*, and *character* of a structure were important to the architect, only the first two of these factors were so considered by the nonarchitects. In a similar survey of exterior housing quality, Peterson et al (1969) reported that sound physical quality and harmony with nature were significant factors affecting housing preference, whereas variety and richness—that is, the "design" or esthetic qualities treasured by architects—rated third in importance.

The issue of designer-user differences is a complex one which cannot be wholly resolved by narrow, somewhat problematical research. We should remind ourselves, too, that not more than 5 percent of all structures in the United States are custom-designed. The user may be his own architect, or he may simply buy standard plans and attempt to adapt them to his requirements. And for others, the architect/planner may have at best a limited awareness of his client's real needs, in part because the client himself may be unaware of them, or is unable to communicate his needs to the architect. The satisfaction of these needs must ultimately be tested through use. The experience of users is, nevertheless, often unknown to the designer. Once completed, buildings are seldom reviewed by those who planned them.

Even when individual and social needs are fully understood, the question arises as to the inherent capacity of design to realize them. Everyday, large-scale environments are generally too complex to permit an easy congruence, let alone "determine" behavior in any unilateral sense. The complexity of behaviors implicated in such environments becomes clear only when a dramatic change is introduced, as in the case of urban renewal or when the individual migrates to a new environment. Then the real effects of the man-made world are most easily discerned.

We find many examples of urbanized settings that have been rejected by their occupants because of the planners' ignorance of human nature, especially on the subcultural level. Turner (1972) notes that the reluctance of many low-income families to exchange poor housing for space in high-rise buildings results from both the financial and personal efforts they have made in improving their own dwelling. The house, however humble, has an existential meaning for them which the high-rise building lacks. Of course, not all instances of large-scale urban change result in disaster. Wilner et al. (1962) have noted cases where change has led to positive effects for low-income residents. Still, these instances are too rare to assume that the designers of the built environment are usually sensitive to the wide range of needs which characterize this group.

The Person and the Built Environment

Up to this point we have dealt with two concepts, environmental determinism and "fit." The latter describes the congruence between the individual or group and the setting, be it the chair one sits in or the house occupied by a family. The former presumes an identifiable cause-and-effect relationship between the physical setting and what takes place within it. We have seen the difficulty of establishing such a relationship when many variables are involved. A more demonstrable explanation of the apparent determinism observed in some situations is this: When we observe behavioral changes which seem to be caused by some environment this change is the result of an interaction between prior behavioral needs and values and the setting's capacity to meet those needs. The environment does not determine the types of behaviors which occur, it only operates in conjunction or disjunction with the values and needs which people are trying to realize in that environment.

But is this also true in one-on-one relationships, where the person as a physical object responds to immediate environmental contacts? Does not the tight shoe make us limp, the hard chair cause us to squirm? Designers are at home in this world of biotechnical environments because it is seemingly easier to achieve a good "fit" between, let us say, a person and a suit of clothes than between the person and a room or building. The overt, physiological processes and skeletomuscular attributes of people are susceptible to exact measurement and therefore capable of being fitted—if not necessarily determined—in very precise ways.

The general term for this phase of design is *anthropometrics*. As a technique, it seeks to establish objective anatomical measurements for different populations as well as subjective responses to specific environmental characteristics such as temperature, sound, and illumination. The data compiled from these measurements form the basis on which clothing, equipment, furniture, and spaces are designed to fit the human body. In the form of building codes and architectural handbooks these data assume the status of standards or norms. The seat of the average chair, for instance, is 1½ feet off the floor; most doors are 6½ feet high. In practice, anthropometric standards are based on statistical averages, which is why very tall men must stoop to go through doors and why the elderly and handicapped find much of their physical environment inadequate. The familiar remark that greeted army recruits prior to World War II—that military uniforms came in two sizes: too big and too small—was not an unjustified observation, as many veterans of older wars can testify.

Anthropometric standards are applied to specific environments. In the industrial and office setting they are covered by the term "ergonomics" and imply that the measurements are used with respect to certain work tasks. How well does the employee "fit" with the machine he is operating or the desk at which he sits? Are light, temperature, and sound levels optimal for the task at hand? Is the equipment safe? Standards for the home, generally speaking, differ considerably from work environments because of the element of personal choice; efficiency of operation is not necessarily the only criterion by which people judge their relationship to the living room or kitchen. In addition, requirements for the house are not only more varied than those of the typical work setting—less defined by a single task—but they reflect a wider array of social roles. There must be more possibilities for the occupant. Public settings show even greater variation in standards; it is up to the user to accommodate himself to what exists. "Poor lighting" is often considered desirable in cocktail lounges. For business reasons, many theaters provide insufficient leg room between rows of seats. On the other hand, good acoustics are essential for the concert hall and anything below a certain standard will not be tolerated.

If physical factors alone were involved in this relationship between man and his proximate environment there would be little reason to discuss them here. In fact, fit can also be experienced psychologically and socially. Wheeler (1967) has written:

> There are clearly healthy and unhealthy buildings in the medical sense, in the psychological sense and in the sociological sense. Our ability to adapt

> is probably why bad elements of architecture are so widely tolerated. After a while they cease to be noticed by those who are continuously exposed to them. This does not mean, however, that adaptation is without cost to humans. It requires energy to move to a new level of adaptation and it requires energy to stay there. Environmental factors that do not conform to some modal value on each of the perceptual dimensions are "expensive" to live with; we pay for "tuning them out" by using more energy or by being less effective in our work or play. [p. 4]

On the physical level there must be some general congruence between the object and the user. The glove must have five fingers or, if it is a mitten, space for the thumb. A man's shirt sleeves should not hang down over his hands. Eyeglasses must fit the wearer and, even more importantly, their lenses should accurately correct for visual defects. In all such relationships, Rapoport and Watson (1972) note, certain limits and ranges are set by man's physiological and anatomical characteristics; the variables, which may imply only a relative fit, are "culturally defined choices." Where criticality is low —that is, when we can get along without an exact fit—choice assumes a more important role. A good example of such criticality is furnished by the prosthetic devices used by the disabled. The object must conform closely to the user's disability or it will not function well.

Even where design standards are regarded as "hard" and quantifiable, they may simply reflect the cultural characteristics of the population at the time they were drawn up. This design lag becomes evident as attitudes and physical dimensions change. Contini (1965) has remarked that much contemporary design is for the population of fifty or seventy-five years ago when people were three inches shorter, on the average, than they are today. In many respects we are living in a physical environment planned for past generations who had quite different requirements. As Kennedy and Highlands (1964) sum up, ". . . rebuilding or remodeling proceeds at a slower pace than the changes which humans make in their use of buildings . . . inhabitants . . . become partially trapped by forms which were designed and constructed to care for the needs of previous generations." [p. 1] Equally important, as Rapoport (1969) notes, is the tendency of immigrants to the United States to use the architecture they brought with them even though it is often unsuitable for the region in which they have chosen to live.

Only in recent years has an interest in anthropometrics been widely extended from military and work environments to the house. Kira's (1967) *The Bathroom,* for instance, studies physical-facility standards for elimination and personal hygiene on the basis of anatomical as well as attitude differences between men and women. Kira sees the bathroom as a compromise that does not work very well for either party; from the designer's viewpoint, however, the significance of the study is in showing that the commonplace environment of a single room can be subjected to a detailed analysis of social and physiological behaviors that leads, in turn, to design recommendations. Parsons (1972) has performed a similar feat for the bedroom.

Sex differences frequently account for the physical standards that apply to many household activity patterns, especially those that take place in the kitchen. Roland (1965) notes that the average house is a recreation area, hospital, scullery, library, theater, school, laundry, sewage-disposal plant, garage, and so on, all of which must be fitted to occupants who differ not only by sex, but by numbers, age, and size.

Except in cases of very high criticality, few physical standards are absolute. For example, illumination and temperature are areas of considerable variability. Recommended daylight standards for English classrooms were changed five times between 1863 and 1951 (Rapoport and Watson 1972). Similar modifications occurred in the United States as lighting research was intensified and new techniques were developed in the use of plate glass. However, in recent years the tendency has been to revert to less glazing, in both office buildings and schools, to prevent overheating in the summer. This has coincided with the improvement in artificial lighting. Here, too, standards have risen consistently throughout the present century but to some extent these are also indicative of the power of persuasion (the advertiser and manufacturer), vogues (fluorescent lighting), and consumer buying power. Temperature preferences, too, reflect notable differences among cultures. In Great Britain the comfort zone has been established at around 63° F.; in the United States the range—often legally set for apartment houses and commercial buildings—is 70–72°. One result of this is that Americans tend to dress more lightly in winter.

It is doubtful if these differences can be traced entirely to physical factors. In both countries living standards and social expectations play a role in defining the comfort zone. The energy crisis of 1973–1974 in the United States, with a consequent reduction of power in many parts of the country, showed the degree to which many offices and homes were heated and illuminated beyond actual need—and our ability to redefine "comfort."

This psychosocial use of the environment is continually at work in determining physical standards. For a good part of the relationship of person to object is rooted, not in biological necessity or even comfort, but rather in our preconscious cultural processes, the established norms of behavior that we take for granted. Such norms dictate that in their homes most Japanese sit and sleep on the floor, whereas Western people sit in chairs and sleep in beds. Irish bathtubs are traditionally much shorter than American tubs; the bather is not accustomed to stretching out. Rapoport and Watson (1972), citing comparative studies of anthropometric standards in Great Britain, India, West Germany, and the United States, note that the variations among the four countries is only partly the result of physical differences in the populations. Spatial norms and not volumetric reasons apparently account for the fact that Indians, facing one another across a dining table, sit eight inches closer than do Americans. In this country the dining table that separates husband and wife by the length of eight feet is not as functional (unless one has servants) as the breakfast nook. It is, however, socially emblematic. This can also be said of certain kinds of contemporary furniture in which style predominates over comfort. Couches, for example, are often so wide that one cannot sit straight and to lean back is awkward. Stairways may tell us more about the homeowner's wealth than the ease with which they can be climbed. "In the various designers' guides to staircase design the suggested proportions change depending upon whether stairs are interior or exterior, domestic or 'grand,' which suggests that the limits set are not *physical* but *contextual.*" [p. 41]

On a social plane intracultural factors are seen in the influence of fashion design on clothing. Few would disagree that comfort and good fit frequently play a secondary role in our choice of a suit or dress; style, dictated temporarily by the arbiters of the fashion industry, becomes the determining factor. High-heeled shoes, precarious to walk on, are an especially good example of an "unnatural" adaptation of the human body to a social fit at the expense of the physical. Such factors are also at work in establishing levels of accessibility to natural light. A good deal will depend upon how much the homeowner prizes (and has access to) an outside view. Hopkinson, Petherbridge, and Longmore write: "If the current fashion is for 'picture windows' and for a seeking after outdoor life, the standard of daylight considered necessary for amenity will be far higher than in a society which considers the outdoor elements to be cruel and inimical to human well-being." [see Rapoport & Watson 1972: 49] To this we can add that in many communities picture windows, although theoretically permitting higher daylight levels, are seldom used for this purpose. To effect privacy, the blinds are frequently drawn and the window itself is simply there to impress the neighbors.

To sum up: our purpose in this section has been to look at a few of the social and psychological determinants underlying what have come to be accepted as physical standards. Among these are custom, fashion, cultural preferences, status, taste, and individual behavior attributes based on age, sex, and personality. Seen in this way, the interface is not a discretely measurable guide for establishing "hard" standards, but a flexible concept that is also meaningful in terms of psychological experience. Thus, beneath a certain critical threshold, adequate lighting may be perceived on the basis of several variables that have little or nothing to do with good visibility. The use of certain types of furniture (modern versus traditional, for instance) is likely to reflect cultural attitudes and life style. The "fit" is psychosocial.

Problems in Using the Built Environment

Up to this point we have discussed the design of environmental settings in terms of the "average" or "normal" person; very little has been said about the human variables, either physical or psychological, that go into the experience from the individual user's point of view. Nor have we dealt with the design implications of larger settings, such as housing environments and institutions where spatial relationships as well as proximate objects contribute to an appropriate fit. It will be helpful here to discuss some of the problems found in the use of settings that are covered later in the chapter. We might begin this section by questioning the adequacy of environmental supports for playing out certain roles and for various interactions. Nowhere is this as clear as in the experience of children, the elderly, and the handicapped. All have been environmentally disfranchised to some extent, for most settings presume that users will possess full size, complete strength, some "average" speed of locomotion, full perceptual powers, and the proper status to use these powers. In fact, few people measure up completely to the demands of their environment; the colorblind or nearsighted no less than the toddler and the disabled will be found wanting in some situations.

Very few settings provide either alternative uses or additional supports for those who require them. Whether it is the bus step too steep for the young child or the elderly, the door height too low for the six-foot-seven-inch basketball player, the bathroom impossible for the person in a wheelchair—all make it difficult for the person to move smoothly and without self-consciousness through the various situations and relationships of a day. These limitations undercut the role one is playing, diminish a sense of competence, and put the individual "in his place," so to speak. We recall the comment of a sensitive architect after he had completed a psychiatric facility for children. Only after having his own children go through the building, prior to its official opening, did he discover some serious flaws. When his five-year-old had difficulty operating the doors, he recognized that they were beyond a child's capacities. (This facility had many doors, as most institutions do.)

Our review of proximity studies has shown the importance of design in promoting social interaction. To this we should add the settings that administratively or symbolically encourage interaction while failing to provide the proper facilities and spaces. A high-rise urban school is an example. With its premium on space, social areas are often eliminated, preventing the casual encounters that contribute to the student's intellectual and social development. Few houses provide the old-fashioned kitchen-meeting-eating-fighting-playing-talking space. The showplace living room may not be an adequate substitute. The architect's conception of a psychological center, the ubiquitous family room, does not quite make it either, perhaps because it seldom serves a consistent and regular function such as food preparation and eating. Also, it tends to be relegated to the basement or a remote portion of the house. For the apartment dweller, and even more for the occupant of a low-cost project, this is an irrelevant issue. They have neither the old-fashioned kitchen nor the family room—nor a stoop for informal neighboring, something that has been linked to much of the dissatisfaction and disorder in public projects.

Another potential problem area concerns the conflict between what is intended by the interaction and what the setting permits. Two separate issues are important here, that of the lack of fit between an interaction and the setting and the question of territorial conflicts. The first of these raises the question of the ways in which social interaction is modified either by settings that no longer work or by changes in the motives and intentions of their occupants. As was noted, we are all living in the relics of the past. This may or may not be important to what we are doing at the moment, but it is difficult to imagine that it cannot have some long-range and subtle effect on behavior. The old-fashioned office with separate rooms may elicit some good feelings, a sense of having an identifiable space in which one belongs, but it may not support communication and shared responsibilities where these are desired. The traditional classroom cluttered with desks and chairs may give each student his own place, but it also may make group projects and individualized teaching difficult, if not impossible.

To some degree the success of these relics depends on how well the occupants understand their own goals, and either manipulate or change the environment to meet them or perhaps reconsider and change the goals. If the teacher, for example, feels defeated by a traditional classroom, if she does not try to work with it and get her children to work with it, then the setting can be an excuse for failure. Too often people fail to see their environment as part of an ongoing activity or relationship and fail to make use of available options, for even the most archaic building has some freedom within it if the person can assume that freedom. People who move into old Victorian brownstones or Revolutionary War farmhouses usually do so with a conception of the potential of their built environment, and even more, an enthusiasm to make these relics appropriate to their own life styles.

Social conflicts in particular settings raise the issues of crowding, territoriality, and privacy. These will be noted in some detail as they apply to office environments, but they are equally relevant to the home, the school, and the neighborhood. People have a need to acquire, personalize, and identify with spaces. Sometimes the setting respects this need and role requirements support it as well. But in some situations and for some persons there is inevitable conflict. A crowded apartment may make it impossible for individual members to find their places; equally undermining are those situations where space is available but where the possibility of retaining it is thwarted by the social reality. One can imagine families whose members have little respect for the spaces, privacy, and possessions of others, where one is not permitted habitually to use an area. The large institution is perhaps a dramatic example of this lack of privacy and territorial space, but it is incorrect to assume that this is true only in large-scale settings. They are likely to be more devastating in the home or neighborhood where one expects a sense of belonging. How can we design to reduce this possibility and, conversely, how can people be sensitized to see these needs operating in their relationships with others?

Design and Social Effect: The Small Group

The theoretical basis for what is loosely called "social design" has been covered in Chapter Six. This approach assumes that it is not sufficient merely to provide sturdy, well-lighted, and perhaps esthetically pleasing structures, but it is necessary to provide as well for desirable levels of privacy and social intercourse, for ease of communication and movement, and for the addition of symbolic references. At the same time, the designer avoids the procrustean approach of cramping the users of a building into a rigid relationship to it; the setting should be congruent with the behaviors enacted in it but need not attempt to regulate them. In Zeisel's (1971) phrase, it "should interfere as little as possible with the way people live . . ." and possess a "physical form compatible with prevalent social patterns." [p. 29]

Given a "prevalent social pattern," or norm, what then are some of the design-influenced effects on the users of specific settings? On the most obvious level, as was noted in the previous section, the design of a structure affects (1) physiological processes. This is clearly an area in which the architect has wide latitude. On a psychological level design may also influence (2) overt individual behavior and (3) overt social activity. Poorly organized space, for example, can be stressful to work in, alienating the individual from his setting and lowering efficiency. In the social sense the arrangement of space can either facilitate cooperative attitudes or cause friction among those using it. Finally, design affects (4) responses which cannot be easily verbalized. Wall colors and similar esthetic considerations constitute independent variables which, unlike the size or shape of a room, are not themselves acted upon by the user; yet in the satisfaction or annoyance evoked they are very much a function of the design process. Visual stimulation, size perception, and mood are affected by color, for instance. One "knows" when he is in pleasant or ugly surroundings. This esthetic response may also affect his judgment of others (Maslow & Mintz 1956).

All buildings imply at least some form of social activity stemming from both their intended function and the random encounters they may generate. The arrangement of partitions, rooms, doors, windows, and hallways serves to encourage or hinder communication and, to this extent, affect social interaction. This can occur at any number of levels and the designer is clearly in control to the degree that he plans the contact points and lanes of access where people come together. He might also, although with perhaps less assurance, decide on the desirability of such contact.

An example of the negative effects of design on social interaction is furnished by Miller in his description of new residence halls at Indiana State University, Terre Haute (see Wheeler 1967). To cut down on noise from the hallway, a divider containing mechanical equipment and service components was installed where a center corridor would otherwise run. "This solution, however, produced a new problem of behavioral or sociological nature: friendship formation was severely curtailed in the new arrangement." [p. 12] In a more recent set of halls designed by Miller both the noise and the interaction factors were provided for by placing the service equipment in a square core surrounded by a student lounge which in turn was ringed by a corridor that gave access to the rooms. The floor traffic that had formerly made the hallway noisy was substantially reduced since students traversed much less corridor space in entering and leaving the building.

Design which is counterproductive (such as Miller's original plans) may produce an effect that is beneficial in other ways. Taylor (quoted by Parsons 1970) concerning the open classroom, notes that

> . . . there is less noise for many reasons, one of which is the lack of reverberating walls. Surprisingly, it usually becomes more difficult to hear [class discussions], consequently an unexpected reward occurs. Teachers and their students tend to be drawn closer together, physically and psychologically. The class often becomes more informal, with students sitting on the carpets rather than on chairs. [1970: p. 2]

We might question the effect of this arrangement when informality is not sought; and Parsons asks whether it was perhaps the lack of walls—the feeling of being overwhelmed by too much space—rather than the difficulty in hearing that brought people closer together. If intimacy is seen as desirable, this open classroom paradoxically encouraged it.

The problem of size and layout frequently turns up in the design of office space. Because this has been a heavily researched area—more so, for instance, than the house—much of what we know empirically about the relation of space and group activity is drawn from office settings. Clearly, this is a special environment. The occupants are united in a common effort, spending as much as seven or eight hours a day in forced propinquity. Under what circumstances does this lead to interoffice intrigue, friendship formation, alliances, and a "group spirit"?

Wells (1972), investigating the layout of an insurance office in Manchester, England, found that the "small office arrangement produces the best possibility for the formation of a group with clear identity and concepts of itself as a discrete and simple entity. On the other hand, the open plan office allows for more *possibilities* of interpersonal contact and group formation." [p. 103] Noting that preferences in both kinds of space were dictated primarily by the sex and age of the workers, Wells concluded that spatial variables did, however, play a significant role.

People in open plan offices had more contact with others in the overall area but also exhibited more diffuse relationships. Workers in the smaller areas made more friends within their own section and, to a lesser extent, their own department; there was also a much greater degree of internal cohesion. Interestingly, however, the small office accounted for a greater number of isolates. Since pressure to share in the group spirit was more pronounced than in the large areas, workers were faced with the alternative of joining in or withdrawing. In both types of space, Wells points out, the "number of sociopreferential choices decreases steadily with distance." [p. 112] In brief, spatial arrangements, to the extent that they bring people together, and in their manner of doing so, underlie much of the social life of the office.

The degree to which social life may be desirable, however, is another question. Functionally, insofar as the work task is concerned, too many opportunities for contact could interfere with efficiency, but just as conceivably an improved morale might make the employee more responsive to his task, particularly in routine situations where social contact is an antidote to boredom. In any case, such matters are frequently handled by administrative control, with regimentation of space—the long rows of cheek-by-jowl desks—precluding either privacy or sociability. This is the typical bullpen, or pool, well-known to every minor-status office worker.

Attempts to design around this problem are documented by Brookes and Kaplan (1970) in their survey of the so-called *Burolandschaft* or office landscape. In these layouts (Fig. 11-1), work groups are scattered over a large open plan; there are no fixed partitions, although furniture arrangement and potted plants are used to define group space; executives share the area with their employees. In a field study on the effects of office design on 120 employees after a change from a conventional mixture of rectilinear open plan, semiprivate, and private offices to a landscaped design, Brookes and Kaplan found "significant increases in judgments of aesthetic value and decreases in judgments of functional efficiency. A perceived increase in noise level, loss of privacy, and increase in visual distractions were chief causes of complaint. There were some positive changes in group sociability." [p. 373]

In general, the authors concluded, the new space did not seem to function as well as the old. It looked better but didn't work better, although this factor might to some extent be attributed to administrative policies which necessarily "managed" the space in terms of corporate goals. They cite Hundert and Greenfield's study comparing landscape and conventional office groups, which found that only information flow was improved by switching to the new plan. "Privacy was lost. Distractions and interruptions were seen as having increased. . . ." Zeitlin (quoted in Brookes and Kaplan 1972: 378) in his report on the use of this type of office by the Port of New York Authority, comments that "attitudinal changes about the work itself, the nature of the job, and the role of the individual with respect to his job changed only minimally. It is clear that the physical design of the office, whether landscaped or not, cannot install motivation within its work force."

Perhaps the negative results that have been obtained from these studies reflect the feeling on the part of the worker that he has no real control over the setting, no matter how pleasant it may be. The totally designed modern office building is notorious for compelling its users to live with it on its own terms. Many offices prohibit the employee, be he executive or clerk, to turn the lights on or off in his office or decorate private spaces; like the heat and air conditioning, these are automatically controlled at a central point.

One of the most extensive studies undertaken in the area of office design was conducted by the Pilkington Research unit in England (Manning 1965). This comprehensive work on design elements and attitudes of users surveyed many offices and included an in-depth study of a new office building. A critical question in this latter study dealt with the response of the employees when they were moved from an old facility to a new open plan arrangement. The exposure and impersonality of the setting seemed to create some dissatisfaction; there was frequent romanticization of the old building where workers felt they had more privacy. These reactions, however, came soon after the move and may not be unusual when a familiar environment is given up for a new one. A follow-up study about a year later found much less concern with the building. Whether the arrangement was one that facilitated social relationships was still open to question, but there did seem to be a more relaxed attitude on the part of the management and many more applications were received for employment in the company. There was also evidence of a general pride on the part of the staff. Perhaps it would not be overstating the case to suggest that a new sense of place identity had evolved.

A decidedly positive attitude toward the landscape office is reported by Zanardelli (1969) from his experience at the Ford Motor Company. As manager of the Engineering Systems Department, Zanardelli found

> . . . much more face-to-face contact than would have been accomplished in a conventional office arrangement—people could better see and sense the total team of which they were a part. The office became a community; a communion between workers and managers developed. [p. 39]

Work spaces were less likely to fill up with out-of-date and unnecessary papers; personal recognition was achieved and rank distinguished through the number of pieces and the color of furniture and the kinds of plants allocated to an individual within a work area. Unwanted interruptions occurred much less frequently; workflow was more streamlined and what Zanardelli terms the "cave mentality" of the cubicle office gave way to a productive accessibility between staff and managers. "[I]t was easier to induce communication with people who would otherwise be reluctant to approach me. I did get to know my people better, and our rapport was unobstructed by artificial physical conditions." [pp. 39–40] It should be pointed out that Zanardelli speaks from the managerial point of view; he believed, nevertheless, that the plan worked to almost everyone's satisfaction.

A quite different approach to office design was Joiner's (1971) comparison of commercial, government, and academic settings in Britain and Sweden. In these studies both the functional and symbolic values of spatial arrangements were considered. Limiting himself to single-person offices, Joiner endeavored to relate position in the space, distance, and symbolic

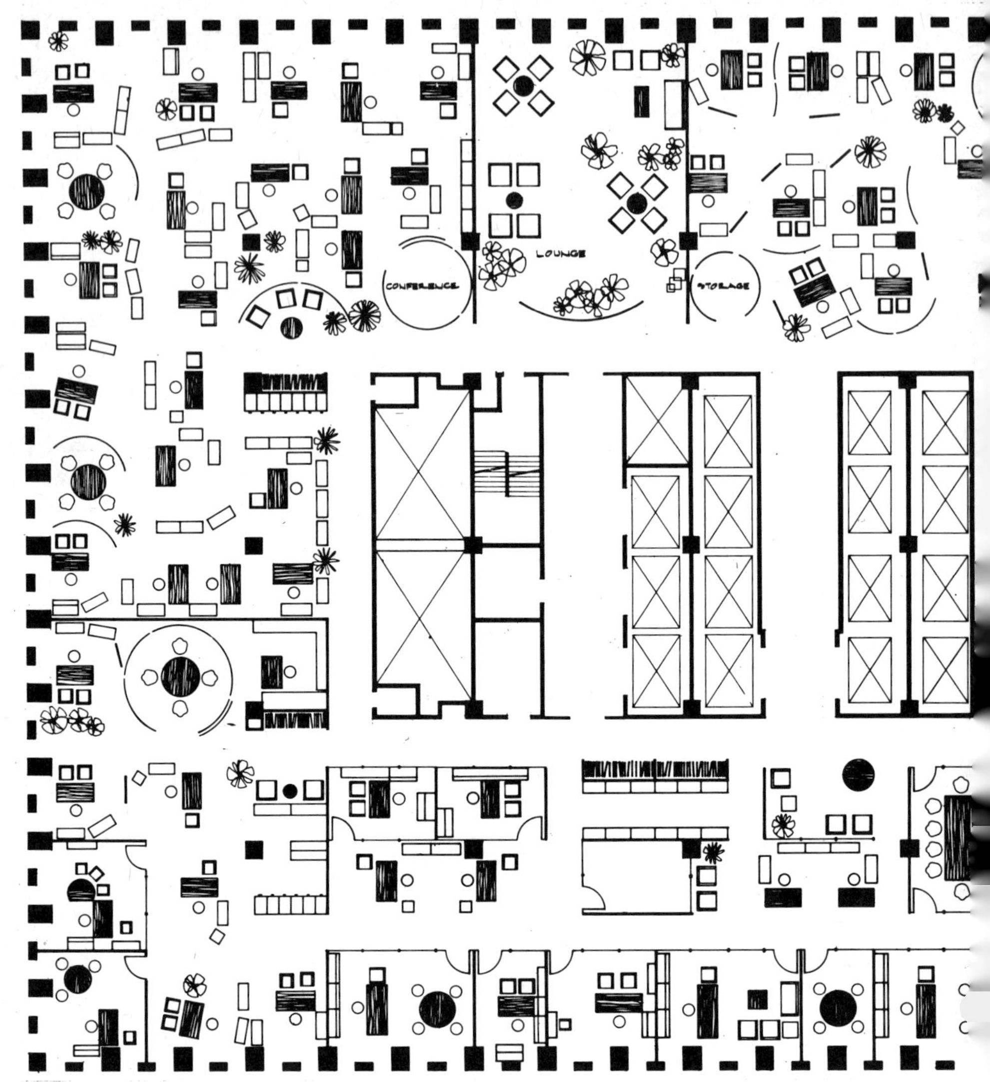

Fig. 11-1 A study for a landscaped or open office plan. Designer: JFN Associates, New York, N.Y.

decoration to the sense of territory created for the occupant. He found, perhaps not surprisingly, that for the person in business and government, status was an important factor in determining the office arrangements. This was not found to be true in academic settings. For nonacademics, high-status persons (executives) tended to position their desks so as to face the door whereas lower-status employees were more often in a side-to-door arrangement.

To face a door is a way of telling visitors to keep their distance; the occupant knows in advance when his area is to be invaded. Academics and those in lower-status business or government jobs, sitting alongside their doors, are more vulnerable to the close proximity of others. In the case of university

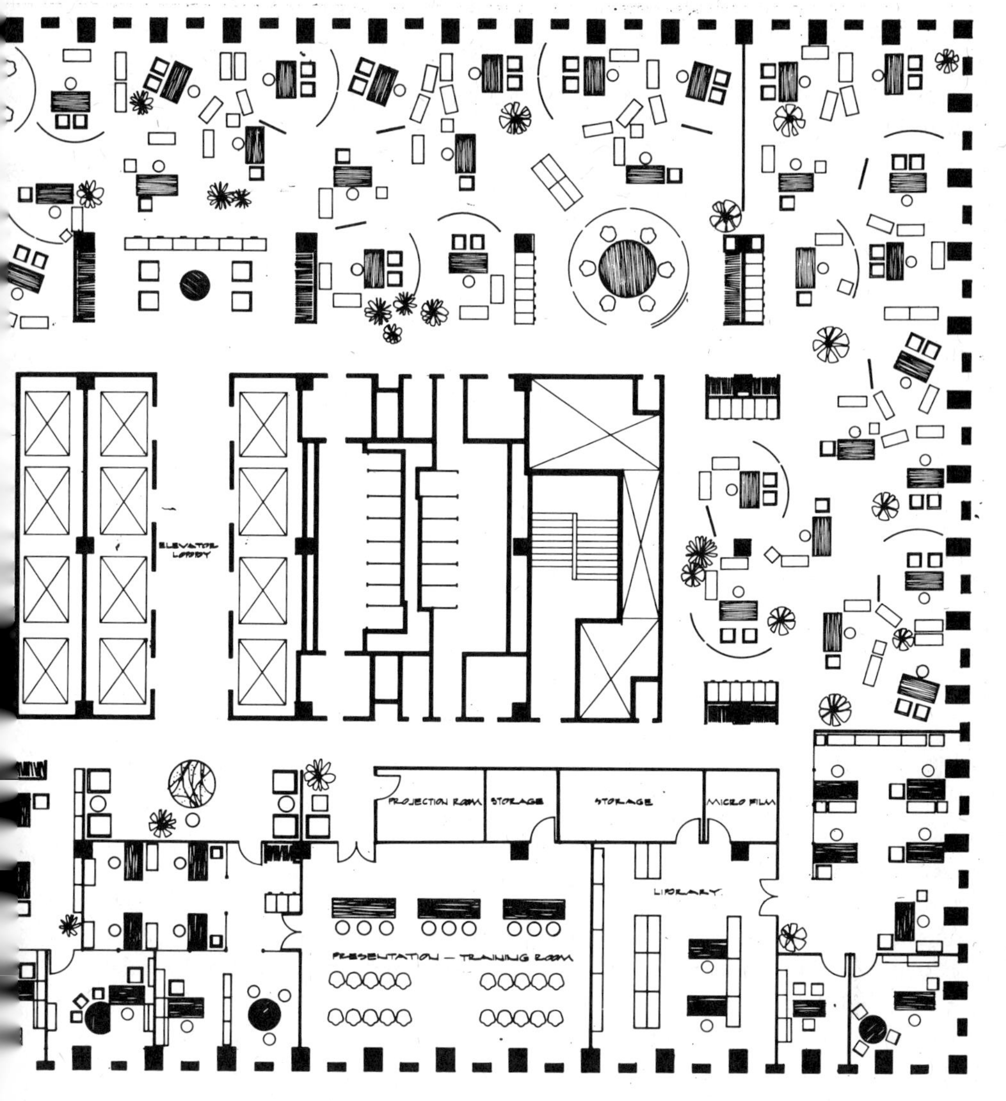

people, who spend a good deal of time with their students, the arrangement serves to decrease the view of them as authority figures, thus decreasing social distance. Joiner suggests that time is also a factor in influencing office arrangement. Those who do spend more time in their offices are more likely to personalize them in terms of furnishings, small details, self-markers (family photographs), and so on. In the open plan office this attempt at creating symbolic space is more difficult.

The conclusion here is simply that the design of interior space influences people on many levels. It sets certain limits on the number of contacts we have, influencing at the same time the establishment of long-or short-range friendships. It provides the necessary framework for functional relationships—the workflow of an office. On a deeper level, it has symbolic meaning, cueing others to our intentions (for example, the office that says "come in" or "keep away"). It encourages or limits the personalization of space and helps define our role in the organization.

Social Design and Site Planning

Our purpose now is to examine some of the design elements that influence behavior in exterior spaces, in larger settings such as institutions, and in planned communities. One such element is the site plan. How does the location and arrangement of buildings affect the issues we have just discussed—the need for social and territorial space, for privacy, and for human interaction?

To site a building is to locate it in relation to its own external space (grounds), other buildings in the immediate area, and the nearby community. Site plans are usually drawn in accordance with features of the physical terrain, amount of land available, the interrelationships of structures in the same development, desirable weather exposures, and the setting—how the building is to be viewed from the street or road. These can be termed the physical aspects of the plan. Their importance as socially mediating factors can be seen by looking at the housing patterns in one's own neighborhood. The cul-de-sac arrangement is likely to bring the residents of a block somewhat closer together if for no other reason than that it better defines the boundaries of their immediate living area. Cluster housing differs from conventionally spaced housing in its relation to common open space; residents form a minicommunity within the larger area. Row houses provide yet another siting arrangement which may affect residential interaction. Merton's (1948) study (cited in Chapter Nine) suggests that the location of front doors is the important factor in neighbor-to-neighbor contact. To take a notably different setting, the typical college quadrangle creates at least a physical sense of community because the buildings face inward. Whether there is much interbuilding social communication is questionable.

In dealing with the social aspects of siting, Gutman (1966) asks two questions: (1) What is the process through which site plans can influence behavior; and (2) What kinds of behavior are conceivably influenced by the site plan? He sees the process operating on both the primitive level of human physiology (lighting, sanitation, temperature control, air circulation) and the more important level of individual and group interaction, or what he terms social effectiveness. The physical network of the plan facilitates or inhibits communication among the residents relative to their location in the scheme. In sum, neighbors hear and see each other. In addition, the plan acquires symbolic meaning (the well-landscaped, spacious grounds imply status) and an esthetic value; thus, the housing "project" can be attractive in its layout and contribute to the users' positive evaluation of the space.

This point was made by the Environmental Research and Development Foundation (1969) in its study of a public housing project in Kansas City,

Kansas. Emphasis was put on the need to "overcompensate, rather than compromise the quality of life for tenants" through better site selection and design in order to overcome the stigma associated with public housing. In many U.S. cities scattersite housing is now the favored solution to the problems of low-income projects. By distributing smaller structures over different neighborhoods, the projects are not only less visible and of lower density but (it is hoped) some of the assumed values of middle-class areas will rub off on the tenants. Resistance to scattersite housing in most American cities indicates skepticism of this solution on the part of the entrenched residents. Social, ethnic, and class prejudices all play an important role.

Some of these difficulties in social design can be laid at the door of the architect-planner as well as the city housing authorities. In general there is often a lack of flexibility in the design stage of the project. Gutman (1972) cites the example of a large urban renewal project in a section of Chicago noted for its juvenile delinquency. Row houses were to surround, on three sides, a large central green space which was to be used as a common area for play, recreation, and community activities. The problem was whether or not to fence the area and provide a locked gate for which only the residents would have a key. This was a clearly defined dilemma. If not fenced and locked, the commons might become a turf for the gangs in the neighborhood. If locked, this might not only discourage use of the area by the tenants but it would also confirm their fears about the hazardous character of the neighborhood. Gutman, who was hired as a consultant on this project, suggested letting the tenants make the decision after they moved in. They could lock the gates if it seemed necessary or remove the fence entirely. To compare results, they might even establish fences in some of the building groups but not in others. It is interesting that the architects rejected this proposal; as Gutman notes, they wanted their solution in advance.

In a comparative study of the effects of site and building form between a high-rise apartment house and a two-story garden type Boyd et al. (1965) hypothesized that the taller building would offer less opportunity for social interaction than the low-rise and that, consequently, high-rise occupants would show less "self to others belongingness," or connection with the outside world. Information was also gathered on the tenants' feelings of alienation, social isolation, anomie, powerlessness, and normlessness. In general test scores confirmed that people who lived in the garden complex made proportionately three times as many friends inside their building area as did occupants of the high-rise. The sense of "belonging"—measured by such feelings as "alienation," "anomie," "powerlessness," and "normlessness"—was definitely lower for the high-rise tenants. However, the sense of social isolation did not seem to be a factor here, and the authors point out that many older people preferred the taller building, probably because it seemed safer. In fact, as we know from Newman's (1972) study, it may not have been. We must also remember that such populations tend to be self-selected, with the younger, more active families preferring the low-rise structures.

How much the siting fostered friendship formation is not clear from this study, although the extent to which the garden-type apartment draws certain types and age groups to it must itself be considered a positive factor.

The kinds of behavior that might be influenced by site plan include the mental health of individual residents, family organization and household life, the social organization of the site residents and the relation of the plan to the larger settlement (Gutman 1972). Most research, however, has concentrated on the latter two factors. Much of this (Cooper 1971; Lee 1968; Merton 1948) has been discussed in connection with the urban environment. Even here the evidence is far from compelling. Whereas community involvement and the use of shopping and recreational facilities may depend on site location (Buttimer 1972; Lee 1968), Gutman (1966) stresses that

> . . . it does not follow that if community facilities are lacking . . . the residential group will not be cohesive. On the contrary, the literature indicates that when dwelling units are far from grocery stores, then their occupants are more likely to borrow food and kitchen supplies from each other; while the absence of a nursery school near the site leads the residents to turn to neighbors for help in caring for infants and young children. [p. 111]

This view is not shared by Madge (1950), who notes that housing estates in England, often isolated from shopping and recreational facilities, have had the effect of ". . . a driving back of attachment to the house itself and its furniture, with a minimum attachment to the locality. Interest and attachment is concentrated on the inside of the house rather than the outside." [p. 191] In the cities, Madge points out, backyard neighboring—the exchange of seeds, for instance—resulted in the formation of Flower Guilds and similar voluntary associations.

Buttimer (1972) has likewise pointed up the role of siting in the residents' use of social space in housing estates. In comparing "planned" versus "less-planned" estates in both central and peripheral areas of Glasgow, Buttimer sought to contrast the conventional standards of the architect-designer with the resident's own attitudes and evaluations of his dwelling area. Since this study points up most of the constructs we have been dealing with, it is worth looking at in some detail.

Four districts were selected, all in the lowest socioeconomic category of the city. Three questions were asked:

1. Were residents in planned districts in general more satisfied than residents of less-planned districts?
2. How did the evaluation of external observers compare and contrast with resident evaluations of the same characteristics? Were criteria such as optimal density, accessibility to various services, design norms for house size and layout, and safety—the elements stressed by architects—also measures of tenant satisfaction?
3. Could residents' satisfaction with their environment be inferred from the evaluation of the external observers—evaluations based on objective criteria?

In answer to the first question Buttimer found that inhabitants of the centrally located "planned" estate were the happiest. There was a high degree of territorial identification. Priorities were cleanliness, view from the living room, neighborly contact, and greenery. Interestingly, although the siting of the less-planned, centrally located estate was in a much less desirable area, residents also experienced a high degree of satisfaction with "life in the area" (58 percent) as compared with the area itself (40 percent). Buttimer suggests that this was because of familiarity with the surroundings, a sense of belonging to the locality. People did not deny the problems and strain but other factors compensated for the lack of amenities.

In comparing the two outlying estates, the planned or less-planned character of each proved a reliable index of satisfaction. The planned peripheral estate was disliked only for its distance from friends and relatives. "The high degree of satisfaction with the area (81%) and with life in the area (65%) reflects the congruence between residential aspiration and achievement." [p. 305] On the other hand, the less-planned estate, which was almost three times as large, also imposed more physical and social isolation on its tenants and accounted for a relatively low degree of territorial identification: 65 percent of them wanted to leave. The second and third questions might be answered, then, by saying that optimum density, accessibility to services, safety, and spatial layout can be planned into an environment and that these elements may be evaluated positively by the residents. Location in itself, however, is not an absolute criterion. The isolated, less-planned estate in a good neighborhood evoked more dissatisfaction than the centrally located less-planned estate in a deteriorating area. But both planned developments rated higher than their counterparts, in part because the sense of belonging—what Buttimer calls the "existential variable" had not been planned out of the setting. An even greater retention of this factor in relocation housing might occur, she believes, if prospective tenants were presented with a range of available choices a year or so beforehand. The conveniences and facilities wanted would be made known to the designer before the plans were developed. Community centers, swimming pools, green space, gardens, walks, and the like "could be decided as need arises and as budgetary and other constraints allow." [p. 312] In short, the business of completing the design of an estate could become a collective decision—something denied to the residents of Gutman's Chicago project.

Institutional Settings

Environmental psychology owes a good part of its genesis to the study of institutional settings. In fact, criticism might be directed to the fact that much of the empirical work in the field has taken place in institutions, especially psychiatric hospitals. Notable in this connection is Sommer's work on seating behavior (Sommer & Ross 1958), spatial invasions (Sommer 1969), Horowitz's studies of the body buffer zone (Horowitz et al. 1964) and the authors' own earlier work (Ittelson, Proshansky, & Rivlin 1970a, 1970b,) all of which studied institutional settings. Most of these studies recognized the danger of generalizing beyond the specific settings, but they also raised issues concerning the meaning of behavior-environment relationships and the legitimacy of examining them as instances of broader environmental behaviors. Because a predictable occurrence takes place in an institutional setting does not necessarily rule out more general implications. In fact, a large part of our lives is spent in institutional settings of one kind or another, and the qualities that make a setting institutional imply some common effects on behavior.

This section will examine four types of institutions, two partial, two total in character (Goffman 1962). For each, the following questions must be considered:

1. What is the relationship between the physical form of the institution and the goals or program (teaching, therapy, rehabilitation, productivity) taking place within it?
2. What evidence, empirical or other, do we have concerning the effects of this specific institutional form on the activities, levels of satisfaction, and the goals of occupants?
3. What are the design implications, if any, of the current state of our knowledge about these institutional forms?

In no way will this represent a complete survey of all types of institutions. That task in itself would require a separate book. We are highlighting a selected cross-section that will give some idea of the kinds of data available and some picture of the application of these data. The total institutions surveyed are the psychiatric hospital and the prison; partial institutions are the day care center and school.

Our interest here is necessarily limited to the physical design aspects of institutions rather than their administrative practices, although it is clear that these two are not unrelated. Physical form can reinforce the therapeutic or rehabilitative "philosophy" of the institution, but when design lags behind newer approaches to institutional treatment, it can make this philosophy harder to carry out. Moreover, the design of institutional buildings generally reflects the attitudes of the larger society toward those who are being institutionalized. The maximum security prison, for example, often resembles a fortress, implying that both social attitudes and administrative practice are punitive; the minimum security facility suggests that a rehabilitative approach is being attempted.

Indeed, we can read the history of society's feelings about the ill, the deviant, the criminal, and the military by looking at the various building forms that house them. In Europe the fourteenth-century monastery might evolve successively into a sixteenth-century fort, an eighteenth-century almshouse, and a nineteenth-century mental hospital (Rothman 1971). All were essentially the same physical structure, but turned to radically different uses. In this country, with few old ruins to be converted, each institutional type evolved its own form at a point in history where institutional architecture had not yet been formalized into a specialty. The result was a great deal of experimentation and, in general, a strongly deterministic view of the role of physical design in the treatment, education, or rehabilitation of inmates.

Goffman (1962) suggests that modern life generally involves social arrangements in which the individual works, plays, and sleeps in different settings, each having different persons as participants, each under a different authority structure, and lacking "an over-all rational plan." [p. 6] This is not true of institutional living, where work, recreation, and sleep all take place in the same place, with the same large group of persons who move through a more-or-less programmed day. Everyone is expected to do much the same thing, at precisely the same time, and the program of the day is imposed by an authority structure, generally in line with some set of goals called "therapeutic philosophy," "rehabilitation program," or the like. Inherent in the total institution is the pronounced demarcation between staff, whose responsibilities are largely those of surveillance, and those whose lives are being managed, generally termed inmates.

As described by Goffman (1962), the total institution can vary in type. Some protect persons unable to fend for themselves (the old, poor, orphaned, or physically handicapped); others care for those who are both incapable of self-care and deemed unintentional threats to the community (persons with severe contagious diseases such as TB, the mentally incapacitated), those who are regarded as threats to the community (the civil or war criminal), and those who require settings to enable them to carry out some work task (this group includes facilities for men in the army, boarding schools, and quarters for servants and colonials). A final type of total institution is the retreat, settings where persons can remove themselves from the outside world, either for religious training, as in the case of monasteries or convents, or for some other purpose.

Goffman (1962) has written extensively of the effects of institutionalization on inmates, particularly the mental patient. In brief, behavior is affected in two broad respects: First, disculturation or "untraining" occurs, rendering the patient unable, at least temporarily, of managing many features of outside life, if he ever returns to it. Second, the person's sense of self is undermined, if unintentionally, through a series of procedures that are degrading and humiliating. Autonomy, freedom of action, and self-determination are lost to the institutional managers. In effect, the patient becomes a nonperson.

Obviously, all patients do not meet the overwhelming conditions of the total institution the same way. A recent study (Braginsky et al. 1969) has documented the varying styles of patient adaptation to the hospital—the major ones being "warders," "workers," and "mobile socializers." Each style was associated with different patient characteristics (in terms of age, attitudes about hospitalization and being a patient, goals, and interests). Each style led to a different hospital outcome, in particular the information the patient acquired, the discharge rate, length of hospitalization, and involvement in therapy. Interestingly, these styles were not related to indices of psychopathology or hospital pressures. The authors cite this as evidence for recognizing that one must use much the same terms in understanding patients as one uses for normals.

Sommer and Osmond (1961) have described the institutional experience as embracing, in addition to disculturation, such factors as *deindividuation*—the impairment of thought and action; *psychological or physical damage* based on hospital experiences; *estrangement* from the civilian world; *isolation* from friends and family; and *stimulus deprivation* resulting from a tempo of hospital life often markedly different from the world outside. In the opinion of some psychotherapists (see, for example, Laing 1969) confinement in psychiatric institutions simply prolongs the patient's illness.

The bleak reading provided by Goffman and others should not obscure the positive side of institutional life. In any case, as Goffman and Braginsky et al. note, various adaptational strategies are employed by inmates in coming to terms with their setting. Quite obviously, too, institutions differ in quality, not least on the scale of how much they respect the inmate as an individual. Finally, it is to be noted that numerous studies over the years testify to the fact that on the order of half of all patients admitted to mental hospitals *show marked improvement despite the absence of any treatment at all.* For such persons the hospital may be, truly, an asylum from the stressful situation which contributed to their illness, a place in which they can gather their own strengths for another assault on life. The environment, qua environment, seems to be therapy.

Nevertheless, the power of an institution to compel certain behaviors—behaviors which are intended to benefit the institution rather than the inmate —is well known. Survival depends upon submission to the institutional norm of behavior; defiance of, or resistance to, such a norm is regarded as evidence of illness or an indication that the inmate lacks the right attitude and is not improving. This may, indeed, be the case. But, again, it may indicate that the person is trying desperately to preserve or regain his own ego integrity. Here, size of institution is seemingly a critical factor; out of sheer administrative necessity the large institution often finds it necessary to regiment inmates to an extent which the smaller institution considers undesirable. As Ullman (1967) suggests, available data tend to confirm the hypothesis that small size and favorable effects are associated. The expedient nature of much institutional behavior is borne out by an incident at the Napa Valley State Hospital in California during the earthquake of 1906. According to reports, damage to hospital facilities forced patients and staff into temporary quarters made up of tents. Both staff morale and patient cooperativeness improved noticeably; epileptic inmates had markedly fewer seizures. This unexpected state of affairs ended when inmates and staff reoccupied the restored buildings. Behavior quickly returned to "normal" (Agron 1971).

Importance of the Physical Environment in Psychiatric Facilities

As a behavior setting there is no single model for the psychiatric hospital. Throughout history the explanation of mental disorders, the treatment prescribed, and the physical context of the care have taken many different forms. The patient has been considered divine, bewitched, ill, evil, unfortunate, in need of protection, rest, treatment, reeducation, punishment, work, and many more. A wide range of settings has been provided, from the temples in ancient Greece and the monasteries of the Middle Ages to the giant state hospitals of today. We associate "modern" treatment techniques and the development of a "moral" treatment view, the conception of the patient as an unfortunate, needing help in returning to normal life, with the nineteenth century. Care was given to details of the setting and personnel that would facilitate treatment. A notable name at this period is the psychiatrist Thomas Kirkbride, head of the Pennsylvania Hospital for the Insane from 1840 to 1883. Kirkbride and his architect, Samuel Sloane, worked out detailed plans that influenced many facilities still in use, although many of their original ideas have been lost in the years of renovation and growth (Goshen 1961). Kirkbride wanted a hospital for no more than 250 patients, located close to the community. The linear plan led to rapid expansion and undermined the original philosophy. Today, most hospitals are too large, too isolated, and often more custodial than therapeutic.

Although anecdotal and of short duration, the experience at Napa Valley points up the kind of role that can be played by the physical setting in the so-called therapeutic environment. To maximize the opportunities for patient interaction, the psychiatrist Humphry Osmond designed a layout for a psychiatric institution at Saskatoon, Canada (1957), providing what he termed sociopetal space, or areas that drew people together. Wards were clustered around central areas, in contrast to the "linear impartiality" (Fields 1971) of the conventional corridor layout. But Osmond cautions that such central dayrooms should not overwhelm the patient with too much space or too many possible two-person relationships. Sommer (1969) has echoed this view in pleading for a recognition of the legitimacy of the schizophrenic's need for isolation in designing hospitals for the mentally ill. Institutional settings of all forms generally organize space to make it difficult for inmates to find a place to withdraw, usually in the interests of staff surveillance. Sommer points up the essential need for schizophrenics to turn within themselves for comfort.

Our knowledge of the role of specific design factors on patient behavior is limited, although we see a good deal said about "appropriate" design—often based upon untested assumptions or the ideas of successful designers and practitioners. Among the latter we might cite the work of Bettelheim, whose Orthogenic School in Chicago provides residential care for extremely disturbed children. Although Bettelheim's treatment philosophy emphasizes psychodynamic factors, the environment is incorporated into the therapy. In *Truants from Life,* Bettelheim (1955) writes:

> The physical setting of an institution acquires its greatest personal significance for the children only as it increasingly becomes the framework within which constructive living can proceed—the safe center of their lives, to whose security they can return from excursions into the outside world, and within whose walls they have the feeling that nothing really bad can happen. [pp. 28–29]

Surely, the qualities Bettelheim writes of are as much a result of staff as housing, but the design and treatment interact with one another. By having dorms, classes, and recreational areas close to each other, physical closeness is enhanced. Bettelheim suggests that a cottage arrangement is attractive, but that the spaces between areas may be frightening to any child; and the disturbed even more, although this view is not universally shared.

It is difficult to evaluate such conclusions, however successful they seem to be in practice. Yet systematic empirical evidence regarding physical factors is really not available. For example, Bayes (1967), a British architect, investigated the role of color and form on the treatment of disturbed children. His review of the state of existing information found no shortage of opinion but many conflicting conclusions. Almost everyone could agree on the need for research. In a later work by Bayes and Francklin (1971) the retarded, the mentally ill, the maladjusted, as well as the handicapped and gifted, were surveyed, with coverage of a broader set of spatial factors such as personal space, privacy, and territoriality. As an example, Bayes and Francklin describe the tremendously difficult problem of designing for the retarded. How can the sense of self and privacy of the institutionalized retarded be enhanced through the design of space? In persons with limited ability to respond to privacy cues this is especially difficult. How does one balance the security of an unchanging setting with the variety and complexity that encourages exploration? The questions they raise go far beyond isolated physical components of the therapeutic setting.

For the child in an institution, perhaps more than for adults, the environment takes on an especially significant role. Whereas the adult learns to manipulate or adapt to the environment, the child's limited powers are likely to make the environment exert a more prominent influence on behavior. This is even more noticeable in managed settings. Tars and Appleby (1973) compared the behavior of a ten-year-old boy before and after he was hospitalized. In the hospital behavior was much more structured. The boy was involved in more activities, but for shorter periods of time. Despite the fact that more people were around him in the hospital setting, he was less likely to interact with them than with people at home. In the hospital, moreover, such interactions were less often self-initiated. The authors suggest that home provided more opportunities for exploration and privacy without interruptions, and that the programmed hospital day curtailed initiative and creativity. This combination of restriction on freedom of choice and limited opportunities for privacy is the essence of institutional life.

Yet an institution, no matter how total, is not deterministic. Not everyone behaves in the same way or uses available space identically. Environmental options are still present. For example, in a partially occupied children's psychiatric hospital, Rivlin and Wolfe (1972) studied the use of space in the large and undermanned building. Children frequently wandered on their own, often into areas that were prohibited. The milieu therapy approach gave them considerable freedom. In response to the wandering and the difficulties in getting children to activities, the staff began to impose a series of changes, some physical but most administrative. Doors were locked, children's time was programmed, and their freedom restricted. Areas became institutionalized in use, their qualities became defined. The house became a place for withdrawal and fewer casual social encounters, talking to staff and other children, were observed.

One cannot place a value judgment on this experience, but we can speculate on other ways to deal with these same problems. If it were possible to control the movement of active young children in a partially unoccupied hospital by architectural rather than programmatic means—by closing off unused spaces or having functional areas in close proximity—one might anticipate a different history of use. For even after the events that precipitate programmatic shifts are long over, the patterns of use that have been established are likely to persist. Very little attention has been given to this aspect of the physical environment as a condition of institutional life. Much of the behavior that we see in institutions seems stimulated as much by the setting as by the characteristics of inmates. Pacing, which might be viewed as schizophrenic activity, is also possibly a result of the physical and social monotony and the existence of long corridors, representing one of the few things to do, given the social-physical setting. Complaints are often made by administrators, nursing staff, and others in psychiatric hospitals that patients congregate in corridors, leaving organized social and activity areas underused. Yet the corridor, in many places, in fact is potentially the most interesting, and certainly the most varied, place to be.

The manipulation of space in treating the mentally ill is based on the frequently erroneous notion that the more contact among patients the better. What is really at issue is the patient's freedom of choice. Private space may actually increase contact (Ittelson, Proshansky, & Rivlin 1970, 1970b), but in any case it is the patient who makes the decision. The French psychiatrist Paul Sivadon (1970) has attacked the problem somewhat differently, at least in dealing with acute stages of schizophrenia. Part of his therapeutic procedure involves the use of space by programming the patients for larger and larger areas with increasing opportunities for contacts, according to their therapeutic needs.

Manipulation studies have provided natural experimental data on various design elements. In a study of the effects of redesigning an area of a psychiatric ward (Ittelson, Proshansky, & Rivlin 1970c), behaviors were observed before and after the changes. It was clear that not only were there differences within the redesigned area, but even more marked were the changes to other ward sectors. The newly designed area, previously a popular spot for more isolated activities, became less appropriate for withdrawal after comfortable seating was provided. The isolated activity did not disappear, but rather, patients found other places to express themselves—the end of the corridor, the dayroom, and some bedrooms. Behavior had redistributed itself.

Another manipulation study (Holahan & Saegert 1973) compared two identical admission wards in a large municipal psychiatric hospital. One ward was extensively remodeled, including repainting and the color-coding of doors; furniture was added in the dayroom and bedrooms and a range of options was created for patients by installing partitions in the bedrooms and providing seating areas in a sector of each bedroom and in the dayrooms. The control ward was identical in form but otherwise unchanged. Patients were randomly admitted to each. Observations of the wards and interviews with patients revealed that the remodeled ward had significantly more socializing and significantly less isolated passive behavior. The authors cite the potential role of the setting in encouraging a new adaptive behavior in contrast to one that fosters the kind of behavior that led to hospitalization in the first place.

The stimulus qualities of an institutional environment account for another source of satisfaction or discomfort. Osmond (1957) has noted the importance of eliminating anything making extraordinary perceptual demands on patients. Izumi (1967) confirmed this observation on a self-induced LSD "trip" which he felt simulated the schizophrenic's perception of a hospital environment: "To be 'startled' by the monotony of one color, such as beige, throughout the institution, was a phenomenon which could immobilize a patient. . . . The ubiquitous terrazzo floor, suspended ceiling and similar 'uniformity' added to the patient's confusion in relating himself to time and space." [p. 4] Izumi's prescription for designing a mental hospital is to emphasize familiarity (and reassurance) in the various building elements and to avoid the illusory qualities that confuse the patient's already impaired sense of reality. One such illusion is simply making a room look larger than it is. Another is the use of "clocks or signs which might appear to be floating, insecure or defying gravity." [p. 8]

The effect of institutional size on a patient's experience has already been stressed; common sense would tell us that a large state institution, with 10,000 inmates, will encourage quite different behavior from the 100-bed private institution. Data compiled by Hyde (reported by Kennedy & Highlands 1964) on Massachusetts mental institutions show that patients recover faster in small hospitals, possibly because these facilities were found to have higher intern and residency requirements. In addition, the bureaucratic inertia of super-hospitals is not as likely to be found in the smaller setting.

An attempt to give the setting a more active role in therapy, especially from the site-planning perspective, is the so-called therapeutic community and recent attempts to create small, community-based residences. In this form of milieu therapy the facility exists not as a place of retreat from the world but as a vital link to it, in which outside social, psychological, and cultural values are kept alive. Milieu therapy stresses the value of the individual, the importance of group process, the need for face-to-face interpersonal relationships. Sivadon (1970), for example, sees the hospital as a natural habitat which duplicates the opportunities for personal growth that are available in the everyday world. And while all this may seem new, it is remarkably similar in many respects to the "moral treatment" practiced 150 years ago.

Whatever approach is emphasized in treating the mentally ill, the physical environment is an independent variable that affects the rate of improvement. Larger size is seen as increasingly counterproductive to the goals of the institution. The setting itself may unintentionally dictate all or part of the therapeutic philosophy. It can function as a container for people who are undergoing treatment, or in its spatial configuration and esthetic qualities it can be a therapeutic tool in itself. The problem is intensified by the wide range of disorders that must be treated, as well as the different philosophies of treatment; nevertheless, mental health specialists are learning that the institution cannot dehumanize the patient and cure him at the same time.

The Prison as a Total Institution

Much of what has been written about mental hospitals also applies to the prison environment. Certainly, their historical perspectives overlap in many details. The inmate is subjected to control by others; his behavior is accountable to institutional rules and regulations, and although ostensibly he is being rehabilitated, he is also being punished (as, indeed, some mental patients are punished for being sick). Above all, prisons, like hospitals, have a high symbolic connotation: The massive, fortresslike structures, with stone walls and guard towers, represent a place to stay out of and a place that contains. They are deterrent environments. Wittman (1972) has noted that prisons also perform a residual function: ". . . their primary purpose can be to prevent certain kinds of social action from occurring outside their walls. . . .Where corrective purposes cannot be carried out in a facility designed for corrections, the facility functions as residual social environment." [p. 12–1–5]

This is not the place to discuss prison philosophy and the problems of rehabilitation. The uprisings that have taken place in many U.S. prisons, culminating in the Attica, New York, revolt of 1971, have included protests against environmental conditions, notably overcrowding. Beyond this there is some indication that the modern prisoner's sense of human rights is in conflict with the inhuman aspects of the setting. The five-tiered, inside cell blocks modeled on Sing Sing (a prison built in 1828), are ostensibly a matter of administrative convenience and security; environmentally, they are gigantic dungeons. "The bars usual in such prisons are usually twice as large, and more than twice as strong, as those used in zoos to restrain lions or giant

Kodiak bears," comments a publication by the U.S. Bureau of Prisons (1949).

In the Bureau's view there is "a lag between correctional ideas and correctional construction"; in terms of its purpose, the fortress-prison is seen as self-defeating.

> The very existence of gloomy, thick-walled bastilles invariably produces mental attitudes on the part of both administrator and inmates which militate strongly against the possibility of putting rehabilitation foremost . . . if the inmates are mentally overwhelmed and dejected by forbidding and repressive surroundings, they can hardly be expected to respond to reformative policies with zest or understanding. [p. 2]

Innovations in minimum security facilities, such as prison farms, point toward greater recognition of the importance of the setting in rehabilitation. Some of the newer medium security prisons now provide dormitories rather than cells for inmates. In Massachusetts the commissioner for Youth Services closed down five of the state's reform schools, transferring their residents to group homes, foster homes, and community-based facilities "from which they could simply walk out at any time." (*The New York Times*, September 1, 1972). The Commissioner, Dr. Jerome G. Miller, notes that in 1970, under the old prison system, the rate of recommitment in the Boston area was 71 percent. In 1971 it dropped to 42 percent—"a decline that coincided with the increased use of alternatives to dormitories." New Jersey's Leesburg prison is attempting to do away with the fortress image by substituting brightly decorated lounges, "homelike" cells that look out on a garden court, and attractive dining pavillions for the bleak and stimulus-bare facilities common to most penal institutions. We hazard the guess that "dungeons" harden the antisocial attitude of prisoners and the disregard of staff who must work in them; humane environments encourage self-respect, but there must obviously be consistency between treatment philosophy and the setting. We also note that such model prisons are still a rarity.

Many of the issues raised in connection with psychiatric hospitals are important to any total institution. For example, the questions of security, bedroom size and privacy, freedom of choice, and territorality have parallels in the prison. Yet prisons vary greatly from maximum to minimum security. There is probably as much difference of opinion regarding design solutions. A basic problem seems to surround the definition of the purpose of incarceration and an explication of a rehabilitation policy. There is considerable disagreement regarding administrative values. To one official a good prison is one with a good security record, to another the low rate of returnees is important, to still others the self-supporting feature is paramount. Some of these issues have design implications. Gilbert (1972), after touring a number of prisons, cites the tendency, noticeable in other institutions (for example, schools and psychiatric hospitals), of perpetuating old architecture forms.

Prison life, by its very nature, is impersonal and anonymous; the inmate has little individual choice. But above all he is confined to an unchanging environment, and within this setting confined again in a cell. In dealing with cell size, Gilbert (1972) found that the degree of confinement was the critical factor. If the prisoner is free to go to other areas in the prison, the actual size of the cell becomes less important to him; the tendency then is to complain about its cleanliness. More important, too, are the physical and programmatic restrictions exemplified in the series of locked doors that are interposed between the prisoner and the "outside." Gilbert writes: "It is more usually the case that internal separations are strictly maintained on the theory that there is a functional relationship between separation and security." [p. 11] The wave of "riots" even in maximum security prisons, indicates that physical restrictions alone do not prevent trouble; on the contrary, they may contribute to the outbreaks. The tendency to build entire complexes to a single level of security—generally maximum—eliminates what might be a more flexible approach, environmentally at least, to prison reform.

To these factors of confinement and restriction, Sommer (1972) adds crowding, lack of privacy, and sensory deprivation. Prisons tend to be stimulus-bare; perhaps because of this, some prisoners experience a kind of "sensory enhancement" in which sounds and odors are especially disturbing. The absence of privacy among inmates, combined with physical barriers between inmates and staff, may also encourage the development of an inmate culture of "criminal values," Sommer believes. He cites the recommendation of Norman Johnson *against* "honor dormitories" because they increase the power of inmate culture. Sommer suggests some form of microenvironment which would permit a degree of privacy in group living. Glaser (1964), however, cites evidence that interinmate socialization does not promote the spread of criminal attitudes as much among older inmates as among the younger, yet current practices usually provide dormitories for juvenile offenders, with little privacy possible. He advocates the single room or cell for all prisoners to prevent contacts during the unprogrammed part of the day.

The problem today, to judge from the newspapers, is essentially one of crowding and lack of privacy. This is not only a stress element in itself, but it encourages the formation of prisoner cliques and tends to break down prison discipline. The individual cell need not be inhumane; what matters more is the time spent in it and the opportunities for exercise, recreation, study, and work made available in the total setting. The architect can design these facilities into the prison complex; he cannot, of course, control their use—in short, design itself will not solve the prison "problem." It can, however, make solutions easier or more difficult for others.

The Partial Institution

It is not always easy to determine where the "outside world" leaves off and institutional life begins. Some prisons give furloughs to trusted inmates; the patient in a psychiatric hospital who spends his weekends at home is only partially institutionalized—indeed, the effort here is to deinstitutionalize him. Half-way houses for recently discharged mental patients, former addicts, or prisoners combine some of the security and therapy of the institution with the freedom and responsibility of the general society.

On another level, most of us are partially "institutionalized" at some time in our lives. Many work settings are institutional in their regimentation of time, activity, and use of the environment—what we cannot do and what we are expected to do. Large corporations impose their own particular constraints on employees and enforce different sartorial regulations, from the smock worn by some clerical workers to the suit and tie that is considered *de rigeur* for the rising executive. Camps, both children's and adults', exemplify degrees of short-term institutional life. The commune, although expressing an ideal of freedom for its members, often regiments its schedule of activities, responsibilities, and use of facilities. Wherever men and women must live or work together toward a common end, some degree of internal social control is necessary. Our interest here is how this institutionally generated social factor interacts with the physical components of a particular setting.

One example, already considered in some detail, is the office environment. Two other partial institutions will be briefly discussed here—the day care center and the school. The first has been selected because it is a relatively new type of behavior setting that is quite literally searching for an appropriate form, creating its own environment as it grows. Schools, about which we have written in previous sections of this book, will be given a final look because their design in recent years has been closely geared to a changing educational philosophy that is intimately bound to the nature of the setting.

The Day Care Center. Although many different settings today identify themselves as day care, the prototype tends to look more like a school than any other form. They are places where very young children are cared for over long periods of time. Day care has come to mean an all-day service, taking the child soon after he awakens in the morning and keeping him until late afternoon when parents return from work. Some twenty-four–hour centers are used by parents with night work. Thus the center, which may seem synonymous with the nursery school, really has many of the components of a home. This implies that both physical form and program must have a wide array of stimulations, adapted to the developmental needs of the children, yet respecting the life styles of the different user groups.

Two basic environmental issues are involved here: the size and the quality and organization of equipment and space. We can summarize the research findings on size by citing the results of an extensive survey of fifty day care centers in Los Angeles County (see Prescott et al. 1971; Prescott & Jones 1971; Prescott 1970). Size, as measured by the number of children, was found to be a reliable predictor of the quality of the program. These investigators indicated that the larger centers, although they tended to have greater resources, better physical conditions, a more highly trained staff, and a lower per-child cost, did not necessarily. exhibit more effective child care. Centers caring for thirty to sixty children tended to be superior to those serving more than sixty. These larger centers were inclined to emphasize rules and to use more restraints; smaller centers were more likely to stress fun, creativity, and social interaction among the children, who seemed to be more enthusiastic and interested. The teachers also differed, with those in smaller centers rated as more sensitive. Children in small centers were less likely to be segregated by age and more inclined to mix as a group in the various activities.

The size of a space, of course, is meaningful only in relation to the number of those using it. A large room may seem impersonal if only a small number of children are in it. Crowded, it may create undesirable competitive and territorial pressures. Chapman and Lazar (1971) provide evidence that increasing the size of a group results in a shift in role identification from adults to peers, but this is by no means a clear finding. Hutt and Vaizey (1966), for instance, found that increasing group size resulted in more dependence on adults and a decrease in social interaction, as well as generally negative behaviors in the direction of aggressiveness and territorial conflict, although each of these was specific to particular types of children. On the other hand, less adult supervision may mean more privacy for children, although Chapman and Lazar (1971) remark that European studies show that very young group-reared children often do not develop a respect for collective ownership.

At this point there is no clear answer either to the question of optimal group size (the activity in question must certainly be considered), child/staff ratio, or total institutional size. Nor is there any clear picture of the necessary amount of inside or outside space per child, although this is universally incorporated into state regulations. In fact, the requirements vary from state to state.

The organization of spaces within the center is an equally complicated problem, embodying many of the controversies in the open versus closed school settings. In Prescott et al. (1967) the role of clear pathways was pointed up as a component of activity and involvement of children. Expectedly, a rich and varied setting, providing a wide array of natural materials and animals, was often associated with involvement and interest on the part of teachers and children. The organization and type of furnishing raises the issue of scale. Should interiors be full or child-scaled? If the day care setting is to have a home quality, at least some full scale objects may provide the sense of home and encourage the necessary skills in learning to use full-sized furnishings. Often, the convenience of staff leads to a child-scaled world on the assumption that children can manage better without supervision. In truth this is so; where things are sized, placed, and arranged on an adult level, they must pass through the adult before the child can manage them. This power and review may limit the child's use of them and create a sense of powerlessness. A balance between the challenge of the full or "real world" setting and the easier manageability of small things seems a reasonable solution.

The School. Turning to schools, we find a long tradition of experiments with architectural forms—forms that reflected, as did the curriculum itself, societies' views of education. The Greeks and Romans considered learning of rudiments as a painful initiation into the community of scholars; students in a typical Roman school sat on backless stools, wrote on wax tablets perched on their knees, and faced the teacher, who sat on a dais in a backed chair (Marrow 1956). Early education in America centered on the classics and the Bible. School sessions were limited and were frequently held in the home of the teacher, who might be a minister. During the post-Revolutionary period the curriculum focused on the "three Rs" and the physical setting had changed to the celebrated one-room schoolhouse, which was often dilapidated, drafty, dimly lit, overcrowded, and colorless. To accommodate the varied ages in crowded quarters (sometimes as many as one hundred students in a room thirty feet square), the older pupils sat on long benches facing three walls on which sloping shelves supported their copy books or slates. Younger children sat on low benches placed within the three-sided arena. In general the environmental props for education during this period were minimal.

By the turn of the century many changes had taken place. Industrialized America required a greater technological and academic expertise of its citizenry. Schools were larger, classrooms were graded, the curriculum was organized, the teachers were trained (Cremin 1968). Perhaps most visible of all was the monumental character of many school buildings. Although the educational approach did not differ materially from what had gone before, these "halls of learning" became physically emblematic of the importance that society attached to the education of its young. This approach stressed the preparatory nature of schooling—and the passive role of the student. However, many extracurricular activities were added, from athletics and baton twirling to social dancing and school bands. Schools became bigger, more specialized in their curricula, and, in the opinion of some critics, less relevant to the real needs of the child. The Little Red Schoolhouse, for all its faults, seemingly provided more individualized instruction than the factory-school that succeeded it.

John Dewey (1938), raising doubts about our educational directions, strongly emphasized the individual pupil. He felt that the child's life in school must be as real and vital to him as his life at home, in his neighborhood, and on the playground, a view close to that expressed by Froebel in the nineteenth century and later by Montessori. If this was to be accomplished, the school, as an "environment for learning," would have to be drastically changed. In Dewey's pragmatic view the child learns, not merely by being lectured at, but by taking apart, reassembling, and experimenting with the world around him. Schools must help him do this.

It is against this background that design, too, began to change, although not always for the reasons implicit in Dewey's educational philosophy. Schools were to be less "institutional" looking, with red brick giving way to glass walls and with low-slung, campus-type structures replacing the old "firehouse" edifices still common in most towns and cities. If nothing else, schools seem pleasanter places to be in—"they don't smell like schools anymore," one of our neighbors commented. Whether they are better educationally is a matter of dispute. The last decade has witnessed a rash of criticism directed toward the still-prevalent passive learning methods, the punitive atmosphere, and the poor educational quality of schools (Holt 1970; Kohl 1967; Kozel 1967; Silberman 1970). A new building does not necessarily mean better teaching, especially if it is large and overcrowded, as many are today.

An important influence in American education today is that of the British "open classroom." The Open Space School Project (1970) revealed that more than half of all schools built since 1967 were of this type. The most distinguishing feature of the open plan ideology is that children learn best when they are free to follow their interests and progress at their own pace (Blackie 1971; Plowden 1967). Although many of Britain's open classes take place in traditional buildings, the emphasis on the use of outdoors, corridor space, and, in fact, all available school space has given a heavy weight to the role of the physical environment as a support for open classroom philosophy. The newer school buildings in Britain are generally based on activity patterns observed by the planning architects; design thus attempts to reflect rather than anticipate behavior. The Plowden Report (1967) describes a new school in this manner:

> The "teaching area" was conceived as the whole school environment, rather than a set of individual rooms. . . . Outside and inside provide an integrated learning environment. Inside there are small working areas each with a degree of privacy and a character of its own, opening into a larger space sufficiently uncluttered to allow children to climb and jump, dance and engage in drama. Among the small working spaces is a sitting room, a library, two workshops with water available, a kitchen and three group study spaces. [Vol. 2, Paragraph 1094, 1967]

Some of the implications of the open classroom for American education have been dealt with earlier. In general, we can sum up by saying that new schools have not been the hoped-for panacea. One reason for this concerns the feasibility of importing and reinterpreting an educational philosophy which is successful in another culture. Another is the order of events. In Britain building renovations followed the program operation and in many instances the training of teachers. Here the open school program frequently follows the move into a radically different environment with little prior teacher or pupil preparation. In other cases it is superimposed on a setting and staff functioning with different philosophies. Criticism of noise levels and distraction felt in the engineered open schools, despite actual noise reduction levels, implies a recognition of teacher attitudes as a crucial factor in their perceptions. In Brunetti's (1972) study, the distractive quality of noise was found to be dependent on the particular tasks the students were engaged in; high density also contributed to the amount of perceived distraction.

Another problem is that not all open schools use their space to the best advantage. Staff leadership would seem to be a critical factor here; for it is not environments that teach, but a combination of teachers interacting with students and stimulating materials. Environments can support improved learning approaches. In a real sense teachers and students must learn to utilize their environments in the interests of their goals, both immediate and long-range. This is a skill in itself and may require a new kind of training for environmental awareness. Given the open plan, it may prove to be that the freedom here actually does foster the child's ability to realize his capacities. At this point, we simply do not know. What appears to be needed now is a closer study of the variety of activities that take place in the open classroom program, where they take place, and how the particular physical setting facilitates or hinders the participants, both teacher and pupil, in reaching their goals. When this is known, the architect/designer can step forward with more confidence than is now the case.

New Towns and Model Cities

Institutional settings are one type of environment where the physical plan serves a regulative function; they are, so to speak, closed environments. To some extent this is true of such subenvironments as the housing project or even the retirement community with its special facilities for a specific age group. Is it possible to extend this concept to the city at large—to design for social effect in more complex settings, yet retain the freedom that is treasured in the noninstitutional world? On the level of urban renewal we have seen the difficulties involved when planning, preoccupied with economic, administrative and budgetary matters, neglects the psychological implications inherent in changing people's city environment (Gans 1962; Newman 1972). Mussen and Slyper (1972), in their plans for urban renewal in Israel, recommend "much more precise definition and measurements of what constitutes 'the successful community'. . . . There would have to be a fuller understanding of desires for choice and variety by urban residents and the ingredients and mixes of ingredients that produce human satisfaction in the urban setting." [p. 124] The authors stress the importance of frequent social evaluation and monitoring of projects during construction and after they are built. The program for the renewed community would be regarded as developmental in nature rather than a completed "package." As changes in living and life styles occur, along with the social and economic contingencies that inevitably grow out of change, urban planning would be adapted to the new behavior:

". . . [T]here would be less reliance on the planner's prejudgments of what constitutes 'the good community.' "

In the United States an effort is being made to see urban renewal as a social as well as physical problem. In the Model Cities Program authorized by Congress in 1966, better education, improved health services, increased income levels and job opportunities, better transportation, and reduced crime are targets for social action. It is not slum clearance per se, but an improved quality of life that is sought. This can best be achieved through the participation of those whom the program is designed to help.

Thus, in analyzing 11 of the 150 cities that have received Model Cities grants, the Department of Housing and Urban Development (HUD) learned that the perceived needs of the residents in all but 3 of the cities were oriented toward social service rather than economic projects. Another interesting finding by HUD is that in neighborhoods with high social turbulence, residents tend to have more influence on the planning process; where residents are "cohesive" and politically organized, they tend to dominate the planning and are able to elicit a more sustained interest on the part of the city government. It is in this direction of democratic participation that urban renewal enjoys its greatest opportunities as designers become much more aware of the variable needs of the inner-city population.

Whether we can in fact save our cities through slum clearance and rebuilding is being increasingly questioned. Yet the question is not new. Cities have always presented seemingly insoluble problems that might best be solved by simply starting over. The New Town movement, which dates back almost three-quarters of a century, approached the issue in just these radical terms. New Towns were designed as avenues of escape from the overburdened, industrialized city, Utopias that shared the advantages of the countryside while retaining the economic viability of the city proper. Old cities, of course, would not disappear; but less pressure would be felt inside them as people moved to these model communities.

Conceived by the Briton Ebenezer Howard, who coined the term "Garden City" to describe his ideal community, the first New Town was built under private auspices at Letchworth, England, in 1904. Howard was one of the first city planners, and for his day, something of a visionary. He believed, with the ancient Greeks, that there was a natural "size" at which an organization could function best; in Mumford's (1961) words, he wanted to restore "the human measure to the new image of the city." However, he also believed that such communities, whose ideal population would be about 32,000 persons, should be self-sustaining. Unlike the promoters of suburbs, he did not want to eliminate industry from his Garden City; what he did want to do was to keep it from growing in the lopsided and specialized way that characterized industrial development in the large metropolis.

Howard's second New Town, Welwyn, was not begun until 1954. His ideas were introduced to the United States, on a minor scale, at Radburn, New Jersey, by Stein and Wright in 1928. However, the seed had been planted, and at the end of World War II the British Labour government for the first time in England's history began a conscious attempt to decentralize the country's urban population. The New Towns Act of 1946 projected a greenbelt around London to prevent further expansion while providing recreation areas for the existing population; the building of new communities and the expansion of smaller ones would house one million persons, as many as three-fourths of these from London proper. By 1968, twenty-eight New Towns had been planned or completed in England and the movement had spread to West Germany, Finland (Tapiola), Brazil (Brasilia), and the United States, where Reston, Virginia, and Columbia, Maryland, have become showcases for the new urban living.

In achieving its present state of development, the New Towns have modified many of Howard's ideas. Some communities in England now foresee a population of half a million persons. Others, in effect, serve as suburbs, with emphasis on commuting. At the same time, modern planners see the New Towns as opportunities to effect changes in the social behavior of their inhabitants. Fava (1970) summed up many of the social questions, which Howard was only partly concerned with, including the quality of neighborhood interaction, high-rise multifamily compared with low-rise single-family dwellings, the effects of density and size of community on the individual's psychological functioning, the importance of propinquity on interpersonal contacts, the value of self-sufficiency for communities, the value of balance and diversity, the way housing is selected, the value of decentralization and local participation.

Criticism of New Towns

The history of Utopias has been the history of sublime failures. Although in some ways they have not lived up to their designers' dreams, the New Towns have not failed. Paradoxically, they have become more, rather than less, Utopian as their underlying philosophy has spread. What Howard saw as a physical setting for a rational and pleasant way of life is now regarded as a cultural and social setting for promoting men's diverse occupational interests, artistic self-expression, and leisure-time hobbies. Concerts, art exhibits, and community activities flourish. But the New Towns were also to be classless towns, and it cannot be said that this ideal has come about.

Both psychologists and social critics note too that whatever their advantages, New Towns fail to provide for certain behavioral needs which the unplanned city often supplies. Planning itself—more properly, overplanning—tends to restrict freedom of choice. Lack of diversity and architectural variety produces a bland response to the physical environment. Most New Towns offer few surprises or opportunities for exploration; in the stimulus sense, they are often "impoverished" and lacking in novelty. In some New Towns life does not seem to be lived spontaneously but according to a master plan.

How valid are these criticisms? Since no two New Towns are exactly alike, there is no way we can generalize. Taken overall, there does seem to be merit in the charge that a community planned wholly in terms of rational living—a community that stresses the orderly and esthetic while excluding outlets for the spontaneous and adventurous side of man's nature—will not be experienced as completely satisfying. Children in particular may be affected by the lack of environmental challenge. In West Germany educators compared the paintings and drawings of young children in three New Towns with those produced by children in traditional cities (see Fellows 1971). They concluded that for the former group the planned character of the environment inhibited the child's natural curiosity and blunted his creativity. City children, on the other hand, tended to be stimulated by their surroundings.

A somewhat extreme example of response to the planned environment is seen in the new capital of Brazil. During construction of Brasilia the temporary town of Ciadade Libre ("Free City") sprang up to accommodate the workmen and their families. It was to this shantytown that many residents of the capital fled for excitement at the end of the day. In Izumi's (1969) words, Brasilia had "visual order" but lacked "the varieties of psychic rhythms that we need to experience in any environment." The result was that upon the completion of Brasilia, Ciadade Libre was incorporated as a satellite town to the capital.

More specific criticism has been leveled at the separation of living from working areas, and, in some New Towns, the isolation of the shopping district from the rest of the community. In a survey of Wolverhampton it was found that families whose wage earner worked outside the area used local shops, library, youth club, clinic, and so on much less than families whose wage earner was employed nearby, "although the members of the family concerned were the housewife and children, not the main earner himself" (Madge 1950).

Attempts to promote social homogeneity through the arrangement of diverse groups in physical proximity have not had much success in the New Towns, in spite of the hopes of their planners. In England self-segregation has been a noticeable feature of these communities and is now "factored into" the plans. This should not be too surprising. It is generally agreed that man needs to belong to social groups where he is known, in stable settings where he can acquire a sense of identification with a place. Beyond this, social exclusiveness may not be so desirable. Fava (1970) believes that New Towns in the United States are becoming economic havens for the middle and upper classes. She cites an in-depth survey of 800 residents of two New Towns in California, in which it was learned that "a major reason for buying in New Towns was the belief that 'planning' protected the community against the intrusion of economic and racial diversity." This, of course, is a knife that cuts both ways. She notes that the black activist-entrepreneur Floyd B. McKissick proposes the New Town of Soul City, near Raleigh, North Carolina. It will be all black.

The "New" New City: Milton Keynes

The New Town movement has become not so much the process of deurbanization envisioned by its early planners as an experiment in reurbanization with explicit and clear-cut social goals. Cities with a population as large as 500,000 are now considered acceptable. Existing towns are being clustered in a cohesive grouping to form the basis for the new community. One of the best known of these New Cities is Milton Keynes, an area northwest of London embracing several small towns totalling about 100,000 people. Now under development, Milton Keynes expects to have 70,000 new population by 1981 and 150,000 by 1990. In the words of its designers (see Llewelyn-Davies et al. 1970), the physical plan of the New City "is not based on any fixed conception of how people ought to live. Nor is it a plan for a 'space-age' super-city, based on technological determinism." [p. 23] On the contrary, Milton Keynes might be very broadly described as an existential community. Open-ended plans call for continuous monitoring and evaluation of resident satisfaction with all aspects of the social and physical environment. This will allow for necessary alterations in design as the city expands. At the same time the shortcomings of the older New Towns are recognized in an effort to prevent their recurrence. It is recognized that people want clutter in their environment as well as order. According to the designers, Milton Keynes promises to supply the need for "surprise, random happenings, unplanned meetings and exciting discoveries."

It is not possible in our brief space to describe in detail the conceptual basis for this New City. For the student of environmental psychology, however, five major themes emerge which illustrate the points we have been making with respect to social design.

1. Opportunity and freedom of choice are provided in the fields of education, employment, housing, health care, and so on. No single "life style" is mandated. Densities of housing areas will allow for considerable variation. To promote interaction homes are oriented toward numerous "activity centers" rather than grouped to form "an inward looking neighborhood unit." Milton Keynes recognizes the neighborhood as a natural ecological unit but avoids turning it into a sanctuary.
2. A good transportation and communication network is planned. Although public transport is provided to high standards, the designers recognize that the automobile is still preferred by many, and no effort is made to make the community a "car-free" city. However, all neighborhood streets are local streets, with no through traffic.
3. The city will have balance and variety. Gross segregation of different kinds of people will be avoided by distributing different kinds of housing over the entire city.
4. Milton Keynes will be attractive. No single architectural style will predominate, and there will be a variety of different building types and forms. "The Corporation will not discourage idiosyncratic taste." Main roads will be designed to

afford a sequence of views and will run at ground level so that travelers "will feel in close touch with the city, and a part of it." Older, historic buildings are to be preserved, and the City Center will exhibit the vitality of any good downtown business district. An intimate scale is sought.
5. The city will encourage an awareness of its physical form—it will be easily cognized. "The city should speak for itself, through its plan and its architecture." People are to acquire a clear working knowledge of the city and its form through direct experience. Light industrial and office development will be interspersed throughout residential areas as a means of diversifying the environment.

At this writing, financial considerations have made it impossible to realize all aspects of this blueprint. Nevertheless, Milton Keynes tries to strike a balance between too high a degree of preconceived finality and the "permissiveness" which characterizes the older, chaotic cities. Not only physically but psychologically it represents a fresh start for its inhabitants. This may be one of the cardinal attractions of the New Town movement. Finally, to a significant degree, such towns might become models for urban redevelopment as our existing cities undergo massive rebuilding during the coming decades.

The Future Environment

New towns are a tentative step into the future. This is not to say that in some sense man has never planned his cities before. The medieval city, for example, was often organized around the market place and with respect to the castle; residential zones were clearly defined for various social classes. Walls were erected for protection. But such planning was crude at best; more often cities simply grew, like Paris and Rome, and what planning occurred came later in an effort to correct the faults of earlier and unsystematic development. As in most human endeavor, in creating cities man learns something from his own mistakes.

But how far can planning go? To what extent can we totally anticipate environmental needs on the urban, or any other, scale? On a purely technical level there is, indeed, very little that cannot be accomplished. We know that men have lived for relatively brief periods on the moon and in space. There have been settlements, exploratory in nature, at the South Pole. All of these, of course, are highly artificial, viable only because they draw their support from more conventionally rooted settlements. Yet, the challenge exists to make such environments habitable, as man once cleared sections of the jungle and the wilderness. With our present know-how this is not simply a dream.

The problem is twofold: the cost of building such communities may be greater than we are willing to pay; and the behavioral demands inherent in living in them may exceed our willingness or even our capacity to adapt. Yet we know that one of the central conditions of modern times is an exploding population growth that not only puts increasing pressure on the world's resources but adds to the social and psychological complexity of experience. Many cities have seemingly reached the limits of their natural capacity to expand and still supply the services and quality of life for which they were intended. Decentralization is proposed by many urban planners as the next step. One such prototype is the Experimental City Project (Spilhaus 1968) sponsored by government agencies and business leaders in collaboration with the University of Minnesota.

The central feature of the project is a system of dispersed cities of controlled size numbering approximately 250,000 people and surrounded by open land. Business and industry would locate in these cities as at present, but almost all service facilities would be underground, including truck deliveries and other forms of commercial transportation. There would be virtually no vehicles on ground level streets. For transporting people, cars and buses would give way to "motorless, driverless, noiseless, semi-private pods, computer-controlled . . . [p. 713]." Density would be regulated by zoning and building size. Changes in the demand for services are anticipated by allowing for considerable flexibility in the structures themselves through the use of adjustable floors, ceiling heights, and walls. One of the more intriguing proposals of the Experimental City envisions inflatable buildings that can be quickly deflated. Parts of the city might also be domed.

Technologically, there is little about such a city that cannot be realized. The decision to build rests with the social and economic planner rather than the urban planner, the willingness of the real estate developers to participate, and the user's conviction that he is not facing simply a different kind of urban nightmare—one based on too much planning rather than not enough. In any case, it is relatively conservative when compared with many theoretical models that have come off the drawing boards in recent years (see Dahinden 1972). Herron's Walking City, designed in 1964, envisions an urban complex of half a dozen mobile, multistoried containers mounted on legs and connected with one another by tubular corridors. The Atelier Warmbronn has designed an inflatable, transparent membrane which can be spread over three square kilometers of arctic landscape, with outside air warmed to a temperate climate, and a mobile electric lamp replacing the sun during the long winter nights. Fuller's proposed geodesic dome for enclosing all or parts of cities is well-known. Fuller has also sketched a tetrahedral, or pyramid-shaped city that would accommodate one million people. Residential units with a garden area would be terraced on the slopes of the pyramid. Fuller's Triton City consists of triangular "islands" built over water and connected to each other and the mainland by decks. The islands would constitute self-contained neighborhoods of not more than 6500 residents.

Visionary cities are also contemplated in the form of funnels (Jonas), mammoth bridges (Shibuya), tripods (Salier et al.), latticeworks bearing prefabricated cells (Cook), masts with clip-on homes (Quarmby), and craters (Chaneac) whose slopes would provide terraces for building sites. Less futuristic, but perhaps more attainable, is the housing unit Habitat, the cliff-dweller design demonstrated at Expo '67 in Montreal and now occupied permanently. Many other examples could be added to this list. Probably the most innovative of all designers of future cities is Paolo Soleri (see Maholy-Nagy 1970) whose Arcology—a term combining architecture and ecology—has provided a detailed philosophy for new and radical urban forms. One of his thirty projects, Acrosanti, is now being constructed in Arizona. Soleri sees his cities as biostructures that "grow" in accordance with the shifting cultural, industrial, living, and leisure needs of their occupants. They are total, but artificial, ecosystems. One such, Asteromo, is literally a space vehicle with its own facilities for gardening and farming. It would accommodate 170,000 people.

There are a number of points to be made about these alternatives in addition to their Utopian intentions and science-fiction appearances. Many, for instance, imply a very high density population. In one way or another, they are high-rise cities in a concentrated form; the urban complex is "shrunk" to more manageable dimensions in opposition to what Soleri calls the automobile mystique and the asphalt nightmare. One of his designs, hexahedronal in shape, calls for 200 occupants per acre (New York City averages 33 occupants per acre). Most visionary cities also strive for functional autonomy; the occupant is a relatively passive object in a push-button environment.

These are examples of highly automated and self-contained cities tracing their lineage to Le Corbusier's (1963) premise that buildings are machines to live in. We might ask, therefore, to what extent future man will be willing to accept the built environment as a totality for which he has little personal feeling. Throughout the visionary city, with all its technical apparatus, convenience, and efficiency, the danger is that inhabitants may find little with which to identify in a personal and creative sense, and little indeed that is built to human scale. Will there be sufficient variety and challenge—will living in them be a stimulating experience? Will residents be able to find social space for their lives amid a functional totality? Since these cities do not exist, there are as yet no answers to our questions. The designer's vision enables us to test the future simply in theoretical terms; yet without that vision there would be little progress.

Design is not imposed on human organization but grows out of an array of cultural and social needs (Rapoport 1969). And only as these needs can be anticipated will the engineering achievements that we know are possible provide the behavioral fit that makes them worthwhile. Here we have a paradox: it is characteristic of all times that the technology of the age determines in large measure what these needs will be. Thus, the designer of future environments is in the difficult position of projecting solutions to problems that his technology may create; unintentionally, he is supplying new difficulties as well as new answers. Above all, in this acceleration of technical mastery he may be thrusting man into the future before he is ready for it.

Yet perhaps the real danger facing future mankind is not so much that the world will be overplanned, but that planning will be neglected—as in the past—in favor of expedient solutions. One characteristic of tomorrow will almost certainly be a high degree of mobility, of dynamic change. The proliferation of mobile homes in this country illustrates the difficulty of planning for long-term growth; when residents can pull up stakes and move their habitat with them, a good part of the urban setting becomes fluid, unplanned, and, in the view of many, unattractive.

In contrast we see too an increasing trend toward age-segregated communities, "leisure villages," and resort cities in which the future is faced by their inhabitants in vastly different ways. For these places design will be related to special functions with relatively less interchangeability among settings than before, and with a deemphasis on the pluralism that historically has marked the forms of our built environment.

Still another facet of this trend is the concentration of technological function in fewer and fewer hands. The individual is divorced from a working relationship with his environment. Although leisure may be his, the sense of belonging and meaningful participation may be lacking. Boguslaw has written: "The current preoccupation with computer-based systems and automation has, unfortunately, left . . . the overwhelming majority of our population occupying the role of bystanders. His characteristic involvement in system-design efforts is *ex post facto* and this greatly circumscribes the range of his possible influence (quoted by Sarason, p. 278)." The dilemma, then, is a future which may be radically overdesigned on the one hand, and chaotic on the other. Somewhere in between is a world that reflects our optimum needs. What compromise is possible between an environment of wholly new forms and tools and the earthbound individual whose values, strengths, and goals will always to some extent be rooted in the past? We cannot amputate man on the scale of history, sending only part of him into the future.

We began this book by describing a theoretical model of environmental man. We saw him as a new kind of man, independent of the religious, economic, and psychological identities of past ages, dependent upon a sound ecological relationship with his present. The historical attitudes that went into this changing perspective were reviewed, and it was suggested that present-day man is faced with restoring the "bits and pieces" of a scientifically modeled world into a whole in which he is organically a part. His perceptual functioning and social behavior were seen as related to this holistic concept of the environment. Two widely contrasting milieus, the urban and the natural, were offered as settings which confront man with specific problems in the realization of biological needs and social and individual goals. In this chapter we have inquired as to how man consciously designs an environment that intervenes in his own favor.

Now, having thrust environmental man into a future of seemingly limitless possibilities as well as unpredicted consequences, we would like to conclude by giving him a soft landing. This future is not entirely mysterious, for man will build it, however metaphorically, in his own image. In many ways our environment will be even more specialized and streamlined than the present, and it will do more for us. Yet there is no reason to believe that all will face this future in the same way. For many reasons man will probably cling to the qualities of his present world that have proved psychologically satisfying. However miraculous its tools, the built environment is a habitat as well as a machine, a context for the participation and challenges, the diversity and personal meanings, the face-to-face and group relationships that transcend the utility of life and make it precious. For whatever its outward form, the future must enclose a world in which we recognize ourselves.

References

Agron, G. Some observations on behavior in institutional settings. *Environment and Behavior,* 1971, *3,* 103–114.

Barker, R. *Ecological psychology.* Stanford, Calif.: Stanford University Press, 1968.

Bayes, K. *The therapeutic effect of environment on emotionally disturbed and mentally subnormal children.* London: Gresham Press, 1967.

Bayes, K., & Francklin, S. The therapeutic environment. In K. Bayes and S. Francklin (Eds.), *Designing for the handicapped.* London: George Godwin, 1971.

Berger, B. *Working class suburb: A study of auto workers in suburbia.* Berkeley, Calif.: University of California Press, 1960.

Bettelheim, B. *Truants from life.* New York: The Free Press, 1955.

Blackie, J. *Inside the primary school.* New York: Schocken Books, 1971.

Boyd, D., Morris, D., & Peel, T. S. Selected social characteristics and multi-family living environment: A pilot study. *Milieu,* 1965, *1,* 5. (News report of the Environmental Research Foundation.)

Braginsky, B. M., Braginsky, D. D., & Ring, K. *Methods of madness: The mental hospital as a last resort.* New York: Holt, Rinehart and Winston, 1969.

Brookes, M., & Kaplan, A. The office environment: Space planning and affective behavior. *Human Factors,* 1972, *14,* 373–391.

Brunetti, F. A. Noise, distraction and privacy in conventional and open school environments. In W. J. Mitchell (Ed.), *Environmental design: Research and practice. Proceedings of the EDRA 3/AR 8 Conference.* Los Angeles: University of California Press, 1972.

Buttimer, A. Social space and the planning of residential areas. *Environment and Behavior,* 1972, *4,* 279–318.

Canter, D. An intergroup comparison of connotative dimensions in architecture. *Environment and Behavior,* 1969, *1,* 37–48.

Canter, D. Attitudes and perception in architecture. *Architectural Association Quarterly,* 1961, *1,* 24–31.

Chapman, J. E., & Lazar, J. B. A review of the present status and future needs in day care research. Washington, D.C.: Interagency Panel on Early Childhood Research and Development, November 1971.

Contini, R. Human behavior and building: An engineer's view. *Building Research,* 1965, *2,* 15.

Cooper, C. St. Francis Square: Attitudes of its residents. *Journal of American Institute of Architects,* 1971, *58,* 22–27.

Cremin, L. A. *Transformation of the school.* New York: Knopf, 1968.

Dewey, J. *Experience and education.* New York: Macmillan, 1938.

Dahinden, J. *Urban structures for the future.* New York: Praeger, 1972.

Environmental Research and Development Foundation. St. Margaret's Park public housing project: An architectural and behavioral description. Mimeographed report. Kansas City, Mo., 1969.

Fava, S. The sociology of new towns in the U.S.: "Balance" of racial and income groups. Paper presented at the meeting of the American Institute of Planners, Minneapolis-St. Paul, Minnesota, October 1970.

Fellman, G., & Brandt, B. A neighborhood a highway would destroy. *Environment and Behavior,* 1970, *2,* 281–301.

Fellman, G., & Brandt, B. Working-class protest against an urban highway: Some meanings, limits and problems. *Environment and Behavior,* 1971, *3,* 61–79.

Fellows, L. Psychological report finds new town in West Germany boring to children. *New York Times,* March 13, 1971, Part I, p. 14.

Fields, H. Environmental design implications of a changing health care system. In W. H. Ittelson (Ed.), *Environment and cognition.* New York: Seminar Press, 1973.

Fitch, J. M. The aesthetics of function. In R. Gutman (Ed.), *People and buildings.* New York: Basic Books, 1972.

Gans, H. *The urban villagers.* New York: The Free Press, 1962.

Gilbert, A. Observations and recent correctional architecture. In National Institute of Law Enforcement and Criminal Justice, *New environments for the encarcerated.* Washington, D.C.: National Institute of Law Enforcement and Criminal Justice, 1972.

Glaser, D. *The effectiveness of a prison and parole system.* Indianapolis: Bobbs-Merrill, 1964. [Excerpts in H. M. Proshansky, W. H. Ittelson, & L. G. Rivlin (Eds.), *Environmental psychology: Man and his physical setting.* New York: Holt, Rinehart and Winston, 1970. Pp. 445–463.]

Goffman, E. *Asylums.* Chicago: Aldine, 1962.

Goshen, C. E. A review of psychiatric architecture in the principles of design. In C. E. Goshen (Ed.), *Psychiatric architecture.* Washington, D.C.: American Psychiatric Association, 1961.

Gump, P. Milieu, environment and behavior. *Design and Environment,* 1971, *2,* No. 4, 48–52.

Gutman, R. Site planning and social behavior. *Journal of Social Issues,* 1966, *22,* 103–105. [Reprinted in H. M. Proshansky, W. H. Ittelson, and L. G. Rivlin (Eds.), *Environmental psychology: Man and his physical setting.* New York: Holt, Rinehart and Winston, 1970. Pp. 509–517.]

Gutman, R. The questions architects ask. In R. Gutman (Ed.), *People and buildings.* New York: Basic Books, 1972. [Originally appeared in *Transactions of the Bartlett Society* (Bartlett School of Architecture, University College, London), 1965–1966, *4,* 49–82.]

Hershberger, R. G. A study of meaning and architecture. *Man and His Environment Newsletter,* 1968, *1,* 6–7.

Holahan, C. J., & Saegert, S. Behavioral and attitudinal effects of large-scale variation in the physical environment of psychiatric wards. *Journal of Abnor-*

mal Psychology, 1973, *82*, 454–462.
Holt, J. *How children fail.* New York: Dell, 1970.
Horowitz, M. J., Duff, D. F., & Stratton, L. O. Body buffer zone: Exploration of personal space. *Archives of General Psychiatry*, 1964, *11*, 651–656. [Reprinted as Personal space and the body-buffer zone. In H. M. Proshansky, W. H. Ittelson, & L. G. Rivlin (Eds.), *Environmental psychology: Man and his physical setting.* New York: Holt, Rinehart and Winston, 1970. Pp. 214–220.]
Huntington, E. *Civilization and climate.* New Haven: Yale University Press, 1915.
Hutt, C., & Vaizey, M. J. Differential effects of group density on social behavior. *Nature,* 1966, *209,* 1371–1372.
Ittelson, W. H., Proshansky, H. M., & Rivlin, L. G. A study of bedroom use on two psychiatric wards. *Hospital and Community Psychiatry,* 1970a, *21,* 177–180.
Ittelson, W. H., Proshansky, H. M., & Rivlin, L. G. Bedroom size and social interaction of the psychiatric ward. *Environment and Behavior,* 1970b, *2,* 255–270.
Ittelson, W. H., Proshansky, H. M., & Rivlin, L. G. The environmental psychology of the psychiatric ward. In H. M. Proshansky, W. H. Ittelson, & L. G. Rivlin (Eds.), *Environmental psychology: Man and his physical setting.* New York: Holt, Rinehart and Winston, 1970c.
Izumi, K. LSD and architectural design. Mimeographed paper, 1967.
Izumi, K. Some psycho-social aspects of environmental design. Mimeographed paper, 1969.
Joiner, D. Office territory. *New Society*, 1971, *23*, 660–663.
Kasmar, J. V., Griffin, W. V., & Mauritzen, J. H. Effect of environmental surroundings on outpatients' mood and perception of psychiatrists. *Journal of Consulting and Clinical Psychology*, 1968, *32*, 223-226.
Kennedy, D., & Highlands, D. Buildings and organizational effectiveness. Paper presented at the 63rd annual meeting of the American Anthropological Association, Detroit, Michigan, November, 1964.
Kira, A. *The bathroom: Criteria for design.* New York: Basic Books, 1967.
Kohl, H. *Thirty-six children.* New York: New American Library, 1967.
Kozol, J. *Death at an early age.* Boston: Houghton Mifflin, 1967.
Laing, R. D. *The divided self.* London: Tavistock Publications, 1969.
Le Corbusier (Jeanneret, C. E.) *Towards a new architecture.* New York: Praeger, 1963.
Lee, T. Urban neighbourhood as a socio-spatial schema. *Human Relations,* 1968, *21*, 241–268. [Reprinted in H. M. Proshanksy, W. H. Ittelson, & L. G. Rivlin (Eds.), *Environmental psychology: Man and his physical setting.* New York: Holt, Rinehart and Winston, 1970. Pp. 349-370.]
Llewelyn-Davies, Weeks, Forestier-Walker, and Bor. *The plan for Milton Keynes.* Wavendon, England: Milton Keynes Development Corp., 1970. 2 Vols.
Madge, C. Private and public places. *Human Relations*, 1950, *3*, 187-199.
Manning, P. (Ed.) *Office design: A study of environment.* Liverpool, England: University of Liverpool, The Pilkington Research Unit, 1965. [Excerpts in H. M. Proshansky, W. H. Ittelson, & L. G. Rivlin (Eds.) *Environmental psychology: Man and his physical setting.* New York: Holt, Rinehart and Winston, 1970. Pp. 463–483.]
Marrow, H. I. *A history of education in antiquity.* New York: Sheed and Ward, 1956.

Maslow, A. H., & Mintz, L. Effects of esthetic surroundings: 1. Initial short-term effects of three esthetic conditions upon perceiving "energy" and "well-being" in faces. *Journal of Psychology*, 1956, *41*, 247-254.

Merton, R. K. The social psychology of housing. In W. Dennis (Ed.), *Current trends in social psychology.* Pittsburgh: University of Pittsburgh Press, 1948.

Michelson, W. *Man and his urban environment: A sociological approach.* Reading, Mass.: Addison-Wesley, 1970.

Moholy-Nagy, S. The arcology of Paolo Soleri. *Architectural Forum*, 1970, *132*, 70-74.

Mumford, L. *The city in history.* New York: Harcourt, Brace & World, 1961.

Mussen, I., & Slyper, J. L. Urban conservation in the context of social improvement and development strategies for the towns of Israel. In R. Alterman with A. Kirschenbaum (Eds.), *Urban renewal planning in Israel.* Haifa, Israel: Center for Urban and Regional Studies, Technion Institute for Research and Development, 1972.

Newman, O. *Defensible space.* New York: Macmillan, 1972.

New York Times. Alternatives to reformatories hailed amid controversy in Massachusetts. September 1, 1972, p. 8.

Open Space School Project Bulletin, School Planning Laboratory, Stanford University, March 1970.

Osmond, H. Function as the basis of psychiatric ward design. *Mental Hospitals* (Architectural Supplement), 1957, *8*, 23-29. [A condensed version appears in H. M. Proshansky, W. H. Ittelson, & L. G. Rivlin (Eds.), *Environmental psychology: Man and his physical setting.* New York: Holt, Rinehart and Winston, 1970. Pp. 560-569.]

Parsons, H. M. Human factors in environmental design: The state of the art. Paper presented to the Metropolitan Chapter of the Human Factors Society, 1970.

Parsons, H. M. The bedroom. *Human Factors*, 1972, *14*, 421-450.

Patri, P. Personal communication, 1971.

Payne, I. Pupillary responses to architectural stimuli. *Man-Environment Systems*, 1969, S11.

Peterson, G. L., Bishop, R. L., & Fitzgerald, R. W. The quality of visual residential environments: Perspectives and preferences. *Man-Environment Systems*, 1969, S 13.

Plowden Report. *Children and their primary schools.* Vol. 1. London: Her Majesty's Stationery Office, 1967.

Prescott, E. The large day care center as a child-rearing environment. *Voice for Children*, 1970, *2* (4).

Prescott, E., & Jones, E. Day care for children: Assets and liabilities. *Children*, 1971, *18* (2), 54-58.

Prescott, E., Jones, E., & Kritchevsky, S. *Group day care as a childrearing environment.* Pasadena, Calif.: Pacific Oaks College, 1967.

Prescott, E., Jones, E., & Kritchevsky, S. Assessment of child-rearing environments: An ecological approach. Report prepared for the Children's Bureau, Office of Child Development, U.S. Department of Health, Education and Welfare, June 1971.

Rapoport, A., & Watson, N. Cultural variability in physical standards. In R. Gutman (Ed.), *People and buildings.* New York: Basic Books, 1972.

Rapoport, A. *House form and culture.* Englewood Cliffs, N.J.: Prentice-Hall, 1969.
Rivlin, L. G., & Wolfe, M. The early history of a psychiatric hospital for children: Expectations and reality. *Environment and Behavior*, 1972, *4*, 33-72.
Roland, G. E. Human factors and building design. *Building Research,* 1965, *2,* 12-14.
Rothman, D. *The discovery of the asylum: Social order and disorder in the new republic.* Boston: Little, Brown, 1971.
Seeley, J. R., Sim, R. A., & Loosley, E. W. *Crestwood Heights.* New York: Basic Books, 1956.
Silberman, C. *Crisis in the classroom.* New York: Random House, 1970.
Sarason, S. *The creation of new settings and future societies.* San Francisco: Jossey-Bass, 1972.
Sivadon, P. Space as experienced: Therapeutic implications. In H. M. Proshansky, W. H. Ittelson, & L. G. Rivlin (Eds.), *Environmental psychology: Man and his physical setting.* New York: Holt, Rinehart and Winston, 1970.
Sommer, R. *Personal space.* Englewood Cliffs, N.J.: Prentice-Hall, 1969.
Sommer, R. The social psychology of the cell environment. In National Institute of Law Enforcement and Criminal Justice, *New environments for the incarcerated.* Washington, D.C.: National Institute of Law Enforcement and Criminal Justice, 1972.
Sommer, R., & Osmond, H. Symptoms of institutional care. *Social Problems,* 1961, *8*, 254-263.
Sommer, R., & Ross, H. Social interaction on a geriatrics ward. *International Journal of Social Psychiatry*, 1958, *4*, 128-133.
Spilhaus, A. The experimental city. *Science*, 1968, *159*, 710-715.
Sprout, H., & Sprout, M. *The ecological perspective on human affairs.* Princeton, N.J.: Princeton University Press, 1965.
Studer, R. The organization of spatial stimuli. In L. Pastalan & D. Carson (Eds.), *The spatial behavior of older people.* Ann Arbor, Mich.: University of Michigan Press, 1970.
Tars, S. E., & Appleby, L. The same child in home and institution: An observational study. *Environment and Behavior*, 1973, *5*, 3-28.
Turner, J. F. C. Housing as a verb. In J. F. C. Turner & R. Fichter (Eds.), *Freedom to build.* New York: Macmillan, 1972.
Ullman, L. *Institution and outcome: A comparative study of psychiatric hospitals.* New York: Pergamon Press, 1967.
U.S. Bureau of Prisons. *Handbook of correctional institution design and construction.* Washington, D.C., 1949.
Wells, B. W. P. The psycho-social influence of building environment: Sociometric findings in large and small office spaces. In R. Gutman (Ed.), *People and buildings.* New York: Basic Books, 1972.
Wheeler, L. *Behavioral research for architectural planning and design.* Terre Haute, Ind.: Ewing Miller Associates, 1967.
Wilner, D. M., Walkley, R. P., Pinkerton, T. C., & Tayback, M. *The housing environment and family life.* Baltimore, Md.: Johns Hopkins Press, 1962.
Wilson, J. *Urban renewal: The record and the controversy.* New York: The Free Press, 1967.
Wittman, F. D. Alcoholism and architecture: The myth of specialized treatment

facilities. In W. J. Mitchell (Ed.), *Environmental design: Research and practice. Proceedings of EDRA 3/AR 8 Conference.* Los Angeles: University of Calfornia Press, 1972.
Young, M., & Willmott, P. *Family and kinship in East London.* New York: The Free Press, 1957.
Zanardelli, H. A. Life in a landscape office. In N. Polites (Ed.), *Improving office enviroment.* Elmhurst, Ill.: The Business Press, 1969.
Zeisel, J. Fundamental values in planning with the non-paying client. In *Architecture for human behavior: Collected papers from a mini-conference.* Philadelphia: Philadelphia Chapter/The American Institute of Architects, 1971.
Zeisel, J. Sociology and architectural planning: Working book 4. Mimeographed paper, 1970.

Suggested Readings

Fitch, J. M. *American building II: The environmental forces that shape it.* Boston: Houghton Mifflin, 1972.
Newman, O. *Defensible space.* New York: Macmillan, 1972.
Gutman, R. (Ed.) *People and buildings.* New York: Basic Books, 1972.
Sommer, R. *Design awareness.* San Francisco: Rinehart Press, 1972.

Index